GUINNESS

AIRCRAFT

FACTS & FEATS

GUINNESS

AIRCRAFT
FACTS & FEATS

MICHAEL TAYLOR & DAVID MONDEY

GUINNESS SUPERLATIVES LIMITED
2 Cecil Court, London Road, Enfield, Middlesex

Editor: Beatrice Frei
Design and layout: Ian Wileman

Published in Great Britain by
Guinness Superlatives Limited, 2 Cecil Court,
London Road, Enfield, Middlesex

Guinness is a registered trade mark of
Arthur Guinness Son & Co. Ltd.

British Library Cataloguing in Publication Data

Taylor, Michael J.H.
    The Guinness book of aircraft facts and feats.
    1. Aeronautics—Flights—History
    I. Title   II. Mondey, David
    629.13'09   TL515

    ISBN 0-85112-406-2

Set in 10/11pt Sabon
Printed and bound in Great Britain by
Butler and Tanner Ltd., Frome, Somerset

Contents

Introduction

Six years have passed since the third edition of *Air Facts and Feats* was published. In the ensuing years many aircraft of all types have been built and flown, records set, and major advances in aerospace technologies accomplished. This period has seen the introduction of NASA's incredible Space Shuttle Orbiter, the world's first reusable spacecraft. But the Orbiter is also an aeroplane, landing on an airstrip using its own retractable landing gear. This capability raises problems for the authors, as the Orbiter clearly has to be recorded in the chapter relating to spaceflight, yet, as an aeroplane, it is the fastest and highest flying, the most expensive to develop and build, and has the most powerful engines. However, whilst the craft has an orbital speed of about 17 600 mph (28 325 km/h) and is fitted with three main engines each rated at 375 000 lb (170 100 kg) static thrust at take off, it lands unpowered at only 208 mph (334 km/h). It is clearly, therefore, a high performer only as a spacecraft, although remaining one of the wonders of our modern age.

It was back in 1909 that the English Channel was first conquered by aeroplane, and by the close of 1918 the stretch of water was regularly crossed by military aeroplanes. When the third edition of this book was published it would have seemed impossible that a fourth edition could record an aeroplane 'first' for this same journey. Yet, whilst the distance across has not changed in the 75 years since Blériot set off, the type of aeroplane used has. On 12 June 1979 Dr Paul MacCready's Gossamer Albatross completed the first air crossing by a man-powered aeroplane. This achievement won him a £100 000 Kremer Prize, a reward very much in the tradition of pioneering flights. Add to this achievement the first solar-powered aircraft crossing of the channel, other records broken by civil and military aircraft, the appearance of even larger hot-air balloons, more diminutive aeroplanes, etc, and it becomes clear that air facts and feats are constantly changing. But, this is not to say that old records are always bettered by new-technology aircraft. In 1983 the world height record for piston-engined aeroplanes was still held by the Caproni Ca 161*bis* of 1938, the Short-Mayo Composite upper aircraft *Mercury* of 1938 still held the distance record in a straight line for seaplanes, a Pratt-Read sailplane retained the height record for two-seat sailplanes it established in 1952, and the Fairey Rotodyne of the late 1950s was still the fastest convertiplane in a 100 km closed circuit.

This fourth edition of the book, now known as *Aircraft Facts and Feats*, is completely revised, with many new entries and illustrations and new chapter groupings. More space has been devoted to rocketry and spaceflight and to lighter-than-air craft, and a greater number of facts on aviation's pioneers prior to the Wright brothers have been included. This is in no way intended to lessen the achievements of the Wrights, who proved once and for all that sustained flight could be achieved by heavier than air powered aeroplanes, but serves to provide a more balanced picture of contemporary experiments. It can be said that only because the Wrights attempted to capitalise financially on their aviation achievements, and in so doing virtually suspended further involved research and development, did European builders eventually catch up technically and then overtake them.

Also new to this edition is a greater attempt to include many of the facts readily associated with Guinness books—such as the fastest, largest, smallest, heaviest. To put all aircraft facts and feats into perspective, as this century has also been one of the motorcar, television, frozen food, the tank, tea bag and nuclear power, a number of the most important non-aviation inventions of each period have been grouped after the records at the end of relevant chapters.

Covering man's achievement in the air, from the tower jumpers to astronauts on the Moon, must rank aviation as unrivalled for adventure and achievement.

Lighter than Air

It is recorded that man first attempted to become airborne using wings of one kind or another, these 'tower jumpers' seeking either to glide to the ground or to flap their way upwards. As the third chapter relates, many died in the attempts. Yet, as aviation in the 1980s is preoccupied with wing-borne flight, it is all too easy to forget that man's first successful ventures into the air were achieved more than one hundred years before the Wright brothers pioneered heavier-than-air powered flight, using hot-air and hydrogen balloons.

1783 can be seen as the foundation year of manned flight proper, largely as the result of the famed Montgolfier brothers' experiments in Paris. The Montgolfiers experimented with hot-air balloons, requiring heated air as the lifting agent. The inherent dangers of carrying a bonfire suspended below the balloon's envelope did not deter the pioneers or those men that actually flew the man-carrying Montgolfier balloons. It is interesting that whilst the name Montgolfier is well known, the names of the men that actually 'piloted' the balloons during these early flights are not well remembered. But, the dangers and restrictions of hot air as the lifting agent divided opinion between this and the use of hydrogen gas, which had already been discovered and could be produced using an expensive process of chemical reaction. Furthermore, hydrogen offered the possibility of longer duration flights. Whilst it was recognised that hydrogen was 'inflammable air', again there seemed no shortage of men and women willing to become airborne. This is especially surprising when one considers that the aeronauts were launching themselves into the unknown, at a time when fear of the sky persisted. More surprising still is that little time passed before tentative ascents gave way to daring feats. Two such daring flights ended in tragedy, resulting in the first deaths of men and woman aeronauts. The first men to lose their lives did so while attempting to cross the English Channel in a combination hot-air/hydrogen balloon, less than two years after the first manned ascent. The first woman aeronaut to die in a ballooning accident had been viewing her own firework party from the vantage point of a

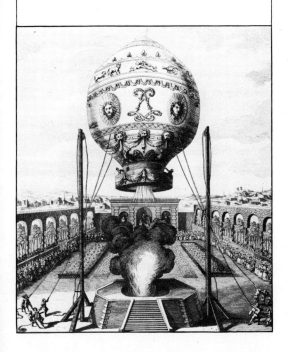

Drawing of a man-carrying Montgolfier hot-air balloon in tethered flight, late 1783, in the grounds of a M. Reveillon. (Science Museum, London)

hydrogen balloon. In both cases the hydrogen gas ignited.

Few appreciate the scale of ballooning in the 19th century, for pleasure, sport, serious experimentation and observation. From the 1860s balloons filtered into military service, aided in the case of America by the Civil War. However, the first major balloon operation took place between 1870 and 1871, when the defenders of Paris eluded the surrounding Prussian army by using hastily fabricated balloons to carry from the besieged city despatches, letters, persons and carrier pigeons. This operation led to the deployment (by the Prussians) of the first purpose-designed wagon-mounted anti-aircraft guns.

When it is appreciated that the period between 1895 and 1914 is termed 'the Golden Age' of ballooning, it becomes clear that this form of flying machine can claim a far longer period of continuous prominence than is the case for heavier-than-air machines. Moreover, the great interest in hot-air ballooning of recent years— using gas cylinders with burners to create hot air (rather than burning solid materials) and using flame-resistant fabric to construct the envelopes—has brought ballooning close to the forefront of sport flying for a second time.

Modern balloons are still subject to the whim of the wind. It was this helplessness that first prompted early pioneers to use propellers and rudders to achieve propulsion and directional control. Success was gained with the invention of the airship (correctly 'dirigible'), which moved away from a spherical envelope but was far larger and much more expensive to construct. Despite greater control, early airships appeared to suffer many accidents which, with cost and size, partly explains why the balloon remained popular. Nevertheless, prior to 1915, with development and a great increase in size, the airship was regarded as the most comfortable and safe form of air travel, one suited to commercial operation, and the most destructive vehicle of war devised by man.

The last decade has seen the construction of the world's first hot-air airship, built by the same British company that has delighted the public with its giant advertising balloons in shapes ranging from stately homes to gollies, a spark plug, peanut men and giant pairs of trousers. Interest is again being shown in airships for commercial and military use, mainly for offshore support and surveillance, and indeed the flying display at the international air show at Farnborough in 1982 was opened by an airship.

The first recorded design for a lighter-than-air craft was attributed to the Jesuit priest Francesco de Lana-Terzi. Dated 1670, this comprised a wooden boat hull for three to four people, lifted into the air by four rope-tethered copper foil spheres from which the air had been extracted to create vacuums. A central mast with square sail was to provide propulsion and a hand-carried oar was to give directional control.

The first successful demonstration of a model hot-air balloon took place on 8 August 1709 in the Ambassadors' drawing-room at the Casa da India, Lisbon, in the presence of King John V of Portugal, Queen Maria Ann, the Papal Nuncio, Cardinal Conti (later Pope Innocent III), princes of the Court, members of the Diplomatic Corps, noblemen and courtiers. The balloon, made and demonstrated by Father Bartolomeu de Gusmão, consisted of a small envelope of thick paper, inflated with hot air produced by 'fire material contained in an earthen bowl encrusted in a waxed-wood tray' which was suspended underneath. The balloon is said to have risen quickly to a height of 12 ft (3·5 m) before being destroyed by two valets who feared that it might set the curtains alight. Suggestions that Gusmão became airborne later in a full-scale version of the balloon, although documented, cannot be substantiated. Interestingly, Gusmão later constructed a model glider.

Hydrogen was first isolated in 1766 by the English scientist Henry Cavendish, who referred to it as 'inflammable air' or Phlogiston. The Royal Society was told of the gas, which is much lighter than atmospheric air.

The first model hot-air balloon demonstrated by Joseph Montgolfier was a silk bag, which rose to the ceiling of a lodging house at Avignon, France, in November 1782.

The first balloon to ascend, capable of sustaining a weight equivalent to that of a man was a hot-air balloon made by the brothers Joseph and Étienne Montgolfier (1740–1810 and 1745–99 respectively). This balloon, calculated as being able to lift 450 lb (205 kg), was released on 25 April 1783, probably at Annonay, France, rose to

Model of de Lana's lighter-than-air craft. (Science Museum London)

about 1000 ft (305 m) and landed about 3000 ft (915 m) from the point of lift-off. The balloon had a diameter of about 39 ft (12 m) and achieved its lift using hot air provided by combustion of solid waste (probably paper, straw and wood) below the neck of the envelope.

The first public demonstration by the Montgolfier brothers was given in the market place at Annonay on 4 June 1783, when a small balloon of about 36 ft (11 m) diameter, constructed from linen and paper, rose to a height of 6000 ft (1830 m). This balloon travelled more than 1 mile (1·6 km) before landing.

The first free ascent by a hydrogen-filled balloon (unmanned) was made on 27 August 1783 from the Champ-de-Mars, Paris, when Jacques Alexandre César Charles (1746–1823) launched a 12 ft (3·5 m) balloon. It was filled with hydrogen that Charles had manufactured and was capable of lifting 20 lb (9 kg).

The balloon drifted for 45 min and came to earth at Gonesse, 15 miles (25 km) from Paris, where it was promptly attacked by a frenzied

mob of panic-stricken peasants, who destroyed the 22 000 ft³ (620 m³) rubber-coated silk envelope.

The first living creatures to become airborne under a balloon were a sheep, a duck and a cock which were lifted by a 41 ft (13 m) diameter hot-air Montgolfier balloon at the Court of Versailles on 19 September 1783 before King Louis XVI, Marie-Antoinette and their Court. The balloon achieved an altitude of 1700 ft (520 m) before descending in the Forest of Vaucresson 8 min later, having travelled about 2 miles (3 km). The occupants were scarcely affected by their flight nor by their landing.

The first known award for an aviation feat was the Order of St Michel presented to the Montgolfier brothers by King Louis XVI after the balloon demonstration of 19 September 1783.

The first man carried aloft in a balloon, and therefore **the world's first aeronaut,** was François Pilâtre de Rozier. On 15 October 1783, he ascended in a tethered 49 ft (15 m) diameter Montgolfier hot-air balloon to 84 ft (26 m), the limit of the restraining rope. The hot air was provided by a straw-fed fire below the fabric envelope and the balloon stayed up for nearly 4½ min. Interestingly, the honour of being the first aeronaut had nearly gone to two criminals, who, as proposed by King Louis XVI, might have gained their freedom by volunteering for the flight. After protests by de Rozier, he was given the opportunity to become airborne instead.

The first men carried in free flight by a balloon, the first pilot and passenger, and **the first men to make an aerial journey** were de Rozier and the Marquis d'Arlandes, who rose in the 49 ft (15 m) diameter Montgolfier balloon at 13·54 h on 21 November 1783 from the gardens of the Château La Muette in the Bois de Boulogne. These first aeronauts were airborne for 25 min and landed on the Butte-aux-Cailles, about 5½ miles (8·5 km) from their point of departure, having drifted to and fro across Paris. Their maximum altitude is unlikely to have been above 1500 ft (450 m).

The first men to be carried in free flight by a hydrogen balloon were Jacques Charles and one of the Robert brothers. The Robert brothers had been responsible for producing rubber coated silk material, ideal for retaining the gas, and indeed had helped construct the balloon for the attempt. They ascended from the gardens of Les Tuileries, Paris, at 13·45 h on 1 December 1783, in a balloon 28 ft 2 in (8·6 m) in diameter before a crowd estimated at 400 000. The craft landed 27 miles (43 km) distant, near the town of Nesles. This flight can be said to have heralded the beginning of the end for the early hot-air balloon, having achieved a distance greater than was possible with the Montgolfier type.

The first unmanned hot-air balloon to be released in the United Kingdom was that constructed by Irishman Riddick. It was flown on 4 February 1784 from the Rotunda Gardens, Dublin.

The first balloon ascent in Italy was made on 25 February 1784, when Chevalier Paolo Andreani and brothers Augustin and Charles Gerli ascended in a Montgolfier balloon from Moncuco, near Milan.

The first manned balloon flight in the United Kingdom was made on 15 April 1784, when Mr Rosseau and a ten-year-old drummer boy took off at 14.00 h from Dublin, Ireland, for a 2 h flight. They eventually landed at Ratoath. This marked also **the first occasion music was played from an aircraft,** as the boy beat a tune on a drum for at least an hour of the flight to indicate their position to the crowd below.

The first women to ascend in a balloon (tethered) were the Marchioness de Montalembert, the Countess de Montalembert, the Countess de Podenas and Mademoiselle de Lagarde, who were lifted into the air by a Montgolfier hot-air balloon on 20 May 1784 from the Faubourg-Saint-Antoine, Paris.

The first woman to be carried in free flight in a balloon was Madame Thible, who ascended in a Montgolfier with Monsieur Fleurant on 4 June 1784 from Lyon, France. The balloon, named *Le Gustav*, reached an altitude of 8500 ft (2600 m) in the presence of the King of Sweden.

The first Scottish aeronaut was James Tytler, who made a balloon ascent from the Comely Gardens, Edinburgh, on 7 August 1784. However, he is better remembered for making an ascent in a Montgolfier-type balloon on 25 August, this time from the city's Heriot's Garden. He is believed to have attained an altitude no greater than 500 ft (150 m).

The first aerial voyage by a hydrogen balloon over Great Britain was made by Vincenzo Lunardi of Lucca, an employee of the Italian Embassy in London. On 15 September 1784 he ascended in a 'charlière' (hydrogen balloon) from the Honourable Artillery Company's training ground at Moorfields, London, and flew northwards to the parish of North Mimms (today the site of the village of Welhamgreen), Hertfordshire, where he landed his cat and jettisoned ballast. This caused him to ascend again and he finally landed at Standon Green End near Ware, Hertfordshire. On the spot where he landed stands a rough stone monument on which a tablet proclaims:

Let Posterity know
And knowing be astonished!
That
On the 15th day of September, 1784
Vincent Lunardi
of
Lucca in Tuscany
The first Aerial Traveller in Britain
Mounting from the Artillery Ground
in London
And traversing the Regions of the Air
For two Hours and fifteen Minutes
in this Spot
Revisited the Earth.
On this rude Monument
For ages be recorded
That wonderous enterprize, successfully
achieved
By the powers of Chymistry
And the fortitude of man
The improvement in Science
Which
The Great Author of all Knowledge
Patronising by his Providence
The inventions of Mankind
Hath generously permitted
To their benefit
And
His own Eternal Glory

The first English aeronaut was James Sadler who, on 4 October 1784, flew in a Montgolfier-type balloon of 170 ft (52 m) circumference at Oxford.

The first application of a propeller to a full-size man-carrying aircraft was recorded on 16 October 1784, when Jean-Pierre Blanchard

Drawing of Blanchard and Jeffries leaving Dover on 7 January 1785. (Science Museum, London)

added a small hand-operated six-blade propeller to the passenger basket of his balloon. As a means of propulsion it was, of course, completely ineffectual.

The first aerial crossing of the English Channel was achieved by the Frenchman Jean-Pierre Blanchard, accompanied by the American Dr John Jeffries. On 7 January 1785 they rose from Dover at 13.00 h and landed in the Forêt de Felmores, France, at approximately 15.30 h, having discarded almost all their clothes to lighten the craft *en route*. Their balloon was hydrogen-filled.

The first attempt to cross the Irish Sea by balloon was made by Richard Crosbie on 19 January 1785. Before a crowd of tens of thousands of onlookers, he set off in his hydrogen balloon from Ranelagh Gardens, Ireland. After a good start to the journey, Crosbie decided to postpone the actual sea crossing as darkness was setting in. He eventually landed safely at Clontarf. On 12 May the same year Crosbie made a second attempt at the crossing, but on this occasion the hydrogen balloon only just managed to lift off from the Dublin Barracks and was soon at rest again. Having yet again charged money for the opportunity of seeing him fly, probably making Crosbie **the first aviation entrepreneur,** he asked the crowd for a volunteer of smaller proportions than himself to attempt the crossing. Richard McGwire stepped forward and indeed took off. Fortunately, he was followed out to sea by a number of boats, which eventually plucked him from the water some miles out. On 19 July Crosbie made his last attempt to cross the Irish Sea by balloon. This might have succeeded but for a

storm, and eventually Crosbie was rescued by a barge.

The first aeronaut to receive a knighthood for attempting an aerial journey was twenty-one-year-old Richard McGwire (see above).

The first aeronauts to be killed while ballooning were François Pilâtre de Rozier and Jules Romain, who were killed while attempting to fly the English Channel from Boulogne on 15 June 1785 in a composite hot-air/hydrogen balloon. It is believed that, when hydrogen was vented from the envelope, the escaping gas was ignited, and the balloon fell at Huitmile Warren, near Boulogne.

The first British woman to travel by balloon in Britain was Mrs Letitia Ann Sage who ascended in Lunardi's hydrogen balloon from St George's Fields, London, on 29 June 1785. Lunardi, who had proclaimed that he would be accompanied by three passengers (Mrs Sage, a Col Hastings and George Biggin), discovered that his balloon's lifting power was not equal to the task. Rather

Richard Crosbie ascending from Ranelagh Gardens on 19 January 1785. (Aer Lingus)

than draw attention to the lady's weight (by her own admission, she weighed more than 200 lb [90 kg]), he stepped down from the basket with Col Hastings. The balloon eventually came to earth near Harrow, Middlesex, where the two occupants were rescued from an irate farmer by the boys of that famous school.

During the period from 1785 to 1789 Jean-Pierre Blanchard made the **first balloon flights in several European countries,** including Germany, Belgium and Switzerland.

The first use of the word 'hydrogen' for the 'inflammable air' used in balloons was made by the French chemist Lavoisier in 1790.

The first free flight by a balloon in the United States of America was made on 9 January 1793 by the Frenchman Jean-Pierre Blanchard, who ascended in a hydrogen balloon from the yard of the old Walnut Street Prison, Philadelphia, and landed in Gloucester County, New Jersey, after a flight of 46 min. Among the vast crowd who turned out to witness this event were the President, George Washington, and four future presidents of the United States: John Adams, Thomas Jefferson, James Madison and James Monroe.

The first use of a man-carrying balloon in war (tethered) was in June 1794, deployed by the French Republican Army at Maubeuge, Belgium. On 26 June, during the battle of Fleurus, Capt Coutelle ascended in the balloon *Entreprenant* to make an aerial reconnaissance of the enemy. Coutelle had been sent to Maubeuge by the Committee of Public Safety but, on arrival, had nearly been executed as a spy by an officer of the French Army whose job it was to ensure that soldiers did not desert the fighting ranks. Both balloon companies attached to the Army were disbanded five years later.

The first man to survive the destruction of his hot-air balloon while in flight was R. Jordarki Kuparanto who, on 24 July 1808, baled out of a Montgolfier balloon that had caught fire. Luckily Kuparanto had taken the precaution of ascending with a parachute as part of his equipment.

The first aerial crossing of the Irish Sea was accomplished on 22 July 1817 by Windham Sadler, son of James Sadler, the first English aero-

naut. His journey took him between the Portobello Barracks and Holyhead, Wales.

The first woman aeronaut to be killed in a flying disaster was Madame Blanchard, widow of the pioneer French aeronaut Jean-Pierre Blanchard (who had died after a heart attack, suffered while ballooning, on 7 March 1809). Madame Blanchard was killed when her hydrogen balloon was ignited during a firework display at the Tivoli Gardens, Paris, on 7 July 1819.

The first aeronaut to record 100 flights was undoubtedly the Englishman Charles Green (1785–1870) who, on 14 May 1832, ascended in a balloon for the 100th time, on this occasion from the Mermaid Tavern, Hackney, London. Green was the pilot of the *Great Nassau Balloon* during Robert Cocking's parachute descent of 24 July 1837 (see following chapter).

The first long distance voyage by air from England was made during 7–8 November 1836 by a hydrogen balloon named *The Royal Vauxhall Balloon*, crewed by Charles Green, Robert Holland MP and Monck Mason. They ascended from Vauxhall Gardens, London, and travelled 480 miles (772 km) to land near Weilberg in the Duchy of Nassau. The balloon was subsequently renamed the *Great Nassau Balloon*.

The first balloon bombing raid was carried out on 22 August 1849, when Austrian unmanned hot-air balloons were launched against Venice. These caused little damage, despite each carrying a 30 lb (14 kg) bomb and time fuse.

The first balloon flight over the Alps was made between Marseilles and Turin on 7 October 1849 by M. F. Farban.

The first hydrogen balloon ascent in Australia was achieved on 29 March 1858, from the Cremorne Gardens, Melbourne, in a balloon named *Australasian*. This was flown by two men named Dean and Brown.

The first long distance balloon flight in America was made on 2 July 1859 by John C. Wise, John La Mountain and O. A. Gager, who covered 1120 miles (1800 km) from St Louis to Henderson, New York.

The first telegraph message transmitted from the air (and then relayed to the President of the

United States) was keyed out by an official telegraph operator who accompanied the flamboyant showman Thaddeus Sobieski Constantine Lowe, during a tethered demonstration flight in the balloon *Enterprise* on 18 June 1861.

The first American Army Balloon Corps was formed on 1 October 1861 with a complement of 50 men under the command of Thaddeus S. C. Lowe who, following his demonstration flight, had been made Chief Aeronaut of the Army of the Potomac. The Corps had originally five balloons, the *Constitution*, *Intrepid*, *Union*, *United States* and *Washington*. Two more, the *Excelsior* and *Eagle*, entered service early in 1862. They were used for reconnaissance and artillery direction. The Corps was disbanded in mid-1863, almost two years before the end of the American Civil War.

The world's first aircraft carrier (defined as a waterborne craft used to tether, transport or launch an aircraft) was the *G W Parke Custis*, a

Intrepid, one of five balloons that formed the initial equipment of the American Army Balloon Corps. (US National Archives)

coal-barge converted during the American Civil War in 1861 under the direction of Thaddeus S. C. Lowe for the transport and towing of observation balloons. The *G W Parke Custis* entered service with General McClellan's Army of the Potomac in November 1861, frequently towing balloons on the Potomac River for the observation of the opposing Confederate forces.

Intrepid, one of the five original hydrogen balloons of the American Army Balloon Corps, was deployed for observation during the Battle of Fair Oaks in the Civil War between 31 May and 1 June 1862. On 11 December one of the balloons was used by the Corps to assist in the crossing of the river Rappahannock, probably the first time a balloon had been used in connection with crossing difficult terrain.

The first military use of balloons in an international war outside Europe was by the Brazilian Marquis de Caxias during the Paraguayan War of 1864-70. This atrocious conflict, which committed the combined forces of Brazil, Argentina and Uruguay against landlocked Paraguay, brought total disaster to the latter nation whose dictator, Francisco Solano López, ordered mass killings among his own people in a savage attempt to compel them towards victory. In the event Brazil occupied Paraguay until 1876; of about 250 000 Paraguayan male nationals before the war, only 28 000 survived in 1871.

The Prussian Army formed two lighter-than-air detachments in 1870, with the assistance of Englishman Henry Coxwell. These were deployed during the Franco-Prussian war (see below).

The first major balloon operation was carried out during the Franco-Prussian War of 1870-1. The Prussian Army had surrounded Paris and had cut off the city from the rest of France. Inside the city were a few skilled balloonists and material for balloon-making. In an attempt to get despatches out of Paris, Jules Duroug ascended in a balloon on 23 September 1870. He flew over the Prussian camp and landed at Evreux three hours later. He was followed by Gaston Tissandier, Eugène Godard and Mangin, who were all fired on. Meanwhile, inside Paris other balloons were being made from available material and sailors from the French Navy were being trained as pilots. Balloon ascents carried on until 28 January 1871, by which time 66 flights had been made, carrying about 110 passengers in addition to the pilots, 2½–3 million letters, and carrier pigeons to fly back to Paris with despatches. In mid-October 1870 a chemist, M Barreswil, suggested the use of microphotography to allow each pigeon to carry a large number of messages. On 18 November **the first official pigeon post** was introduced between Tours and Paris. This microphotography system was reintroduced during the Second World War as the Airgraph service, coping with large volumes of forces and civilian airmail.

The first crossing of the North Sea was made from Paris, France, on 1 November 1870 in the hydrogen balloon *Ville d'Orleans*. The 774 mile (1246 km) journey ended at Blefjell in Norway.

The first attempt to fly across the Atlantic in a hydrogen balloon was made by John Wise in 1873. Sponsored by the *New York Daily Graphic*, the attempt had to be abandoned after only 41 miles (66 km) following an accident.

The first practical development of balloons in the British Army dates from 1878 when the **first 'air estimates'** by the War Office allocated the sum of £150 for the construction of a balloon. Capt J. L. B. Templer of the Middlesex Militia (later KRRC(M)) and Capt H.P.Lee, RE, were appointed to carry out the necessary development work. Although Capt Templer was thus the **first British Air Commander** and an aeronaut in his own right (and the owner of the balloon *Crusader*, which became the **first balloon used by the British Army** in 1879), the **first two aeronauts in the British Army** were Lt (later Capt) G. E. Grover, RE, and Capt F. Beaumont, RE, who had been attached as aeronauts to the Federal Army during the American Civil War from 1862. The **first British Army Balloon**, a coal-gas balloon named *Pioneer*, was made during 1879, costing £71 from the £150 appropriation, and had a capacity of 10 000 ft³ (283·2 m³).

The first balloon ascent in Canada was made on 31 July 1879 by a hydrogen balloon manned by Richard Cowan, Charles Grimley and Charles Page at Montreal.

The first military use of a man-carrying balloon in Britain was that by a balloon detachment during military manoeuvres at Aldershot, Hampshire, on 24 June 1880. A balloon detachment accompanied the British military expedition to Bechuanaland, leaving on 26 November 1884 and arriving at Cape Town on 19 December. Another accompanied the expeditionary force to the Sudan, departing from Britain on 15 February 1885.

The first attempt to carry out an exploration of the Arctic by free balloon was made on 11 July 1897, when Salomon August Andrée and two companions took off from Danes Island, Spitzbergen. Their 160 000 ft³ (4531 m³) capacity balloon had a sail attached to a complicated arrangement of drag ropes, with which it was hoped to steer the craft. Nothing was known of the explorers' fate until their bodies were discovered on White Island, Franz Josef Land, on 6 August 1930.

The first American pilot to be shot down in war was Sgt Ivy Baldwin, Army Signal Corps. In 1898 America and Spain went to war and Baldwin successfully persuaded the Army to deploy a balloon for observation. During the Battle of Santiago, Cuba, Baldwin ascended and gave important information on Spanish troop movements. Seeing the tethered balloon, and in the knowledge of the soldiers below, Spanish troops opened fire on the envelope and it dropped into water, causing only slight injuries to Baldwin. He eventually died in 1955.

The first ratified altitude record for balloons was that achieved on 30 June 1901 by Professors Berson and Suring of the Berliner Verein für Luftschiffahrt who attained a height of 35 435 ft (10 800 m). At the time of this record's ratification there was much controversy with those who still firmly believed that James Glaisher had achieved a height of 37 000 ft (11 275 m) on 5 September 1862; as instrumentation to confirm this altitude with any chance of accuracy did not exist at the time, ratification of the Berson and Suring record was upheld; this record remained unbroken for 30 years (although exceeded on a number of occasions by aeroplanes). Berson and Suring's record was beaten in 1931 when the Swiss physicist Prof Auguste Piccard, carried in a sealed capsule suspended beneath a balloon, made **the first balloon flight into the stratosphere** with an altitude of 50 135 ft (15 281 m). In the following year he increased this to 53 153 ft

(16 201 m). On 11 November 1935 Capt Orvil Anderson and Capt Albert Stevens of the USA attained an altitude of 72 395 ft (22 066 m) in a balloon in which they ascended from a point 11 miles (17 km) south-west of Rapid City, South Dakota, and landed 12 miles (19 km) south of White Lake, South Dakota.

The first official balloon race in Great Britain, organised by the Aero Club, took place on 7 July 1906. Seven balloons competed, taking off from the grounds of the Ranelagh Club at Barn Elms, London. Winner of the event was Frank Hedges Butler, accompanied by Col J. C. and Mrs Capper.

The first international balloon race, and also **the first of the balloon races for the Gordon Bennett Trophy,** attracted an entry of 16 balloons. Flown from the gardens of the Tuileries, Paris, on 30 September 1906, it was won by Lt Frank P. Lahm of the US Army who covered a distance of 402 miles (647 km) before landing at Fylingdales Moor, near Whitby, Yorkshire.

Without doubt, the Gordon Bennett contest for a trophy and an annual prize of 12 500 francs, presented by the expatriate American James Gordon Bennett, became the most famous international balloon event.

On 15 June 1924 Lt Ernest Demuyter of Belgium, flying the balloon *Belgica*, won the trophy outright, having won also the two previous contests. His winning distance was 466 miles (750 km), reaching St Abbs Head, Berwick, Scotland. This distance, however, was one of the shortest in the first series of contests. Sportingly, the trophy was represented for competition, leading to the second series, won by Capt W. E. Kepner, US Army, on 30 June 1928; a third series, won in 1930 by W. T. van Orman of the USA; and a fourth series, with the 1938 and last contest being won by Janusz of Poland, with a flight of 1013 miles (1630 km).

The second but most famous air crossing of the North Sea was made during 12 to 13 October 1907 by the hydrogen balloon *Mammoth,* manned by Frenchman Monsieur A. F. Gaudron and two others. They ascended from Crystal Palace, London, and landed at Brackan on the shore of Lake Vänern in Sweden. The straight-line distance flown was about 720 miles (1160 km).

The first international balloon race in Great Britain, on 30 May 1908, began at the grounds of the Hurlingham Club, Fulham, London. Thirty balloons competed, representing five European nations.

The first National Balloon Race held in America was won by John Berry and Paul McCullough on 5 June 1909. Their distance covered was about 378 miles (608 km).

The greatest 'balloon buster' of the First World War was French Sous-Lieutenant Michel Coiffard, whose 34 air 'victories' included the destruction of 28 observation balloons.

The second greatest 'balloon buster' of the First World War was the Belgian ace of aces Willy Coppens, who included 26 balloons within his total of 37 war victories.

The German pilot responsible for the destruction of the greatest number of enemy balloons during the First World War was Leutnant Heinrich Gontermann, who destroyed 18, including three confirmed in one day.

The British and Empire pilot credited with the destruction of the greatest number of balloons during the First World War was Capt Andrew Wetherby Beauchamp-Proctor, a South African pilot serving with the RFC/RAF. His war total of 54 air victories included 16 balloons. Beauchamp-Proctor was the fifth highest-ranking British and Empire pilot of the war and he received the Victoria Cross.

The greatest American 'balloon buster' of the First World War and undoubtedly the best remembered of all balloon busters was 2nd Lt Frank Luke, a fighter pilot of the 27th Aero (Pursuit) Squadron. Born in 1897, Luke enlisted in the US Signal Corps (Aviation Section) in September 1917 and was commissioned in January 1918. He was sent to France in March 1918, where, after completing advanced flying and aerial gunnery training, he initially ferried aircraft. However, he was posted to the 27th Aero (Pursuit) Squadron in late July. On 16 August he broke formation against orders and scored his first aerial victory. This was only the first of many brushes with authority. Luke formed a close friendship with Lt Wehner and together they became balloon busters of great skill. The first balloon to fall to Luke's guns was destroyed

2nd Lt Frank Luke, the great American 'balloon buster' fighter pilot of the First World War. (US National Archives)

on 12 September, near Marrieulle. Between this date and his death while on an unauthorised balloon busting mission, on 28 September, Luke shot down a further 14 balloons. With aeroplanes destroyed, his total of air victories was 21, making him America's second ranking ace of the war. He was awarded a posthumous Congressional Medal of Honor.

The first operational use of intercontinental bomb-carrying balloons was made on 3 November 1944, when the Japanese initiated an assault on the United States. An ingenious constant-altitude device was intended to ensure that the balloon remained aloft in the prevailing jet stream which carried the balloons 6200 miles (9978 km) across the Pacific Ocean. Each carried a payload of one 33 lb (15 kg) anti-personnel bomb and two incendiary weapons. More than 9000 of these balloons were launched, and it is estimated that approximately 1000 completed the crossing. Because of a self-destruct device, there were only 285 recorded incidents as a result of their use, and only six persons are known to have been killed by them.

The first ratified altitude record for a manned balloon of over 100 000 ft (30 480 m) was achieved by Maj David G. Simons, a medical officer of the US Air Force, who reached an altitude of 101 516 ft (30 942 m) on 19–20 August 1957 in the 3 000 000 ft³ (84 950 m³) balloon *AF-WRI-1*. He took off from Crosby, Minnesota, on 19 August to gather scientific data in the stratosphere and landed at Frederick, South Dakota, the following day.

The current world altitude record for manned free balloons is held by Commander Malcolm D. Ross of the United States Navy Reserve who, on 4 May 1961, ascended over the Gulf of Mexico to an altitude of 113 739·9 ft (34 668 m) in the Lee Lewis Memorial Winzen Research balloon.

The first hot-air balloon record to be ratified by the FAI, a height of 9770 ft (2978 m), was achieved by B. Bogan in the USA on 13 September 1965.

The first crossing of the Swiss Alps by hot-air balloon was achieved on 21 August 1972 by Cameron A-140, crewed by Don Cameron and Mark Yarry. The flight was from Zermatt, Switzerland, to Biella, Italy.

The first transatlantic crossing by a gas balloon

Japanese intercontinental bomb-carrying balloon photographed over the Pacific Ocean. (US Army)

Awaiting vertical alignment of the balloon AFWRI–1 that took Maj David G. Simons to a new altitude record of nearly 102,000 ft (31 000 m).

Maj David G. Simons inside the small gondola of AFWRI–1, on 19 August 1957. (US National Archives)

was achieved by *Double Eagle II*, crewed by Ben L. Abruzzo, Maxie L. Anderson and Larry M. Newman. This achievement, made between 12 and 17 August 1978, established new world distance and duration records for gas balloons of 3107·62 miles (5001·22 km) and 137 h 5 min 50 s respectively.

After travelling some 2900 miles (4667 km), balloonists Maxie Anderson and Don Ida were compelled to call off **their attempt to complete the first round-the-world balloon flight** on 14 February 1981. They had taken off two days earlier at Luxor, Egypt, but problems with their balloon *Jules Verne* caused them to abandon the flight near New Delhi, India.

The first non-stop balloon flight across the American continent was achieved by Fred Gorrell and John Shoecroft in the helium-filled balloon *Superchicken III*. Launched from a site near Los Angeles, California, on 9 October 1981, a landing was made in Georgia 55 h 25 min later.

The world's largest hot-air balloon and the holder of the current world distance and duration records for manned hot-air balloons is Cameron A-530 *Semiramis*. Having a capacity of 529 720 ft³ (15 000 m³), it was flown by the French balloonists Hélène Dorigny and Michel Arnould

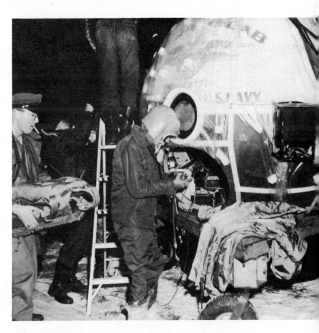

Malcolm D. Ross preparing to enter the gondola of his balloon that achieved an altitude of 76 000 ft (23 165 m) on 8 November 1956, in the US Navy's Stratolab Project. A flight by Ross on 4 May 1961 set the current world altitude record for manned free balloons. (US National Archives)

for a distance of 717.52 miles (1154.74 km) during 25–26 November 1981, not only establishing a world distance record for hot-air balloons but a new duration record of 29 h 5 min and 48 s.

The current world altitude record for manned hot-air balloons was set by Julian Nott of Great Britain on 31 October 1980. Flown from Longmont, Colorado, USA, the Cameron balloon A-375 attained an altitude of 55 137 ft (16 805 m).

The current world distance record for a manned balloon was established during 9–12 November 1981 by the helium-filled Raven balloon *Double Eagle V*. Crewed by Ben L. Abruzzo, Rocky Aoki, Ron Clark and Larry M. Newman, it travelled 5208·68 miles (8382·54 km) between Nagashima, Japan, and Covello, California, USA. This was also **the first manned balloon crossing of the Pacific Ocean.**

The largest balloon ever built was constructed by Winzen Research Inc, Minnesota, USA, with an inflatable volume of 70 000 000 ft³ (2 000 000 m³).

The most unusual hot-air balloon ever flown is probably the representation of the Château de Balerot, one of the many special shape hot-air balloons currently produced by Cameron Balloons of England.

Cameron A–530 Semiramis, *the world's largest hot-air balloon, alongside one of the smallest.* (Cameron Balloons)

Cameron's Château de Balerot. (Cameron Balloons)

Having become airborne in hot-air and hydrogen balloons, it was not long before the more inventive aeronauts attempted to overcome the unpredictable nature of ballooning by seeking ways and means of steering and propulsion. With these, the aeronaut would be able to travel in a direction other than that dictated by the wind. The result was the navigable airship, known correctly as the dirigible.

The first published design for a dirigible was that conceived by French Lt Jean-Baptiste Marie Meusnier, Corps of Engineers, in 1784. This was submitted to the Académie des Sciences but was never constructed. The design called for inner and outer envelopes, the latter to maintain the craft's steerable cigar shape when gas was released, and three large two-blade propellers were to provide propulsion, turned by 80 crew members prior to development of a suitable engine.

The world's first powered, manned dirigible made its first flight on 24 September 1852, when the Frenchman Henri Giffard rose in a steam-powered balloon from the Paris Hippodrome and travelled approximately 17 miles (27 km) to Trappes. His average speed for the journey was 5 mph (8 km/h). The envelope was 144 ft (43·89 m) in length and had a capacity of 88 000 ft³ (2492 m³); the steam engine developed about 3 hp and drove an 11 ft (3·35 m) diameter three-blade propeller.

The world's first aircraft to be powered by an internal combustion engine was that built and flown by Austrian Paul Hänlein in 1872. Approximately 164 ft (50 m) in length and 29 ft 6 in (9 m)

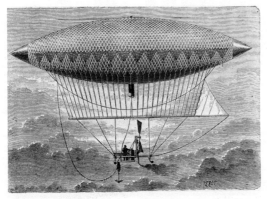

The world's first powered, manned dirigible was designed by Henri Giffard. (Science Museum, London)

maximum diameter, the 85 000 ft³ (2407 m³) craft was powered by a 5 hp Lenoir-type four-cylinder gas engine which consumed gas from the envelope. This turned a 15 ft (4.57 m) diameter propeller at about 40 rpm, using 250 ft³ (7·08 m³) of gas per hour. Only tethered flights were made and lack of capital prevented further development.

Among the first hangars built specifically to house dirigibles was one erected at Chalais-Meudon for an exhibition of 1878. This became **the first French government-owned dirigible hangar** in 1879.

The first great German dirigible pioneer was Dr Karl Wölfert who, in 1880, ascended in a dirigible fitted with a small engine. His flying companion was Herr Baumgarten. Load distribution problems caused the dirigible to crash, prompting Baumgarten to abandon the project. However, Wölfert was not so discouraged and on 5 March 1882 he ascended in a dirigible at Charlottenburg, when he attempted unsuccessfully to propel it using a hand-turned propeller.

The first dirigible fitted with an electric motor was that flown on 8 October 1883 by Frenchman Gaston Tissandier. The motor was produced by Siemens and was powered by 24 bichromate of potash batteries.

The world's first fully controllable powered dirigible was *La France*, an electric-powered craft which, flown by Capt Charles Renard and Lt Arthur Krebs of the French Corps of Engineers, took off on 9 August 1884 from Chalais-Meudon, France, flew a circular course of about 5 miles (8 km), returned to their point of departure and landed safely. The 9 hp Gramme electric motor drove a 23 ft (7·01 m) four-blade wooden tractor propeller. A maximum speed of 14½ mph (23·5 km/h) was achieved during the 23 min flight.

The first successful use of a petrol engine in a dirigible was by Dr Karl Wölfert, who designed and built a small balloon to which he fitted a 2 hp single-cylinder Daimler engine in 1888. Its first flight was carried out at Seelberg in Germany on Sunday, 12 August that year, probably flown by a young mechanic named Michaël.

A name later to become synonymous with airships was that of Count Ferdinand von Zeppelin,

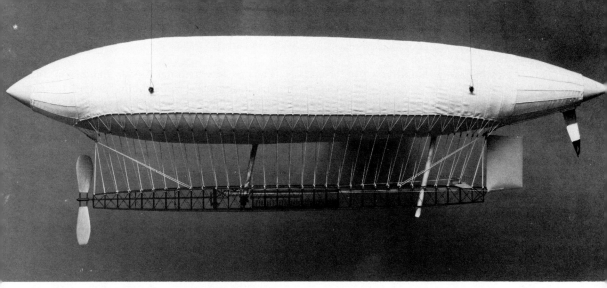

Model of La France (British Crown Copyright, Science Museum, London)

who had his first design for a passenger-carrying airship rejected by the German government's technical commission in 1894. Not too discouraged, in the following year he was granted the first patent for his method of constructing rigid airships, and in 1896 he raised the princely sum of 800 000 Reichmarks to found the Joint Stock Company for Promotion of Airship Flight. Zeppelin died on 8 March 1917, having seen the heyday of the airship as a strategic bomber.

The first people to be killed in a dirigible accident were Dr Karl Wölfert and mechanic Herr Knabe, when *Deutschland*'s engine vaporiser set fire to the envelope, resulting in a gas explosion, on 14 June 1897.

The first all-metal dirigible, the German Schwartz *Metallballon*, made its only ascent on 3 November 1897.

The first floating dirigible hangar was that constructed in 1899 to house Zeppelin LZ 1, which floated on Lake Constance.

The first flight of a Zeppelin dirigible was made by Count Ferdinand von Zeppelin's LZ 1 on 2 July 1900. This flight, carrying five persons and lasting about 20 min, was from the floating hangar on Lake Constance and showed that the airship lacked control. LZ 1 was 420 ft (128 m) long, had a diameter of 38 ft 6 in (11·73 m) and a volume of 400 000 ft³ (11 327 m³). Power was provided by two Daimler engines, each rated at 16 hp.

An early demonstration of controlled flying in a dirigible was made on 19 October 1901, when Brazilian-born Alberto Santos-Dumont flew his airship No 6 round the Eiffel Tower in Paris, France, winning a 100 000 franc prize. With an overall length of 108 ft (33 m), maximum diameter of 19 ft 6 in (6 m) and capacity of 22 200 ft³ (630 m³), it was powered by a 20 hp Buchet/ Santos-Dumont water-cooled petrol engine, driving a two-blade propeller.

The first practical dirigible was designed by the Lebaudy brothers and first flew on 12 November 1903. The flight of 37 miles (60 km) was from Moisson to the Champ-de-Mars, Paris. This was the **first fully controlled air journey in history.**

The first of many Zeppelin dirigibles to be destroyed in bad weather was LZ 2, which had made its first and only ascent on 17 January 1906 and was lost in a gale while moored at Kisslegg the following day. (LZ 1 had been broken up after three flights, in 1901.)

Zeppelin LZ 3 was first flown on 9 October 1906. This became **the first military Zeppelin** on 20

Wölfert dirigible in the 1890s.

June 1909, when it was handed over to the German Army as Z1.

The first British Army airship, Dirigible No 1 (popularly known as *Nulli Secundus*), was first flown on 10 September 1907 with three occupants: Col John Capper, RE, pilot; Capt W.A.C. King, Adj of the British Army Balloon School; Mr Samuel Cody, 'in charge of the engine'. The engine was a 50 hp Antoinette. The airship was 122 ft (37 m) long, 26 ft (8 m) in diameter and had a capacity of 55 000 ft³ (1555 m³). The second and third Army airships were *Beta* (35 hp Green engine) and *Gamma* (80 hp Green engine) respectively.

The République was the first dirigible to be used by the French Army on manoeuvres, in 1908.

The first dirigible to be used to bring attention to a political cause was one flown over the British House of Commons by a suffragette on 21 June 1908, from which leaflets were dropped.

The first dirigible to be used by a commercial airline was Zeppelin LZ 6, which was first flown on 26 May 1909. (Details of the airline, Delag, can be found below.) LZ 6 was 472 ft (144 m) long, had a maximum diameter of 42 ft 6 in (13 m) and a volume of 565 035 ft³ (16 000 m³). Power was provided by a 145 hp Maybach and two 115 hp Daimler engines, giving a maximum speed of 37 mph (60 km/h).

Nulli Secundus, *the first British Army airship, in 1907.* (Science Museum, London)

The first International Airship Exhibition (ILA) was staged at Frankfurt/Main between July and October 1909. Zeppelin LZ 5 was flown to the exhibition.

The first occasion on which four people lost their lives in an air accident was on 25 September 1909 when the French dirigible *République* lost a propeller which pierced the gasbag; the craft fell from 400 ft (122 m) at Avrilly, near Moulins, the crew of four being killed.

The world's first commercial airline was formed as Delag (Die Deutsche Luftschiffahrt Aktiengesellschaft) by Count Ferdinand von Zeppelin on 16 October 1909. Between 1910 and November 1913 the airline carried more than 34 000 passengers between major German cities without injury, although, of the six original airships employed on the services, three were lost.

The first non-rigid dirigible to be moored by mast was the British Army's *Beta 1*, which first flew on 3 June 1910. This was also **the first British dirigible to have wireless telegraphy installed.**

The first occasion on which five people lost their lives in an air accident was on 13 July 1910 when a German non-rigid dirigible, of the Erbslön type, suffered an explosion of the gasbag and fell from 920 ft (280 m) near Opladen, Germany. The crew of five, including Oscar Erbslön, were killed.

The first flight of an airship from England to France was achieved by E.T. Willows in the *Willows III* on 4 November 1910.

The first British rigid dirigible was the Vickers R1 *Mayfly*. It was 512 ft (156 m) long and was destroyed in a handling accident at Barrow on 24 September 1911 before making a single flight.

The first airmail carried in Germany was flown on an experimental service between Darmstadt and Frankfurt/Main by the dirigibles *Schwaben* and *Gelber Hund*. This service lasted from 10 to 22 June 1912.

The first international commercial airship service was begun by the Delag dirigible *Hansa* on 19 September 1912, flying between Hamburg, Copenhagen (Denmark) and Malmö (Sweden).

The first Zeppelin dirigible designed to be capable of reaching Britain in case of war (with a bomb load) and the largest airship completed before the outbreak of the First World War was LZ 18, designated L2 in German naval service. Launched on 9 September 1913, L2 was 518 ft 4 in (158 m) long and had a volume of 953 500 ft³ (27 000 m³). Power was provided by four 165 hp Maybach engines. Intended to be the first of ten large dirigibles to equip two Navy units, it was lost, however, on 17 October 1913, when it caught fire while airborne. All 28 crew were killed.

The first dirigible with a volume of more than one million ft³ was the German Navy's Schütte-Lanz SL 3, which was completed in February

Britain's first rigid airship was the Vickers R.1 Mayfly, damaged beyond repair before making its first flight.

1915. Powered by four 210 hp Maybach engines, it was 502 ft 4 in (153 m) in length and had a volume of 1 144 200 ft³ (32 400 m³). This airship was lost in 1916.

The first successful mission by a German dirigible during the First World War was carried out on 12 August 1914, when L3 located the Dutch battleship *de Zeven Provincien* and destroyers close to the island of Terschelling, Waddeneilanden.

The first bombing attack of the First World War was made by an aeroplane flown by Lt Césari and Corp Prudhommeau, French Aviation Militaire, against the Zeppelin sheds at Metz-Frescaty, on 14 August 1914.

The first dirigible to be shot down by French infantry was *Dupuy-de-Lôme* on 24 August 1914, a French airship mistakenly identified as a Zeppelin.

The first British air raid on Germany was by four aircraft of the Eastchurch RNAS Squadron. On 22 September 1914 two aircraft took off from Antwerp to attack the airship sheds at Düsseldorf, two to attack the airship sheds at Cologne. Only the aircraft flown by Flt Lt Collet found the target—the sheds at Düsseldorf—and his three

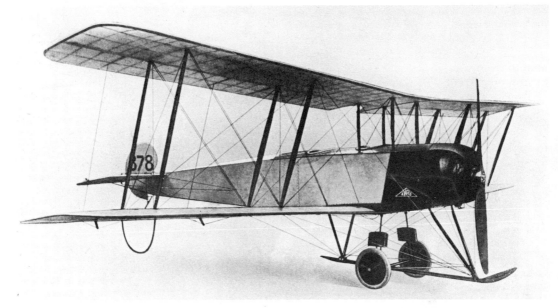

20 lb (9 kg) Hales bombs, while probably on target, failed to explode. All aircraft returned safely.

The first successful British air raid on Germany took place on 8 October 1914. Sqn Cdr D.A. Spenser-Grey and Flt Lt R.L.G. Marix of the Eastchurch RNAS Squadron flew from Antwerp in Sopwith Tabloids (Nos 167 and 168) to attack airship sheds at Düsseldorf and Cologne with 20 lb (9 kg) Hales bombs. Grey failed to find the target, bombed Cologne Railway Station and returned to Antwerp. Marix reached his target at Düsseldorf, bombed the shed from 600 ft (183 m) and destroyed it and Zeppelin LZ25/ Z.IX inside. His aircraft was damaged by gunfire, and he eventually crash-landed 20 miles (30 km) from Antwerp, returning to the city on a bicycle borrowed from a peasant.

The first ever strategic bombing raid by a formation of aircraft was launched on 21 November 1914 against the Zeppelin sheds at Friedrichshafen. Sqn Cdr E.F. Briggs, leading the attack, was accompanied by Flt Cdr J.T. Babington and Flt Lt S.V. Sippé, also on Avro 504s of the Royal Naval Air Service. The aircraft flew from Belfort in France, each carrying four 20 lb bombs, with which Zeppelin LZ32 (L7) was damaged in its shed and the gasworks destroyed. Briggs was wounded in the head by heavy defending machine-gun fire and taken prisoner.

The Avro 504 flown by Sqn Cdr E.F. Briggs during the attack on the Zeppelin sheds at Friedrichshafen, 21 November 1914.

The heaviest bomb dropped by an aircraft by the end of 1914 weighed 661 lb (300 kg), released during experiments from the new German semi-rigid dirigible *M IV*, on 18 December 1914. This dirigible had been commissioned only days before.

The first airship raid on Great Britain was carried out on 19 January 1915 by three German Navy Zeppelins, L3, L4 and L6. They took off from Fuhlsbüttel and Nordholz. L6 was forced to return through engine trouble but L3 and L4 arrived over the Norfolk coast at about 20.00 h; nine bombs were dropped in the Great Yarmouth area at 20.25 h by L3, killing two persons and wounding three others. Meanwhile L4 had gone north-west towards Bacton and dropped incendiary bombs on Sheringham, Thornham and Brancaster as well as a high-explosive bomb on Hunstanton wireless station. Following that, it dropped bombs on Heacham, Snettisham and King's Lynn, where seven high-explosive bombs were dropped and an incendiary, killing two people and injuring 13. The two airships were both wrecked on the coast of Jutland on 17 February 1915, after running into a gale on their homeward journey from a mission to spot the British Fleet.

The first partially successful attack on a submarine by an airship was performed in the early afternoon of 3 May 1915, when Zeppelin LZ36 (L9) spotted four British submarines and managed to damage the conning tower of one, D4, by dropping five 50 kg bombs from an altitude of about 3280 ft (1000 m).

The first air raid on London was by Zeppelin LZ38 on 31 May 1915. The Kaiser had authorised bombing of London, east of the Tower, a few days before and on the night of the 31st 3000 lb (1360 kg) of bombs were dropped on north-east London, killing seven people and injuring 14 others.

The first dirigible of the US Navy to fly was the DN-1 (A1) which was acquired under contract on 1 June 1915 from the Connecticut Aircraft Company. As originally built with two engines it was too heavy to leave the ground; after redesign with only one engine it made its first of three flights on 20 April 1917 at Pensacola, Florida. It was subsequently damaged and not repaired.

The first airship to be brought down by air attack was Zeppelin LZ37 on the night of 6 to 7 June 1915. In company with LZ38 and LZ39, the airship set out from Bruges to bomb London but adverse weather later forced them to alter course for their secondary targets—railways in the Calais area. LZ37 was located and attacked by Flt Sub Lt R.A.J. Warneford of No 1 Squadron, RNAS, flying a Morane-Saulnier Parasol from Dunkirk. Warneford's only means of attack were six 20 lb (9 kg) bombs; he followed the airship from Ostend to Ghent, being forced to keep his distance by fire from the airship's gunners. He made a single pass over the airship dropping all six bombs from about 150 ft (45 m) above it. The sixth exploded, and the airship fell in flames on a suburb of Ghent killing two nuns. Only one member of Oberleutnant Otto van de Haegen's crew survived. Warneford returned safely to base after making a forced landing to repair a broken fuel line. He was informed the following evening that he had been awarded the Victoria Cross; he died 12 days later when the tail of a Henry Farman pusher biplane collapsed in mid-air.

The first German airship to be brought down on British soil was the Schutte-Lanz SL XI, which was attacked on the night of 2 September 1916 by Lt W. Leefe Robinson, RFC, using the

Although Zeppelin raids on England resulting in death or injury to British people ended in April 1918, other raids followed. LZ112 (L70) raided England on the night of 5–6 August 1918 but was shot down by Maj Egbert Cadbury flying a DH4. Twenty-two crew died.

newly-invented Pomeroy incendiary ammunition. It crashed in flames near Cuffley, Hertfordshire. Robinson was awarded the VC. This action demoralised German airship crews, particularly because it had demonstrated the effectiveness of British defences, and is said to have prevented a large-scale airship attack on London. However, on the night of 23 to 24 September eleven Zeppelins raided England, three with London as their target. One airship, LZ76 (L33), was hit by anti-aircraft fire and landed at Little Wigborough and another, LZ74 (L32), was shot down by a British aircraft (flown by 2nd Lt Sowrey) over Great Burstead.

The first successful dirigible of the US Navy was the Goodyear FB-1 acquired under contract on 14 March 1917 and first flown from Chicago, Illinois, to Wingfoot Lake, near Akron, Ohio, on 30 May 1917.

The greatest losses suffered by the German Naval Airship Division on a single day of operational missions were five Zeppelins that failed to return to base on 20 October 1917. LZ85 (L45) and LZ96 (L49) force landed in France, LZ 93 (L44) was shot down over France, LZ 89 (L50) was lost over the Mediterranean and LZ 101 (L55) force landed in Germany. LZ 50 (L16) had also been wrecked the previous day. On 5 January 1918 five Navy dirigibles were destroyed in an explosion at the Ahlhorn sheds, raising the total number of airships lost to the German Navy in three months from October 1917 to twelve.

The last German airship attack on England which resulted in death or injury was made on 12 April 1918. Altogether, during the 51 Zeppelin airship raids on Great Britain during the war, 196 tons (199 tonnes) of bombs were dropped, killing 557 people and injuring many more.

The greatest number of rigid airships operated by an armed service was the 69 Zeppelins and Schütte-Lanz craft flown by the German Naval Airship Division during the First World War. This service also suffered the greatest proportion of fatalities of any armed force, with approximately 40 per cent of its total personnel being killed.

The first airship crossing, and first two-way crossing of the Atlantic by any type of aircraft, were achieved by the British airship R-34 between 2 and 6 July (westward) and 9 and 13 July (eastward), 1919. Commanded by Sqn Ldr G.H. Scott, with a crew of 30, the R-34 set out from East Fortune, Scotland, and flew to New York, returning afterwards to Pulham, Norfolk, England. The total distance covered, 6330 miles (10 187 km) in 183 h 8 min, constituted a world record for airships.

Delag, the pre-war commercial airline flying dirigibles, reopened services on 24 August 1919 with the airship *Bodensee*, flying the route between Friedrichshafen and Berlin. However, this service was suspended on 1 December by order of the Allied Control Commission. Between these dates about 103 flights had been made, carrying 2400 passengers and 66 140 lb (30 000 kg) of cargo. Each flight carried 23 passengers.

The first dirigible with a volume of more than $2\frac{1}{2}$ million ft^3 was the British Shorts R-38. Launched in 1921, it was **then the largest airship in the world,** with a length of 695 ft (212 m), maximum diameter of 85 ft (26 m) and volume of 2 740 000 ft^3 (77 600 m^3). Power was provided by six Cossack engines with a total output of 2100 hp. It was destroyed when it broke up over Hull, England, on 24 August 1921. It was to have been sold to the United States and at the time of the disaster there were 16 Americans aboard in

ZR-1 Shenandoah, a helium-filled rigid airship, seen here at its mooring mast. Between September 1923 and its loss in September 1925, ZR-1 made 57 flights.

addition to the crew of 33. All the Americans and 28 of the British lost their lives.

The first airship to use helium gas instead of hydrogen was Goodyear C 7, one of 16 C series non-rigid airships ordered for the US Navy as coastal patrol and convoy craft. This made its first flight on 1 December 1921. The first C series airship, the C 1 launched in September 1918, was the first non-rigid dirigible to demonstrate the 'parasite' concept, when on 12 December 1918 it lifted a Curtiss Jenny biplane to an altitude of 2500 ft (760 m) and successfully released it. Previous experiments in Germany and Britain using the rigid airships L35 and R-23 had seen the air launch of an Albatros D.III and Sopwith Camel respectively. The Albatros had been released on 26 January 1918, making this **the first demonstration of the parasite fighter concept**. The first British parasite experiment was conducted on 6 November 1918.

The first helium-filled American rigid airship was the Zeppelin-type ZR-1 *Shenandoah*, which first flew on 4 September 1923 at Lakehurst, New Jersey, USA. On 3 September 1925 it was destroyed in a storm over Caldwell, Ohio, with heavy loss of life.

The only dirigible received by the US Navy from Germany as war reparations was the newly-built LZ 126, known as ZR-3 *Los Angeles*. This was

Italia at King's Bay in May 1928.

flown from Friedrichshafen to Lakehurst, USA, during 12 to 14 October 1924. A very successful airship that made well over 300 flights up to 1932, it was initially filled with hydrogen gas.

The French rigid airship *Dixmude*, in fact Zeppelin LZ 114 (L72), received as war reparations, remained airborne for 118 hours and 41 minutes in September 1925, landing on the 25th. This was by far the greatest duration flight of the period.

The first airship flight over the North Pole was made by the Italian-built N-class semi-rigid airship N.1, subsequently named *Norge* by Roald Amundsen who bought the airship for Arctic exploration. During the period from 11 to 14 May 1926, the *Norge* was flown from Spitzbergen to Teller, Alaska. Among the distinguished crew were Amundsen, Umberto Nobile and Lincoln Ellsworth, who dropped Norwegian, Italian and American flags at the Pole on 12 May. On 23 May 1928 Nobile set off in another attempt to fly over the North Pole, in the Italian dirigible *Italia*. This crashed on the return journey. Nobile survived this but Amundsen, who set out to rescue the crew of *Italia*, died.

N.1 Norge *in flight.* (Real Photographs)

The greatest straight-line distance ever flown by an airship is 3967.137 miles (6384.50 km), achieved by the German passenger dirigible LZ 127 *Graf Zeppelin* between 29 October and 1 November 1928. Captain was the legendary Dr Hugo Eckener.

The first airship flight round the world was accomplished by the German *Graf Zeppelin* between 8 and 29 August 1929. Captained by Dr Hugo Eckener, the craft set out from Lakehurst, New Jersey, and flew via Friedrichshafen, Germany, Tokyo, Japan, and Los Angeles, California, returning to Lakehurst in 21 days, 5 h and 31 min. This total distance covered was more than 21 870 miles (35 200 km). Most successful of all the passenger-carrying airships, the *Graf* had flown well over a million miles and had carried a total of some 13 100 passengers before

Graf Zeppelin moored in the USA in late 1929, seen alongside the small Goodyear-built US Navy non-rigid blimp Volunteer

being scrapped at the beginning of the Second World War.

The last commercial airships to be developed by Great Britain were the R-100 and R-101. The latter crashed on 5 October 1930 at Beauvais, France, on a flight from Cardington, Bedfordshire, England, to Egypt and India. The accident, which destroyed the airship and killed 48 of the 54 occupants (including Lord Thomson, Secretary of State for Air, and Maj Gen Sir Sefton Brancker, Director of Civil Aviation), brought to an end the development of passenger-carrying airships in Great Britain. The R-101 was, however, the largest ever British airship, with a length of 777 ft (236·8 m) and volume of 5 508 800 ft³ (155 995 m³). The R-100 was designed by Barnes Neville Wallis (later Sir Barnes) for the Airship Guarantee Company. It was for this craft that he originated his unique geodetic form of basic airframe structure, used later in the construction of Vickers Wellesley and Wellington bomber aircraft. In a test on 16 January 1930 the R-100

achieved a speed of 81½ mph (131 km/h), making it **the fastest airship in the world.**

During July and August 1930 the R-100 made a double Atlantic crossing, flying between Cardington and Montreal, Canada. But, following the R-101 disaster, it was scrapped.

The world's first fighter-carrying airship intended for operational service, USS _Akron_, was flown for the first time on 25 September 1931. This operated successfully with its six Curtiss F9C-2 Sparrowhawk fighters until 4 April 1933 when it crashed into the sea off the New Jersey coast during a storm. (See below.) On 3 November 1931 _Akron_ ascended with 207 persons on board, **the greatest number ever carried by an airship.**

The first and only American operational fighters to serve aboard airships were naval Curtiss F9C Sparrowhawk biplanes, which served on board the US airships _Akron_ and _Macon_ between 1932 and 1935. The prototype Sparrowhawk (_XF9C-1_) achieved the first 'hook-on' on the airship _Los_

Britain's ill-fated R-101 leaving its mooring mast at Cardington. (Science Museum, London).

USS Akron, *the first fighter-carrying operational airship.*

The crew of the US Navy airship ZPG 2, after making the longest unrefuelled duration flight. Lt. Moore is standing eighth from the left.

Angeles on 27 October 1931, and the first production aircraft hooked-on to *Akron* on 29 June 1932.

The last major airship disaster involved the destruction of the German *Hindenburg*, then the world's largest airship, on 6 May 1937. It was destroyed by fire when approaching its moorings at Lakehurst, New Jersey, USA, after a flight from Frankfurt, Germany. Thirty-five of the 97 occupants were killed in the fire which engulfed the huge craft and which was attributed to the use of hydrogen—the only gas available to Germany owing to the United States' refusal to supply commercial quantities of helium. With its sister craft, the LZ 130 *Graf Zeppelin II*, it was the largest rigid airship ever built, with a length of 803 ft 10 in (245 m) and a volume of 7 062 100 ft³ (199 981 m³).

The first airship built in Britain following the R-101 disaster made its first flight at Cardington, Bedfordshire, on 19 July 1951. This was a small airship named *Bournemouth*, built by the Airship Club of Great Britain under the leadership of Lord Ventry.

Hindenburg engulfed in flames at Lakehurst on 6 May 1937. (US National Archives)

The longest duration flight by a non-rigid dirigible without refuelling is 264 h 12 min, established between 4 and 15 March 1957 by a US Navy Goodyear ZPG 2 class craft. This flight, crewed by Cdr J.R. Hunt, Lt Cdr Robert S. Bowser and twelve others, began from South Weymouth NAS, Massachusetts, and ended at Key West, Florida. The distance flown was 9448 miles (15 205 km), a record for lighter-than-air craft.

The largest non-rigid airships ever built were four Goodyear ZPG 3-W early warning radar craft ordered for the US Navy. The first of these was launched on 21 July 1958 but crashed in 1960. All remaining craft were deleted in 1962. Each was 403 ft 4 in (122·9 m) long and had a volume of 1 516 300 ft³ (42 937 m³).

The longest duration flight (without refuelling) by a fully equipped non-rigid dirigible on a mission is 95 h 30 min, achieved by the crew of a US

Navy ZPG 2 airship between 25 and 29 March 1960. In command of the crew of 19 was Lt Lundi A. Moore.

The world's first hot-air airship was first flown on 3 January 1973 at Newbury, England. Constructed by Cameron Balloons, D-96 (G-BAMK) was 100 ft (30·5 m) in length, with a maximum diameter of 45 ft (13·72 m). It was powered by a converted Volkswagen motorcar engine and had a speed of 17 mph (27·5 km/h). The lightweight nylon fabric envelope had a gross capacity of 96 000 ft³ (2718 m³) and was inflated by hot air generated by a propane gas burner carried in the lightweight tubular-metal gondola. More developed hot-air airships have followed from Cameron.

The producer of the largest number of airships is the Goodyear Tire & Rubber Company, which has built well over 300. The company also operates the largest current fleet of airships, comprising four non-rigid craft for public relations and advertising.

The first hot-air airship, known as the Cameron D-96.

Pioneers of Flying

Myths, fantasies, and early accounts of intrepid tower jumpers who often as not leapt to their deaths clutching ill-conceived 'flying' apparatus, all serve to show that man has always considered assisted flying possible. A glance skyward to see birds in flight was the inspiration for early myths and fantasies, when stories were told of gods and mortals who had flown with bird-like wings. Perhaps the best remembered of these was the flight to freedom by Icarus and Daedalus from imprisonment by Minos, King of Crete. Such tales, which science tells us could have had no basis in reality, bear further examination. For example, whilst some gods were pictured with wings as part of their divine forms, earth-bound humans were required to build wings, thereby constructing flying apparatus. Furthermore, whilst civilisations like the Egyptians in the centuries BC had their own winged gods, some historians believe that basic understanding of

aerodynamics for flight might have been understood in Egypt 2300 years ago.

The first of the recorded tower jumpers was Bladud, the ninth king of Britain who, in about 843BC, jumped to his death from the Temple of Apollo in Trinavantum (London) adorned with wings of feathers. Many centuries later, tower jumpers were still leaping off high places, with little chance of a second attempt at flight! Then, in the 11th century, two well-recorded leaps appeared to have shown some promise, although ending in one death and serious injury to the other would-be flier.

In the meantime, in China in the 4th century BC the kite had been invented for pleasure and war. In about 200 BC Chinese General Han Hsin used a kite to calculate the distance between his army and the enemy during a battle, and eight centuries later the Chinese are known to have used kites to pass military signals by semaphore. Amazingly, it was the kite that first gave man a taste of flying, as recorded in later paragraphs.

Free flight was still the aim of most would-be fliers and an important step forward was made in 1250 AD. In this year an English Franciscan monk named Roger Bacon completed a book entitled *Secrets of Art and Nature*, in which he mentioned 'Engines for flying, a man sitting in the midst thereof, by turning only about an Instrument, which moves artificiall Wings made to beat the Aire, much after the fashion of a Bird's flight'. At last the need for mechanical assistance had been appreciated, although Bacon's thoughts were directed to what we know today as the ornithopter with flapping wings. More than two centuries later the Italian Leonardo da Vinci also designed an ornithopter, giving further proof that it had been appreciated that man's muscle power without assistance was insufficient for flight. This was endorsed by the Italian Giovanni Borelli in 1680, in his book *De Motu Animalium*. Unfortunately, the ornithopter remained the number one concept for manned powered flight right up to the invention of man-carrying balloons, a dead-end concept that has still to be mastered in the late 20th

century. Interestingly, whilst the ornithopter proved to be no way forward in itself, recent years have witnessed that engine power is not always necessary for powered and sustained flight. The development of pedal-power aircraft, albeit using modern technology in their configuration and construction, has shown that man's muscles can generate sufficient power for sustained flight if matched mechanically to a sufficiently lightweight and high-lift airframe. Perhaps the real measure of Bacon's, da Vinci's and Borelli's understanding of mechanical flight is that they never felt the need to put their theories to the test.

It is generally accepted that Sir George Cayley (1773–1857) was the 'Father of Aerial Navigation'. Unlike the eminent persons mentioned previously, he believed that wings should be left to produce lift only and that another system of propulsion should be sought. This, instantly, rejected the ornithopter. He is credited with designing the first aircraft with a fixed and cambered wing, set at a modest angle of attack, a tail unit with horizontal and vertical surfaces, and a man-carrying body. Although a piloted aircraft of this general configuration and capable of powered flight was some decades away, the foundations for such a machine had been laid.

The earliest known model that could have represented a flying machine was a carved wooden bird, thought to be some 2300 years old. Originally discovered at Saqqara, Egypt, in 1898, and rediscovered in a storage box at the Cairo museum by Dr Khalil Messiha in 1972, it has a high-mounted wing with a finely carved aerofoil section, a body with the rear portion of narrow elliptical shape, and a deep vertical tail-fin with a groove for a horizontal surface.

The first 'tower jumper' to achieve some measure of gliding flight was probably the English Benedictine monk Oliver of Malmesbury, in about 1020 AD. Known as 'the Flying Monk', he jumped from Malmesbury Abbey with wings. A measure of gliding flight must have been achieved, as his only injuries were two broken legs. To Oliver can also be attributed **the first practical lesson in heavier-than-air gliding flight,** as his injuries convinced him of the necessity for tail surfaces attached to the feet.

The first known printed illustration of a flight is this woodcut entitled 'The Flight of Daedalus and Fall of Icarus', from Riederer Spiegel der Währen Rhetoric, Frieburg 1493. (Science Museum, London)

Another important and recorded attempt at gliding flight in the 11th century, but one that ended in fatality, was that made by Saracen of Constantinople. For the attempt he wore a cloak fitted with stiffening ribs. Unfortunately, one rib snapped and he plunged to the ground. This must rank as the best recorded case of early structural failure.

The first helicopters to fly were small models powered by the string-pull method, the first of which appeared in the 14th century. One such toy was illustrated in a Flemish manuscript of 1325.

The first witnessed and properly recorded manned flights took place in Cathay (China) in the 14th century. These were recorded by the Venetian merchant traveller Marco Polo, while in Cathay with his father and an uncle. He witnessed man-carrying tethered kites and a translation of his report appears in *The Description of the World*, edited by A. C. Moule and P. Pelliot and published in London in 1938; it goes like this:

And so we will tell you how, when any ship must go on a voyage, they prove whether its business will go well or ill on that voyage. The men of the ship indeed will have a hurdle, that is a grating, of withies, and at each corner and side of the hurdle will be tied a cord, so that there will be eight cords, and they will all be tied at the other end with a long rope. Again they will find someone stupid or drunken and will bind him on the hurdle; for no wise man nor undepraved would expose himself to that danger. And this is done when a strong wind prevails. They indeed set up the hurdle opposite the wind, and the wind lifts the hurdle and carries it into the sky and the men hold on by the long rope. And if while it is in the air the hurdle leans towards the way of the wind, they pull the rope to them a little and then the hurdle is set upright, and they let out some rope and the hurdle rises.... The proof is made in this way, namely that if the hurdle going straight up makes for the sky, they say that the ship for which that proof has been made will make a quick and prosperous voyage, and all the merchants run together to her for the sake of sailing and going with her. And if the hurdle has not been able to go up, no merchant will be willing to enter the ship for

This work by Prater c 1803 depicts Blanchard releasing animals over Vienna on 2 August 1791. (Science Museum, London)

which the proof was made, because they say that she could not finish her voyage and many ills would oppress her. And so that ship stays in port that year.

The first recorded successful quasi-parachute jumps were made in China in 1306, as part of the celebrations during the coronation of Fo-Kin.

The first aerial bombers were bomb-carrying pennon kites, first illustrated in Europe in 1326.

The first known design for a parachute proper was that by the Italian Leonardo da Vinci, dated about 1485. This square-section parachute was drawn to be hand held.

The first design for a parachute to appear in published form was to be found in *Machinae novae*, a Venetian work of 1595 by Fausto Veranzio. This was a square cloth attached to a frame, the corners of which were roped to a body harness.

The first powered model aeroplane to have flown is thought to have been that constructed in 1647 by the Italian Titus Livio Burattini, then residing at the court of King Wladyslaw IV of Poland. It is recorded to have had four sets of wings in tandem and a tail unit, the two centre pairs fixed and the forward and rear pairs for propulsion as an ornithopter. Drive was via springs. (Eight years later, Englishman Robert Hooke also flew a model ornithopter.)

A recorded parachute jump successfully made outside China was performed by an athlete in 1687, in the presence of the King of Siam and courtiers. Detailed by M de la Loubères, following a journey to Siam, the athlete is said to have jumped from height with two umbrellas, the handles of which were attached to his girdle.

Perhaps the first sustained flight by a man-carrying glider was performed in the 17th century by Hezarfen Celebi of Turkey. Leaping from a tower at Galata, he is said to have covered some distance before meeting the ground.

A clockwork-powered model helicopter, with two contra-rotating rotors, was constructed and flown in 1754 by the Russian Michael Vasilyevitch Lomonosov. This was probably **the first self-propelled model helicopter**. (A similar type of model helicopter was constructed by Jacob Degen in 1816.)

The first demonstration in Europe of a quasi-parachute was given by the Frenchman Sebastien le Normand, who, in 1783, jumped from an observation tower at Montpellier (at a height equivalent to a first floor) under a braced conical canopy of 2 ft 6 in (0.76 m) diameter.

The first recognised self-propelled model helicopter appears to have been that demonstrated on 28 April 1784, in France, by Launoy and Bienvenu. It consisted of a stick with a two-blade propeller at each end. The model was powered by a bowdrill arrangement; as the string of the bowdrill unwound the propellers counter-rotated. It was on this model that Sir George Cayley based his model helicopter in 1796, using a similar bowdrill arrangement but powering two four-blade rotors made from feathers.

The first living creatures to descend by parachute from a balloon were animals released on 2 August 1791 over Vienna by the famous aeronaut Jean-Pierre Blanchard. (Following this and the release of a dog over Strasbourg, Blanchard made a parachute descent at Basle but broke a leg, in 1793.)

The first parachute descent ever performed successfully by man from a vehicle was accomplished by the Frenchman, André Jacques Garnerin, who jumped from a balloon at 2230 ft (680 m) having ascended from the Parc Monçeau near Paris on 22 October 1797.

The first man in the world to identify and correctly record the parameters of heavier-than-air flight was the Englishman, Sir George Cayley, sixth Baronet (born 27 December 1773; died 15 December 1857). Sir George Cayley succeeded to the Baronetcy in a long and distinguished line of Cayleys whose origins are traceable back to Sir Hugo de Cayly, Knight, of Owby, who lived early in the 12th century. Sir William Cayley was created first Baronet by Charles II on 26 April 1661 for services in the Civil War. It was at Brompton Hall, near Scarborough, in the 1790s, that young George Cayley had carried out some of his early experiments with model aeroplanes. The following is a list of notable achievements by this remarkable scientist who was first to:
☐ set down the mathematical principles of heavier-than-air flight (ie lift, thrust and drag)
☐ make use of models for flying research, among them a simple glider—the first mono-

plane with fixed wing amidships, and fuselage terminating in vertical and horizontal tail surfaces; this was constructed in 1804

☐ draw attention to the importance of streamlining (in his definition of 'drag')

☐ suggest the benefits of biplanes and triplanes to provide increased lift with minimum weight

☐ construct and fly a man-carrying glider

☐ demonstrate the means by which a curved 'aerofoil' provided 'lift' by creating reduced pressure over the upper surface when moved through the air

Handbill advertising Robert Cocking's parachute descent at the Royal Gardens. Vauxhall. (Science Museum, London)

☐ suggest the use of an internal-combustion engine for aeroplanes and constructed a model gunpowder engine in the absence of low-flash-point fuel oil.

The first parachute descent in England was made by André Jacques Garnerin on 21 September 1802. However, he was injured in the descent, when one strap supporting the basket snapped.

The first man to survive the destruction of his hot-air balloon while in flight by the use of a parachute (see Lighter-than-air.)

The first parachute descent from a balloon in America was that made by Charles Guille who, on 2 August 1819, jumped from a hydrogen balloon at a height of about 8000 ft (2440 m) and landed at New Bushwick, Long Island, New York.

To demonstrate the effectiveness of his man-lifting kites, English school teacher George Pocock attached one of his kites to a road carriage in 1827 and was pulled at speed between the cities of Bristol and Marlborough.

The first public demonstration of a new form of parachute with an upside-down canopy to prevent oscillations, designed by Briton Robert Cocking and released from about 6600 ft (2000 m) on 24 July 1837, ended in tragedy. Lifted to height under the *Great Nassau Balloon*, the parachute, with Cocking underneath in a basket, descended well after release until the upper rim collapsed and he plunged to his death.

The first model helicopter to use a pressure-jet system to drive the rotor was that flown by Englishman W. H. Phillips in 1842. Steam passed through the tips of the blades to turn the rotor.

Sir George Cayley's 'Aerial Carriage', designed in 1843, was perhaps the first attempt at a convertiplane. It had four circular wings, in pairs, mounted on outriggers from the boat-like wheeled fuselage. When the rotating wings were needed to provide lift, they were designed to open out into eight-bladed propellers. Forward propulsion was by two rear-mounted propellers.

The first modern aeroplane design, incorporating wire-braced constant chord wings (constructed using spars and cambered ribs, with double skinning), an enclosed fuselage for the crew and passengers and housing the power

Model of Sir George Cayley's Aerial Carriage *of 1843*. (British Crown Copyright. Science Museum, London)

This engraving of the full-size Aerial Steam Carriage *or* Ariel *is inscribed to the Directors of The Aerial Transit Company*. (Science Museum, London)

plant, propellers, a fixed tricycle landing gear, and a vertical tail and large-area tailplane, was the *Aerial Steam Carriage* (also known as the *Ariel*). Designed by Englishman William Samuel Henson (1812–88) from 1842, the design received a patent in 1843 and was expected to be built for service with the proposed Aerial Transit Company, **the first ever projected commercial airline.** The full-size *Aerial Steam Carriage* was to have had a span of 150 ft (45·72 m), a wing chord of 30 ft (9·14 m), and a length of about 84 ft 9 in (25·83 m), and the single 25–30 hp Henson steam engine was expected to drive two 10 ft (3·05 m) diameter six-blade pusher propellers. Although the subject of many engravings, it was never built. This is partly because of the failure of a scale model of the *Aerial Steam Carriage* to make a sustained flight. This model, with a span of 20 ft (6·10 m) and also steam powered, was tested between 1844 and 1847. Although launched using a ramp, it proved incapable of sustaining flight. Having seen the failure of his dreams, Henson emigrated to America in 1848. However, this model was **the first to be powered by a steam engine.**

The first powered model aeroplane to fly successfully is the subject of some controversy. The first claim is made for John Stringfellow, an associate of Henson who was to have been the co-founder of the Aerial Transit Company (had the founding of this public company for worldwide air travel been accepted more favourably). Continuing Henson's work, but using a 10 ft 6 in (3·20 m) span steam-driven model with curved wings, Stringfellow launched his model from a high cable at Chard, Somerset, England in 1848 but this is thought not to have sustained flight. However, Stringfellow is also remembered for a model triplane exhibited at the first aeronautical exhibition at the Crystal Palace in 1868, which, although unsuccessful in flight, introduced the concept of superimposed straight wings on a model. (It should be remembered that the triplane concept in itself was not new, Cayley having produced a triplane glider with superimposed wings in 1849—see below.)

The person credited with producing **the first powered model aeroplane to fly successfully** was Frenchman Félix du Temple de la Croix, who in 1857–58 flew a model powered successively by clockwork and steam.

The first person to be carried aloft in a heavier-than-air craft in sustained (gliding) flight was a ten-year-old boy who became airborne in a glider constructed by Sir George Cayley at Brompton Hall, near Scarborough, Yorkshire, in 1849. The glider became airborne after being towed by manpower down a hill against a light breeze.

The first man to be carried aloft in a heavier-than-air craft, but not in control of its flight, was Sir George Cayley's coachman at Brompton Hall, reputedly in June 1853. A witness of the event stated that after he had landed, the coachman struggled clear and shouted 'Please, Sir George, I wish to give notice. I was hired to drive, not to fly.' No record has ever been traced giving the name of either the ten-year-old or of the coachman. The decennial census of 1851, however, records the name of John Appleby as being the most probable member of Sir George's staff. With regard to the young boy, Sir George had no son or grandson of this age at the time of his experiments, so the first 'pilot' may have been a servant's son.

The first aircraft designed to save life was the man-carrying sea rescue kite developed by Irishman Cordner and first flown in 1859.

The world's first aircraft carrier (see Lighter than air.)

The first design for a jet-propelled aeroplane in the modern sense (remembering the rocket-powered model bird designed by the Italian Joanes Fontana in about 1420, and before this the wooden model bird propelled by steam or compressed air jet demonstrated in about 400–350 BC by Greek-born Archytas of Tarentum, Italy) was produced by Frenchman Charles de Louvrie in 1865. Known as the *Aéronave*, it had a canopy-type wing supported on a strut above a wheeled cart which carried twin jetpipes through which vaporised oil or similar fuel was to have been burned and ejected. This was not constructed.

The Aeronautical Society of Great Britain was founded on 12 January 1866. In 1868 it staged the **first ever aeronautical exhibition,** held at Crystal Palace. The exhibits included model engines driven by steam, oil gas and guncotton.

The first design for a powered delta-winged aeroplane was that by Englishmen J. W. Butler and E. Edwards and patented in 1867. This was also the **first British design for a jet-propelled aeroplane.**

Undoubtedly the first ornithopter to fly successfully was completed in 1870 by Gustave Trouvé. This bird-like model was powered by revolver cartridges which, when fired, forced down the wings, which returned by springs. It was reported that flights of 195 ft (60 m) were possible.

The first scientist correctly to deduce the main properties (ie lift distribution) of a cambered aerofoil was F. H. Wenham (1824–1908) who built various gliders during the mid-19th century to test his theories. In collaboration with John Browning, Wenham built **the world's first wind tunnel** in 1871 for the Aeronautical Society of Great Britain.

The first powered man-carrying aeroplane to achieve a brief 'hop', after gaining speed down a ramp, was a monoplane with swept-forward wings built by Félix du Temple and piloted by an unidentified young sailor, at Brest in about 1874. The power plant was a hot-air or steam engine, driving a tractor propeller.

The first unmanned aeroplane to fly from level ground was the *Aerial Steamer*, designed and built by Englishman Thomas Moy. A tandem wing craft with two six-blade pusher paddle-like propellers positioned between the wings and powered by a 3 hp steam engine, it lifted a few inches from the ground in 1875 in tethered flight from a circular track.

The four-stroke cycle gas engine was patented by Nikolaus Otto in Germany in 1876, and in 1877 he invented the four-stroke petrol internal combustion engine.

Among the first manned and powered aeroplanes to achieve a 'hop' flight after gaining speed down a slope was the huge monoplane built by Russian Alexander Fedorovich Mozhaiski and hopped in 1884. With a wing 74 ft 10 in (22·80 m) in span and 46 ft 7 in (14·20 m) in chord, and powered by a 20 hp steam engine driving a four-blade tractor propeller forward of the wings and a 10 hp steam engine driving two smaller pusher propellers inset in the wings, it was piloted by I. N. Golubev at Krasnoye Selo.

The first ever aeronautical exhibition was held at the Crystal Palace in 1868. Among that depicted can be seen a Stringfellow triplane hanging from the roof, kites, an airship, model ornithopters and a boy carrying a toy helicopter. (Lent to Science Museum, London)

The first man-carrying aeroplane to achieve a powered 'hop' after rising from supposedly level ground was the bat-winged *Éole* monoplane built and flown by Clément Ader (1841-1925), at Armainvilliers, France, on 9 October 1890. Powered by an 18-20 hp steam engine, the Éole covered about 165 ft (50 m), but never achieved sustained or controlled flight. Ader's second aeroplane, the *Avion III*, was tested twice on 12-14 August 1897 but did not fly.

The first contract for a military aeroplane was awarded to Clément Ader (see above) on 3 February 1892, to construct a two-seater capable of lifting a bomb-load of 165 lb (75 kg). This contract was not fulfilled, as the aeroplane failed to fly at Satorg, France, on 14 October 1897.

The first British powered aeroplane to fly tethered from a circular track, with a load equivalent to that of a pilot, was probably an early example of the *Multiplane*, a steam-powered multi-winged aeroplane designed by Horatio Phillips and flown at Harrow, England, with a 72 lb (33 kg) load in May 1893. This had 41 wings, each 19 ft (5·8 m) in span and with a chord of only 1½ in (3·8 cm). This type of wing set the pattern for his later successful aircraft.

The three most outstanding pioneers of gliding flight prior to successful powered flight were the German Otto Lilienthal (1848-96), the American Dr Octave Chanute (1832-1910), and the Englishman Percy S Pilcher (1866-99). Their achievements may be summarised as follows:

Otto Lilienthal, German civil engineer, published a classic aeronautical textbook *Der Vogelflug als Grundlage der Fliegekunst* (The Flight of Birds as the Basis of Aviation) in 1899. Although he remained convinced that powered flight would ultimately be achieved by wing-flapping (ie in the ornithopter), Lilienthal constructed five fixed-wing monoplane gliders and two biplane gliders between 1891 and 1896. Tested near Berlin and at the Rhinower Hills near Stöllen, these gliders managed sustained gliding flight; the pilot, usually Lilienthal himself, supported himself by his arms, holding the centre section of the glider. Thus, he could run forward and launch himself off the hills. During this period he achieved gliding distances ranging from 330 ft (100 m) to more than 820 ft (250 m). Although he had been experimenting with a

small carbonic acid gas engine, he died on 10 August 1896 after one of his gliders crashed on the Rhinower Hills on 9 August before he could progress further with powered flight.

Octave Chanute, American railroad engineer, was born in Paris, France, on 18 February 1832. His book *Progress in Flying Machines*, published in 1894, was the first comprehensive history of heavier-than-air flight and is still regarded as a classic of aviation literature. As well as providing a valuable information service for pioneers on both sides of the Atlantic, he began designing and building improved Lilienthal-type hang-gliders in 1896. After experimenting with multi-planes fitted with up to eight pairs of pivoting wings and a top fixed surface, he evolved the

Otto Lilienthal, airborne in a biplane glider in 1896
(Science Museum, London)

classic and successful biplane configuration. Flight-testing of his gliders was performed mainly by Augustus M. Herring (1867–1926), as Chanute was too old to fly himself. The Wright brothers gained early inspiration from *Progress in Flying Machines*, became close friends of Chanute, and learned from him the advantages offered by a Pratt-trussed biplane structure and, later, a catapult launching system for their wheel-less aircraft.

Percy S. Pilcher, English marine engineer, built his first glider, the *Bat*, in 1895 and flew that year on the banks of the River Clyde. Following advice by Lilienthal, as well as early practical experiments, Pilcher added a tailplane to the *Bat* and achieved numerous successful flights. This aircraft was followed by others (christened the *Beetle, Gull* and *Hawk*), the last of which was constructed in 1896 and included a fixed fin, a tailplane and a wheel undercarriage. It had a cambered wing with a span of 23 ft 4 in and an area of 180 ft² (7 m and 16·72 m² respectively). Pilcher had always set his sights upon powered

Octave Chanute. (US National Archives).

Percy Pilcher and Ella with the glider Beetle *at Cordross in 1895.*

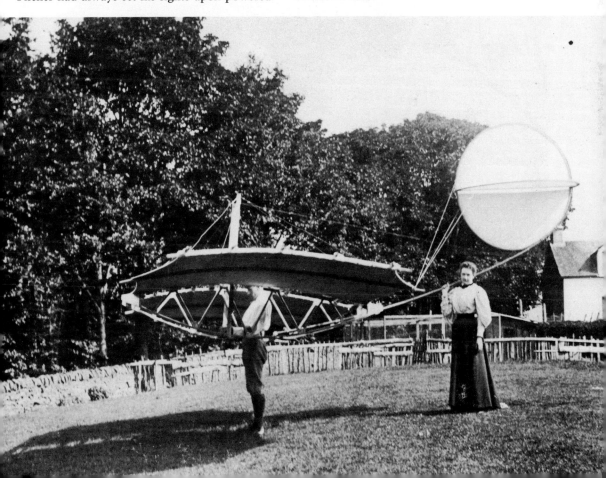

flight and was engaged in developing a light 4 hp oil engine (probably for installation in his *Hawk*) when, having been towed off the ground by a team of horses, he crashed in the *Hawk* at Stanford Park, Market Harborough, on 30 September 1899, and died two days later.

The box-kite structure was invented in 1893 by an Australian, Lawrence Hargrave (1850–1915). This simple structure provided good lift and stability and formed the basis of early aeroplanes such as the Voisin.

The largest aeroplane to lift itself off the ground briefly in the 19th century was designed and built by Sir Hiram Maxim (1840–1916). Basically a biplane test rig with 4000 ft² (372 m²) of lifting area, it was powered by two 180 hp steam engines and ran along a railway track 1800 ft (550 m) long which was fitted with wooden re-

straining guard-rails to prevent the machine from rising too high.

On 31 July 1894, during a test run, the machine lifted about 2 ft (60 cm) before fouling the guard-rails and coming to rest.

The Aéro Club de France was founded in 1898.

The Wright brothers (Wilbur and Orville) used a 5 ft (1·5 m) span biplane kite to test their theories on wing warping for the first time in August 1899.

American-born Samuel Franklin Cody (1861–1913) began his experiments to develop a man-lifting kite in 1899. His experiments at Farnborough, England, led to the development

Lawrence Hargrave testing a box-kite structure tethered to a pole and attached to a strain gauge to measure lift, in 1893.

of the military observation kite, as used during the First World War.

In 1900 the Wright brothers constructed and flew their No 1 glider. A biplane, it was flown also as a kite but had insufficient span. Using wing warping for lateral control, it was their first man-carrying aircraft and the first to be tested at the later famous Kill Devil Hills, North Carolina. Wing span was 17 ft (5·18 m). The Wrights' No 2 glider was built in 1901. Of increased span, it was not as successful as hoped and resulted in the decision to undertake further research on aerofoils, using models. The No 3 glider, built during August and September 1902, reflected this

Sir Hiram Maxim's giant biplane test rig before flight in 1894.

research and flew a great many times. This formed the basis of the powered *Flyer*.

The first man to achieve sustained powered flight with an unmanned heavier-than-air craft was the American Samuel Pierpont Langley (born 22 August 1834 at Roxbury, Massachusetts; died 27 February 1906, at Aiken, South Carolina). Mathematician and solar radiation physicist, Langley commenced building powered model aeroplanes during the 1890s, launching them from the top of a houseboat on the Potomac River near Quantico. His 14 ft (4·25 m) span models achieved sustained flights of up to 4200 ft (1280 m) from 6 May 1896 and incorporated a single steam engine mounted amidships, driving a pair of propellers. Langley's use of the name *Aerodrome* was derived incorrectly from the Greek αερο-δρόμος (*aerodromos*) supposedly meaning 'air runner'; the word, however, is cor-

Langley reflects on the time prior to launch of the full-size Aerodrome. *(Smithsonian Institution).*

rectly defined as the location of a running event and cannot be held to mean the participant in a running event. Thus in the context of an *airfield* the word 'aerodrome', as originally applied to Hendon in Middlesex, England, is correct. In 1898 Langley was requested to continue his experiments with a $50 000 State subsidy and set about the design and construction of a full-scale version. As an intermediate step he built a quarter-scale model which, in June 1903, became **the world's first aeroplane powered by a petrol engine to achieve sustained flight.** His full-size *Aerodrome*, with a span of 48 ft (14·6 m) and powered by a 52 hp Manly-Balzer five-cylinder radial petrol engine, was completed in 1903, and attempts to fly this over the Potomac River with Charles M. Manly at the controls were made on 7 October and 8 December 1903. On both occasions the aeroplane fouled the launcher and dropped into the river. In view of the Wright brothers' success immediately thereafter, the American Government withdrew its support from Langley and his project was abandoned.

The first 'hop' from water by a seaplane was probably performed by Austrian Wilhelm Kress in a tandem-winged machine, powered by a 30 hp Daimler petrol engine, in October 1901. There is some doubt, as a few sources claim that

he capsized the seaplane before leaving the water during the taxying phase. The trials were conducted on the Tullnerbach reservoir. This seaplane preceded Langley's full-size *Aerodrome* as **the first manned aeroplane fitted with a petrol engine.**

Perhaps now considered the most controversial figure of 1901-2 was Bavarian born Gustav Whitehead, whose claimed aviation feats are not officially recognised and often divide opinion. On 14 August 1901 at Bridgeport, Connecticut (having emigrated to America), he is said to have piloted in sustained flight an aeroplane of his own design, covering a distance of about 880 ft (270 m) at an altitude of 50 ft (15 m). The single engine powered both the propellers and the landing gear wheels. On 17 January 1902 Whitehead is reported to have flown a controllable twin-engined flying-boat over a circular distance of about 7 miles (11 km), finally alighting on water. Other flights and achievements are said to have followed these. Photographs of Whitehead and his aircraft on the ground appeared in the press and he was the subject of many contemporary write-ups. Others stated thereafter that they saw him fly.

In Britain the Aero Club was founded on 29 October 1901, becoming the Royal Aero Club on 15 February 1910.

Non-aviation inventions of the period

The pulley Recognised as the invention of Archytas of Tarentum, Italy, in about 400–350 BC. (See First design for a jet-propelled aeroplane.)

Clock Mechanical clock dates from China in AD 725, by I. Hsing and Liang Lingtsan.

Anti-shipping mine Used by the Dutch during a raid on Antwerp, Belgium, in 1585.

Camera Earliest photograph was taken in 1826 by French physician and scientist Joseph Nicéphore Niepce, depicting a scene at Gras, near St Loup-de-Varennes.

Telephone By the American Alexander Graham Bell in 1876.

Turbine-powered ship Designed by the Hon Sir Charles Parsons, Great Britain, and built as the *Turbinia* in 1894. Power was provided by three steam turbines.

At last—Flight

This chapter covers little more than a single decade, yet spans the period between the first officially recognised manned, sustained, controlled and powered flight and the time when nations began preparing for the greatest and most destructive war the world had ever known. But, by accepting (as we do) that the Wright brothers' initial flight of 17 December 1903 was the first flight proper, injustices are heaped upon some other pioneers of the air that managed to achieve at least most of the above criteria for flight and who are known, or are thought by some, to have flown over respectable distances prior to 17 December.

To understand why the Wrights are accepted as having been the founders of aeroplane flight proper, it is important to keep in mind a single word, *controllable*. Theirs was the first powered aeroplane to succeed in making a sustained flight with the pilot having some real measure of control. Of course the term 'sustained' is relative to

Wilbur Wright looks on as Orville pilots the Flyer on the first powered, sustained and controlled flight by an aeroplane.

the period and indeed the first flight by the Wrights on 17 December was little more than a long leap into the air, lasting just twelve seconds from beginning to end.

But what of the other aviators? Among the pioneers who are credited with powered flight before the Wright brothers was the German civil servant from Hanover, Karl Jatho. His aircraft is normally referred to as a semi-biplane, having an unusually shaped bottom wing and a similarly configured but much smaller upper wing. No tailplane was fitted, but between the wings were substantial rudder surfaces and elevators were carried. The small 9 hp petrol engine drove a paddle-like pusher propeller. On 18 August 1903 Jatho 'hopped' the aeroplane over a distance of 59 ft (18 m), which can barely be considered 'sustained'. However, in November he covered 195 ft (60 m). This, in fact, represents a flight more than 50 per cent longer in distance than the first made by Orville Wright on the 17th of the following month. However, this 'flight' on the Vahrenwalder Heide lacked that essential, control, and was not the victim of discrimination on the basis that the Wright *Flyer* looked a real plane and the Jatho aerodyne appeared from its design capable of little more than marginal flight, though in truth it did lack the development potential of the *Flyer*. Also to be remembered is that on 17 December the *Flyer* was flown four times, the longest flight lasting nearly a minute.

If Jatho can be considered to have been a 'possible', then there were also 'probables' about whom far too little is known and therefore acknowledged. One such aviator was the American Lyman Gilmore who, in 1896, is said to have flown a steam-powered aeroplane on about a dozen occasions, the longest of these covering a distance of approximately 4 miles (6·4 km) after launch from a track. Certainly, Gilmore produced aeroplanes during this period that might have been capable of sustained flight. One, photographed when nearing completion, was a 60 ft (18·3 m) span airliner with heavily strut-braced bird-like wings, featuring a round-section fuselage (with windows) that offered interior seating for ten passengers. Unfortunately, this giant was destroyed by fire while in its hangar. If the claim for Gilmore's 1896 steam-powered aeroplane could be substantiated and officially recognised, aviation history would need to be rewritten. At the very least his steam plane must be a frontrunner for the accolade 'the most successful early steam-powered aeroplane flown' (assuming it did!).

There is no doubt that the Wrights took a very professional attitude to flying, not only in the amount of original research carried out to achieve a satisfactory flying machine but also in terms of exploitation of their achievements. In March 1903 they patented an aeroplane design to protect their work, based on their No 3 glider, and between the close of 1903 and October 1905 they managed to perfect the *Flyer*. Then, extraordinarily, they stopped flying and began to capitalise on the *Flyer*. In January 1905, when the US government opened negotiations for the purchase of an aeroplane for military use, no other could come close to the *Flyer*, a position endorsed in mid-year with the appearance of the fully-controllable and refined *Flyer III*. Yet, by the time a Wright aeroplane was delivered to the US Army, the brothers were well on their way to losing their hitherto seemingly unassailable lead in design and performance. A further year and European aeroplanes were foremost.

The first aeroplane to achieve man-carrying, powered, sustained flight in the world was the *Flyer*, designed and constructed by the brothers Wilbur and Orville Wright, which first achieved such flight at 10.35 h on Thursday, 17 December 1903, at Kill Devil Hills, Kitty Hawk, North Carolina, with an undulating flight of 120 ft (36·5 m) in about 12 s. Three further flights were made on the same day, the longest of which covered a ground distance of 852 ft (260 m) and lasted 59 s. It should be emphasised that these flights were the natural culmination of some four years' experimenting by the Wrights with a number of gliders, during 1899-1903. Details of the powered *Flyer* were as follows:

Wright Flyer No 1 (1903)
Wing span: 40 ft 4 in (12·3 m).
Overall length: 21 ft 1 in (6·43 m).
Wing chord: 6 ft 6 in (1·98 m).
Wing area: 510 ft² (47·38 m²).
Empty weight: 605 lb (274 kg).
Loaded weight: Approximately 750 lb (340 kg).
Wing loading: 1·47 lb/ft² (7·2 kg/m²).
Power plant: 12 bhp four-cylinder water-cooled engine lying on its side and driving two 8 ft 6 in (2·59 m) diameter propellers by chains, one of which was crossed to achieve counter-

rotation. Engine weight with fuel (0·33 imp gal), approximately 200 lb (90 kg).

Speed: 30 mile/h (approximately 48 km/h).

Launching: The *Flyer* took off under its own power from a dolly which ran on two bicycle hubs along a 60 ft (18 m) wooden rail.

The first full-size aeroplane to feature ailerons was a biplane flown by Frenchman Robert Esnault-Pelterie in October 1904.

The first aeroplane flight with a duration of more than five minutes was that by Wilbur Wright in the *Flyer II*, which covered 2¾ miles (4·4 km) on 9 November 1904.

The first glider flight from a balloon was performed by American Daniel Maloney on 29 April 1905. In a similar flight on 18 July Maloney lost his life.

The Aero Club of America was founded on 30 November 1905.

The world's first full-time air correspondent was Englishman Harry Harper, who began this position with the *Daily Mail* newspaper in 1906.

The first tethered sustained flight in Europe was made by the Danish engineer Jacob C.H. Ellehammer on 12 September 1906. Piloting a curi-

Before Jacob Ellehammer achieved the first sustained but tethered flight in Europe, in September 1906, he had attempted flight with an earlier machine. Here, in 1905, Ellehammer and associates withdraw his aircraft from a specially constructed hangar on Lindholm island, site of his later achievement.

Santos-Dumont's 14-bis tail-first biplane.

ous and primitive biplane fitted with a 20 hp radial engine, he covered about 140 ft (43 m) in circular flight, as the biplane was tethered to a post. For this the rudder had been fixed, making the flight uncontrollable by the pilot.

The first accredited sustained flight (ie other than a 'hop') achieved by a manned, powered aeroplane in Europe was made on 12 November 1906 by the Brazilian constructor-pilot Alberto Santos-Dumont (1873–1932), a resident of Paris, France, who flew his '*14-bis*' 722 ft (220 m) in 21·2 s; his aeroplane was in effect a tail-first box-kite powered by a 50 hp Antoinette engine, and this flight won for him the Aéro-Club de France's prize of 1500 francs for the first officially observed flight of more than 100 m. A previous flight, carried out on 23 October, covered 197 ft (60 m) and had won Santos-Dumont the Archdeacon Prize of 3000 francs for the first sustained flight of more than 25 m. Santos-Dumont's flight on 12 November was the first ever FAI recognised world record for distance flown. (See 26 October 1907.)

The first powered aeroplane flight in Great Britain, though not officially recognised, was almost certainly made by Horatio Phillips (1845–1924) in a 22 hp *Multiplane* in 1907. The aircraft had four of Phillips's unique narrow 'Venetian blind' wing-frames in tandem. It covered a distance of about 500 ft (152 m).

The first of many Daily Mail prizes offered for aeroplane achievements was one for a model aeroplane exhibition and competition held at the Agricultural Hall, London, on 6 April 1907. In a fly-off finish at Alexandra Palace, Alliott Verdon Roe was awarded £75 for the flight of his model biplane. With this prize, Roe went on to construct a full-size aeroplane.

The first aeroplane to be flown with cantilever wings was Louis Blériot's Type VI *Libellule*, which also featured wingtip ailerons. The Type VI made its first flight on 11 July 1907.

The Aeronautical Division of the Signal Corps, US Army, was founded on 1 August 1907.

The first helicopter to lift a man from the ground was the French Breguet-Richet helicopter of 1907. Although the craft lifted off the ground at Douai, France, on 29 September that year, it did not constitute a free flight as four men on the ground steadied the machine with long poles which, while not contributing to the aircraft's lift, constituted a form of control restriction. Power was provided by a 50 hp Antoinette engine.

The second official distance record was set by Frenchman Henry Farman in the Voisin-Farman I at 2530 ft (771 m), on 26 October 1907. This aeroplane had first flown on 30 September. To be official as a world record, the achievement had to be recognised by the FAI, which had been established in France on 14 October 1905.

The first monoplane with tractor engine, enclosed fuselage, rear-mounted tail-unit and two-wheel main undercarriage with tailwheel was the Blériot VII powered by a 50 hp Antoinette engine. This was Louis Blériot's third full-size monoplane and was built during the autumn of 1907 and first flown by him at Issy-les-Moulineaux, France, on 10 November 1907. Before crashing this aeroplane on 18 December that year Blériot had achieved six flights, the longest of which was more than 1640 ft (500 m). This success confirmed to the designer that his basic configuration was sound—so much so that despite a 30-year deviation into biplane design, Blériot's basic configuration is still regarded as fundamentally conventional among propeller-driven aeroplanes of today.

The first true free flight by a man-carrying helicopter was performed by Paul Cornu in his 24 hp Antoinette-powered twin-rotor (each 19 ft 8 in [6·0 m] diameter) aircraft near Lisieux, France, on 13 November 1907. The flight, which lasted only 20 s, attained a height of 1 ft (0·3 m).

Breguet-Richet helicopter in September 1907.

The first US aeroplane company was formed on 30 November 1907 by Glenn Curtiss as the Curtiss Aeroplane Company.

The first specification for a military aeroplane ever issued for commercial tender was drawn up by Brig-Gen James Allen, Chief Signal Officer of the US Army, on 23 December 1907. The specification (main points) was as follows:

- ☐ Drawings to scale showing general dimensions, shape, designed speed, total surface area of supporting planes, weight, description of the engine and materials.
- ☐ The flying machine should be quick and easy to assemble and should be able to be taken apart and packed for transportation.
- ☐ Must be designed to carry two persons having a combined weight of about 350 lb and sufficient fuel for a flight of 125 miles.
- ☐ Should be designed to have a speed of at least 40 mile/h in still air.
- ☐ The speed accomplished during the trial flight will be determined by taking an average of the time over a measured course of more than 5 miles, against and with the wind.
- ☐ Before acceptance a trial endurance flight will be required of at least 1 h.
- ☐ Three trials will be allowed for speed. The place for delivery to the Government and trial flights will be Fort Myer, Virginia.
- ☐ It should be designed to ascend in any country which may be encountered in field service. The starting device must be simple and transportable. It should also land in a field without requiring a specially prepared spot, and without damaging its structure.
- ☐ It should be provided with some device to permit of a safe descent in case of an accident to the propelling machine.
- ☐ It should be sufficiently simple in its construction and operation to permit an intelligent man to become proficient in its use within a reasonable length of time.

The first circuit flight made in Europe was undertaken by Henry Farman on 13 January 1908 in his modified Voisin biplane at Issy-les-Moulineaux when he took off, circumnavigated a pylon 1625 ft (500 m) away and returned to his point of departure. By so doing, Farman won the Grand Prix d'Aviation, a prize of 50 000 francs offered by Henry Deutsch de la Meurthe and Ernest Archdeacon to the first pilot to cover a kilometre. The flight took 1 min 28 s and, owing to the distance taken in turning, probably covered 4875 ft (1500 m).

The first tenders accepted by the US Army for military aeroplanes were received on 6 February 1908. These came from A. Herring, the Wright brothers and J. Scott. Contracts for these aircraft were signed four days later but only the Wright brothers eventually delivered an aeroplane for testing. Interestingly, on 15 February Captain Thomas Baldwin's tender for the US Army's first dirigible was delivered.

The first aeroplane flight in Italy was made by the French sculptor-turned aviator Léon Delagrange in a Voisin in May 1908. At this time, aircraft built by the French brothers Gabriel and Charles Voisin were flown by two pilots, Henry Farman and Léon Delagrange. Henry Farman was born in England in 1874 and retained his English citizenship until 1937 when he became a naturalised Frenchman. Having turned from painting to cycling before the turn of the century, he progressed to racing Panhard motor cars and at one time owned the largest garage in Paris. Gabriel Voisin later remarked that Farman possessed considerable mechanical and manipulative skill, whereas Delagrange 'was not the sporting type' and knew nothing about running an engine. Delagrange was killed flying a Blériot monoplane on 4 January 1910. Farman, having abandoned flying to pursue the business of aeroplane manufacture, died on 17 July 1958.

The first aeroplane flight in Belgium was made by Henry Farman, at Ghent, in May 1908.

The first passenger ever to fly in an aeroplane was Charles W. Furnas who was taken aloft by Wilbur Wright on 14 May 1908 for a flight covering 1968 ft (600 m) of 28·6 s duration. Later the same morning Orville Wright flew Furnas for a distance of about 2½ miles (4000 m), which was covered in 3 min 40 s. Interestingly, it was only on 6 May that the Wrights had begun flying again after a three-year self-imposed absence.

The first passenger to be carried in an aeroplane in Europe was Ernest Archdeacon, the Frenchman whose substantial prizes contributed such stimulus to European aviation, who was flown by Henry Farman on 29 May 1908.

The first American to fly after the Wright brothers was Glenn H. Curtiss, who flew his *June Bug* for the first time on 20 June 1908. During this flight Curtiss covered a distance of 1266 ft (386 m) and exactly a fortnight later, on 4 July, he made a flight of 5090 ft (1550 m) in 102·2 s to win the *Scientific American* trophy for the first official public flight in the United States of more than one kilometre.

The first aeroplane flight in Germany was made by the Dane J.C.H. Ellehammer, in his No IV machine at Kiel on 28 June 1908. However, this flight had a duration of only 11 s. A development of this aeroplane was flown by **the first German pilot,** Hans Grade, at Magdeburg in October 1908.

The world's first woman passenger to fly in an aeroplane was Madame Thérèse Peltier who, on 8 July 1908, accompanied Léon Delagrange at Turin, Italy, in his Voisin for a flight of 500 ft (150 m). She soon afterwards became the first woman to fly solo, but never was a qualified pilot.

The world's first full-size triplane to fly was the French Goupy I, which first took to the air on 5 September 1908. Built by Ambroise Goupy, it was powered by a 50 hp Renault engine. The later Goupy II, actually built by Blériot and first flown in March 1909, is recognised as the first of the classic tractor-engined biplanes.

The first flight in Europe of about 30 min duration was performed on 6 September 1908 by Léon Delagrange at Issy-les-Moulineaux, when he covered a distance of 15¼ miles (24·4 km) in 29 min 53 s.

The first fatality to the occupant of a powered aeroplane occurred on 17 September 1908 at Fort Myer, Virginia, when a Wright biplane flown by Orville Wright crashed killing the passenger, Lt Thomas Etholen Selfridge, US Army Signal Corps. Wright was seriously injured. The accident happened during US Army acceptance trials of the Wright biplane and was caused by a failure in one of the propeller blades. This imbalanced the good blade, which tore loose one of the wires bracing the rudder-outriggers to the wings, and so sending the aircraft crashing to the ground from about 75 ft (25 m).

The most important endurance flight to date was made by Wilbur Wright on 21 September 1908, when he covered 41⅓ miles (66·5 km) in France.

The first resident Englishmen to fly in an aeroplane (albeit as passengers) were Griffith Brewer (the first), the Hon C.S. Rolls, Frank Hedges Butler and Maj B.F.S. Baden-Powell, who were taken aloft in turn by Wilbur Wright in his biplane at Camp d'Auvours on 8 October 1908. Butler had founded the Aero Club of Great Britain, while Baden-Powell was Secretary of the Aeronautical Society. The 'resident' qualification is necessary here as of course the English-born, French-resident Henry Farman had been flying for more than a year by the time the four Englishmen were taken aloft by Wright.

The first officially recognised aeroplane flight in Great Britain was made by the American (later naturalised British citizen) Samuel Franklin Cody in his *British Army Aeroplane No 1*, powered by a 50 hp Antoinette engine. The flight of 1390 ft (424 m) was made at Farnborough, Hampshire, on 16 October 1908 and ended with a crash-landing, but without physical injury to Cody.

The first European cross-country flight was made by Henry Farman on 30 October 1908, when he flew from Châlons to Reims, a distance of about 16 miles (26 km).

The longest flight by the end of 1908 was by Wilbur Wright on 31 December 1908, at Camp d'Auvours, where he achieved a stupendous 77 miles (124 km) in 2 h 20 min. This won for him the Michelin prize of 20 000 francs—apart from breaking all his own records. Details of the longest flights made by Wilbur Wright in 1908 follow, together with a list of the more significant flights made by other aviators that year.

The British Army Aeroplane No 1 *at Farnborough.*

Wilbur Wright

14 May 1908	Kill Devil Hills	5 miles	(8 km)	In 7 min 29 s.
8 August 1908	Hunaudières, France	—	—	Demonstration flight 1 min 45 s.
16 September 1908	Auvours, France	—	—	Flight taking 39 min 18 s.
21 September 1908	Auvours, France	41⅓ miles	(66·5 km)	First major endurance flight. Flew more than 100 times at this location.
3 October 1908	Auvours, France	34¾ miles	(56 km)	In 55 min 37 s.
10 October 1908	Auvours, France	46 miles	(74 km)	In 1 h 9 min 45 s, with M. Painleve as passenger.
18 December 1908	Auvours, France	62 miles	(99·8 km)	In 1 h 54 min 53 s. Climbed to 330 ft (100 m) to establish new altitude record.
31 December 1908	Auvours, France	77 miles	(124 km)	In 2 h 20 min 23 s, to win Michelin prize and set up new world record.

Léon Delagrange

11 April 1908	Covered over 2½ miles (3·9 km) at Issy-les-Moulineaux.
23 June 1908	Covered 8¾ miles (14·08 km) in 18 min 30 s at Milan, Italy.
6 September 1908	Covered 15¼ miles (24·4 km) in 29 min 53 s at Issy-les-Moulineaux.
17 September 1908	Flight lasting 30 min 27 s at Issy-les-Moulineaux.

Henry Farman

13 January 1908	Covered a 1 km circuit in 1 min 28 s at Issy-les-Moulineaux.
6 July 1908	Covered 12½ miles (20 km) in 20 min 20 s.
30 October 1908	Covered 17 miles (27·3 km) in 20 min on cross-country flight from Châlons to Reims.

Glenn H. Curtiss

4 July 1908	Covered 5090 ft (1550 m) in 1 min 42 s to win *Scientific American* trophy.

The first successful Russian aeroplane was the Gakkel-3 of 1909, designed by Yakov M. Gakkel.

The first German aviator to fly a German aeroplane was Hans Grade who, on 12 January 1909, flew a triplane of his own design at Magdeburg.

Probably the most successful monoplane designed and built before the First World War was the French Blériot XI, the work of Louis Blériot and first flown on 23 January 1909 while powered by a 30 hp REP engine.

The first aerodrome to be prepared as such in England was the flying-ground between Leysdown and Shellness, Isle of Sheppey (known as 'Shellbeach'), where limited established facilities were provided. It was opened in February 1909 by the joint effort of the Aero Club of Great Britain and Short Bros Ltd.

The first aeroplanes to be manufactured in series were six Wright biplanes produced by the British Short Brothers under an agreement concluded between Wilbur Wright and Eustace Short in February 1909. Therefore, Short Brothers was the first aircraft manufacturing company proper in aviation history.

The world's first aeroplane production line: Short-built Wright biplanes were constructed in the company's principal erecting shop. Then Short Brothers employed 80 men.

The Roe I triplane nearing completion at Lea Marshes in June 1909. A.V. Roe works on, second from right. (Science Museum, London)

The first sustained, powered flight by an aeroplane in the British Empire was made on 23 February 1909 by J.A.D. McCurdy, a Canadian, over Baddeck Bay, Nova Scotia, in the Aerial Experimental Association's biplane *Silver Dart*, which he had designed. He had made his own first flight at Hammondsport, New York, USA, the previous December.

The first aeroplane flight in Austria was made by the Frenchman G. Legagneux, at Vienna in April 1909 in his Voisin. **The first Austrian** to fly was Igo Etrich, in his *Taube* at Wiener-Neustadt in November of that year. This aircraft gave its name to the type in fairly widespread use by Germany at the beginning of the First World War.

The first cinematographer to be taken up in an aeroplane was at Centocelle, near Rome, on 24 April 1909, in a Wright biplane flown by Wilbur Wright.

The first resident Englishman to make an officially recognised aeroplane flight in England was J.T.C. Moore-Brabazon (later Lord Brabazon of Tara) who made three sustained flights of 450, 600 and 1500 ft (137, 180 and 450 m) between 30 April and 2 May 1909 at Leysdown, Isle of Sheppey, in his Voisin biplane. He had learned to fly in France during the previous year and on 30 October 1909 won the £1000 *Daily Mail* prize for the first Briton to cover a mile (closed circuit) in a British aeroplane—a Short-Wright biplane. He was awarded the Royal Aero Club of Great Britain's Aviator Certificate No 1 on 8 March 1910. Lord Brabazon died in 1969.

The first aeroplane flight of more than one mile in Britain was achieved on 14 May 1909 by Samuel Cody who flew the *British Army Aeroplane No 1* from Laffan's Plain to Danger Hill, Hampshire—a distance of just over 1 mile—and landed without incident. The Prince of Wales requested a repeat performance during the same afternoon, but Cody, turning to avoid some troops, crashed into an embankment and demolished the tail of his aeroplane.

The first aeroplane flight in France of one hour endurance was performed by Frenchman Paul Tissandier in a Wright biplane on 20 May 1909. He also set the first official FAI world speed record for aeroplanes (see end of section).

The first aeroplane to carry a pilot and two passengers was the Blériot XII, piloted on 12 June 1909 by Louis Blériot and with passengers Santos-Dumont and Fournier.

The first apprentice to an aeroplane manufacturing company was Howard (Dinger) Bell, who joined Short Brothers on 10 July 1909. His father, nicknamed 'Father Bell' by the employees, was the company's first foreman.

The first Briton to fly an all-British aeroplane was Alliott Verdon Roe (1877–1958), in his Roe I triplane on 13 July 1909 at Lea Marshes, Essex. Lack of funds to build the triplane had forced Roe to construct it from wood instead of light-gauge steel tubing, to cover the wings with paper and to use the same 9 hp JAP engine that had powered his unsuccessful biplane. The 100 ft (30 m) flight that was achieved on the 13th was

Blériot passes over beach huts and out into the Channel sky. (Science Museum, London)

Hubert Latham in his Antoinette. (Science Museum, London)

much improved upon on the 23rd, when he flew 900 ft (274 m) at an average height of 10 ft (3 m).

Conquest of the English Channel. In response to an offer by the *Daily Mail* of a prize of £1000 for the first pilot (of any nationality) to fly an aeroplane across the Channel, **the first attempt** was made by an Englishman, Hubert Latham, flying an Antoinette IV. He took off from Sangatte, near Calais, at 06.42 h on Monday, 19 July 1909, but alighted in the sea after only 6–8 miles (10–13 km) following engine failure which could not be rectified in the air. He was picked up by the French naval vessel *Harpon*. The occasion of this attempt was also the **first instance of wireless telegraphy being used to obtain weather reports,** the first report being transmitted from Sangatte,

near Calais, to the Lord Warden Hotel, Dover, at 04.30 h on that morning.

Despite working furiously to get a replacement Antoinette, Latham was beaten by Louis Blériot. The Frenchman took off in his Blériot XI monoplane at 04.41 h, from Les Baraques, on Sunday, 25 July 1909, and landed at 05.17·5 h in the Northfall Meadow by Dover Castle to become **the first man to cross the English Channel in an aeroplane.**

Latham made a second attempt to fly the Channel two days later (on 27 July), taking off at 05.50 h from Cap Blanc Nez. When only 1

Miss Columbia after being equipped with a wheeled landing gear. (US National Archives)

mile (1·6 km) from the Dover cliffs, his engine failed and once again he had to alight in the sea.

The first aeroplane flight in Sweden was made by the Frenchman Legagneux at Stockholm in his Voisin biplane on 29 July 1909.

The first woman passenger to fly in an aeroplane in England was Mrs Cody, wife of Samuel, who was taken up by her husband during the last week of July 1909 over Laffan's Plain, Hants, in the *British Army Aeroplane No 1*.

The first passenger to be carried by an aeroplane in Canada was F.W. 'Casey' Baldwin who was taken aloft on 2 August 1909 at Petawawa, Ontario, in an aeroplane flown by J.A.D. McCurdy.

The first aeroplane purchased by the American Government was a Wright Model A biplane, subsequently named *Miss Columbia*, sold by the Wright brothers on 2 August 1909. The price was $25 000, but a bonus of $5000 was awarded as the specified maximum speed of 40 mile/h (64 km/h) was exceeded. The aircraft was constructed at Dayton, Ohio.

The first International Aviation Meeting in the world opened on 22 August 1909 at Reims, and lasted until 29 August 1909. Thirty-eight aeroplanes were entered to participate, although only 23 managed to leave the ground; the meeting also attracted aviators and aeroplane-designers from all over Europe and did much to arouse widespread public interest in flying. The types of aeroplanes which flew were: Antoinette, Blériot XI, Blériot XII, Blériot XIII, Breguet, Curtiss, Henry Farman, REP, Voisin, and Wright.

The world's first speed record over 100 km was established by the Englishman, Hubert Latham, during the Reims International Meeting (see above) between 22 and 29 August 1909. Flying an Antoinette (powered by a 50 hp eight-cylinder Antoinette engine) he covered the distance in 1 h 28 min 17 s, at an average speed of 42 mph (67 km/h). In so doing he won the second largest prize of the meeting amounting to 42 000 francs. Latham also won the altitude competition by reaching 508 ft (155 m). First prize went to Henry Farman who, flying a Gnôme-powered Farman, set up new world records for duration and distance in a closed circuit, covering 111·847 miles (180 km) in 3 h 4 min 56·4 s, winning 63 000 francs.

Poster advertising the first aviation meeting held in Great Britain. (Science Museum, London)

The first pilot to be killed flying a powered aeroplane was Eugène Lefebvre, on 7 September 1909; he crashed while flying a new Wright type A at Port Aviation Juvisy. Soon afterwards, on 22 September, Captain Ferber was killed when his Voisin hit a ditch while preparing for take-off.

The first aeroplane flight in Denmark was made by Léon Delagrange in September 1909.

The first Aviation Meeting held in Great Britain was that organised by the Doncaster Aviation Committee on the Doncaster Racecourse between 15 and 23 October 1909. This meeting was not governed by rules laid down by the FAI, nor was it officially recognised by the Aero Club of Great Britain. Twelve aeroplanes constituted the field, of which five managed to fly. **The first**

officially recognised meeting was held at Squires Gate, Blackpool, between 18 and 23 October 1909, being organised by the Blackpool Corporation and the Lancashire Aero Club; seven of the dozen participants were coaxed into the air.

The first American woman passenger in an aeroplane was Mrs Ralph van Deman, who flew with Wilbur Wright on 27 October 1909.

The first major prize in Great Britain for all-British aviation activity was the £1000 offered by the *Daily Mail* to the first British pilot to complete a circular flight of 1 mile (1·6 km) in an all-British aeroplane. This prize was won by J.T.C. Moore-Brabazon on 30 October 1909 at Shell-beach when, flying the Short Biplane No 2, he achieved the one mile flight in a time of 2 m 36 s. Similar in configuration to the Short-built Wright biplanes, the Short No 2 differed considerably in detail and was powered by a 50–60 hp Green four-cylinder inline engine.

The first piglet to fly in a powered aeroplane in Britain took to the air as J.T.C. Moore-Brabazon's passenger on 4 November 1909. Intended to debunk the old adage that 'pigs can't fly', pig and pilot did admirably with a 3·5 mile (5·6 km) cross-country flight.

The first successful still photographs taken from an aeroplane were by M Meurisse, in December 1909, and showed the flying-fields at Mourmelon and Châlons. The aeroplane was an Antoinette piloted by Latham.

The first aeroplane flight in Australia was made by Colin Defries on 9 December 1909. Defries, a well-known racing driver, flew an imported Wright biplane over a distance of 1 mile (1·6 km) at a height of 35 ft (11 m) at Victoria Park Racecourse, Sydney, New South Wales.

The first American monoplane to fly was the Walden III, designed by Dr Henry W. Walden and flown on 9 December 1909 at Mineola, Long Island, New York. It was powered by a 22 hp Anzani engine.

The first passenger to be carried by aeroplane in Australia was Mr C.S. Magennis, who flew with Colin Defries on 10 December 1909.

The first aeroplane flight in Ireland was made by Harry G. Ferguson of Belfast on 31 December 1909. The aeroplane was of his own design and

Harry Ferguson posing in the cockpit of his monoplane, 1909. (Aer Lingus)

manufacture; it resembled a Blériot, and was powered by an eight-cylinder 35 hp air-cooled JAP engine.

The first flight at an altitude of 1000 m (3280 ft) was achieved by Hubert Latham on 7 January 1910 at Châlons, France, flying an Antoinette VII monoplane.

The first aeroplane meeting to be held in the USA was organised by the Aero Club of California at the Dominguez Field, Los Angeles on 10 January 1910.

The first man to drop missiles from an aeroplane was Lt Paul Beck on 19 January 1910, when he released sandbags (representing bombs) over Los Angeles from an aeroplane piloted by Louis Paulhan. On 30 June, the same year, Glenn Hammond Curtiss dropped dummy bombs from a height of 50 ft (15 m) on the shape of a battleship marked by buoys on Lake Keuka.

The first helicopter to be built by Igor Sikorsky (who later became one of the greatest helicopter designers in the world) was a twin contra-rotating rotor machine which appeared in 1910. Each rotor consisted of two long-chord wing-type planes and an aerodynamically-shaped spar; the fuselage was a simple upright structure designed to hold an engine to drive the rotors via a belt. The whole apparatus was mounted on rails. However, the helicopter did not fly and it was to be a quarter of a century before Sikorsky would fly successfully in a helicopter of his design.

The first Aviation Certificate awarded by the Royal Aero Club was received by Moore-

Mme la Baronne de Laroche, the first certificated woman pilot.

Brabazon on 8 March 1910. The Aero Club had become the Royal Aero Club on 15 February 1910.

The first military pilot to get the Brevet of the Aéro-Club de France was Lt Camerman on 7 March 1910, receiving Brevet No 33.

The first certificated woman pilot in the world was Mme la Baronne de Laroche, a Frenchwoman, who received her Pilot's Certificate No 36 on 8 March 1910, having qualified on a Voisin biplane. She was killed in 1919 in an aeroplane accident.

The first night flights were made by Emil Aubrun, a Frenchman, on 10 March 1910 flying a Blériot monoplane. Each of the two flights began and ended at Villalugano, Buenos Aires, Argentina, and was about 12·4 miles (20 km) long.

The first aeroplane flight in Switzerland was made by Capt Engelhardt on 13 March 1910.

The first take-off from water by an aeroplane was made by Henri Fabre, a Frenchman, in his Gnome-powered seaplane *Hydravion* at La Mède harbour, Martigues, France, on 28 March 1910.

The first recorded night flight in Great Britain was made by Claude Grahame-White from 27 to 28 April 1910, in an attempt to overhaul Louis Paulhan competing in the *Daily Mail* £10 000 London to Manchester race (which had to be started from a point within 5 miles of the newspaper's London offices and finish at a point within 5 miles of its Manchester offices). This was the first aeroplane event in Britain to offer a £10 000 prize. Paulhan, who eventually won despite Grahame-White's night flight, thus made the first London to Manchester aeroplane flight and the first straight line aeroplane flight in Britain of more than 100 km.

The first aeroplane to be 'forced down' by the action of another was the Henry Farman biplane of Mr A. Rawlinson during the Aviation Meeting at Nice, France, in mid-April 1910. Mr Rawlinson was flying his new Farman over the sea when the Russian Effimov passed so close above him (also in a Farman) that his downdraught forced the Englishman into the water. The Russian was severely reprimanded for dangerous flying and fined 100 francs.

The first British woman to fly solo in an aeroplane was almost certainly Miss Edith Maud Cook, who performed various aerial acts under the name of Miss 'Spencer Kavanagh'. She achieved several solo flights on Blériot monoplanes with the Grahame-White Flying School at Pau in the Pyrenees in early 1910. She was also a professional parachute-jumper, known as 'Viola Spencer', and was killed after making a jump from a balloon near Coventry, England, in July 1910.

The first aeroplane flights in Spain were made by Gaudart, Poillot, Le Blond, Mamet and Olieslaegers between March and April 1910.

The first England to France and two-way crossing of the English Channel was accomplished by the Hon C.S. Rolls (the 'Rolls' of 'Rolls-Royce')

George William Patrick Dawes in the uniform of the RFC. (Wilma V. Dawes)

flying a French-built Wright biplane on 2 June 1910. He took off from Broadlees, Dover, at 18.30·5 h, dropped a letter addressed to the Aéro Club de France near Sangatte at 19.15 h, then flew back to England and made a perfect landing near his starting-rail at 20.06 h. He was thus the **first man to fly from England to France in an aeroplane, the first man to make a non-stop two-way crossing, and the first cross-Channel pilot to land at a pre-arranged spot without damage to his aeroplane.**

The first French reconnaissance flight was undertaken by Lt Féquant in a Henry Farman biplane on 9 June 1910. The following day a Wright biplane was accepted into French Army service.

The first naval officer in the world to learn to fly was Lt G.C. Colmore, Royal Navy, who took flying lessons on the Short S.26 biplane at Eastchurch, England, at his own expense and was awarded British Pilot's Certificate No 15 on 21 June 1910.

The first Romanian aeroplane to fly was the *Vlaicu I* parasol-wing monoplane, designed by Aurel Vlaicu and flown on 17 June 1910. This date is marked as the National Aviation Day in that country.

The first pilot to fly at a height of over 1 mile was American Walter Brookins on 10 July 1910, when he piloted a Wright biplane at Indianapolis to about 6230 ft (1900 m).

The first British pilot to lose his life while flying an aeroplane was the Hon. Charles Stewart Rolls (born in London, 27 August 1877, the third son of the first Baron Llangattock), who was killed at the Bournemouth Aviation Week on 12 July 1910 when his French-built Wright biplane suffered a structural failure in flight.

The first flight in Australia by an Australian in an indigenous aeroplane was made by John R. Duigan of Mia Mia, Victoria, on 16 July 1910 in an aeroplane constructed from photographs of the Wright *Flyer*. On that day Duigan flew only 28 ft (8·5 m), but on 7 October he covered 588 ft (179 m) at a height of about 12 ft (3·65 m).

The first patent for a device to allow a fixed machine-gun to be fired from an aeroplane was received by German August Euler on 24 July

1910. This was subsequently demonstrated on the biplane *Gelber Hund*.

The first German active duty officer to receive a Pilot's Licence was Lt Richard von Tiedemann, a Hussar officer. He first flew solo on 23 July 1910.

The first serving officer of the British Army to be awarded a Pilot's Certificate in England was Capt George William Patrick Dawes who was awarded Certificate No 17 for qualification on a Humber monoplane at Wolverhampton on 26 July 1910.

Dawes died on 17 March 1960 aged 80. He had served in South Africa between 1900 and 1902 when he was awarded the Queen's Medal with three clasps, and the King's Medal with two clasps. He took up flying privately in 1909 and was posted to the RFC on its formation in 1912. He commanded the Corps in the Balkans from 1916 to 1918 as Acting General but used his permanent rank of Lt Col, during which time he was awarded the DSO and the AFC, was mentioned in despatches seven times, and awarded the Croix de Guerre with three palms, the Serbian Order of the White Eagle, the Order of the Redeemer of Greece and created Officer of the Légion d'honneur. He served with the Royal Air Force in the Second World War as a Wing Commander, retiring in 1946 with the MBE. He thus was one of the very few officers who served actively in the Boer War and both world wars. Dawes is also credited with having made the first flight in the Indian sub-continent.

The first mail carried unofficially in an aeroplane in Great Britain was flown by Claude Grahame-White on 10 August 1910 in a Blériot monoplane from Squires Gate, Blackpool; he did not reach his destination at Southport, having been forced to land by bad weather.

The first Channel crossing with a passenger was by Franco-American John B. Moisant and his mechanic in a Blériot two-seater aeroplane, from Calais to Dover, on 17 August 1910.

The first military firearm to be fired from an aeroplane was a rifle used by Lt Jacob Earl Fickel, US Army, from a two-seater Curtiss biplane at a target at Sheepshead Bay, New York City, on 20 August 1910.

The first use of radio between an aeroplane and the ground was on 27 August 1910 when James McCurdy, flying a Curtiss, sent and received messages via an HM Horton wireless set at Sheepshead Bay, NY State.

The first American woman to fly solo in an aeroplane was Blanche Scott on 2 September 1910.

The first air collision in the world occurred on 8 September 1910 between two aeroplanes piloted by brothers named Warchalovski at Wiener-Neustadt, Austria. One of the pilots suffered a broken leg. A passenger on one of the aircraft was the Archduke Léopold Salvator of Austria.

The first crossing of the Irish Sea was made by Robert Loraine who, flying a Farman biplane on 11 September 1910, set off from Holyhead, Anglesey. Although engine failure forced him down in the sea 180 ft (55 m) offshore from the Irish coast near Baily Lighthouse, Howth, he was generally considered to have been the first to accomplish the crossing.

The first flight over the Alps was made by the Peruvian Georges Chavez in a Blériot on 23 September 1910. His flight from Brig, Switzerland, to Domodossola, Italy, via the Simplon Pass, ended in disaster when he crashed on landing and was killed.

The first ever carriage of freight by air was undertaken on 7 November 1910. On this occasion

Max Morehouse alongside the pilot for the first freight flight, Philip O. Parmalee (on right).

it had been arranged between the Wright Company and the Morehouse-Martens Company of Columbus, Ohio, which operated an emporium named The Home Dry Goods Store, for two packages of silk to be transported by air between Dayton and Columbus to bring attention to a sale. A Wright Model B, at the last minute piloted by Philip O. Parmalee (see below), was used to carry nearly 542 yds of silk, at a cost to the company of $5000. Despite this carriage fee, the store made a profit of more than $1000, partly by cutting up some of the material and selling it in small pieces as souvenirs mounted on postcards.

The first aeroplane to take off from a ship was a Curtiss biplane flown by Eugene B. Ely from an 83 ft (25 m) platform built over the bows of the American light cruiser USS *Birmingham*, 3750 tons (3810 tonnes), on 14 November 1910. It has often been averred that the vessel was anchored at the time of take-off; this is not correct as it had been proposed to take off as the ship steamed at 20 knots into the wind. In the event, the *Birmingham* had weighed anchor in Hampton Roads, Virginia, but, impatient to take off, Ely gave the signal to release his aircraft at 15.16 h before the ship was under way. With only 57 ft (17 m) of platform ahead of the Curtiss, the aircraft flew off but touched the water and damaged its propeller; the pilot managed to maintain control and landed at Willoughby Spit, 2½ miles (4 km) distant. As Ely became airborne from the cruiser, the *Birmingham* sent an historic radio message 'Ely's just gone.'

The first explosive bombs dropped by American pilots were those dropped by Lt Myron Sidney

Eugene B. Ely made the aircraft carrier for aeroplanes a reality by flying off USS Birmingham *on 14 November 1910.* (US National Archives)

Crissy and Philip O. Parmalee, from a Wright biplane, during trials on 7 January 1911 at San Francisco, California.

The first aeroplane to land on a ship was also a Curtiss biplane flown by Ely, on 18 January 1911, when he landed on a 119 ft 4 in (36 m) long platform constructed over the stern of the American armoured cruiser, USS *Pennsylvania*, 13 680 tons (13 900 tonnes), anchored in San Francisco Bay. It had been intended that the vessel would be under way during the landing, but the Captain considered that there was insufficient sea space to manoeuvre and the *Pennsylvania* remained at anchor. Despite landing downwind the Curtiss rolled to a stop at 11.01 h after a run of only 30 ft (9 m). Capt C.F. Pond is reputed to have remarked that 'this is the most important landing of a bird since the dove flew back to the Ark'. After lunch Ely successfully took off again from the *Pennsylvania* at 11.58 h and returned to his airfield near San Francisco.

The first aeroplane to perform a premeditated landing on water, taxi and then take off was a Curtiss 'hydroaeroplane' flown by Glenn Curtiss on 26 January 1911. He took off and then landed in San Diego Harbor, turned round and took off again, flying about 1 mile (1·6 km) before coming down near his starting point. A Curtiss A-1 'hydroaeroplane' was the US Navy's first aeroplane, first flown on 1 July 1911.

The first British pilot to survive a spin (probably first in the world) was Fred Raynham who, flying an Avro biplane during 1911, stalled while climbing through fog. The stall occurred after he had stooped to adjust his compass as he thought that it was malfunctioning; the next he knew was that he was standing upright on the rudder pedals with his aeroplane whirling round. Quite how he recovered from the spin will never known, for his recollection was that he *pulled the stick back*; notwithstanding this he caught sight of the ground and was able to perform a controlled landing.

The first flight in New Zealand by an aeroplane was made by a Howard Wright type biplane piloted by Vivian C. Walsh at Auckland on 5 February 1911. With his brother Leo, Vivian Walsh imported materials from England with which to build the aircraft and installed a 60 hp ENV engine. Vivian Walsh also made **the first seaplane flight in New Zealand** on 1 January 1914.

The first Government (official) air-mail flight in the world was undertaken on 18 February 1911 when the French pilot Henri Pequet flew a Humber biplane from Allahabad to Naini Junction, a distance of about 5 miles (8 km) across the Jumna River, with some 6500 letters. The regular service was established four days later as part of the Universal Postal Exhibition, Allahabad, India, the flights being shared by Capt W.G. Windham and Pequet. The envelopes of this first air-mail service were franked 'First Aerial Post, UP Exhibition, Allahabad, 1911' and are highly prized among collectors.

The first torpedo drop from an aeroplane was achieved in 1911 by the Italian Capitano Guidoni, flying a Farman biplane. The torpedo weighed 352 lb (160 kg).

Eleven passengers were first carried in an aeroplane on 23 March 1911 by Louis Breguet over a distance of 3·1 miles (5 km) at Douai, France, in a huge aircraft of his own design. **Twelve passengers were first carried in an aeroplane** on 24 March 1911 by Roger Sommer over a distance of 2625 ft (800 m) in a Sommer biplane powered by a 70 hp engine.

The first non-stop flight from London to Paris was made on 12 April 1911 by Pierre Prier in 3 h 56 min, flying a Blériot monoplane powered by a 50 hp Gnôme engine. Prier, who was Chief Flying Instructor at the Blériot Flying School, Hendon,

took off from Hendon and landed at Issy-les-Moulineaux.

The first recorded carriage of freight by air in Britain was a box of Osram lamps carried on 4 July 1911 by a Valkyrie monoplane flown by Horatio Barber from Shoreham to Hove in Sussex, England, on behalf of the General Electric Company who paid £100 for the flight.

The first American woman pilot was Harriet Quimby who, on 2 August 1911, gained her licence. On 16 April 1912 she became **the first woman to fly an aeroplane across the English Channel.**

The first British woman pilot was Mrs Hilda B. Hewlett, who gained Pilot's Certificate No 122 on 29 August 1911.

The first official mail to be carried by air in Great Britain was entrusted to the staff pilots of the Grahame-White and Blériot flying schools who commenced carrying the mail between Hendon and Windsor on Saturday, 9 September 1911. The first flight was undertaken on that day by Gustav Hamel in a Blériot monoplane, covering the route in 10 min at a ground speed of over 105 mph (169 km/h) with a strong tailwind. The service lasted until 26 September, having been instituted to commemorate the Coronation of HM King George V. The total weight of mail carried between the Hendon flying-field and Royal Farm, Windsor was 1015 lb (460·4 kg).

The first coast-to-coast flight across America was made by Calbraith P. Rodgers between 17 September and 5 November 1911. Rodgers, trying to win a $50 000 prize offered by William Randolph Hearst, flew from New York to Pasadena in a Burgess-Wright biplane. Making a series of short flights, he arrived at the destination 19 days outside the specified 30-day limit and so failed to qualify for the prize.

The first Italian airmail service started on 19 September 1911 and covered Bologna, Venice and Rimini.

The first official carriage of mail by air in the USA was by Earl L. Ovington on 23 September 1911 in a Blériot-type monoplane known as the Queen monoplane. The journey of 6 miles (9·6 km) began from Nassau Boulevard, New York. Ovington became *Air Mail Pilot No 1*, a

Earl Ovington, the first duly sworn US airmail pilot, accepts mail from Postmaster General Hitchcock. (US National Archives)

Short S.38 on board HMS Africa *in January 1912.*

title given to him by Postmaster-General Hitchcock.

The first gallantry decoration to be 'earned' by a marine aviator was the Distinguished Flying Cross awarded posthumously to Eugene B. Ely, who was killed while flying on 14 October 1911. The award of the DFC was made 25 years later in recognition of his outstanding contributions to marine aviation during 1910 and 1911. His sole reward during his life was an award of $500 made by the US Aeronautical Reserve during 1911.

The first time an aeroplane was used in war was on 22 October 1911 when an Italian Blériot, piloted by Capitano Piazza, Italian Air Flotilla, made a reconnaissance flight from Tripoli to Azizia to view the Turkish positions.

The first bombs dropped from an aeroplane in war were small Cipelli grenades, hand-released from an Italian Air Flotilla aircraft (piloted by 2nd Lt Giulio Gavotti) over Turkish positions at Taguira Oasis and Ain Zara, on 1 November 1911.

The first officer of the Royal Navy to take off from a ship in an aeroplane was Lt Charles Rumney Samson who is said to have made a secret flight in a Short biplane from a platform on the bows of the British battleship, HMS *Africa*, 17 500 tons (17 780 tonnes), moored in Sheerness Harbour during December 1911. His first officially recorded take-off was from HMS

Africa at 14.20 h on 10 January 1912, flying a Short S.38 biplane. Cdr Samson was appointed Officer Commanding the Naval Wing of the Royal Flying Corps in October 1912.

The first parachute descent from an aeroplane in America was performed by Capt Albert Berry who, on 1 March 1912, jumped from a Benoist aircraft flown by Anthony Jannus at 1 500 ft (460 m) over Jefferson Barracks, St Louis, Missouri.

The first seaplane competition was held at Monaco in March 1912. Seven pilots attended (Fischer, Renaux, Paulhan, Robinson, Caudron, Benoit, Rugère), the winner being Fischer on a Henry Farman biplane.

The first instance of a Government ordering the grounding of a specific type of aircraft occurred in March 1912 when the French Government ordered all Blériot monoplanes of the French Army to be prohibited from flying until they had been rebuilt so that their wings were braced to withstand a degree of negative-G. Five distinguished French pilots had been killed following the collapse of the Blériot's wings, but the ban was short-lived and the aircraft were flying again within a fortnight. The weakness was spotlighted by Louis Blériot himself who, despite the likely loss of prestige, published a short report explaining the weakness in his own aeroplanes. There is no doubt that his frankness increased—rather than detracted from—his very high standing in aviation circles.

Denys Corbett Wilson's aeroplane at Co. Wexford on 22 April 1912, after the first aeroplane crossing from Great Britain to Ireland. (Aer Lingus)

The first of the great flying days at Hendon was held on 20 April 1912, when approximately 15 000 spectators paid to gain admission to the 6d, 1s and 2s 6d enclosures.

The first completed crossing from Great Britain to Ireland by aeroplane was achieved by Englishman Denys Corbett Wilson on 22 April 1912, flying across the St Georges Channel.

The first recognised flight in an aeroplane with a fully enclosed cabin for the pilot was made by A.V. Roe on 1 May 1912, in his Avro Type F.

The first pilot in the world to take off in an aeroplane from a ship under way was Cdr Samson, who took off in a Short pusher biplane amphibian from the forecastle of the battleship HMS *Hibernia* while it steamed at 10·5 knots off Portland during the Naval Review on 9 May 1912. At the conclusion of the Review, Cdr Samson was one of the officers commanded to dine with HM King George V on board the *Victoria and Albert*.

The first single-seat scout aeroplane was the Farnborough BS1 of 1912, which was designed mainly by Geoffrey de Havilland. Powered by a 100 hp Gnome rotary engine, this very advanced aeroplane demonstrated a speed of over 91 mph (147 km/h) over a mile course.

Another Farnborough aeroplane, the BE1, made **the first successful artillery-spotting flight** over Salisbury Plain in 1912.

The first all-metal aeroplane to fly was the *Tubavion* monoplane built by the Frenchmen Ponche and Primard in 1912. A fatal accident brought its tests to a halt.

The Royal Flying Corps was founded on 13 May 1912 from the Air Battalion of the Royal Engineers, British Army. This day also marked the founding of the Naval Wing. The formation dates of the early squadrons are listed on p. 73.

The largest 'Golli' in the world must be this hot-air balloon built by Cameron Balloons.

Alcock and Brown's Vimy takes off.

Goodyear Europa, *a non-rigid airship with thousands of lamps on each side of the envelope to light-up static or animated slogans for advertising and public relations.* (Air Photo Supply)

Replica of the Ryan NYP Spirit of St Louis *in which Charles Lindbergh flew the Atlantic solo in 1927.*

English Electric Wren, as entered in the 1923 Lympne lightplane competition, with a replica Bristol Boxkite and Blériot XI monoplane to the rear. (Kenneth Brookes)

Lockheed P-38 Lightning long-range fighter of the Second World War.

Second of two Lockheed XP-80A Shooting Stars, prototype of the USAAF/USAF's first operational jet fighter and first flown in mid-1944.

The Boeing Model 377 Stratocruiser was delivered to airlines from 1949. It set new standards of luxury for the air traveller, with both standard seating and sleeper interior arrangements available.

The first European fully swept-wing jet fighter was the Swedish Saab J 29, nicknamed Tunnan (barrel). These two J 29Fs carry Sidewinder air-to-air missiles.

Jet Provost trainers, for many years the RAF's main two-seat basic jet trainer.

Convair B-36 had the greatest wing span of any operational bomber. It was also the only post-war bomber with six pusher engines.

North American P-51 Mustang fighters of the USAAF's 8th Air Force based in England during the Second World War.

Entering service with the RAF in 1956, the Avro Vulcan was the last of Britain's three types of V-bomber to remain operational in an offensive role. Along with the USAF's B-52 Stratofortress, the Vulcan was evaluated as a carrier for the Douglas Skybolt air-launched ballistic missile. Neither type of bomber was to be assigned Skybolt operationally.

Perhaps the most unusual form of flying machine was the Bell Jet Belt, first demonstrated in 1969 as a way of giving Army personnel a fast method of crossing water or difficult terrain. Other stated uses included reconnaissance and amphibious landings.

France's first and only supersonic strategic bomber is the Dassault Mirage IV-A, first flown in 1959 and originally intended to carry a single free-fall nuclear weapon semi-recessed into the under-fuselage. A new supersonic nuclear stand-off missile is currently under development to arm 15 Mirage IV-As and other French aircraft.

Dornier Do 31-E, an experimental V/STOL transport of the latter 1960s using two underwing turbofans for horizontal flight and no fewer than 14 lift-jets for vertical flight.

Squadron	Date	Remarks
No 1 (Airship and Kite)	13 May 1912	Formed out of No 1 Airship Company, Air Battalion.
No 2 (Aeroplane)	13 May 1912	Formed from scratch.
No 3 (Aeroplane)	13 May 1912	Formed out of No 2 Aeroplane Company, Air Battalion.
No 4 (Aeroplane)	16 May 1912	Formed from scratch.
No 5 (Aeroplane)	26 July 1913	Formed from scratch at Farnborough.
No 6 (Aeroplane)	31 January 1914	Formed from scratch at Farnborough.
No 7 (Aeroplane)	May 1914	Formed from scratch.
No 8 (Aeroplane)	May 1914	Formed out of No 1 Airship and Kite Squadron, RFC.

The first American aeroplane armed with a machine-gun was a Wright Model B biplane flown by Lt Thomas de Witt Milling at College Park, Maryland, on 2 June 1912. The gunner, who was armed with a Lewis gun, was Capt Charles de Forest Chandler of the US Army Signal Corps.

The first American woman to be killed in an aeroplane accident was Julie Clark of Denver, Colorado, whose Curtiss biplane struck a tree on 17 June 1912 at Springfield, Illinois, and turned turtle. She had qualified for her Pilot's Certificate on 19 May 1912.

The Central Flying School of the RFC was established at Upavon, England, on 19 June 1912.

The first American woman to make a parachute descent in the USA was Tina Broadwick, on 21 June 1912.

The first crossing of the English Channel by an aeroplane with a pilot and two passengers was made on 4 August 1912 by W.B. Rhodes Moorhouse (later, as a Lt in the Royal Flying Corps, the first British airman to be awarded the Victoria Cross, on 26 April 1915) who, accompanied by his wife and a friend, flew a Breguet tractor biplane from Douai, France, via Boulogne and Dungeness, to Bethersden, near Ashford, Kent, where they crashed in bad weather. Nobody was hurt.

The first man to fly underneath all the Thames bridges in London between Tower Bridge and Westminster was F.K. McClean who, flying the Short S·33 pusher biplane from Harty Ferry, Isle of Sheppey, on 10 August 1912, passed between the upper and lower spans of Tower Bridge, and then underflew all the remaining bridges to Westminster where he landed on the river. No regulations forbade this escapade, but the police instructed McClean to taxi all the way back to Shadwell Basin before mooring! On the return trip the aeroplane side-slipped soon after take-off and damaged one of the floats after hitting a barge. The machine was then towed into Shadwell Dock and dismantled for the return by road to Eastchurch.

Avro Type F with an enclosed cockpit for the pilot.

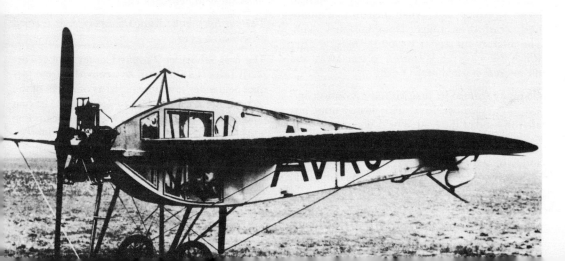

US Army Signal Corps aeroplanes were used on Army manoeuvres for the first time on 10 August 1912.

The first military aeroplane trials to be held in Great Britain took place at Larkhill, Salisbury Plain, in August 1912. The most important section, the speed competition, was won by Samuel Franklin Cody flying his primitive *Cathedral* biplane. Of about 30 British and French aircraft that took part, the most advanced was the Farnborough BE2, a development of the BE1.

The first pilot to perform, recover from and demonstrate recovery from a spin was Lt Wilfred Parke, Royal Navy, on 25 August 1912 while flying the Avro cabin tractor biplane during the Military Trials of that year. On this occasion Parke and his observer, Lt Le Breton, RFC, were flying at about 600 ft (183 m) and commenced a spiral glide prior to landing; finding that the glide was too steep, Parke pulled the stick back, promptly stalled and entered a spin. With no established procedure in mind for recovery he attempted to extricate himself from danger by pulling the stick further back and applying rudder *into* the direction of spin, and found that the spin merely tightened. After carefully noting this phenomenon he decided, *when only 50 ft (15 m) from the ground*—and from disaster—to reverse the rudder, and the machine recovered instantly. Parke was able to give a carefully reasoned résumé of his corrective actions, thereby contributing immeasurably to the progress of aviation.

The first officer of the Royal Flying Corps Reserves to be killed while engaged on military flying duties was 2nd Lt E. Hotchkiss (the Bristol Company's Chief Flying Instructor at Brooklands) who, with Lt C.A. Bettington, was killed on 10 September 1912 when their Bristol monoplane crashed on a flight from Salisbury Plain. The aircraft suffered a structural failure, after which the wing fabric started to tear away and the aircraft crashed near Oxford.

Germany formed its first Military Aviation Service on 1 October 1912. This lasted until just after the end of the First World War.

The first trials in America to determine the suitability of aeroplanes for anti-submarine warfare began on 26 October 1912, under the command of Lt John H. Towers.

The first aeroplane to be successfully catapult-launched from a boat was a Curtiss A-1 Triad hydroaeroplane, piloted by Lt T. Ellyson, on 12 November 1912. The operation was performed from an anchored barge, at the Washington Navy Yard, using a compressed-air launcher invented by Capt W.I. Chambers.

The number of Pilots' Certificates which had been awarded in the world by the end of 1912 was 2490, though the number of actual pilots was slightly smaller as some had been awarded certificates in more than one country. One or two others had received certificates in countries which were not members of the Fédération Aéronautique Internationale. The massive superiority of France at this time is evident:

1	France .	966	10	Holland .	26
2	Great Britain	382	11	Argentine	
3	Germany .	345		Republic .	15
4	United States of			Spain .	15
	America .	193	13	Sweden .	10
5	Italy .	186	14	Denmark .	8
6	Russia .	162	15	Hungary .	7
7	Austria .	84	16	Norway .	5
8	Belgium .	58	17	Egypt .	1
9	Switzerland .	27			—
				Total	2490

The first Russian aeroplane with a machine-gun fitted was the Dux-1, a pusher-engined biplane intended for ground attack. This appeared in 1913.

The first British aeroplane designed and built as an armed fighting machine was the Vickers Destroyer EFB 1, ordered by the British Admiralty in November 1912 and displayed at the Olympia Aero Show in February 1913.

The 1st Aero Squadron, US Army, was formed on 5 March 1913.

The first Schneider Trophy Contest (more correctly titled 'La Coupe d' Aviation Maritime Jacques Schneider'), was included as one item of the second international Hydro-aeroplane Meeting held at Monaco during the two weeks beginning 3 April 1913. It created initially little interest, with only seven entries for the first contest, reduced to four starters after the eliminating trials. The course consisted of twenty-eight 10 km laps and this 1913 contest, flown on 16 April, was

Vickers Destroyer EFB 1 at the Olympia Aero Show in 1913. (Flight International)

won by Maurice Prévost flying a 160 hp Gnome-powered Deperdussin. This pilot was under the impression that he should alight and taxi across the finishing line, but in fact this was invalid and it was required that he should fly the aircraft across the line. He was accordingly sent off again to complete a further lap which, including a period spent ashore, deciding whether to continue or not, added about an hour to his time, so that his average speed is recorded in the official results as being 45·75 mph (73·63 km/h). Second was late-starter Roland Garros, flying a Morane-Saulnier monoplane powered by an 80 hp Gnome engine.

The first gyroscopic automatic stabiliser was successfully demonstrated by the Americans, Lawrence B. Sperry and Lt Patrick Nelson Lynch Bellinger, in a Curtiss F flying-boat in 1913. The aircraft was longitudinally and laterally stabilised.

The first non-stop aeroplane flight between England and Germany was made by Gustav Hamel on 17 April 1913, flying a military-type Blériot XI monoplane between Dover and Cologne in a time of 4 h 18 min.

The first bombs to be dropped by aeroplane on an enemy warship were those released by Didier Masson, a supporter of General Alvarado Obregon, on Mexican gunships in the Guaymas Bay, on 10 May 1913.

The first four-engined aeroplane to fly was the *Le Grand* ('The Great One', known also as *Russky Vityaz* or Russian Knight) biplane designed, and first flown on 13 May 1913 at St Petersburg, by Igor Sikorsky, then Head of the Aeronautical Department of the Russian Baltic Railway Car Factory at Petrograd. It had a wing span of over 92 ft (28 m) and was powered by four 100 hp Argus engines, originally mounted in tandem pairs but later in all-tractor configuration (from June). The first flight lasted under ten minutes.

Sikorsky Le Grand. (Real Photographs)

From *Le Grand* was evolved the Ilya Mourometz, which became the **first four-engined bomber to see active service.**

The first parachute descent by a woman from an aeroplane was made by the 18-year-old American girl, Georgia ('Tiny') Broadwick who, using an 11 lb (5 kg) silk parachute, jumped from an aircraft flown by Glenn Martin at about 1000 ft (305 m) over Griffith Field, Los Angeles, California, on 21 June 1913.

The first major British competition for seaplanes was the *Daily Mail* Hydro-Aeroplane Trial, started on 16 August 1913. The regulations stated a specified course round Britain, involving a distance to be flown of 1540 miles (2478 km) by an all-British aircraft before 30 August. Four aircraft were entered, but Samuel Cody was killed in a crash at Laffan's Plain on 7 August. F.K. McClean withdrew his Short S.68 due to engine trouble, and the Radley-England Waterplane was scratched for the same reason. This left Harry Hawker, accompanied by his mechanic H.A. Kauper, as the only contender. He left the water at Southampton at 11.47 h, in a Sopwith three-seater tractor biplane which was powered by a 100 hp Green six-cylinder inline engine. The route was from Southampton via Ramsgate, Yarmouth, Scarborough, Aberdeen, Cromarty, Oban, Dublin, Falmouth and back to Southampton. After an abortive attempt, which ended at Yarmouth owing to a cracked engine cylinder, Hawker took off again from Southampton on 25 August. He managed to fly round the course as far as Dublin when, just before alighting on the water, his foot slipped off the rudder-bar and the aircraft struck the water and broke up. The *Daily Mail* prize of £5000 was not awarded, but Hawker received £1000 as consolation.

The first pilot in the world to perform a loop was Lt Nesterov of the Imperial Russian Army who, flying a Nieuport Type IV monoplane, performed the manoeuvre at Kiev on 27 August 1913.

The first pilot to fly inverted in sustained flight (as distinct from becoming inverted during the course of the looping manoeuvre) was Adolphe Pégoud who, on 21 September 1913, flew a Blériot monoplane inverted at Buc, France. Notwithstanding the above definition, Pégoud's manoeuvre involved two 'halves' of a loop, in that he assumed the inverted position by means of a half-loop, and after sustained inverted flight recovered by means of a 'pull-through'. He thus did not resort to a roll or half-roll, which manoeuvre had not apparently been achieved at this time. As a means of acclimatising himself for the ordeal of inverted flight, Pégoud had had his Blériot mounted inverted upon trestles and had remained strapped in the cockpit for periods of up to 20 min at a time!

The first air crossing of the Mediterranean was achieved on 23 September 1913 by a Morane-Saulnier monoplane piloted by Roland Garros, who flew 453 miles (730 km) from Saint-Raphaël, France, to Bizerte, Tunisia, in 7 h 53 min.

The first 'over 200 km/h' world speed record was set by Frenchman Maurice Prévost in the Deperdussin 'monocoque' of 1913 at Reims on 29 September 1913, at 126·666 mph (203·850 km/h). This was **officially the fastest aircraft prior to the First World War,** as no further records were set until 1920.

The first ever aerial combat between aircraft took place in November 1913, when, over Mexico, an aeroplane piloted by Phillip Rader in support of General Huerta exchanged pistol shots with one flown by Dean Ivan Lamb operating with the forces of Venustiano Carranza.

The first flight from France to Egypt was accomplished by Jules Védrines in a Blériot powered by an 80 hp Gnôme engine, between 29 November and 29 December 1913. Setting out from Nancy, France, his route was via Würzburg, Prague, Vienna, Belgrade, Sofia, Constantinople, Tripoli (Syria), Jaffa and Cairo.

Non-aviation inventions of the period

Tracked agricultural tractor Produced by the American Holt Manufacturing Company, and steam powered, in 1906.

Talking motion film Sound-on-film process was patented by Eugène Augustin Lauste in 1906.

Geiger counter The work of the German physicist Hans Geiger to measure radiation, dating from 1908.

Progressive world absolute speed records achieved by man in the atmosphere

Speed mph	km/h	Pilot	Nationality	Aircraft	Location of achievement	Date
34·03	54·77	Paul Tissandier	France	Wright biplane	Pau, France	20 May 1909
43·34	69·75	Glenn Curtiss	USA	Herring-Curtiss biplane	Reims, France	23 Aug 1909
46·17	74·30	Louis Blériot	France	Blériot monoplane	Reims, France	24 Aug 1909
47·84	76·99	Louis Blériot	France	Blériot monoplane	Reims, France	28 Aug 1909
48·20	77·57	Hubert Latham	France	Antoinette monoplane	Nice, France	23 Apr 1910
66·18	106·50	Léon Morane	France	Blériot monoplane	Reims, France	10 July 1910
68·18	109·73	Alfred Leblanc	France	Blériot monoplane	Belmont Park, Long Island, USA	29 Oct 1910
69·46	111·79	Alfred Léblanc	France	Blériot monoplane		12 Apr 1911
74·40	119·74	Édouard Nieuport	France	Nieuport biplane		11 May 1911
77·67	124·99	Alfred Léblanc	France	Blériot monoplane		12 June 1911
80·80	130·04	Édouard Nieuport	France	Nieuport biplane	Châlons, France	16 June 1911
82·71	133·11	Édouard Nieuport	France	Nieuport biplane	Châlons, France	21 June 1911
90·18	145·13	Jules Védrines	France	Deperdussin monoplane	Pau, France	13 Jan 1912
100·21	161·27	Jules Védrines	France	Deperdussin monoplane	Pau, France	22 Feb 1912
100·99	162·53	Jules Védrines	France	Deperdussin monoplane	Pau, France	29 Feb 1912
103·64	166·79	Jules Védrines	France	Deperdussin monoplane	Pau, France	1 Mar 1912
104·32	167·88	Jules Védrines	France	Deperdussin monoplane	Pau, France	2 Mar 1912
106·10	170·75	Jules Védrines	France	Deperdussin monoplane		13 July 1912
108·16	174·06	Jules Védrines	France	Deperdussin monoplane	Chicago, Illinois, USA	9 Sept 1912
111·72	179·79	Maurice Prévost	France	Deperdussin monoplane		17 June 1913
119·22	191·87	Maurice Prévost	France	Deperdussin monoplane	Reims, France	27 Sept 1913
126·666	203·85	Maurice Prévost	France	Deperdussin monoplane	Reims, France	29 Sept 1913

Progressive world absolute height records achieved by man in the atmosphere

Height ft	m	Pilot	Nationality	Aircraft	Location	Date
508	155	H. Latham	GB	Antoinette	Reims, France	29 Aug 1909
984	300	Comte Charles de Lambert	France	Wright	Paris, France	18 Oct 1909
1486	453	H. Latham	GB	Antoinette	Châlons, France	1 Dec 1909
3281	1000	H. Latham	GB	Antoinette	France	7 Jan 1910
3966	1209	L. Paulhan	France	Henry Farman	Los Angeles, USA	12 Jan 1910
4380	1335	W. Brookins	USA	Wright	Indianapolis, USA	14 June 1910
4540	1384	H. Latham	GB	Antoinette	Reims, France	7 July 1910
6234	1900	W. Brookins	USA	Wright	Atlantic City, USA	10 July 1910
6601	2012	A. Drexel	USA	Blériot	Lanark, Scotland	11 Aug 1910
8471	2582	Léon Morane	France	Blériot	Deauville, France	3 Sept 1910
8488	2587	G. Chavez	France	Blériot	Issy-les-Moulineaux, France	8 Sept 1910
9120	2780	H. Wynmalen	France	Henry Farman	Mourmelon, France	1 Oct 1910
9449	2880	A. Drexel	USA	Blériot	Philadelphia, USA	Oct 1910
9711	2960	R. Johnston	USA	Wright	Belmont Park, USA	31 Oct 1910
10170	3100	G. Legagneux	France	Blériot	Pau, France	8 Dec 1910
10423	3177	M. Loridan	France	Henry Farman	Châlons, France	8 July 1911
10466	3190	Capt Félix	France	Blériot	Etampes, France	9 Aug 1911
12828	3910	Roland Garros	France	Blériot XI	St-Malo, France	4 Sept 1911
16076	4900	Roland Garros	France	Blériot XI	Houlgate, France	6 Sept 1912
17880	5450	G. Legagneux	France	Morane-Saulnier	Corbeaulieu, France	17 Sept 1912
18405	5610	Roland Garros	France	Morane-Saulnier	Tunis	11 Dec 1912
19291	5880	M. Perreyon	France	Blériot XI	Buc, France	11 Mar 1913
20079	6120	G. Legagneux	France	Nieuport	St-Raphael, France	28 Dec 1913

Progressive world absolute distance records achieved by man in the atmosphere

Distance						
miles	km	Pilot	Nationality	Aircraft	Location of start	Date
722 ft	220 m	A. Santos-Dumont	Brazil	Santos-Dumont 14bis	Bagatelle, France	12 Nov 1906
2530 ft	771 m	H. Farman	France	Voisin	Issy-les-Moulineaux, France	26 Oct 1907
0·62	1	H. Farman	France	Voisin	Issy-les-Moulineaux, France	13 Jan 1908
1·25	2·004	H. Farman	France	Voisin	Issy-les-Moulineaux, France	21 Mar 1908
2·44	3·925	L. Delagrange	France	Voisin	Issy-les-Moulineaux, France	11 Apr 1908
7·92	12·75	L. Delagrange	France	Voisin	Centocelle	30 May 1908
14·99	24·125	L. Delagrange	France	Voisin	Issy-les-Moulineaux, France	17 Sept 1908
41·38	66·60	Wilbur Wright	USA	Wright	Auvours, France	21 Sept 1908
62	99·8	Wilbur Wright	USA	Wright	Auvours, France	18 Dec 1908
77·48	124·7	Wilbur Wright	USA	Wright	Auvours, France	31 Dec 1908
83·26	134	Louis Paulhan	France	Voisin	Betheny	25 Aug 1909
96·08	154·62	H. Latham	GB	Antoinette	Betheny	26 Aug 1909
111·8	180	H. Farman	France	Farman	Betheny	27 Aug 1909
145·53	234·21	H. Farman	France	Farman	Mourmelon	4 Nov 1909
244	392·75	Jan Olieslagers	Belgium	Blériot	Mourmelon	20 July 1910
289·4	465·72	M. Tabuteau	France	Maurice Farman	Etampes, France	28 Oct 1910
320·6	515·9	G. Legagneux	France	Blériot	Pau, France	11 Dec 1910
363·35	584·75	M. Tabuteau	France	Maurice Farman	Buc, France	30 Dec 1910
388·4	625	Jan Olieslagers	Belgium	Nieuport monoplane	Kiewit	16 July 1911
449·21	722·94	Fourny	France	Maurice Farman	Buc, France	1 Sept 1911
460	740·3	Gobé	France	Nieuport monoplane	Pau, France	24 Dec 1911
628·1	1010·9	Fourny	France	Maurice Farman	Etampes, France	11 Sept 1912
634·5	1021·2	A. Seguin	France	Henry Farman	Buc, France	13 Oct 1913

First World War

In the widest sense, the genesis of aerial warfare lay in the bomb-carrying pennon kites of the 14th century, and the hydrogen balloons used for observation and bomb-carrying hot-air balloons of the 18th and 19th centuries. With the invention of the aeroplane came new horizons for military planners and, as recorded in the previous section, the very first contract for a military aeroplane bomber was drawn up as early as 1892. Interestingly, though in retrospect the latter was clearly an impracticable project, given the state of the art, it is worth noting here, that when the first aeroplane was taken into military service, it was not intended for offensive use.

Aeroplanes as platforms for guns and bombs started appearing in 1911 and 1912, and it was also in 1911 that Italian airmen dropped Cipelli grenades by hand on Turkish ground forces in Libya. This, undoubtedly the lightest bombing attack in aviation history, can be said to have

laid the foundations for the attacks made during the two world wars and beyond, in fact to Laos during the Vietnam war of the 1960s and early 70s, which received approximately 2½ million tons of bombs over a nine-year period and was the most heavily bombed country ever.

Despite the appearance of purpose-designed 'fighting' aeroplanes, the invention of mechanical gear that would allow a machine-gun to fire through a propeller arc, and other far-sighted concepts, by the outbreak of the First World War little had been done to develop the aeroplane into an efficient attacking machine. Indeed, the first German aeroplanes to bomb Paris and other European cities were Taube monoplanes, bird-winged aeroplanes whose origins can be traced to Austria of 1909.

When war was declared in August 1914, the Imperial German Army and Navy air services had about 280 assorted aircraft and nine airships. Austria–Hungary had 36, Britain about 180, Belgium 24, and France 160 aircraft and 15 airships. These were used initially for reconnaissance, artillery spotting and light bombing duties, and soon became the eyes of the armies. This pointed, inevitably, to the need for armed aircraft or fighter-scouts to destroy opposing machines before vital information could reach enemy land forces.

Arming an aeroplane was far from easy until the re-invention of interrupter gear, which allowed a machine-gun to fire between the rotating propeller blades. The Germans were first to fit such an arrangement, on the Fokker Eindecker, and gained almost complete control of the skies over the Western Front during the winter of 1915-16. The British answer was to build pusher fighters, or aircraft with rear-mounted engines and propellers, so leaving a clear forward field of fire. However, the future lay with front-engined aircraft, and the Allies had to invent their own interrupter gear. Superiority was held first by one side, then the other, as each air force gained that slight advantage in speed or manoeuvrability over its enemies, with more (or over) stable two-seat observation aircraft the most numerous victim.

Sopwith 2F.1 Camel fighters. This variant was produced specially for use on board ship, with a detachable rear fuselage/tail unit and one Vickers gun being supplemented by an upper wing Lewis.

After the Allies had won the war, in November 1918, hostilities continued in Russia during 1919. Thereafter there were other troubles nearer home to embroil some survivors of the war, typified by the death of the sixth-ranking German fighter ace of the war, in 1920. Hauptmann Rudolph Berthold, who had gained 44 'air victories', found himself leading an anti-communist band known as the Eiserne Schar Berthold until he was besieged in a school house at Harburg by German opponents and struck down on 15 March 1920. A stone marks this spot, inscribed Flieger Hauptmann Berthold, dated and carrying the insignia of the 20th Regiment Graf Tauentzien.

Returning to 1914, the year began with a non-military aviation event of very great significance. The story of the world's first scheduled airline service using aeroplanes really begins in 1909, when businessman Thomas Benoist formed the Aeronautic Supply Company (later Benoist Aircraft Company) to give exhibition flights and lessons in aircraft he had designed. He later turned to flying-boats and was second only to Glenn Curtiss in this field in America. In that year, 1912, a Benoist machine was flown by Anthony H. Jannus on a 1970 mile (3170 km) journey between Omaha and New Orleans. In stages this took more than a month, but actual flying time was under 32 hours. Hearing about this feat, a man named Percival E. Fansler got in touch with Benoist and eventually, in 1913, the two decided to form an airline using new Benoist flying-boats. The route chosen was between St Petersburg and Tampa, Florida.

The pilot for the service was Jannus, who therefore became **the world's first airline pilot** (flying aeroplanes). On 1 January 1914 all was readied for the first of two scheduled flights for the day. This was clearly history in the making and a crowd of several thousand onlookers had gathered. An auction was held to see who was to be **the world's first passenger on a scheduled commercial aeroplane flight.** This raised a much needed $400 and soon Mr A.C. Pheil, once mayor of St Petersburg, climbed on board the open cockpit biplane flying-boat. Right on schedule, at 10.00 h, the flying-boat took off, reaching its destination half an hour later. By 11.30 h Jannus was back at St Petersburg. Scheduled airline services using aeroplanes had arrived!

The first scheduled airline using aeroplanes was the St Petersburg–Tampa Airboat Line, which started its operations on 1 January 1914, flying between St Petersburg and Tampa, Florida. The aircraft was a Benoist flying-boat piloted by Anthony Jannus. The operation lasted four months.

The first French airmen to be killed on active service were Capt Hervé and his observer, named Roëland. During the colonial campaign in Morocco, early in 1914, they made a forced landing in the desert and were killed by local Arabs.

The first military operations involving the use of American aeroplanes were those during the Vera Cruz incident (Mexico) in April 1914, when five Curtiss AB flying-boats were carried to the port on board the battleship USS *Mississippi* and the

The US Navy's AB-3 flying-boat, flown on the first mission during the Vera Cruz incident, was also one of the first aircraft ever to be catapulted from a ship, following AB-2 off USS North Carolina. *(US National Archives)*

cruiser USS *Birmingham*. The first such military flight was undertaken by Lt (Jg) P.N.L. Bellinger, who took off in the Curtiss AB-3 flying-boat on 25 April in order to search for mines in the harbour. The AB flying-boats flew on 43 consecutive days, and some damage was sustained from rifle fire. Bellinger's aircraft sustained the first damage by ground fire, on 6 May while on a reconnaissance flight, **the first US military aeroplane to be hit by enemy fire while on active service.**

The first British aeroplane to beat all comers in a major international competitive event was the Sopwith Tabloid. Designed as a small, fast biplane scout aircraft, it first flew in the autumn of 1913. Official tests at Farnborough on 29 November 1913 showed it had exceptional performance, with a maximum rate of climb of 1200 ft (366 m)/min and a maximum speed of 92 mph (148 km/h). Its outstanding competitive success was its victory in the second contest for the Schneider Trophy held at Monaco on 20 April

Sopwith Tabloid, winner of the second Schneider Trophy contest.

1914 when, equipped as a floatplane, the aircraft was flown by Howard Pixton over the 280 km course at an average speed of 86·78 mph (139·66 km/h). After completing the race, Pixton continued for two extra laps to establish a new world speed record for seaplanes at 86·6 mph (139·37 km/h) over a measured 300 km course.

The first parachute drop from an aeroplane over Great Britain was made by W. Newell at Hendon on 9 May 1914 from a Grahame-White Charabanc flown by R. H. Carr. Newell sat on a short rope attached to the port undercarriage, clutching his 40 lb (18 kg) parachute in his lap; when the aeroplane had climbed to 2000 ft (610 m) F. W. Gooden, seated on the lower wing, prised Newell off his perch with his foot! The parachute was 26 ft (7·9 m) in diameter and the drop occupied 2 min 22 s.

The first air service of the US Army was established on 18 July 1914, when the Aviation Section was formed as part of the Signal Corps with a 'paper' strength of 60 officers and 260 men, plus six aeroplanes. This superseded the Aeronautical Division of the Signal Corps.

The first standard naval torpedo dropped by a naval airman in a naval aircraft was a 14 in (35·6 cm) torpedo weighing 810 lb (367 kg), dropped by a Short seaplane flown by Sqn Cdr Arthur Longmore, RN (Royal Aero Club Pilot's Certificate No 72), on 28 July 1914. This followed a similar demonstration by Short's test pilot, Gordon Bell, the previous day.

The first flight across the North Sea by an aeroplane was achieved by the Norwegian pilot Tryggve Gran flying a Blériot monoplane on 30 July 1914.

The world's first four-engined bomber and reconnaissance aircraft to be accepted into military service was the Russian Army's *Ilya Mourometz*, in August 1914.

A brief list of the declarations of war by the major powers, and other dates, which formed the basis for the First World War.
On 1 August 1914 Germany declared war on Russia.
On 2 August 1914 Germany invaded Luxembourg.
On 3 August 1914 Germany declared war on France.
On 3 August 1914 Germany invaded Belgium.
On 4 August 1914 Britain declared war on Germany.
On 5 August 1914 Austria-Hungary declared war on Russia.
On 6 August 1914 Serbia declared war on Germany.
On 10 August 1914 France declared war on Austria-Hungary.
On 12 August 1914 Britain declared war on Austria-Hungary.

On 23 August 1914 Japan declared war on Germany.

On 25 August 1914 Austria-Hungary declared war on Japan.

On 28 August 1914 Austria-Hungary declared war on Belgium.

On 31 October 1914 Russia declared war on Turkey.

On 5 November 1914 Britain declared war on Turkey.

On 24 May 1915 Italy declared war on Austria-Hungary.

On 14 September 1915 Bulgaria declared war on Serbia.

On 15 September 1915 Britain declared war on Bulgaria.

On 16 September 1915 France declared war on Bulgaria.

On 27 August 1916 Italy declared war on Germany.

On 27 August 1916 Romania declared war on Austria-Hungary.

On 28 August 1916 Germany declared war on Romania.

On 30 August 1916 Turkey declared war on Romania.

On 1 September 1916 Bulgaria declared war on Romania.

On 6 April 1917 the United States of America declared war on Germany.

On 7 December 1917 the United States of America declared war on Austria-Hungary.

The last aviation sporting events to be held in Britain before the outbreak of the First World War took place at Hendon on 3 August 1914. They consisted of a cross-country and a speed handicap race, the former being won by R. J. Lillywhite, the latter by the American W. L. Brock.

The era of unrestricted flying over Great Britain came to an end with the outbreak of the First World War. On 4 August 1914 the Home Office issued the following order severely curtailing the flying of aeroplanes over the country:

'In pursuance of the powers conferred on me by the Aerial Navigation Acts 1911 and 1913, I hereby make, for the purposes of the safety and defence of the Realm, the following Order:

'I prohibit the navigation of aircraft of every class and description over the whole area of the United Kingdom, and over the whole of the coastline thereof and territorial waters adjacent thereto.

'This order shall not apply to Naval or Military aircraft or to aircraft flying under Naval or Military orders, nor shall it apply to any aircraft flying within three miles of a recognised aerodrome.

R. McKenna.
One of His Majesty's Principal Secretaries of State.'

The first French airman to be wounded in action was the observer of a French reconnaissance plane, hit by a rifle bullet from German troops. The pilot of the aircraft was Sadi Lecointe.

The first British airmen killed on active service were 2nd Lt R.B. Skene and a mechanic R.K. Barlow, of No 3 Squadron, RFC, on 12 August 1914. Flying from Netheravon to Dover to form up for the Channel crossing, their aircraft, a Blériot two-seater of 'C' Flight, landed because of engine trouble. Shortly after taking off again, the aircraft crashed into trees and both occupants were killed.

The first German Air Service pilot to be killed on active service was Oberleutnant Reinhold Jahnow. He was fatally injured in a crash at Malmédy, Belgium, on 12 August 1914. He was holder of German Pilot's Licence No 80, and a veteran of several reconnaissance flights for the Turks during the Balkan campaign of 1912.

The first British squadrons to fly over the English Channel to France after the outbreak of war were numbers 2, 3, 4 and 5, equipped with BE2s, Blériots and Farman biplanes; BE2s and Farmans; and BE8s and Avro 504s respectively, starting on 13 August 1914. The first of these aircraft to land was BE2a No 347, flown by Lt H.D. Harvey-Kelly. Farmans of No 4 Squadron were later **the first British armed aircraft to be flown in action.**

The first bombing attack of the war: see Lighter than air—dirigibles (14 August 1914).

The most widely used aeroplane type in military service on the outbreak of war was the Etrich Taube. Designed in Austria-Hungary in 1909, it was a 'bird-winged' monoplane powered by a single engine of 85–120 hp. Maximum speed was 72 mph (116 km/h). In August 1914, about half of all the aircraft in German service were of this type and others were operated by the Austro-Hungarian air service. Intended mainly for reconnaissance and training duties, Taubes were often used for dropping light bombs. Germany alone licence-built some 500, examples of which remained in service until 1916.

The first British reconnaissance flight over German territory was carried out by Lt G. Mappleback and Capt P. Joubert de la Ferté of No 4 Squadron, RFC, flying a BE2a and a Blériot monoplane respectively. The flight took place on 19 August 1914.

The first RFC aeroplane to be brought down in action was an Avro 504 of No 5 Squadron, piloted by Lt V. Waterfall, on 22 August 1914. The aircraft was shot down by rifle fire from troops in Belgium.

The first RFC 'air victory' was achieved on 25 August 1914, when Lt Harvey-Kelly flying an unarmed reconnaissance machine, in company with two other unarmed planes from No 2 Squadron, forced a German two-seater to land.

The first aeroplane to be destroyed by ramming was an Austrian two-seater flown by Leutnant Baron von Rosenthal, rammed over the air base at Sholkiv on 26 August 1914 by Staff Capt Petr Nikolaevich Nesterov of the Imperial Russian XI Corps Air Squadron, who was flying an unarmed Morane Type M monoplane scout. Both pilots were killed. Nesterov (remembered also as the **first pilot to loop the loop**) was the Imperial Air Service's **first battle casualty**.

The first British military aircraft insignia consisted of Union Jacks painted in rectangular and shield-shape forms on RFC aircraft. This was necessitated by the fact that RFC aircraft had been fired on by French and British ground-troops, who mistook them for German types. RNAS aircraft were instructed to bear the Union Jack on 26 October 1914. **The roundel was adopted by the RFC from 11 December 1914,** following the French example. On 11 December 1914, the RNAS adopted a roundel for the wings only, consisting initially of a red outer circle and a white centre.

The Iron Cross insignia was adopted for German aircraft in September 1914.

The first great land battle in which victory was generally attributed to aerial reconnaissance was the battle of Tannenberg, where 120 000 Russian soldiers and 500 guns were captured by German forces in late August 1914.

The first RNAS Squadron to fly to France after the start of the war was the Eastchurch Squadron, led by Wg Cdr C.R. Samson (the first British pilot to take off in an aeroplane from a ship). Arriving at Ostend on 27 August 1914, its equipment included two Sopwith Tabloids, three BEs, two Blériots, one Short seaplane, one Bristol biplane and one Farman biplane. The only armed aircraft attached to the Squadron was the Astra-Torres airship No 3.

The first bombs to be dropped upon a capital city from an aircraft fell on Paris, on 30 August 1914. The pilot of the Taube monoplane is thought to have been Leutnant Ferdinand von Hiddessen, who dropped five bombs and a message on the Quai de Valmy, killing one woman and injuring two other people.

The first air operations undertaken by airmen of the Royal Navy during the First World War were reconnaissance flights by Eastchurch Squadron commanded by Wg Cdr Charles Samson in support of a Brigade of Royal Marines on the Belgian coast in August 1914.

The first British air raid on Germany: See Lighter than air—dirigibles (22 September 1914).

Fléchettes were first dropped from aeroplanes of No 3 Squadron RFC in the autumn of 1914. These were steel darts about 5 in (12·7 cm) in length which were carried in containers. Over the target, some 250 fléchettes were dropped from each container on to enemy ground concentrations. Casualties or damage were rare in such attacks.

The first Japanese naval vessel converted to support seaplanes was the 7600-ton (7722 tonnes) *Wakamiya Maru*, converted in 1913. It began operations against German forces at Kiaochow Bay, China, on 1 September 1914, using Farman seaplanes. Dropping improvised bombs made from naval shells, the Farmans succeeded in sinking a German minelayer before being damaged

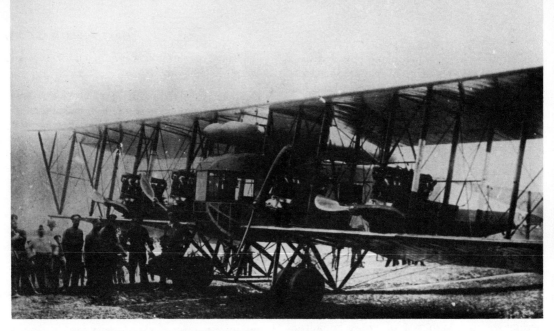

by a mine. The minelayer was **the first warship sunk from the air.**

The first French bomber Groupe was formed on 27 September 1914, equipped with Voisin pusher biplanes nicknamed 'Chicken Coops'.

The first aeroplane in the world to be shot down and destroyed by another was a German two-seater, possibly an Aviatik, shot down at Jonchery, near Reims on 5 October 1914 by Sergent Joseph Frantz and Caporal Quénault in a Voisin pusher of Escadrille VB24. The weapon used is believed to have been a Hotchkiss machine-gun.

The first successful British air raid on Germany: See Lighter than air—dirigibles (8 October 1914).

The first ever strategic bombing raid by a formation of aircraft: See Lighter than air—dirigibles (21 November 1914).

The Sopwith Tabloid was the first single-seat scout to enter production for military service in the world. Designed before the war, a Tabloid won the 1914 Schneider Trophy contest, and later became standard equipment of the early RNAS. Examples serving with the Eastchurch Squadron were armed with a wing-mounted machine-gun from February 1915.

The first operational seaplane unit of the Imperial German Navy was formed on 4 December 1914, moving to its base at Zeebrugge two days later.

Sikorsky Ilya Mouron metz *bomber in service with the EVK.*

The first operational four-engined bombers and reconnaissance aircraft were *Ilya Mouron metz* biplanes, which equipped the Flotilla of Flying Ships (EVK), Russian Army, from 10 December 1914 (formation date of the EVK). This force eventually operated at a strength of between 40 and 50 of these giants. The total number of these bombers built was 73 and those not used for training made about 400 bombing raids, the first against a Polish target on 15 February 1915. Powered by four 125-220 hp engines, the *Ilya Mouron metz* could fly at 60-80 mph (97-129 km/h) and could carry up to 1500 lb (680 kg) of bombs. It carried up to 16 crew members and, as with the German R-Type bombers of 1918, routine servicing and minor repairs could be performed in flight.

The first aeroplane raid on Great Britain, by one aircraft, took place on 21 December 1914. Two bombs fell in the sea near Admiralty Pier at Dover.

The first bomb dropped by an enemy aircraft on British soil, and the second aeroplane raid on Great Britain, again by one aircraft, took place on 24 December 1914. One bomb exploded near Dover Castle.

The first airship raid on Great Britain: See Lighter than air—dirigibles (19 January 1915).

The first Russian aircraft designed for air fighting was the two-seat Sikorsky S-16 biplane, which appeared in January 1915. Fitted with a type of synchronised machine-gun arrangement, S-16s were initially delivered in March to the EVK, as experimental escorts for the *Ilya Mourometz* bombers.

The first use of aeroplanes in military operations in South America was in February 1915, by the Brazilian Army in the State of Santa Catarina.

The first aeroplane to be designed and built for aerial fighting was the Vickers FB5 Gunbus. Armed with one forward-firing machine-gun, which was operated by a second crew member, FB5s started reaching units in France in February 1915, and the first FB5 fighter squadron was formed in July. Powered by a 100 hp Gnôme rotary engine in 'pusher' configuration, the FB5 had a maximum speed of 70 mph (113 km/h).

Turkey's attack on the Suez Canal, which began on 3 February 1915, was repelled partly because of an aerial reconnaissance carried out on 23 January which located the advancing Turkish troops as they approached the area.

The first naval vessel fully converted for aircraft duties, while still under construction, was HMS *Ark Royal*, and as such was the first ship in the world to be completed as an aircraft (seaplane) carrier. Launched in 1914, *Ark Royal* became the first aircraft carrier to operate aeroplanes against the enemy in Europe when, arriving at the entrance to the Dardanelles on 17 February 1915, one of her seaplanes was sent on reconnaissance against the Turks.

NACA, the National Advisory Committee for Aeronautics, was founded in America on 3 March 1915.

The first British bombing raid in direct tactical support of a ground operation occurred on 10 March 1915. It comprised attacks on railways bringing up German reinforcements in the Menin and Courtrai areas (Second Wing) and

Vickers FB5 Gunbus, with the machine-gun removed from the nose but the mounting remaining visible.

the railway stations at Lille, Douai and Don (bombed by the Third Wing), during the Neuve Chapelle offensive. The Divisional Headquarters at Fournes was also bombed by three aircraft of No 3 Squadron piloted by Capt E.L. Conran, Lt W.C. Birch and Lt D.R. Hanlon.

The first single-seat fighter to destroy an enemy aircraft using a machine-gun that fired through the propeller disc was a French Morane-Saulnier Type L, piloted by Roland Garros. Having first fitted deflector plates to the propeller to prevent the bullets from hitting the rotating blades, Garros claimed his first victory using this method on 1 April 1915. On 19 April Garros had to make an emergency landing behind German lines and his aircraft, along with its secret, was captured.

The first air Victoria Cross was awarded posthumously to Lt W.B. Rhodes Moorhouse, pilot of a BE2c of No 2 Squadron, RFC, for gallantry in a low-level bombing attack on Courtrai railway station on 26 April 1915.

The aircraft sent by the Allies to take part in the campaign against German controlled South West Africa were three Henry Farman and two Royal Aircraft Factory BE2c biplanes. These arrived on the last day of April 1915 at Walvis Bay and were used in conjunction with the Union Expeditionary Force. The campaign was successfully concluded on 9 July 1915. The Allied unit comprised mostly South African personnel.

The first intentional air attack by an armed German aircraft on an armed enemy aircraft was made on 26 May 1915, when an armed Halberstadt C, crewed by Oberleutnant Kästner and Leutnant Langhoff, attacked and shot down a French Voisin biplane that was making a reconnaissance over the airfield at Douai.

The first air raid on London: See Lighter than air—dirigibles (31 May 1915).

The first airship to be brought down by air attack: See Lighter than air—dirigibles (6/7 June 1915).

The first single-seat fighter to enter service with the RFC was the Airco (de Havilland) DH2, the prototype of which made its first flight on 1 June 1915. Powered by a 100 hp Gnôme rotary engine, mounted in a 'pusher' configuration, the DH2 had a maximum speed of 93 mph (150 km/h) and

was armed with one forward-firing Lewis machine-gun. It entered service with the RFC in early 1916, and was one of the fighters which ended the supremacy of the Fokker Eindecker. DH2s served, latterly in Palestine, until mid-1917. About 400 were built.

The first American forest fire to be observed by aeroplane is thought to have been one blazing in Wisconsin, on 22 June 1915.

The first fighter to be fitted with a successful synchronised machine-gun, firing forward between the propeller blades, was the German Fokker E series Eindecker. The first E.Is arrived at the Douai airfield on the Western Front for operational trials in July 1915. Eventually, about 425 'E' series monoplanes were built. None flew faster than 87 mph (140 km/h), but they caused such havoc in attacks on Allied aircraft that their activities for ten months in 1915–16 are remembered as the 'Fokker Scourge'. The inherently stable BE2cs of the RFC suffered particularly heavy casualties. First Eindecker victory was achieved on 1 August 1915 by Leutnant Max Immelmann, who had prepared for its use by flying a Fokker M8 on 30 July 1915. Previously, on 1 July, a Fokker M5K (considered the prototype to the E.I) had been flown by Leutnant Kurt Wintgens when he shot down a French Morane-Saulnier, probably **the first air victory using a synchronised machine-gun.** The 'scourge' ended only with the introduction into service of new Allied aircraft such as the RFC's DH2.

France's second most successful fighter pilot was Capitaine Georges Marie Ludovic Jules Guynemer, who served in the 'Cigognes' group with Escadrille MS3/N3/SPA3 and achieved the first of his 54 confirmed victories on 19 July 1915 while in a Morane-Saulnier Parasol. He failed to return from a flight over Poelcapelle (Belgium) on 11 September 1917 and he has no known grave. However, although it is often asserted that no trace of his body or aircraft has ever been found, the records of the 413th Württemberg Regiment, which held that section of the German line on the date in question, show that both were indeed found and identified and that various papers on Guynemer at the time were removed. There is some question as to the identity of the pilot who shot down Guynemer, although

Pilots of No 32 Squadron, RFC, flying Airco DH2 pusher-engined biplane fighters when this photograph was taken in July 1916.

usually Leutnant Kurt Wisseman, Jagdstaffel 3, is credited. Wisseman himself was shot down and killed on 28 September 1917.

One of Germany's first two great fighter aces was Leutnant Max Immelmann, 'The Eagle of Lille'. He was serving with Feldfliegerabteilung No 62 at Douai when the first Fokker monoplane scouts became available. Hauptmann Kastner instructed Boelcke in the subtleties of the new machine, and Boelcke taught Immelmann. On 1 August 1915 Immelmann was responsible for the first victory by a Fokker E.I fighter with synchronised machine-gun, but he met his death on 18 June 1916 when an FE2b of No 25 Squadron, RFC, shot him down near Lens. Immelmann had, by then, gained 15 'air victories'.

The first air attack using a torpedo dropped by an aeroplane was carried out by Flt Cdr C.H. Edmonds, flying a Short 184 seaplane from HMS *Ben-My-Chree* on 12 August 1915, against a 5000 ton (5080 tonne) Turkish supply ship in the Sea of Marmara. Although the enemy ship was hit and sunk, the captain of a British submarine claimed to have fired a torpedo simultaneously and sunk the ship. It was further stated that the British submarine *E14* had attacked and immobilised the ship four days earlier. However on 17 August 1915 another Turkish ship was sunk by a torpedo of whose origin there can be no doubt.

Captured Fokker E.I Eindecker exhibited in Horse Guard's Parade. The Spandau machine-gun had been removed.

On this occasion Flt Cdr C.H. Edmonds, flying a Short 184, torpedoed a Turkish steamer a few miles north of the Dardanelles. His formation colleague, Flt Lt G.B. Dacre, was forced to land on the water owing to engine trouble but, seeing an enemy tug close by, taxied up to it and released his torpedo. The tug blew up and sank. Thereafter Dacre was able to take off and return to the *Ben-My-Chree*.

The first sustained strategic bombing offensive was opened by Italy on 20 August 1915, following its declaration of war against Austria–Hungary on 24 May. Major aircraft type used in the early raids was the Caproni Ca 2 three-engined biplane (100 hp Fiat A10s), of which 31 were delivered in 1915 and 133 in 1916. The Ca 2 was used in the first Italian night bombing raids. It carried a crew of four.

The first launching of an aeroplane by catapult on board ship (excluding anchored barge), took place on 5 November 1915 when an AB-2 flying-boat was catapulted from the stern of the American battleship USS *North Carolina*, anchored in Pensacola Bay, Florida. On the following day AB-2, piloted by Lt Cdr Henry Mustin, was catapulted from USS *North Carolina* while the ship was moving.

The first product of the German Junkers company and **the world's first all-metal monoplane to fly** was the Junkers J1, which took to the air for the first time on 12 December 1915. Intended as a reconnaissance and close-support aircraft, it had cantilever wings and the complete airframe was skinned in sheet iron. Power was provided

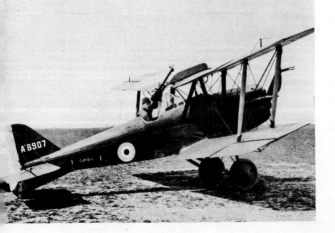

by a 120 hp Mercedes DII engine. Only the single prototype was built.

The first great British ace, Capt Albert Ball, joined No 13 Squadron, RFC, in France on 15 February 1916, his first operational squadron. His first mount was a BE2c used on artillery-spotting flights. In May he was posted to No 11 Squadron, equipped with Nieuport scouts. His first two air victories came on 22 May, when he drove down an Albatros DI and forced an LVG two-seater to land. Only the latter was confirmed. His last squadron was No 56, which flew the new SE5 fighter and the Nieuport Ball loved to fly. As Flt Cdr, Ball gained his 47th and last victory on 6 May 1917. The following evening he dived an SE5 into dense cloud while chasing a German two-seater near Lens and was never seen alive again. His wrecked aircraft and his body were found by the Germans. His Victoria Cross was gazetted on 3 June 1917.

The first major battle to see the use of large formations of fighter aircraft was Verdun, which began on 21 February 1916.

The famed French squadron for volunteer American pilots, later known as the 'Lafayette Escadrille' but originally Escadrille Américaine, was formed on 20 April 1916. Its initial equipment was the Nieuport 11 Bébé.

Parasite fighter experiments began on 17 May 1916, when a Bristol Scout was launched from a Porte Baby flying-boat. (See also lighter than air—dirigibles.)

The first pilot of the Escadrille Américaine to gain an 'air victory' was Lt Kiffin Rockwell, while escorting bombers near Mulhouse on 18 May 1916. Rockwell was killed on 23 September.

The first triplane fighter to enter service was the British Sopwith Triplane, a single-seater nicknamed 'Tripehound'. The prototype flew for the first time on 28 May 1916. Later production aircraft were so successful that the Germans developed their own triplanes, leading to the introduction of the Fokker Dr I.

The first major fleet battle in which an aeroplane was used was the Battle of Jutland on 31 May 1916, when Flt Lt F.J. Rutland (accompanied by

Capt Albert Ball with the Lewis gun lowered on his SE5. (Imperial War Museum)

his observer, Assistant Paymaster G.S. Trewin) spotted and shadowed a force of German light cruisers and destroyers. Taking off from alongside HM seaplane carrier *Engadine* at about 15.10h, Rutland sighted the enemy ships and continued to radio position reports to the *Engadine*.

The first American pilot to be killed in the First World War was Victor Emmanuel Chapman of the Lafayette Escadrille, who was shot down near Verdun on 23 June 1916.

Considered the best single-engined day bomber of the First World War was the British Airco (de Havilland) DH4. The prototype first flew in August 1916, at Hendon, and production aircraft served with the RFC/RAF, RNAS and American Expeditionary Force. Various engines were fitted, including a 375 hp Rolls-Royce Eagle VIII, which gave a maximum speed of 143 mph (230 km/h). Bomb load was up to 460 lb (209 kg).

The greatest Allied ace of the First World War was Capitaine René Paul Fonck, who served with Escadrille SPA103, one of the units of the famous Groupe de Combat No 12 'Les Cigognes'. Officially Fonck is credited with 75 victories; his own personal estimate, including aircraft destroyed but not confirmed by Allied ground observers, was 127. His first victory came on 6 August 1916, when he forced down a Rumpler while flying a Caudron G IV reconnaissance and bombing biplane. His second victory, gained on 17 March 1917, was against one of five attacking Albatros fighters. This second confirmed victory led to his transfer to the 'Cigognes' group a month later. On 9 May 1918 he achieved no fewer than six confirmed 'kills'—including three two-seaters destroyed in 45 s, the three wrecks being found in a radius of 1200 ft (365 m). On 26 September he again shot down six aircraft, comprising a two-seater, four Fokker D VIIs, and an Albatros D V. Fonck's last victory was over a leaflet-dropping two-seater on 1 November 1918. Fonck died peacefully in his sleep at his Paris home on 18 June 1953.

The United States Naval Flying Corps was founded on 29 August 1916.

Curtiss-built Hewitt-Sperry biplane flying bomb. (US National Archives)

The first German airship to be brought down on British soil was the Schutte-Lanz SL XI, which was attacked on the night of 2 September 1916 by a BE2c flown by Lt W. Leefe Robinson, RFC: see Lighter than air—dirigibles.

The first radio-guided flying-bomb was tested on 12 September 1916. It was called the 'Hewitt-Sperry biplane' and was built by Curtiss. Powered by a 40 hp engine, it was capable of covering 50 miles (80 km) carrying a 308 lb (140 kg) bomb-load.

The first submarine to be sunk by an aeroplane was the French submarine *Foucault*, on 15 September 1916, by an Austrian Löhner flying-boat.

Albatros D I single-seat fighters, the first of the famous Albatros D series fighters which were partly responsible for giving Germany its second period of air supremacy over the Western Front, in early 1917, were used operationally for the first time on 17 September 1916. In command was Oswald Boelcke.

The greatest ace of the First World War, in terms of confirmed aerial victories, was Rittmeister (Cavalry Captain) Manfred, Freiherr von Richthofen—the so-called 'Red Baron'. The eldest son of an aristocratic Silesian family, he was born on 2 May 1892 and was killed in action on 21 April 1918, by which time he had been credited with 80 victories, had been awarded his country's highest decoration, commanded the élite unit of the Imperial German Air Service

Albatros D I biplane fighter. (Imperial War Museum)

(Luftstreitkräfte), and was the object of great adulation in his homeland and an ungrudging respect among his enemies. Early in the war, Richthofen served on the Eastern Front as an officer in Uhlan Regiment Nr 1 'Kaiser Alexander III', and transferred to the Air Service in May 1915. His first operational posting was to Feldfliegerabteilung Nr 69; with this unit he flew two-seater reconnaissance machines in the East—without apparently any unusual skill. In September 1916 he was selected for Jagdstaffel 2, the scout squadron led by Oswald Boelcke (q.v.). His first officially recognised victory was over an FE2b of No 11 Squadron, RFC; Richthofen, flying an Albatros D II scout, shot down this aircraft on 17 September 1916; the crew, 2nd Lt L.B.F. Morris and Lt T. Rees, lost their lives. Richthofen continued to score steadily, and in January 1917 was awarded the coveted 'Blue Max', the Ordre pour le Mérite. He was given command of Jagdstaffel 11, and characteristically maintained a collection of silver cups, each engraved with the particulars of a victim. The silversmith's most lucrative month was 'Bloody April' of 1917, when Richthofen shot down 21 aircraft. In June 1917 he was given command of a new formation, Jagdgeschwader Nr 1, com-

Still with head bandages from a wound received in combat, von Richthofen salutes Kaiser Wilhelm II.

prising Jastas 4, 6, 10 and 11; this group of squadrons became known to the Allies as 'Richthofen's Flying Circus', because of the bright colours of their aircraft. Contrary to popular legend Richthofen did not invariably fly a personal all-red aircraft but a variety of Albatros D IIIs and Fokker Dr Is, some of which were painted blood-red all over and some only partially red. Richthofen's death on 21 April 1918 has been the subject of controversy ever since. He was flying Fokker Dr I number 425/17 when he became engaged in combat with Sopwith Camels of No 209 Squadron, RAF, over Sailly-le-Sec. At one point, 2nd Lt W.R. May was flying at low altitude with Richthofen in pursuit and the aircraft of Capt A. Roy Brown, DSC, diving to attack the German. Brown opened fire in an attempt to save the inexperienced May from the enemy ace, and Richthofen's triplane was then seen to break away and crash-land. Richthofen was found dead in his cockpit with a bullet wound in the chest. At about the same time as Brown attacked, machine-gunners of an Australian Field Artillery battery fired at Richthofen's aircraft. Although Brown was officially credited with the 'kill', it has never been established who fired the fatal shot.

The first British airline company to be registered was Aircraft Transport and Travel Ltd., in London on 5 October 1916 by George Holt Thomas.

The most successful fighter pilot of the Royal Naval Air Service during the First World War, and, with 60 confirmed victories, third in the over-all British and Empire aces' list, was Raymond Collishaw. A member of No 3 Wing, RNAS, he gained his first air victory on 12 October 1916. In February 1917 he joined a scout unit, No 3 (Naval) Squadron, and in April was posted to No 10 (Naval) Squadron as commander of 'B' Flight. Equipped with Sopwith Triplanes, the 'Black Flight' of 'Naval Ten' earned a reputation as one of the most formidable Allied units of the war. The Flight was composed entirely of Canadians; their aircraft were decorated with black paint, and named *Black Maria* (Collishaw), *Black Prince*, *Black Sheep*, *Black Roger* and *Black Death*. Between May and July 1917 the Flight destroyed 87 enemy aircraft, and during June Collishaw himself shot down 16 in 27 days. After the Armistice, Collishaw commanded No 47 Squadron in the Russian cam-

paign of 1919-20, where he destroyed two more aircraft. He remained in the Royal Air Force, serving in the Second World War and reaching the rank of Air Vice-Marshal, CB, with the DSO and Bar, DSC, DFC and Croix de Guerre, as well as both military and civil grades of the OBE.

The first true fighter leader of the First World War was Hauptmann Oswald Boelcke. He became interested in aviation during army manoeuvres, and gained his Pilot's Certificate at the Halberstadt Flying School on 15 August 1914. He was posted to La Ferte to join Feldfliegerabteilung Nr 13 in September and, with his brother Wilhelm as observer, soon amassed a considerable number of sorties in Army Co-operation Albatros B II biplanes. By early 1915 he had 42 missions in his log-book, and had been awarded the Iron Cross, Second Class. The visit of Leutnant Parschau to his unit to demonstrate the Fokker M8 monoplane scout fired him with enthusiasm; and in April, having received the Iron Cross, First Class, he secured a posting to Hauptmann Kastner's Feldfliegerabteilung Nr 62, where he flew an armed machine for the first time—an Albatros C I, number 162/15. Before long, he was selected to fly early examples of Fokker's E-series armed monoplane scouts; few were available, and Boelcke, Kastner and Leutnant Max Immelmann at first took turns to fly them. After a tour of other fronts in early 1916, Boelcke returned to the West and was given command of the new Jagdstaffel Nr 2 (Jasta 2) which was equipped with Albatros D I and D II scouts. Boelcke was killed on 28 October 1916 during an engagement in which one of his colleagues, Leutnant Boehme, who was flying close to him, banked sharply. Boehme's undercarriage struck the wing of his Albatros, which spiralled to the ground. He was 25 years old, a holder of the Ordre Pour le Mérite and numerous other decorations, the victor of 40 aerial combats, and the idol of his country.

The first bombs to fall on London from an aeroplane were six small bombs dropped from a German LVG C11 on 28 November 1916, falling near Victoria Station. The pilot of the attacking aircraft was Deck Offizier P. Brandt.

The first intentional air victory achieved at night was gained on the night of 11 to 12 February

1917, by Leutnant Peter and Leutnant Frohwein flying a DFW CV. On this occasion they destroyed two bombers landing at Malzeville.

The first British unit to be formed specifically for night bombing operations was No 100 Squadron, RFC, which formed at Hingham, Norfolk, in February 1917, and crossed to France on 21 March. A week later the unit received its first aircraft, 12 FE2bs, then being based at Saint-André-aux-Bois. Moving to Le Hameau on 1 April 1917, the squadron received four BE2es. The first operations were two raids on the night of 5 to 6 April 1917 on Douai Airfield, home base of the 'Richthofen Circus'. One FE2b failed to return; four hangars were badly damaged by bombs.

The second most successful British and Empire pilot of the war was a Canadian, William Avery Bishop, born on 8 February 1894 in Ontario. While in England as a cavalry subaltern in the Canadian Mounted Rifles in 1915, Bishop de-

Royal Aircraft Factory FE2b, seen here as a night bomber armed with small and large bombs. (Imperial War Museum)

cided he would see more action as a pilot, and transferred to the Royal Flying Corps in July of that year. He flew in France as an observer with No 21 Squadron for several months, and was hospitalised as the result of a crash-landing and frostbite. He trained subsequently as a pilot and joined No 60 Squadron in March 1917. The squadron was at that time equipped with Nieuport 17 scouts, an aircraft which Bishop was to handle brilliantly. On 25 March he scored his first victory over an Albatros and subsequently gained many honours including the Victoria Cross for his action over an enemy airfield on 2 June. When his score reached 45, Bishop was promoted Major and awarded a Bar to his DSO. Late in 1917 and early in 1918 he carried out a number of non-combat duties, including recruiting drives in Canada and instructing at an aerial gunnery school. He was subsequently given command of No 85 Squadron, flying SE5as, and went back to France on 22 May 1918. After gaining 27 more victories, he was recalled to England, and never flew operationally again. His DFC was gazetted on 2 July. Bishop remained in the service, rising to the rank of Honorary Air Marshal

in the Royal Canadian Air Force. He died in Florida, USA, in September 1956.

The first vessel in the world to be defined as an aircraft carrier (in the modern sense, ie equipped with a flying deck for operation of landplanes) was the light battle-cruiser HMS *Furious*. Construction of this ship began shortly after the outbreak of the First World War, it being intended to arm her with a pair of 18 in (457 mm) guns. In March 1917 authority to alter her design was issued, and at the expense of one of these huge guns she was completed with a hangar and flight deck on her forecastle. With a speed of 31·5 knots, she carried six Sopwith Pups in addition to four seaplanes. Her first Senior Flying Officer was Sqn Cdr E.H. Dunning. HMS *Furious* became the **longest-lived active carrier in the world.** Between 1921 and 1925 the midships superstructure was eliminated and she emerged as a flush-deck carrier displacing 22 450 tons (22 809 tonnes), with two aircraft lifts and an aircraft capacity of 33. Her overall length was 786 ft (239 m). After an extraordinarily active and exciting career in the Second World War (and a near head-on collision at night in the Atlantic with a troopship which passed so close as to carry away some of the carrier's radio masts), she was finally scrapped in 1949.

One of the longest-serving aircraft that was designed in the First World War was the two-seat Bristol Fighter. No fewer than 3101 were built during the war, the type first becoming operational on the Western Front in early April 1917. Further production was carried out until 1927. Some of the latter examples were equipped for use in tropical climates, and were used for patrol duty in countries like India, Iraq, Palestine and Egypt. Many were exported, serving in New Zealand up to 1936. The F2B Mk II version was powered by a 280 hp Rolls-Royce Falcon II engine, and had a maximum speed of 125 mph (201 km/h).

The worst month in terms of losses for the RFC was April 1917, 'Bloody April', when nearly 140 of the 365 RFC aircraft mustered for an offensive were lost in the first half of the month.

Britain's most successful fighter pilot in the First World War was Major Edward 'Mick' Mannock. His score of combat victories stands at 73, but he is known to have insisted that several additional victories justly attributable to him should be credited to other pilots. Born on 24 May 1887, the son of a soldier, Mannock was working in Constantinople when the war broke out, and was interned by the Turks. He was repatriated in April 1915 on health grounds and rejoined the Territorial Army medical unit to which he had belonged before leaving the country. He was commissioned in the Royal Engineers on 1 April 1916 and finally transferred to the Royal Flying Corps in August 1916. His acceptance for flying duties was remarkable as he suffered from astigmatism in the left eye, and must have passed his medical by a ruse. He gained his Pilot's Certificate on 28 November 1916, and was posted to No 40 Squadron, France, on 6 April 1917, the unit being equipped at that time with Nieuport scouts. He shot down a balloon on 7 May, and on 7 June scored his first victory over an aeroplane. Returning from leave in July he shot down two-seaters on the 12th and 13th of that month, and his Military Cross was gazetted. He was promoted Captain, and took command of a flight. His score grew rapidly, as he was possessed by a bitter and ruthless hatred of the enemy, uncommon among his contemporaries. His care of the pilots under his command, however, was irreproachable, and he has been judged the greatest patrol leader of any combatant air force. In January 1918 he returned to England to take enforced leave, by which time his score stood at 23. He returned to France in March as a Flt Cdr in the newly formed No 74 ('Tiger') Squadron, equipped with the SE5a, and in his three months with the unit added 39 to his score. He was promoted Major in mid-June, and was given leave before taking command of No 85 Squadron. With No 85 he raised his score to 73 before being shot down on 26 July by German ground fire that hit his petrol tank. His grave has never been found and it was nearly a year later that he was awarded a posthumous Victoria Cross.

The first German submarine to be sunk by an aeroplane was the German U-36, which was attacked in the North Sea by a Large America flying-boat piloted by Flt Sub-Lt C.R. Morrish on 20 May 1917.

Official carriage of mail by aeroplane in Italy began on 22 May 1917, when military flights started between the cities of Turin and Rome.

The first mass bombing raid on England by Gotha heavy bombers was made on 25 May 1917, when 21 aircraft attacked several towns, including Folkestone and Shorncliffe. About 95 people were killed and 260 more were injured.

The first mass bombing raid on London was by German Gotha heavy bombers on 13 June 1917. Fourteen bombers attacked an area around Liverpool Street Station, dropping 72 bombs and causing 162 deaths, with 432 people injured. This was the worst bombing raid of the war in terms of dead and injured. The last major bombing raid on England in daylight was on 12 August 1917.

The most successful fighter aeroplane of the war was the Sopwith Camel, which achieved no fewer than 1294 victories over enemy aircraft. Production Camels were operated by the RFC and RNAS from July 1917; a total of 5490 was built. Possessing excellent manoeuvrability, the Camel had a maximum speed of 115 mph (185 km/h).

Fokker Dr I triplane, a highly manoeuvrable fighter based on the British Sopwith Triplane, but with a maximum speed of only 103 mph (165 km/h).

The first landing in the world by an aeroplane upon a ship under-way was carried out by Sqn Cdr E.H. Dunning who flew a Sopwith Pup on to the deck of HMS *Furious* on 2 August 1917. Steaming at 26 knots into a wind of 21 knots, *Furious* thus provided a 47 knot headwind for Dunning who flew his Pup for'ard along the starboard side of the ship before side-slipping towards the deck located on the forecastle. Men then grabbed straps on the aircraft and brought it to a standstill. On 7 August Dunning attempted to repeat the operation in an even greater headwind but stalled as he attempted to overshoot and was killed when his aircraft was blown over the side of the ship.

Crew of HMS Furious *rush to bring to a halt Dunning's Pup fighter.*

The first enemy night bomber to be destroyed over Germany was shot down on the night of 8 to 9 August 1917 near Frankfurt/Main.

The first French mail to be carried by aeroplane was flown between Paris, Le Mans and St Nazaire on 17 August 1917. A regular service was established thereafter.

The first of Germany's new Fokker F I (Dr I) triplane fighters arrived at Courtrai on 21 August 1917. Lt Werner Voss was the first to fly one into action, destroying an RFC aircraft on 30 August.

The first German armoured aeroplane, designed for ground attack and low-level reconnaissance missions, was the Junkers J1 biplane, of which 227 were built. Fitted with 5 mm steel plating,

Junkers JI armoured biplane, its construction earning it the nickname 'furniture van'.

the type entered service in the latter half of 1917 and was armed with three machine-guns.

The first mass bombing raid at night by Gotha aeroplanes on Britain was made on the night of 2 to 3 September 1917. The target was Dover.

The American 1st Aero Squadron arrived in France on 3 September 1917. Brig Gen William L. Kenly became the AEF's (American Expeditionary Force) first Chief of Air Service the same day.

The first raid on Britain by German 'R' type bombers was made on 17 September 1917. German Staaken R VI giant bombers were capable of

Staaken RVI serial R28 very heavy bomber. (P. L. Gray)

dropping 1000 kg bombs, which were the largest bombs of the war.

The first RFC unit to be formed to carry out strategic bombing of targets inside Germany was the 41st Wing, which came into being on 11 October 1917.

The first Gotha bomber to be shot down at night during a bombing raid was destroyed in January 1918 by two Sopwith Camels of No 44 Squadron, RFC, at Wickford, Essex. This proved that even at night the Gotha could be intercepted, and night raids on England ceased in May 1918.

The first combat aeroplane to enter production in the United States was the British de Havilland DH4. The first machine was completed in February 1918.

The first US fighter squadron to arrive in France from America was the 95th Aero (Pursuit) Squadron, on 18 February 1918.

The first US pilot to gain a victory while serving with an American squadron was Lt Stephen W. Thompson, in February 1918. His squadron, the 103rd Pursuit Squadron, had been formed from the Lafayette Escadrille on 18 February but was then still operating with French forces.

The first scheduled regular international airmail service in the world was inaugurated between Vienna and Kiev, via Kraków, Lvóv and Proskurov on 11 March 1918. The service was principally for military mail and was operated with Hansa-Brandenburg C I biplanes, continuing until November 1918.

The most successful American pilot of the First World War was Capt Edward Vernon Rickenbacker, with 26 confirmed aerial victories. Born on 8 October 1890 in Columbus, Ohio, Rickenbacker made a considerable name for himself between 1910 and 1917 as one of America's leading racing motorists. While in England in 1917, he became interested in flying and when America entered the war he returned home and advanced the idea of a squadron composed entirely of racing drivers. The idea did not arouse official interest, but a meeting with Gen Pershing in Washington led to Rickenbacker's enlistment and sent him to France as the General's chauffeur. In August 1917 he transferred to the Aviation Section, and his mechanical expertise led to a posting to the 3rd Aviation Instruction Center at Issoudun as Chief Engineering Officer. In his own time he completed advanced flying and gunnery courses, and on 4 March 1918 finally secured a transfer to the 94th Aero Squadron—the 'Hat-in-the-Ring' squadron commanded by Raoul Lufbery, the Escadrille Lafayette ace. With Lufbery and Douglas Campbell, Rickenbacker flew **the first American patrol over enemy lines** on 19 March, and on 29 April he shot down his first victim, an Albatros scout. On 30 May his fifth victory qualified him as an ace, but it was to be his last for four months. An ear infection put him in hospital and convalescence until mid-September, when he returned to the squadron as a Captain and Flight Commander. He took over command of the 94th on 25 September, and continued to score heavily until the Armistice. Capt Rickenbacker was active in the automobile and airline industries between the wars, and was largely responsible for building up Eastern Air Lines, of which corporation he became Chairman in 1953. During the Second World War he toured widely, visiting Air Force units abroad and undertaking various missions for his Government. In the course of a flight over the Pacific his aircraft was forced to ditch, and Rickenbacker and the crew survived 21 days on a life-raft before being picked up. He remained active in various public fields until his death on 23 July 1973, at the age of 82. His many American and foreign decorations included his country's highest award for gallantry, the Congressional Medal of Honor.

The most successful German fighter of the war was the Fokker D VII, which first became operational on the Western Front in April 1918, with Jagdgeschwader I. The type also served with several air forces after the war. Powered by a 185 hp BMW inline engine, it had a maximum speed of 124 mph (200 km/h) and excellent manoeuvrability. By the autumn of 1918, D VIIs equipped over 40 Jastas of the German air force.

The RFC and RNAS combined to become the RAF on 1 April 1918.

The first mission by the newly formed RAF was performed by No 22 Squadron on 1 April 1918. This squadron was equipped with Bristol F2B Fighters.

The first flush-deck aircraft carrier in the world

was HMS *Argus*, 15 775 tons (16 027 tonnes). Originally laid down in 1914 as the Italian liner *Conte Rosso*, she was purchased by Great Britain and launched in 1917, and completed in 1918. She featured an unrestricted flight deck of 565 ft (172 m) length and could accommodate 20 aircraft. She was ultimately scrapped in 1947. She was **the first carrier in the world to embark a full squadron of torpedo-carrying landplanes**, when in October 1918 a squadron of Sopwith Cuckoos was activated. They did not, however, see action.

The first American observation aircraft to fly over enemy lines were from I Corps Observation Squadron, on 11 April 1918.

The first air crossing of the Andes was achieved by the Argentine army pilot Teniente Luis C. Candelaria, flying a Morane-Saulnier parasol monoplane on 13 April 1918 from Zapala, Argentina, to Cunço, Chile, a distance of approximately 124 miles (200 km). The maximum altitude was about 13 000 ft (4000 m). Candelaria had attended the fifth military flying course at El Palomar which commenced in September 1916.

The first American-trained pilots to shoot down enemy aircraft were 1st Lt Douglas Campbell and 2nd Lt Alan Winslow of the 94th Aero (Pursuit) Squadron, on 14 April 1918. Having taken off at 08.50 h, they intercepted an Albatros D V (flown by Corp Simon) and a Pfalz D IIIa (flown by Sgt Maj Wronieki) of Jagdstaffel 64 in the area of Toul, and shot both down. Both pilots survived. The first to fall was the Albatros, to the guns of Winslow. The American pilots flew Nieuport 28s. Campbell was **the first US pilot, serving under American colours, to become an ace,** gaining his fifth victory on 31 May 1918.

The first experimental airmail service in the USA was flown by US Army Signal Corps Curtiss JN-4 and Standard J aircraft on 15 May 1918, between Washington, DC, and New York City. Lt Torrey H. Webb was the first pilot.

The first US bomber squadron of the AEF was formed in France on 18 May 1918, as the 96th Aero Squadron. The squadron's first raid was against the railway at Dommany-Baroncourt, on 12 June.

The night of 19 to 20 May marked the end of German Gotha bomber raids on Britain, as losses had become unacceptably high.

The Independent Force of the RAF was established on 5 June 1918 to carry out strategic bombing raids on German industrial and military targets. It was this force that dropped **the largest Allied bombs of the war**, the 1650 lb

Airco DH9, one of the types used by the Independent Force from mid-1918.

(750 kg) 'block busters'. The first heavy bombers of the Force were Handley Page O/100s and O/400s, supplemented by the lighter Airco (de Havilland) DH4s, DH9s, DH9As and Royal Aircraft Factory FE2bs.

The first official airmail flight in Canada was flown on 24 June 1918 in a Curtiss JN-4 from Montreal to Toronto by Capt Brian A. Peck, RAF, accompanied by Corp Mathers.

The first flight from England to Egypt was accomplished by Maj A.S. MacLaren and Brig Gen A.E. Borton, flying a Handley Page O/400 bomber, between 28 July and 8 August 1918.

The first pilot to take off successfully from a towed barge in an aeroplane was the American-born Flt Sub-Lt Stuart Culley, RN, who on 1 August 1918 rose from a barge towed by HMS *Redoubt* at 35 knots. At 08.41 h on 11 August 1918 Culley took off from the barge while being towed off the Dutch coast and climbed to 18 000 ft (5500 m) to shoot down the German Zeppelin L53 using incendiary ammunition. He was thus **the first (and probably the only) pilot to shoot down an enemy aircraft after taking off from a towed vessel.** Landing in the sea alongside his towing destroyer, HMS *Redoubt*, he was rescued—and later awarded the DSO for his

French-built Spad XIII fighter, one of the fastest combat aircraft of the First World War, operated by the AEF.

Italian Ansaldo SVA 5.

feat—and his Camel was salvaged by a derrick (invented by Col Samson). The only survivor of the Zeppelin baled out from 19 000 ft (5800 m)—almost certainly a record at that time.

The largest aeroplane force assembled during the war for a single military operation was that used during the battle for the Saint-Mihiel salient between 11 and 15 September 1918. In command of 1483 fighter, observation and bombing aircraft was Gen William Mitchell of the US Air Service.

The first US fighter patrol at night was undertaken by the 185th Aero (Pursuit) Squadron on 12 October 1918.

The First World War came to an end on the 11th hour of the 11th day of the 11th month, 1918.

The largest German aeroplane built during the First World War was the Aviatik R-Type (Riesenflugzeug) giant heavy bomber; basically a Zeppelin Staaken R VI built under licence by Automobil und Aviatik AG, this colossal aeroplane had a wing span of 180 ft 5½ in (55 m) and a length of 88 ft 7 in (27 m). It was powered by four 530 hp Benz Bz VI engines which gave it a maximum speed of 90 mph (145 km/h).

The fastest German fighter of the war to become operational was the Fokker D VIII parasol-wing monoplane, with a speed of nearly 127 mph (204 km/h).

The fastest German fighters produced to prototype stage were probably the AEG D I biplane and Siemens-Schuckert D VI parasol-wing monoplane, both achieving nearly 137 mph (220 km/h).

The fastest British and French operational combat aircraft of the First World War appear to have been the British Airco DH4 day bomber, when Eagle VIII powered, and the French Spad XIII fighter, with speeds of 143 mph (230 km/h) and 138 mph (222 km/h) respectively.

The fastest Italian operational aircraft of the First World War was probably the Ansaldo SVA 5 reconnaissance and bombing biplane, with a speed of 143 mph (230 km/h). Variants of this aircraft, tested with other engines than the standard 220 hp SPA 6A, achieved even higher speeds.

The Great Air Fighters of the First World War

The six most successful British and Empire pilots of the First World War

*Bar to award

Maj Edward Mannock, VC, DSO**, MC	73
Maj W.A. Bishop, VC, DSO*, MC, DFC, L D'H, C D E G	72
Maj R. Collishaw, DSO*, DSC, DFC, C D E G	60
Maj J.T.B. McCudden, VC, DSO*, MC*, MM, C D E G	57
Capt A.W. Beauchamp-Proctor, VC, DSO, MC*, DFC	54
Capt D.R. MacLaren, DSO, MC*, DFC, L D'H, C D E G	54

In addition to the above

    8 pilots gained between 40 and 52 victories
   11 pilots gained between 30 and 39 victories
   57 pilots gained between 20 and 29 victories
  226 pilots gained between 10 and 19 victories
  476 pilots gained between 5 and 9 victories
Thus by the 'five victory' convention, the British and Empire air forces of the First World War produced 784 aces.

The six most successful German pilots of the First World War

Rittmeister Manfred, Freiherr von Richthofen	80
Oberleutnant Ernst Udet	62
Oberleutnant Erich Loewenhardt	53
Leutnant Werner Voss	48
Leutnant Fritz Rumey	45
Hauptmann Rudolph Berthold	44

All of these pilots were decorated with the Ordre Pour le Mérite.

In addition to the above

    6 pilots gained between 40 and 43 victories
   21 pilots gained between 30 and 39 victories
   38 pilots gained between 20 and 29 victories
   96 pilots gained between 10 and 19 victories
  196 pilots gained between 5 and 9 victories
Thus by the 'five victory' convention, the Imperial German air forces of the First World War produced 363 aces.

The four most successful French pilots of the First World War

Capitaine René P. Fonck	75
Capitaine Georges M.L.J. Guynemer	54
Lieutenant Charles E.J.M. Nungesser	45
Capitaine Georges F. Madon	41

In addition to the above

    2 pilots gained between 30 and 39 victories
    8 pilots gained between 20 and 29 victories
   39 pilots gained between 10 and 19 victories
  105 pilots gained between 5 and 9 victories
Thus the French air forces of the First World War produced 158 aces.

The four most successful American pilots of the First World War

Capt Edward V. Rickenbacker, CMH, DSC, L D'H, C D E G	26
2nd Lt Frank Luke Jr, CMH, DSC, C D E G	21
Maj G. Raoul Lufbery, L D'H, MM, C D E G, MC	17
Lt G.A. Vaughn Jr, DSC, DFC	13

The largest and first four-engined British bomber of the First World War was the Handley Page V/1500 biplane, with a wing span of 126 ft (38·4 m) and a length of 64 ft (19·5 m).

The largest and first four-engined British bomber of the First World War was the Handley Page V/1500.

The ugliest aircraft flown during the First World War was probably the German Linke-Hofmann R I biplane bomber. Powered by four Mercedes engines, carried in a fuselage that filled the entire wide interplane gap and driving two huge tractor propellers, both prototypes crashed during flight testing in 1917.

In addition to the above
84 pilots gained between 5 and 12 victories; thus America produced during the First World War 88 aces. (It should be noted that the above figures include pilots who served with foreign air forces only, pilots who served with the American forces only, and pilots with mixed service, and all victories gained by these pilots irrespective of service.)

The four most successful Italian pilots of the First World War

Maggiore Francesco Baracca	.	. . 34
Tenente Silvio Scaroni	.	. . . 26
Tenente-Colonnello Pier Ruggiero Piccio	.	24
Tenente Flavio Torello Baracchini	.	. 21

In addition to the above
39 pilots gained between 5 and 20 victories; thus Italy produced 43 aces during the First World War.

The four most successful Austro–Hungarian pilots of the First World War

Hauptmann Godwin Brumowski	.	. 35–40
Offizierstellvertreter Julius Arigi	.	. 26–32
Oberleutnant Frank Linke-Crawford	.	27–30
Oberleutnant Benno Fiala, Ritter von Fernbrugg	. . . . .	. 27–29

(It should be noted that Austrian, Hungarian and Italian sources disagree as to the absolute accuracy of these pilots' scores.)

In addition to the above
Approximately 26 pilots gained between 5 and 19 victories. Thus it can be stated with reasonable certainty that the Austro–Hungarian Imperial air forces produced between 25 and 30 aces during the First World War.

The four most successful Imperial Russian pilots of the First World War

Staff Capt A.A. Kazakov, DSO, MC, DFC, L D'H	. . . . .	. 17
Capt P.V. d'Argueeff	. . .	. 15
Lt Cdr A.P. Seversky	. . .	. 13
Lt I.W. Smirnoff	. . . .	. 12

In addition to the above
Either 14 or 15 pilots gained between 5 and 11 victories; thus the Imperial Russian air forces produced either 18 or 19 known aces during the First World War. Other Russian pilots became aces, but the records are incomplete.

The four most successful Belgian pilots of the First World War

2nd Lt Willy Coppens, DSO	. .	. 37
Adj André de Meulemeester	. . .	. 11
2nd Lt Edmond Thieffry	. . .	. 10
Capt Fernand Jacquet, DFC	. .	. 7

Confirmation of aerial victories during the First World War was subject to the most stringent regulations, and this has led to confusion over the actual number of victories achieved by various pilots. The figures quoted earlier are, with certain exceptions, those accepted officially as accurate in the countries of origin, and refer only to confirmed victories within the letter of the regulations. They are thus more liable to err on the side of under- rather than overstatement.

The first variable-incidence variable-geometry aeroplane in the world was the Swedish Pålson Type i single-seat sporting aircraft of 1918–19. It is said that the aircraft featured a system of cranks to alter the position of the biplane's top wing as well as its angle of incidence as a means of achieving optimum lift/drag in cruising flight. It is not known what success attended flight trials (if any).

The first flight from Egypt to India was accomplished by Capt Ross M. Smith, Brig Gen A.E. Borton, Maj Gen W. Salmond and crew of a Handley Page O/400, between 29 November and 12 December 1918. Their journey took them from Heliopolis to Karachi.

The first US Army coast-to-coast flight across the USA was made by four Curtiss JN-4 Jennies between 4 and 22 December 1918. The points spanned were San Diego and Jacksonville.

Non-aviation inventions of the period

Traffic lights Positioned in Cleveland, Ohio, by the American Traffic Signal Company, in 1914.

Battle tank Designed by Englishmen William Tritton and Walter Wilson in 1915.

Between the World Wars

The 'war to end wars' was over; ahead was a bright new future with peace assured for generations to come. And then came disillusionment, because somehow or other it had been overlooked that four terrible years of war would have to be paid for. The giant air fleets of the combatant nations and the enormous number of men, and indeed women, needed to support, maintain and fly them, were axed overnight. Major aircraft builders around the world found themselves without work, and many without hope of work just faded away. Those that believed there was a future for aviation fought for survival, revising their factories to manufacture urgently-needed consumer goods until civil avia-

tion could find its feet. And some, with management that could see beyond the immediate scene of despair, realised that the days of military aviation had not ended for ever.

What had the First World War done for the emancipation of the aeroplane? Surprisingly little. By far the majority of all aircraft retained drag-inducing biplane structures, heavy fixed landing gear and open cockpits. The biggest change had come in the development of more reliable and more powerful engines, and the availability of such powerplant had, perhaps, made it easier for aircraft designers to build bigger and more effective aircraft without any significant improvement in design or technology. But the wide-scale use of military aircraft had made people more aware of aviation and its potential for civil use.

This section highlights the progress of aviation in the two decades before the world was again faced with a major conflict, a period in which civil aviation began to reach out across the seas that separated nations. But that was a slow process, conditioned not only by the aircraft available for the task, but also by the acceptance of air travel by the 'man in the street'. By 1938 the world's airlines were carrying less than three million passengers a year: today, just one airport, Chicago O'Hare, handles more than this number in a single month.

Military aviation had a slower 'new start', with air forces short of funds and compelled to make-do with aircraft that had survived the war. Only when the 'clouds of war' were gathering again in the 1930s was money found to design and build military aircraft in large quantity. Let us look, then, at the year of 1919 and the first efforts to rebuild the aircraft industry and to introduce aviation to the people of the world.

Stalwart of the post-war RAF was the de Havilland DH9A, which was used by that service from 1918 to 1931. 'Nine-Acks' were in use for the last months of the war on the Western Front, and subsequently in Russia, in their designated role as day-bombers, Thereafter, the DH9A is best remembered as a general-purpose aircraft, operating in Iraq and India until replaced by Westland Wapitis. For tropical operations the aircraft were given an additional radiator and fuel tank,

Refined version of the Thomas Morse MB-3 fighter, produced by Boeing as the MB-3A.

and were sometimes provided with a spare wheel, pilot's survival rations and other equipment, which was hung all over the airframe.

The first helicopters to demonstrate cyclic pitch control successfully were those designed and constructed by the Marquis de Pescara, an Argentinian, in France and Spain between 1919 and 1925. Although demonstrating this feature successfully, these aircraft were directionally unstable as the result of inadequate torque counteraction.

The first passenger and mail services between London and Paris were initiated on 10 January 1919 by No 2 (Communications) Squadron, RAF. Aircraft used were Airco (de Havilland) DH4As, which were DH4s modified to provide enclosed accommodation for two passengers. This service, intended for communications to and from the Peace Conference at Versailles, was terminated in September 1919.

The first sustained commercial daily passenger service was by Deutsche Luft-Reederei, which operated between Berlin and Weimar, Germany, from 5 February 1919. Aircraft used on the service were five-seat AEG biplanes and two-seat DFWs. The 120 mile (193 km) flight took 2 h 18 min.

The first airline passenger flight between Paris and London was made on 8 February 1919 by a Farman F60 Goliath, owned by the Farman brothers and piloted by Lucien Bossoutrot. As civil flying was not then permitted in the UK, the token payload consisted of military passengers, who flew from Toussus le Noble to Kenley. The flight is not recognised as a genuine scheduled operation.

The first US-designed fighter to enter large-scale production was the Thomas Morse MB-3, the prototype of which made its maiden flight on 21 February 1919.

The first purely commercial aircraft to be built for passenger carrying in Britain after the First World War, one of the first new civil types in the world, was the de Havilland DH16, the prototype of which flew for the first time in March 1919. The type entered service with Aircraft Transport and Travel Ltd in May. Altogether, nine DH16s were built by June 1920; the first six

Aircraft Transport and Travel DH16

were powered by the 320 hp Rolls-Royce Eagle VIII engine; the others had a 450 hp Napier Lion engine. Accommodation was for four passengers. The last DH16 was withdrawn from use in August 1923.

The first American international air mail was inaugurated between Seattle, Washington, and Victoria, British Columbia, Canada, by the Hubbard Air Service on 3 March 1919, using a Boeing Model CL-4S aircraft. The service was regularised by contract on 14 October 1920.

The first sustained (but not daily) regular international service for commercial passengers was opened between Paris and Brussels by the Farman brothers on 22 March 1919. The fare for the 2 h 50 min flight was 365 francs. The pilot was again Lucien Bossoutrot. **The first Customs examination of passengers** took place at Brussels after the third of the weekly flights, on 6 April.

The first recorded free-fall jump from an aeroplane, before deployment of the parachute, was made by Leslie Leroy Irvin on 19 April 1919.

The first British aeroplane to carry civil markings (K-100) was a de Havilland DH6 in 1919. It was sold to the Marconi Wireless Telegraph Co Ltd, and used for radio trials; it became the second aircraft entered on the British Civil Register (as G-EAAB; see below).

The first British civil aeroplane (ie the first on the British Civil Register proper) was a de Havilland DH9 (G-EAAA, previously C6054), operated as

a mailplane by Aircraft Transport and Travel Ltd in mid-1919, between London and Paris.

The first British Certificate of Airworthiness was issued on 1 May 1919 to the Handley Page O/400 (F5414) which thereafter became registered as G-EAAF, owned by Handley Page Air Transport Ltd.

Civil flying in Britain restarted, after the First World War, on 1 May 1919, following publication of the Air Navigation Regulations.

The first occasion on which newspapers were distributed by an aircraft on a daily basis was in May 1919. A Fairey IIIC seaplane was used on a week-long experimental freighting service to distribute the *Evening News* from the Thames, near Westminster Bridge, to coastal towns in Kent. This service saved about two hours' distribution time.

The first Transatlantic crossing by air was achieved by the American Navy/Curtiss NC-4 flying-boat commanded by Lt Cdr A.C. Read between 8 May and 31 May 1919. Three flying-boats, the NC-1, NC-3 and NC-4, under the command of Cdr John H. Towers, had set out from Rockaway, New York, on 8 May. Only NC-4 completed the crossing, arriving at Plymouth, England on 31 May, having landed en route at Chatham, Massachusetts; Halifax, Nova Scotia; Trespassey Bay, Newfoundland;

William Boeing and Edward Hubbard with mail from the first international airmail service.

Navy/Curtiss NC-4 in flight prior to setting off on its transatlantic journey. (US National Archives)

Horta, Azores; Ponta Delgarda, Azores; Lisbon, Portugal; and Ferrol del Caudillo, Spain. The total distance flown was 3925 miles (6315 km) in 57 h 16 min flying time, at a speed of 68 mph (110 km/h). Both NC-1 and NC-3 were forced down on the sea short of the Azores, and NC-1 sank, its crew being rescued. NC-3, with Cdr Towers aboard, taxied the remaining 200 miles (320 km) to the Azores.

The first practical light aeroplane to be produced in Britain after the First World War was the Avro 534 Baby. The prototype crashed after its first take-off on 10 May 1919, but its 35 hp Green water-cooled engine was salvaged and installed in the second aircraft, which won the handicap section of the Aerial Derby flown on 21 June 1919.

The first regular civil air service in England was started by A. V. Roe and Co on 10 May 1919 and discontinued on 30 September 1919. Using three-seat Avro aircraft, services were flown from Alexander Park, Manchester, to Southport, and also to Blackpool. One hundred and ninety-four scheduled flights were made during this period; the cost of a one-way flight was four guineas.

The first stage of a planned US transcontinental air mail service was inaugurated on 15 May 1919, between Chicago and Cleveland. Realising that

only a really long air route would show any advantage over surface transportation in terms of journey time, the US Post Office had purchased more than 125 ex-military aircraft, mostly de Havilland DH4Ms, with which it hoped to carry airmail between New York and San Francisco at the standard first class surface rate of 2 cents per ounce. The final link from Omaha to Sacramento, over the Rockies, was proved practicable on 8 September 1920. After months of careful planning, **the first coast-to-coast airmail** in the USA left San Francisco at 04.30 h on 22 February 1921 and arrived at

US airmail DH-4M, powered by an American Liberty engine.

Mineola, Long Island, New York, at 16.50 h the following day. It was carried from San Francisco to North Platte, Nebraska, by a succession of pilots. At North Platte, it was taken over by a pilot named Jack Knight, flying one of the open-cockpit DH4Ms. When he reached Omaha, weather conditions along the route were so bad that the pilot scheduled to fly the next stage to Chicago had not put in an appearance. So Knight carried on through the darkness to Chicago, over unfamiliar country, becoming a national hero for 'saving the mail service'. A system of lighting for safer flying by night was installed along part of the route in 1923. Regular transcontinental night mail flights were inaugurated on 1 July 1924.

The first post-war aviation event to be held in Britain took place at Hendon on 7 June 1919, when Lt G.R. Hicks won a cross-country handicap race flying an Avro 504K.

Alcock and Brown's Vimy in the bog at Clifden, Co. Galway, after making the first non-stop flight across the Atlantic. (Aer Lingus)

Alcock and Brown (in uniform) receive a tremendous welcome in Ireland. (Aer Lingus)

The first non-stop air crossing of the Atlantic took place on 14-15 June 1919 by Capt John Alcock and Lt Arthur Whitten Brown who flew in a Vickers Vimy bomber from St John's, Newfoundland, to Clifden, County Galway, Ireland. Powered by two Rolls-Royce engines, the Vimy was equipped with long-range fuel tanks and achieved a coast-to-coast time of 15 h 57 min. Total flying time was 16 h 27 min. Both Alcock and Brown were knighted in recognition of this achievement; Sir John Alcock, as Chief Test Pilot of Vickers, was killed on 18 December 1919 in a flying accident caused by bad weather near Rouen, France.

The first military aircraft designed and built in Czechoslovakia, the Letov S1 reconnaissance and light bombing biplane, was introduced in 1919-20. Power was provided by a 260 hp Maybach Mb IVa engine and a total of 90 S1 and S2 versions was built. The SH-1 variant had a maximum speed of 120 mph (193 km/h).

The world's first purpose-built all-metal commercial transport aircraft was flown in Germany. This was the F13 designed by Hugo Junkers, of which 322 were built eventually.

The first London airport at which customs clearance could be obtained for outward bound flights was at Hounslow, Middlesex, in operation from July 1919.

The first non-stop flight between Rome and Paris was made on 14 July 1919 by an Italian Fiat BR light bomber.

The first flight across the Canadian Rocky Mountains, and also the first airmail flight across the Rockies, was made on 7 August 1919 in a Curtiss Jenny flown by Capt Ernest C. Hoy. He flew from Vancouver to Calgary via Lethbridge in 16 h 42 min.

The first scheduled daily international commercial airline flight anywhere in the world was from London to Paris on 25 August 1919. It was made in a de Havilland DH16 flown by Cyril Patteson of Aircraft Transport and Travel Ltd, which took off from Hounslow with four passengers and landed at Le Bourget, Paris, 2 h 30 min later. The fare was £21 for the one-way crossing.

The first two women passengers to fly on an airline service between England and France, on 26 August 1919, were carried in an aircraft of Handley Page Transport.

The first Schneider Trophy Contest to take place off the British coast was that flown at Bournemouth, Hampshire, on 10 September 1919. Fog turned the event into chaos and it was eventually abandoned. Guido Janello of Italy completed eleven laps, but as there was doubt concerning one of his turning points it was not allowed to

Junkers F 13, the world's first purpose-built all-metal airliner.

count as a victory. As a gesture, Italy was asked to organise the next event. The 1919 Contest at Bournemouth was the first in which an aircraft was involved that had been especially prepared by R. J. Mitchell, a 24-year-old recruit of the Supermarine Company.

The first Dutch national airline, KLM (Royal Dutch Airlines), was founded on 7 October 1919. It is the oldest airline in the world still operating under its original name.

The first airline to provide food on its services was Handley Page Transport, on 11 October 1919, when it introduced lunch baskets at a cost of 3 shillings each.

The first American international scheduled passenger air service was inaugurated on 1 November 1919 by Aeromarine West Indies Airways between Key West, Florida, and Havana, Cuba. On 1 November 1920 the airline was awarded the first American foreign airmail contract.

The first flight from Britain to Australia was completed between 12 November and 10 December 1919 by two Australian brothers, Capt Ross Smith and Lt Keith Smith, with two other crew members. They set out from Hounslow, Middlesex, in a Vickers Vimy bomber powered by two Rolls-Royce Eagle engines, and flew to Darwin, a distance of 11 294 miles (18 175 km) in under 28 days. Their feat earned them the Australian government's prize of £10 000 ($40 000) and knighthoods. Sir Ross Smith was killed in a flying accident near Brooklands Aerodrome, England, on 13 April 1922. By tragic coincidence, both Sir Ross and Sir John Alcock (famous for his Atlantic crossing, see above) were killed in Vickers Viking amphibians.

The first men to fly across Australia were Capt H. N. Wrigley and Lt A. W. Murphy, from Melbourne to Darwin in a BE2e between 16 November and 12 December 1919 in 46 h flying time.

One of the first purpose-built British airliners to fly after the First World War, the prototype of the Handley Page W8 made its maiden flight on 2 December 1919.

The airline with the longest continuous record of scheduled services, Aerovias Nacionales de Colombia SA (Avianca), was founded on 5 December 1919.

Dayton-Wright RB Racer, the first aeroplane with a practical retractable landing gear.

The first Boeing commercial aircraft, the B-1 flying-boat of its own design, made its maiden flight on 27 December 1919.

The first automatic pilot to be installed in a British commercial aircraft, the Aveline Stabiliser, was fitted in a Handley Page O/10 during 1920.

The first aeroplane with a practical form of retractable landing gear was the Dayton-Wright RB Racer, designed and built to compete in the 1920 Gordon Bennett Aviation Cup Race.

The first glider competition was held during 1920 at Rhon, Germany, organised by the Aero Technical Association of Dresden.

The first American aircraft carrier was the USS *Jupiter*, an ex-collier of 11 050 tons (11 227 tonnes), which was converted during 1920 to provide a stem-to-stern flight deck. Later named USS *Langley*.

The first flight from Britain to South Africa was made between 4 February and 20 March 1920 by Lt Col Pierre van Ryneveld and Sqn Ldr Christopher Quintin Brand. They set out from Brooklands in a Vickers Vimy bomber but crashed at Wadi Halfa, Sudan, while attempting an emergency landing. The South African government provided the pilots with another Vimy aircraft and after eleven days they set off again, only to crash at Bulawayo, Southern Rhodesia, on 6 March. Once again the government provided an aircraft, a war-surplus DH9, and on 17 March they set off again. Finally, on 20 March, they reached Wynberg Aerodrome, Cape Town. They received subsequently £5000 prize-money and were knighted by HM King George V.

The first post-war world speed record was set in France on 7 February 1920 by Sadi Lecointe at a speed of 171·01 mph (275·22 km/h), flying a Nieuport-Delage 29.

The first regular use of Croydon as London's air terminal began on 29 March 1920. On that date the main airport facilities were transferred from Hounslow, Middlesex, to Croydon—or Waddon, as the airport was known originally. It was opened officially on 31 March 1921.

The oldest airline route still operated by the original airline company is the London–Amsterdam service which was first flown by KLM (Royal Dutch Airlines) on 17 May 1920. The aircraft used for the pioneer flight was an Eagle-engined DH16 (G-EALU) of Aircraft Transport and Travel, piloted by H. 'Jerry' Shaw. After that date, all early KLM services were operated by this British airline under charter.

The first Australian commercial airline, QANTAS (Queensland and Northern Territory Aerial Service) was registered on 16 November 1920 for air taxi and regular air services in Australia. The company's first Chairman was Sir Fergus McMaster (1879-1950), and its first scheduled services began on 2 November 1922 with flights between Charlesville and Cloncurry, Queensland.

The Dornier Delphin flying-boat prototype made its first flight as a five/six-seat commercial aircraft on 24 November 1920. Later versions could seat up to 13 passengers.

The first Pulitzer Trophy Race was flown on 25 November 1920 from Mitchell Field, Long Island, New York. It was won by Capt. Corliss C. Moseley flying a Verville-Packard 600.

First flight of the Blériot-Spad 33 four/five-passenger airliner, one of the most successful early French commercial aircraft, was made on 12 December 1920.

The first fatal accident on a scheduled British commercial flight occurred on 14 December 1920 when a Handley Page O/400 crashed soon after take-off in fog at Cricklewood, London. Pilot R. Bager, his engineer and two passengers were killed, but four other passengers escaped.

The first Japanese fighter built for operation from an aircraft carrier was the Mitsubishi 1MF1, designed by the Englishman Herbert Smith. First flown in 1921, the 1MF1 proved very successful during flight trials.

The Soviet Union's first internal airline service, between Sarapul and Yekaterinburg, was flown during January 1920 by demilitarised *Ilya Mourometz* bombers.

The first solo coast-to-coast flight across the United States was recorded between 21 and 24 February 1921 by Lt William D. Coney of the US Army Air Service. His route, from Rockwell Field, San Diego, to Jacksonville, Florida, was completed in a flying time of 22 h 27 min.

Mitsubishi 1MF1, the first Japanese carrier fighter.

Boeing GA-1 armoured aeroplane.

The first flying-boat designed and built by Short Brothers, the N.3 Cromarty, recorded its maiden flight on 19 April 1921.

The US Army's first production armoured aeroplane, the Boeing GA-1, was flown for the first time during May 1921. In addition to very heavy protective armour plating, it carried eight 0·30 in machine-guns, a 37 mm Baldwin cannon, and ten 25 lb fragmentation bombs.

The only Oxford versus Cambridge University Air Race ever staged was flown on 16 July 1921 and resulted in a flyaway victory for Cambridge. Each team flew three SE5as and the 129 mile (208 km) course of three laps lay along the route from Hendon via Epping and Hertford, returning to Hendon. Cambridge gained maximum points by achieving the first three places, the fastest lap being flown at an average speed of 118·55 mph (190·79 km/h). One of the Oxford aircraft failed to complete the course.

The Vickers Vernon biplane was the first troop transport designed as such from the outset. About 60 were built in three versions, with 360 hp Rolls-Royce Eagle VIIIs, 450 hp Napier Lion II, and Lion III engines respectively. They first entered RAF service in August 1921.

The first Air League Challenge Cup Race was flown at Croydon on 17 September 1921. Because there were then so few civil aircraft available for competitive events, it was decided to award the cup initially to RAF teams. The first winners were a team from No 24 Squadron, then based at RAF Kenley, Surrey.

Japan's first aircraft carrier, the *Hosho*, was launched during November 1921.

The first regular scheduled air services in Australia were inaugurated by West Australian Airways on 5 December 1921.

The first aircraft designed by the Soviet Union's Andrei N. Tupolev, the ANT-1 light sporting monoplane, was flown for the first time during 1922.

The first experiments with a pressurised cabin were made on a de Havilland D.H.4 at Wright Field in the USA during 1922.

A South Atlantic flight attempt was started on 13 March 1922 by Portuguese pilots Capt Gago Coutinho and Capt Sacadura Cabral. Taking off from Lisbon in a Fairey IIIC, they arrived in Brazil on 16 June in the Fairey IIID *Santa Cruz*, the original aircraft having been wrecked *en route*.

The US Navy's first aircraft carrier, the USS *Langley*, was commissioned on 20 March 1922.

The first air collision between airliners on scheduled flights occurred on 7 April 1922, between a Daimler Airways de Havilland DH18 (G-EAWO) flown by Robin Duke from Croydon, and a Farman Goliath of Grands Express Aériens flown by M Mier from Le Bourget. The two aircraft, which were following a road on a reciprocal course, collided over Thieuloy-Saint-Antoine 18 miles (29 km) north of Beauvais. All seven occupants were killed.

The first flight of the prototype Breguet 19 bomber/reconnaissance aircraft was made during May 1922. The Breguet 19 was one of the most extensively-used military types of the 'between-wars' years.

The first glider flight of more than one hour duration was made in Germany on 18 August 1922, by pilot Martens in a *Vampyr*.

The first coast-to-coast crossing of the United States in a single day was made by Lt James H. Doolittle who flew a modified DH4B from Pablo Beach, Florida, to Rockwell Field, San Diego, California, on 4 September 1922. Actual flying time to cover the 2163 miles (3480 km) was 21 h 19 min; elapsed time with a refuelling stop at Kelly Field, Texas, was 22 h 35 min.

The first King's Cup Air Race, over a course from Croydon, England, to Glasgow, Scotland, and return, was won during 8 to 9 September 1922 by Capt F.F. Barnard piloting a de Havilland DH4A.

The first over 200 mph world speed record was set by Sadi Lecointe on 20 September 1922, flying a Nieuport-Delage 29.

The first demonstration of radar signatures was made by technicians at Anacostia Naval Aircraft Radio Laboratory, USA, on 27 September 1922.

The first air control operation, in which an air force became entirely responsible for the internal security of a nation, began in October 1922. The RAF assumed responsibility for maintaining peace in Iraq, replacing the former large army garrison with two squadrons of Vernon transports, four of DH9As, one of Bristol Fighters and one of Snipe fighters.

The first take-off from an American aircraft carrier, the USS *Langley*, was made on 17 October 1922 by Lt V.C. Griffin flying a Vought VE-7SF fighter.

The first American to escape from a disabled aeroplane by parachute was Lt Harold R. Harris, US Army, who on 20 October 1922 jumped from a Loening monoplane at 2000 ft (610 m) over North Dayton, Ohio.

The first flight was recorded in France of the Oehmichen No 2 multi-rotor helicopter on 11 November 1922. Within less than 18 months, on 17 April 1924, Etienne Oehmichen had established with this aircraft a helicopter record for distance in a straight line of 1722 ft (525 m).

Japan's first purpose-built aircraft carrier, the *Hosho*, was commissioned on 27 December 1922. It survived the Second World War and was decommissioned after the Japanese surrender.

The first German aeroplane to land in the UK post-war was a Dornier Komet four-passenger airliner (D-223) of Deutsche Luft-Reederei, which landed at Lympne Aerodrome, Kent, on 31 December 1922.

The first variable-pitch aeroplane propeller, designed by Turnbull in America, was demonstrated during 1923.

The first German aircraft to land in the UK after the First World War was Dornier Komet D-223.

Aero Ab 11, a version of the A 11, arriving back from a touring flight to Prague. (Aero Vodochody Národní Podnik)

The first examples of the Czechoslovakian Aero A 11 were flown in 1923. This highly successful general purpose biplane, of which some 440 examples were built, established several duration records and, in 1926, one completed a 9320 mile (15 000 km) intercontinental flight.

The first successful flight of the C4 Autogiro, designed by Spain's Juan de la Cierva, was made on 9 January 1923. He was to continue the development of these rotary wing aircraft in Britain.

The first take-off and landing on Japan's new aircraft carrier, the *Hosho*, were made in February 1923 by a Mitsubishi 1MF1 flown by a British pilot, Capt Jordan.

The first scheduled air service between London and Berlin was inaugurated by Daimler Airways on 10 April 1923, with intermediate landings at Bremen and Hamburg.

The Soviet Union's first state airline, Dobrolet, was established during March 1923, its initial operations carried out with assistance from the Air Force.

The first Czechoslovakian national airline, Ceskoslovenske Statni Aerolinie (CSA), began its first operations on 1 March 1923.

The first non-stop air crossing of the United States by an aeroplane was achieved on 2-3 May 1923 by Lts O.G. Kelly and J.A. Macready, USAAS, in a Fokker T-2 aircraft. Taking off from Roosevelt Field, Long Island, at 12.36 h (Eastern Time) on 2 May, they arrived at Rockwell Field, San Diego, California at 12.26 h (Pacific Time) on 3 May. They overflew Dayton, Ohio; Indianapolis, Indiana; St Louis, Missouri; Kansas City, Missouri; Tucumcari, New Mex-

ico; and Wickenburg, Arizona. The distance flown, 2516 miles (4050 km), was covered in 26 h 50 min. Kelly and Macready had also established a new world endurance record for aeroplanes, on 16-17 April 1923, flying the Fokker T-2 a distance of 2518 miles (4052 km) over a measured course in 36 h 5 min.

The first Grosvenor Challenge Cup contest, for British aircraft with engines of under 150 hp, was won on 23 June 1923 by Flt Lt W.H. Longton, RAF, flying a Sopwith Gnu.

The first successful in-flight refuelling of an aeroplane was accomplished by Capt L.H. Smith and Lt J.P. Richter in a de Havilland DH4B on 27 June 1923 at San Diego, California. Smith and Richter established a new world endurance record by remaining airborne for 37 h 15 min 43·8 s from 27 to 28 August 1923, covering a distance of 3293·26 miles (5299·9 km) over a measured 50 km course at San Diego. Their DH4B was flight-refuelled 15 times.

The first use of electric beacons mounted on the ground, to provide flight directions for night flying operations, were introduced in the USA on 21 August 1923.

The first six-engined American aircraft, the Barling XNBL-1 triplane bomber, was flown for the first time on 22 August 1923. Then the largest aeroplane in the world, it proved to be underpowered and no further examples were built.

The Soviet Union's first fighter aircraft to be built in series, the Polikarpov I-1 (Il-400) was flown for the first time in prototype form on 23 August 1923. A cantilever low-wing monoplane, it was then powered by an American Liberty engine.

The RAF's first new fighter after the end of the First World War, the Gloster Grebe biplane, entered service during October 1923.

The first lightplane competition held in Great Britain was at Lympne, Kent, in October 1923, organised by the Royal Aero Club. The competition was for single-seat aircraft, and the prizes included £1000 offered by the *Daily Mail* and £500 by the Duke of Sutherland for the longest flight on one Imperial gallon of petrol made by an aircraft with an engine not exceeding 750 cc capacity. The prize money for the one-gallon flight was shared between Flt Lt Walter Longton, who flew an English Electric Wren, and Jimmy H. James in an ANEC monoplane, both flying 87·5 miles (140·8 km). Another prize of £500, offered by the Abdulla Company for the highest speed over two laps, was won in a Parnall Pixie by Capt Norman Macmillan, who attained an average speed of 76·1 mph (122·5 km/h).

Most widely-used inter-war military aircraft produced by the Fokker company, which moved back to Holland in 1918, was the CV. Provisions for fitting wings of differing area, and various engines, enabled many combat and observation roles to be performed. Five main variants were produced, designated CV-A to CV-E, of which the last two were most extensively used. CVs

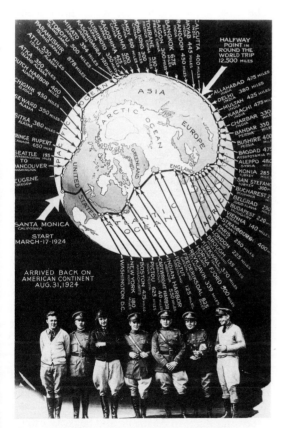

Crews of the Douglas DWCs with an illustration of their route around the world. A noteworthy point is that the illustration shows the start to have been at Santa Monica on 17 March, but it is generally accepted that Seattle was the actual start point. (US National Archives)

served with many air forces, including those of Finland, Hungary, Italy, the Netherlands, Norway, Sweden and Switzerland. The prototype first flew in 1924 and some CVs were still in service during the early years of the Second World War.

The world's first aerial crop-dusting company, Huff Daland Dusters, was formed at Macon, Georgia, in 1924. It became named Delta Air Service, now Delta Air Lines, when passenger services were initiated during 1929.

The first British national airline, Imperial Airways, was formed on 1 April 1924. This was the manifestation of the British government's determination to develop air transport, and the company was to receive preferential air subsidies, having acquired the businesses of British Marine Air Navigation Co, Daimler Airway, Handley Page Transport and Instone Air Lines. Its fleet consisted of seven DH34s, two Sea Eagles, three Handley Page W8bs and one Vickers Vimy.

The first successful round-the world flight was accomplished by two Douglas DWCs (Douglas World Cruisers) between 6 April and 28 September 1924. Four DWCs set out from Seattle, Washington, and two of them circumnavigated the world. The flagplane (named *Seattle* and piloted by the commander of the flight, Maj F. Martin) only reached Alaska, where it crashed on a mountain on 30 April; the crew returned to the USA. Another (the *Boston*) was forced to alight in the ocean near the Faeroes, and eventually sank after being cut loose from the crew's rescue ship, the USS *Richmond*. The crews of the two successful aircraft were as follows:
CHICAGO (Aircraft No 2): Lt Lowell H. Smith, deputy flight commander and pilot; Lt Leslie P. Arnold, mechanic and second pilot.
NEW ORLEANS (Aircraft No 4): Lt Erik Nelson, pilot and engineer officer; Lt John Harding Jr, mechanic and maintenance officer.
   The total mileage by each of the two aircraft which completed the historic flight was 27 553 (44 340 km) and the elapsed time 175 days. The flying time was given as 371 h 11 min. It should be noted that this flight included the first staged crossing of the Pacific Ocean as well as the first staged east-west crossing of the North Atlantic. (Two of these aircraft are preserved to this day, one at the Smithsonian Institution in Washing-

ton, the other in the Air Force Museum at Wright–Patterson Air Force Base.)

The first all-metal aircraft to be built in the Soviet Union, the ANT-2, made its maiden flight on 26 May 1924. Designed by Andrei N. Tupolev, its method of construction was based on that of the German Junkers types.

The first Light Aeroplane Competition for two-seat aircraft, organised by the Royal Aero Club, was held at Lympne, Kent, between 27 September and 4 October 1924. Lightest aircraft in the competition was the Hawker Cygnet, which had an empty weight of 373 lb (169 kg). Two examples were built, G-EBMB and G-EBJH, the former powered originally by a 34 hp British Anzani two-cylinder engine, the latter with a 34 hp ABC Scorpion, also of two cylinder configuration. The Cygnet was also Sydney Camm's first design for the H.G. Hawker Engineering Company. Winner of the competition, and the Air Ministry's £3000 prize, was Mr Piercy with the Beardmore Wee Bee monoplane, powered by a 32 hp Bristol Cherub engine.

First new Italian-designed fighter aircraft to be adopted by the Regia Aeronautica, the Fiat C.R.1 single-seat biplane fighter was demonstrated during this air force's annual review on 4 November 1924.

One of the most successful French aircraft produced between the wars was the Potez 25 reconnaissance and light bombing biplane, first flown during 1925. About 4000 examples were produced, in 87 variants, operated in France and by the armed forces of some 20 countries. Engines from several French manufacturers were installed, ranging from 450 to 600 hp. Accommodation was for two, and the Potez 25 had a maximum speed of 136 mph (219 km/h) with a 450 hp engine.

The fastest light bomber of the mid-1920s was the Fairey Fox. The prototype was first flown on 3 January 1925, powered by a 480 hp Curtiss D12 engine, and had a maximum speed of 156 mph (251 km/h). The first of 28 production Foxes were delivered in August 1926 to No 12 Squadron RAF, which has since used a fox's head as a badge. Much faster than other bombers of their time, Foxes could outpace then-current fighters. No further production was undertaken for the

RAF, but later versions were built in Belgium by Avions Fairey, and some of these were used in action against the invading German forces in 1940.

The prototype of the last biplane fighter of wooden basic construction to serve with the RAF, the Gloster Gamecock, was flown for the first time during February 1925.

The prototype of the de Havilland DH60 Moth, a small **two-seat biplane that revolutionised private flying** and was the true starting point of the flying club movement, was flown for the first time on 22 February 1925.

Henry Ford initiated **the first regular US air freight service,** linking Detroit, Michigan and Chicago, on 13 April 1925.

The first three-engined all-metal monoplane transport in the world to enter commercial airline service was the Junkers G 23, four of which served with Swedish Air Lines (AB Aerotransport) on the Malmo–Hamburg–Amsterdam route from 15 May 1925. This aircraft, built in Germany and Sweden, provided the basis for the later and famous Junkers Ju 52/3m, and set the pattern for low-wing multi-engined monoplanes thereafter.

A contemporary of the above, and **another of the world's famous commercial airliners,** the Fokker F.VIIa-3m three-engined monoplane flew for the first time in prototype form on 4 September 1925.

The first aeroplane flight between London and Cape Town was made by Alan Cobham, with his mechanic A.B. Elliott and cine photographer B.W.G. Emmott, in the second de Havilland DH50 that was built (G-EBFO). They left Croydon on 16 November 1925 and reached Cape Town on 17 February 1926. Cobham landed back at Croydon after the 16 000 mile (25 750 km) round trip on 13 March 1926. Three months later, on 30 June, Cobham and Elliott took off from the River Medway in the same aircraft, converted into a seaplane for the largely overwater flight to Australia and back. G-EBFO returned to a triumphant welcome on the Thames, at Westminster, on 1 October. The suc-

Early production example of the de Havilland DH60 Moth.

cess was marred by the death of Elliott, who had been killed by a stray bullet fired by a bedouin while flying over the desert between Baghdad and Bazra on the outward leg. Cobham was knighted for these flights, which pioneered future Empire air routes.

Flying a Dornier Wal flying-boat, Commandante Franco achieved the **first staged east-west air crossing of the South Atlantic** between 22 January and 10 February 1926.

The most extensively used Fleet Air Arm aircraft of the inter-war period was the Fairey IIIF. The prototype made its first flight on 19 March 1926. Production totalled about 620 aircraft, of which more than 230 were operated by the RAF for general-purpose duties and some 365 by the Fleet Air Arm as spotter-reconnaissance general-purpose biplanes. The last FAA version was the Mk IIIB, powered by a 570 hp Napier Lion XIA engine and with a maximum speed of 120 mph (193 km/h). Fairey IIIFs were operated from land bases, used as seaplanes and catapulted from naval vessels. The type was pronounced obsolete by the FAA in 1940.

The first commercial airmail flights in the USA were started on 6 April 1926 by Varney Speed Lines. These were flown between Pasco and Elko using Swallow biplanes.

On 1 May 1926 Deutsche Luft-Hansa began the world's first night passenger services, flying between Berlin and Königsberg. (Lufthansa)

The first aeroplane flight over the North Pole was accomplished by Lt Cdr Richard E. Byrd (USN) and Floyd Bennett, in the Fokker F.VIIA/3m *Josephine Ford* on 9 May 1926. The total distance flown was 1600 miles (2575 km).

The first successful passenger aircraft built in America was the Ford 4-AT Trimotor, which first flew on 11 June 1926. Powered by three 220 hp engines, it could accommodate ten passengers and had a cruising speed of 105 mph (169 km/h). From 1926 to 1933, Ford built around 200 Trimotors, designated from 3-AT to 7-AT, and this aircraft was operated by many airlines.

The first landing by night on an aircraft carrier was accomplished by Flt Lt Boyce, RAF, on 1 July 26, piloting the Blackburn Dart N.9804 to the deck of HMS *Furious*.

Two great airliners of the mid-1920s were the de Havilland DH66 Hercules and the Armstrong Whitworth Argosy. The Hercules was a 79 ft 6 in (24·23 m) span biplane, powered by three 420 hp Bristol Jupiter VI engines. It was designed to the requirements of Imperial Airways, to fulfil the need for a large multi-engined transport suitable for tropical operations, when the airline agreed to take on the airmail services from Cairo to Baghdad that had been pioneered by the RAF. The prototype was flown first on 30 September 1926 and, following minor modifications, was despatched to Heliopolis on 18 December. Named *City of Cairo*, the DH66 made its first commercial flight on 12 January 1927. Altogether, eleven DH66s were built, seven for Imperial Airways and four for West Australian Airways. The last to survive was *City of Adelaide*, which was destroyed in New Guinea during 1942. The British aircraft normally accommodated a crew of three, seven passengers and mail. The Australian aircraft carried 14 passengers. The Armstrong Whitworth Argosy, a 20-passenger airliner, was powered by three 420 hp Jaguar engines. It was the Argosy that flew the Imperial Airways' lunchtime 'Silver-Wing' service from London to Paris.

The first known use of aircraft for violence in civil crime occurred on 12 November 1926, when three small bombs (which failed to explode) were dropped from an aeroplane on to a farmhouse in Williamson County, Illinois. The raid was carried out by a member of the Shelton gang, against members of the rival Birger gang, in a Prohibition feud involving illicit supplies of beer and rum.

The first light aeroplane flight from London to Karachi, India, was flown by T. Neville Stack in the de Havilland DH60 Moth G-EBMO (Cirrus II engine), accompanied by B.S. Leete in a similar aircraft, G-EBKU, between 15 November 1926 and 8 January 1927.

The mainstays of US Army Air Corps bomber units from 1927 to the mid-1930s were Huff-Daland/Keystone twin-engined biplane bombers, built in many small production versions. All were basically similar externally, differing mainly in engines, tail units and wing configurations. The largest production version was the Keystone B-3A, of which 36 were built, each powered by two 525 hp Pratt & Whitney Hornet engines and having a maximum speed of 114 mph (183 km/h). Bomb load was 2500 lb (1134 kg).

The first non-stop solo air crossing of the North Atlantic was made by Capt Charles Lindbergh during 20–21 May 1927 in the Ryan NYP high-wing monoplane, *Spirit of St Louis*. Taking off from Long Island, New York, on 20 May 1927, his epic flight to Paris of 3610 miles (5810 km) was accomplished in 33 h 39 min at an average speed of 107·5 mph (173 km/h).

Charles Lindbergh working on details of the Spirit of St Louis *as the plane was being constructed.*

Spirit of St Louis

The first French aircraft carrier, named *Béarn*, was completed on 27 May 1927 after almost seven years of construction.

The first non-stop flight between the United States and Hawaii was achieved by Lts Albert F. Hegenberger and Lester J. Maitland during 28–29 June 1927. Flying the US Army Fokker C-2 monoplane *Bird of Paradise*, they covered the 2407 miles (3874 km) from Oakland, California, to Honolulu, Hawaii, in 25 h 30 min.

The world's first charter flight, flown in both directions between Amsterdam and Jakarta, was completed between 15 June and 23 July 1927. The Fokker F.VIIa (H-NADP) was chartered by an American, W. van Lear Black, and flown a total out and return distance of 18 710 miles (30 111 km) under the command of Capt G. J. Geysendorffer.

The first two-seat autogiro, Juan de la Cierva's C6D, made its first flight on 29 July 1927. On the following day, Spaniard de la Cierva became the **first passenger to be carried in a rotating-wing aircraft.**

The first flight by a light aircraft from London to Cape Town, South Africa, was accomplished by Lt R. R. Bentley, SAAF, flying the de Havilland DH60X Moth *Dorys*. Taking off on 1 September 1927, the flight was completed on the 28th of the month.

The first non-stop air crossing of the South Atlantic by an aeroplane was made on 14-15 October 1927. Capt Dieudonne Costes and Lt Cdr Le Brix flew the Breguet XIX *Nungesser-Coli* from Saint-Louis, Senegal, to Port Natal, Brazil, a distance of 2125 miles (3420 km) in 19 h 50 min.

The first air service by Pan American Airways was inaugurated on 19 October 1927 on the 90 mile (145 km) route between Key West, Florida, and Havana, Cuba.

One of the Soviet Union's most enduring aircraft, the Polikarpov U-2 biplane trainer, was flown for the first time on 7 January 1928. Ordered into production in 1930, it was to be built in very large numbers until 1945 and remained in service until 1962.

The first solo flight from England to Australia was made by Sqn Ldr H. J. L. ('Bert') Hinkler in the Avro 581 Avian light aircraft prototype G-EBOV. Flying from Croydon to Darwin, between 7 and 22 February 1928, his 11 005 mile (17 711 km) route was via Rome, Malta, Tobruk, Ramleh, Basra, Jask, Karachi, Cawnpore, Calcutta, Rangoon, Victoria Point, Singapore, Bandoeng and Bima. His aircraft was placed on permanent exhibition in the Brisbane Museum.

The first flight by a woman from South Africa to England was achieved by Lady Heath in an Avro Avian III, flying from Cape Town to Croydon between 12 February and 17 May 1928. This was **also the first solo flight from South Africa to Britain and,** en route, **the first solo flight from the Cape to Cairo.**

The first solo return flight by a woman between London and South Africa was achieved by Lady Bailey who, in a de Havilland Moth (G-EBSF), left London on 9 March 1928. This aircraft was damaged beyond repair at Tabora a month later, but the pilot completed her flight to the Cape in a replacement Moth, G-EBTG. She subsequently toured round Africa before returning to London on 16 January 1929.

The first world speed record in excess of 500 km/h and 300 mph was established by Maj Mario di Bernardi of the Italian Air Force. Flying a Macchi M.52*bis* floatplane, he attained a ratified speed of 318·57 mph (512·69 km/h) on 30 March 1928.

The first east-west air crossing of the North Atlantic, between Baldonnel, Ireland, and Greenly Island, Labrador, was recorded during 12-13 April 1928. This was achieved by Hermann Kohn, the Irish Capt J. Fitzmaurice and Baron von Hunefeld, flying the Junkers W33 *Bremen*.

The first west–east crossing of the Arctic was achieved by Capt G. H. Wilkins and Lt Carl B. Eielson flying a Lockheed Vega monoplane. Taking off from Point Barrow, Alaska, on 15 April 1928, they were within half-an-hour's flying time of their destination when they were forced by poor weather to land on Dead Man's Island. There they sheltered in the cabin of their aircraft for five days before taking off and landing on Spitzbergen on 21 April.

The Australian Flying Doctor Service was inaugurated on 15 May 1928, using the joint services of the Australian Inland Mission and QANTAS at Cloncurry. The first aircraft was a de Havil-

Bremen, *photographed in a hangar at Baldonnel aerodrome.* (Aer Lingus)

land DH50 *Victory*, modified to accommodate two stretchers; its first pilot was A. Affleck and the first flying doctor was Dr K.H. Vincent Welsh. The founder of the service was the Rev J. Flynn, OBE.

The first true trans-Pacific flight, discounting that of the Douglas World Cruisers, was that accomplished by the Fokker F.VIIB-3m *Southern Cross*, flown by Capt Charles Kingsford Smith and C.T.P. Ulm (pilots), accompanied by Harry Lyon (navigator) and James Warner (radio operator). Taking off from Oakland Field, San Francisco, California, on 31 May 1928, their route was via Honolulu, Hawaii, and Suva, Fiji, landing at Eagle Farm, Brisbane, on 9 June 1928. The flight covered 7389 miles (11 890 km), with a flying time of 83 h 38 min. The *Southern Cross* has been preserved and is displayed at Eagle Farm Airport. It was the **first aircraft ever to land in Fiji.**

A de Havilland DH61 aircraft was modified during August 1928 to provide **a flying office** for the British *Daily Mail* newspaper. It was equipped with a typewriter and desk, photographer's dark room, and even had a motor cycle for a reporter to get to the scene of an event.

The first air crossing of the Tasman Sea was made by the *Southern Cross* during 10-11 Sep-

tember 1928. Again piloted by Charles Kingsford Smith and C.T.P. Ulm, the aircraft flew from Richmond Aerodrome, Sydney, to Wigram, Christchurch, New Zealand.

The first rotating-wing aircraft to fly the English Channel was the Cierva C8L Mark II (G-EBYY) Autogiro, flown by Juan de la Cierva with a passenger from Croydon to Le Bourget on 18 · September 1928.

The first successful autogyro of American design was flown by Harold Pitcairn in Philadelphia on 19 December 1928.

The world's first large-scale airlift evacuation of civilians was undertaken by transport aircraft of the Royal Air Force between 23 December 1928 and 25 February 1929. Five hundred and eighty-six people and 24 193 lb (10 975 kg) of luggage were airlifted from the town of Kabul, Afghanistan, during inter-tribal disturbances. They were carried over treacherous country using eight Vickers Victoria transports of No 70 Squadron RAF, and a Handley Page Hinadai.

The prototype of the Gloster Gauntlet, the **last open cockpit biplane to serve with the Royal Air Force,** was flown for the first time during January 1929. In November 1936, three Gauntlets of No 32 Squadron were directed by experimental ground radar to intercept a civil airliner, the

The gigantic Dornier Do X flying-boat. (Conrad Smit)

world's first successful radar–controlled interception.

The first commercial air route between London and India was inaugurated by Imperial Airways on 30 March 1929. The route was from London to Basle, Switzerland, by air (Armstrong Whitworth Argosy aircraft); Basle to Genoa, Italy, by train; Genoa to Alexandria, Egypt, by air (Short Calcutta flying-boats); and Alexandria to Karachi, India, by air (de Havilland DH66 Hercules aircraft). The total journey from Croydon to Karachi occupied seven days, for which the single fare was £130. The stage travelled by train was necessary as Italy forbade the air entry of British aircraft, an embargo which lasted several years and substantially frustrated Imperial Airways' efforts to develop the Far East route.

The first electro-mechanical flight simulator was the Link Trainer which was patented on 14 April 1929. It comprised a replica of an aeroplane, with full controls and instruments, which did not leave the ground; instead it was 'attached' to a mechanical crab that traced a path over a large scale map in such a way as to represent heading, speed and time of the replica aircraft 'flown' by

its occupant. Invented by Edward Albert Link, who sold his first model in 1919, it was adopted by the US Navy in 1931 and by the US Army in 1934. By 1939 there was scarcely an air force in the world that was not using Link Trainers. They can be regarded as the forerunners of today's complex flight simulators.

The first non-stop flight from Great Britain to India was accomplished by Sqn Ldr A.G. Jones Williams and Flt Lt N.H. Jenkins (pilot and navigator respectively) between 24 and 26 April 1929. Flying from Cranwell, Lincolnshire, to Karachi, India, in the Fairey Long Range Monoplane J9479, they covered the 4130 miles (6647 km) in 50 h 37 min. It had been intended to fly to Bangalore to establish a world distance record but the attempt was abandoned owing to headwinds. Another Fairey Long Range Monoplane, K1991, crewed by Sqn Ldr O.R. Gayford and Flt Lt G.E. Nicholetts, made **the first non-stop flight from England to South Africa,** between 6 and 8 February 1933. The total distance covered from Cranwell to Walvis Bay, South-

West Africa, was 5309 miles (8544 km), which was completed in 57 h and 25 min and set a new world distance record.

The largest flying-boat built between the wars was the Dornier Do X, the prototype of which made its maiden flight on 25 July 1929, at which time it was also **the largest aeroplane of any kind in the world.** Powered by 12 engines (initially 525 hp Siemens Jupiters, later 600 hp Curtiss Conquerors), mounted in tandem pairs on the 157 ft 5¾ in (48·00 m) monoplane wing, the Do X once carried (on 21 October 1929) a crew of ten and 159 passengers (nine of whom were stowaways). Altogether three Do Xs were built. The most famous flight was that made by the prototype from Germany to New York, which took from 2 November 1930 to 27 August 1931 because of damage to the wing and hull and lengthy stops at various places including Amsterdam, Calshot, Lisbon, the Canary Islands, Portuguese Guinea and Rio de Janeiro. In commercial terms the Do X was quite impracticable, and the two examples delivered to an Italian airline were never put into service. Although it had a respectable maximum speed of 134 mph (216 km/h), the Do X weighed 123 460 lb (56 000 kg) with full load and had a service ceiling of 1640 ft (500 m).

The first blind-flight take-off, level flight and landing was accomplished by Lt James H. Doolittle on 24 September 1929, at Mitchell Field, Long Island, New York.

The only operational European submarine designed to carry an aircraft was launched on 18 October 1929. Named *Sourcouf*, this submarine cruiser carried a small folding-wing seaplane in a watertight container on the deck.

The Junkers G38 was the largest landplane in the world at the time of the maiden flight of the first of two of these giant monoplanes, on 6 November 1929. The aircraft had a wing span of 144 ft 4 in (44·00 m). Powered by four wing-mounted engines, it accommodated 34 passengers comprising 26 in the main fuselage cabin, three in each of two wing-root cabins and two in the fuselage nose.

The first flight over the South Pole was made during 28–29 November 1929 by the Ford 4-AT Trimotor *Floyd Bennett*. Its crew was Cdr R.E. Byrd, US Navy, with Bernt Balchen (pilot), Harold June (radio operator) and Ashley McKinley (survey).

The first solo flight by a woman from Great Britain to Australia was achieved by Amy Johnson, between 5 and 24 May 1930, flying the de Havilland DH60G Gipsy Moth *Jason* (G-AAAH) from Croydon to Darwin.

The Boeing Company's first commercial monoplane, the Model 200 *Monomail*, made its first flight on 6 May 1930. This significant aeroplane, used as a mail/cargo carrier, introduced a cantilever low-set monoplane wing, retractable landing gear and other advanced features.

The first airline stewardess was Ellen Church, a nurse who, with Boeing Air Transport (later absorbed into United Air Lines), made her first flight, between San Francisco, California, and Cheyenne, Wyoming, on 15 May 1930.

The RAF's last heavy bomber of biplane configuration, the Handley Page HP38 Heyford, was first flown in prototype form on 12 June 1930.

The first east–west staged crossing of the North Atlantic in a flying-boat was achieved by a Dornier Wal piloted by Capt Wolfgang von Gronau. Taking off from the island of Sylt, on 18 August 1930, with co-pilot Edward Zimmer, Fritz Albrecht (radio) and Franz Hack (mechanic), a landing in New York harbour was made on 26 August.

The prototype of the Polish PZL P-7 single-seat fighter was flown during October 1930. When the type equipped all Polish Air Force fighter squadrons in 1933, it was **the first air force in the world to have only all-metal monoplane fighters in first-line service.**

The first coast-to-coast all-air passenger service in the United States was inaugurated by Transcontinental and Western Air, between New York and Los Angeles, California, on 25 October 1930.

The first flight of the Handley Page 42E Hannibal four-engined biplane airliner prototype, G-AAGX, was made on 14 November 1930. The stately HP 42/45 class brought new standards of luxury and reliability to air travel besides providing the backbone of Imperial Airways' fleet during the 1930s. Eight aeroplanes were pro-

Handley Page HP 42
Heracles, *the first 'W'
Western, delivered to
Imperial Airways in 1931.*

duced in two versions, the 'E' (Eastern) and 'W' (Western), carrying 24 and 38 passengers respectively.

The prototype of the Fairey Hendon, **the first monoplane heavy bomber to enter operational service with the RAF,** made its first flight on 25 November 1930.

The Tupolev ANT-6 prototype recorded its first flight on 22 December 1930. When it entered service as the TB-3, it was **the Soviet Union's first four-engined monoplane heavy bomber.**

Imperial Airways' first monoplane airliner was the Armstrong Whitworth AW15 Atalanta, eight of which were built for the airline in 1931 and 1932. Accommodation was for nine passengers plus cargo or mail, and the aircraft were used on the Nairobi–Cape Town and Karachi–Singapore routes.

The largest Japanese military aircraft built between the wars was the Mitsubishi Ki-20, the basic design of which originated in Germany as the Junkers G 38. The first Ki-20 was completed in secrecy during 1931; by 1934 it had been joined by five others, the later examples built from Japanese components. The Japanese Army Air Force was not impressed by the aircraft, and the Ki-20s never saw action. Each had a wing span of 144 ft 4 in (44·00 m).

The first formation flight across the South Atlantic, from Portuguese Guinea to Natal, Brazil, was made on 6 January 1931 by ten Savoia-Marchetti S55 flying-boats, commanded by Italian Air Minister General Italo Balbo. In 1933, from 1 to 15 July, General Balbo led **the first formation flight across the North Atlantic.** Taking off from Orbetello, Italy, the 24 S55s flew to the Century of Progress Exposition in Chicago, their route being via Holland, Iceland, Labrador and New Brunswick, Canada.

The first commercial air route between London and Central Africa was inaugurated on 28 February 1931 by Imperial Airways. The route lay from Croydon to Alexandria (using Argosy aircraft from Croydon to Athens, and Calcutta flying-boats from Athens to Alexandria via Crete), and from Cairo to Mwanza, on Lake Victoria (using Argosy aircraft). Passengers were taken only as far as Khartoum, mail being carried over the remainder of the route.

A remarkable feat of navigation was achieved by Francis Chichester (later Sir Francis), flying his DH60G Gipsy Moth G-AAKK *Mme Elijah* over the Tasman Sea. Taking off from Norfolk Island on 1 April 1931 to make a landfall on Lord Howe Island 561 miles (903 km) distant, an error of more than half a degree could have been fatal, but he landed there safely after a flight of 7 h 40 min.

The RAF's first fighter aircraft able to exceed 200 mph (322 km/h) in level flight, the Hawker Fury I biplane first entered service with No 43

Squadron at Tangmere, Sussex, in May 1931. Powered by a 525 hp Rolls-Royce Kestrel IIS liquid-cooled engine and armed with two synchronised machine-guns, the Fury, designed by the late Sir Sydney Camm, had a top speed of 207 mph (333 km/h) at 14 000 ft (4270 m).

A record round-the-world flight of 8 d 15 h 51 min was recorded between 23 June and 1 July 1931 by the Lockheed Vega *Winnie Mae*. Piloted by Wiley Post, with Harold Gatty as navigator, the flight from and to New York covered a distance of nearly 15 500 miles (24 945 km) in about 106 flying hours, following a route via Chester (UK), Berlin, Irkutsk (Soviet Union) and Alaska.

Flying her Puss Moth G-AAZV *Jason II*, Amy Johnson achieved a **flight from England to Japan in less than nine days.** Taking off from Lympne, Kent on 28 July 1931, she arrived at Tokyo on 6 August in a total flying time of 79 h.

Piloting the Supermarine S.6B S1595 on 13 September 1931, Flt Lt J.N. Boothman **won the Schneider Trophy Contest outright for Great Britain** at 340·08 mph (547·31 km/h); during the course of the seven laps he also set a new 100 km closed-circuit record of 342·87 mph (551·79 km/h). During that afternoon, flying the reserve S.6B S1596, Flt Lt G.H. Stainforth established a new world speed record of 379·05 mph (610·02 km/h).

The first over 400 mph speed record was also set by Flt Lt G.H. Stainforth on 29 September 1931, this time flying the Supermarine S.6B S1595. Making six runs over the set course he achieved an average speed of 407·5 mph (655·81 km/h).

The first non-stop flight from Japan to the United States was achieved by Hugh Herndon Jr and Clyde E. Pangborn flying a Bellanca monoplane. Taking off from Samushiro Beach, some 300 miles (483 km) north of Tokyo, on 4 October 1931, they landed at Wenatchee, Washington, on 5 October after 41 h 13 min.

One of the classic two-seat trainers of all time, for both civil and military use, the prototype of the de Havilland DH82A Tiger Moth was flown for the first time on 26 October 1931.

Two out of every three fighters in service with the French Air Force in 1932 were Nieuport-Delage 62s. Three main versions were produced: the ND62 powered by a 500 hp Hispano-Suiza

12 Mb engine (345 built), the ND622 with a 500 hp H-S 12 Md engine (330 built) and the ND629 with a 500 hp H-S 12 Mdsh supercharged engine (50 built). Others were exported. Maximum speed of the initial production version was 150 mph (241 km/h).

Landing at Stag Lane aerodrome on 16 January 1932 in the DH80A Puss Moth G-ABJO, Wg Cdr R.H. McIntosh and the Hon Mrs R. Westenra completed a journey to Africa, around the continent and back to London. During the course of this trip they recorded **the first British flight across the Sahara, and the first by a lightplane.**

The International Disarmament Conference began in Geneva on 2 February 1932. However, Japan left the League of Nations on 27 March 1933 and Germany on 14 October 1933.

The first twin-engined bomber to be designed for the clandestine German Luftwaffe was the Dornier Do 11. Designated originally Dornier Do F, the prototype first flew on 7 May 1932, disguised as the last of a batch of mail/cargo transport aircraft. Powered by two 650 hp Siemens-Jupiter engines, some 77 Do 11s were produced.

Flying a Consolidated NY-2 trainer at Dayton, Ohio, on 9 May 1931, Capt A.F. Hegenberger made **the first blind solo flight entirely on instruments** with no check pilot on board the aircraft.

The first solo crossing of the North Atlantic by a woman was achieved by the American pilot

Amelia Earhart during a 'screen interview' at Springfield, Londonderry.

Amelia Earhart's Vega under guard at Londonderry.

Miss Amelia Earhart (Mrs Putnam). Taking off from Harbor Grace, Newfoundland, in a Lockheed Vega monoplane on 20 May 1932, she landed at Londonderry, Northern Ireland, on the following day.

The first cantilever low-wing monoplane fighter to serve with the French Armée de l'Air was the Dewoitine D500. First flown in prototype form on 18 June 1932, the production aircraft did not begin to enter service until 1935 due to wing structural weakness. Variants included the D501 and D510 and many examples of the series were exported, China being the largest foreign operator with 34 D510s.

The first east-west solo flight across the North Atlantic, from Portmanock Strand north of Dublin to Pennfield Ridge, New Brunswick, was achieved by J.A. Mollison. Flying the DH80A Puss Moth *The Hearts Content* (G-ABXY), he took off on 18 August 1932, recording a flight time of 31 h 20 min.

The first non-stop transcontinental flight by a woman across the United States, from Los Angeles, California, to Newark, New Jersey, was achieved by Amelia Earhart in a Lockheed Vega on 25 August 1932.

A Travel Air biplane with a steam engine power plant was flown successfully in the United States during 1933. Its Besler two-cylinder double-acting vee engine developed 150 hp at a boiler pressure of 1200 lb/in² (84·37 kg/cm²).

The last operational US biplane to remain in production was the Curtiss SBC Helldiver, which first flew as the parasol monoplane XF12C-1 in 1933. It was almost immediately redesigned as a biplane, and remained in production in the United States until 1941. At the time of the Japanese attack on Pearl Harbor in December 1941, the US Navy still retained 186 Helldivers on strength.

The true ancestor of modern airliners, with all-metal structure, cantilever low wings and retractable landing gear, was the Boeing Model 247, the prototype of which was flown on 8 February 1933. A total of 75 was built. The major production version was the Model 247D, powered by two 550 hp Pratt & Whitney Wasp engines driving controllable-pitch propellers. Cruising speed with ten passengers and 400 lb (181 kg) of mail was 189 mph (304 km/h).

Landing at Port Natal, Brazil, on 9 February 1933, after a flight from Lympne, Kent, in the Puss Moth *The Hearts Content*, J.A. Mollison had attained a remarkable series of achievements. He was **the first pilot to make a solo flight between England and South America, the first to fly the South Atlantic solo from east to west, and the first to have made solo flights across both the North and South Atlantic.**

The first flights over Mount Everest were made on 3 April 1933 by the Marquess of Clydesdale in a Westland PV-3, and by Flt Lt D.F. McIntyre piloting a Westland Wallace, each with one passenger.

The Polish RWD 5*bis* SP-AJU, piloted by Capt Stanislaw Skarzynski, was flown from St Louis, Senegal, to Maceio, Brazil, from 7 to 8 May 1933, recording a non-stop flight of 20 h 30 min. The RWD 5*bis* is claimed to be **the lightest fixed-wing aircraft to have flown across the South Atlantic.**

Germany's first new post-war fighters, built to equip the secret Luftwaffe in the early 1930s, were the Heinkel He 51 and the Arado Ar 68. Many He 51s were built, in several versions, and 135 were operated by the Spanish and German air forces during the Spanish Civil War. Their useful life in this role was curtailed when the Republican forces started flying the Russian Polikarpov I-15. The He 51B-1, powered by a

750 hp BMW VI engine, had a maximum speed of 205 mph (330 km/h). The first prototype Ar 68 flew initially in 1933; the major production version was the Ar 68E which entered service from 1937, although small numbers of Ar 68Fs had entered service in 1935. Powered by a 690 hp Junkers Jumo 210D engine, the Ar 68E had a maximum speed of 208 mph (335 km/h).

The first multi-engined bombers of the clandestine German Luftwaffe to be used in combat were Junkers Ju 52/3m transports, converted as bombers. Each had a bucket-like retractable ventral gun position and were operated pending delivery of Dornier Do 17s and Heinkel He 111s. Some served in Spain with the German Legion Condor during the civil war.

The first aeroplane with retractable landing gear to be flown by the US Navy was the Grumman XFF-1 biplane fighter which, as the FF-1, began to enter service on 21 June 1933.

The Douglas DC-1 first flew on 1 July 1933 at Clover Field, Santa Monica, California. Only one was built, flying mainly in TWA insignia. After service during the Spanish Civil War, it was written-off following a take-off accident near Malaga, Spain, in December 1940. From it were developed the famous DC-2 and DC-3, which established the reputation of Douglas as an airliner manufacturer.

The first solo flight around the world was achieved by Wiley Post between 15 and 22 July 1933, when he flew his Lockheed Vega monoplane, *Winnie Mae*, from Floyd Bennett Field, New York, for a distance of 15 596 miles (25 099 km) in 7 d 18 h 49 min. His route was via Berlin, Moscow, Irkutsk and Alaska, back to New York. Post later pioneered the development of an early pressure suit during high altitude flights in *Winnie Mae*. He was killed in a crash in 1935, together with the famous comedian/philosopher Will Rogers.

Indian National Airways began **the first daily air service in India** on 1 December 1933, with inauguration of a passenger, freight and mail service between Calcutta and Dacca.

The first monoplane fighter with a fully enclosed cockpit and fully retractable landing gear to enter squadron service anywhere in the world

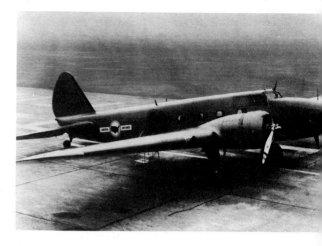

Boeing Model 247D, the true ancestor of the modern airliner.

was the Polikarpov I-16 Ishak ('Little Donkey'). The prototype was flown first on 31 December 1933, and deliveries of the Type I production fighter to Soviet squadrons began during the summer of 1934. The I-16 Type I was powered by a 450 hp M22 engine, had a top speed of 224 mph (360 km/h) at sea level, and was armed with two 7·62 mm ShKAS machine-guns.

The largest French bomber to enter service between the wars was the Farman F221 which, with its derivatives, was the mainstay of the French bomber force for several years. Production began in 1934 with 12 F221s. Later versions included the F222, F222/2, F223 and F2233. The F221 had a wing span of 118 ft 1½ in (36 m) and was powered by four 800 hp Gnome-Rhône 14 Kbrs engines. Maximum speed was 185 mph (297 km/h).

The impressive Farman F221 heavy bomber, featuring tandem-mounted engines and gun turrets.

The first RAF bomber incorporating a power-operated enclosed gun turret was the Boulton Paul Overstrand, 24 of which were built and entered service in 1934. Power was provided by two 580 hp Bristol Pegasus II M3 engines; a bomb load of 1600 lb (725 kg) could be carried.

A new world distance record in the FAI's C-2 seaplane Class of 2399 miles (3861 km) was set during 10–11 January 1934. It was recorded by six Consolidated P2Y-1 flying-boats making a non-stop formation flight from San Francisco, California, to Pearl Harbor, Hawaii.

First flown during April 1934, the Curtiss SOC Seagull served on every aircraft carrier, battleship and cruiser of the US Navy from 1935 to 1945. Designed as a scouting-observation biplane, the first production version was the SOC-1, armed with one 0·30 in forward-firing Browning machine-gun and with a similar gun in the rear cockpit. Two 116 lb bombs could also be carried. Following the original order for 135 SOC-1s, 40 SOC-2s and 130 SOC-3/SON-1s were built. Powered by a 600 hp Pratt & Whitney Wasp engine, the SOC-1 had a maximum speed of 165 mph (265 km/h). It remained in service longer than two types of aircraft built to replace it.

The most famous torpedo-bomber/reconnaissance aircraft ever built, the Fairey Swordfish (nicknamed 'Stringbag' because of its profusion of bracing struts and wires) was a 138 mph (222 km/h) biplane in a world of fast low-wing monoplanes. The prototype first flew on 17 April 1934 (as the TSR 2) and production Mk Is entered service with the FAA in July 1935. By the beginning of the Second World War, 13 squadrons were equipped with the type, 12 more being formed during the war. Among its epic victories were the attack on the Italian fleet at Taranto on 11 November 1940, and the crippling of the German battleship *Bismarck*. A total of 2391 Swordfish was built, the Mk I version being powered by a 690 hp Bristol Pegasus III M3 engine.

Beating by more than four days the England–Australia record set in 1930 by Amy Johnson, New Zealand airwoman Jean Batten, flying a de Havilland DH60M Moth (G-AARB), took 14 d 22 h 30 min for the flight from Lympne, Kent, to Darwin, Australia, during the period 8–23 May 1934.

The first regular internal airmail service in Great Britain was started by Highland Airways on 29 May 1934. The de Havilland Dragon G-ACCE, flown by E.E. Fresson, carried 6000 letters on this first flight from Inverness to Kirkwall, and the service operated thereafter on every weekday.

The first non-stop flight from Canada to England was made during 8–9 August 1934 by L.G. Reid and J.R. Ayling, flying the de Havilland Dragon (G-ACJM) *Trail of the Caribou*. Their flight, from Wasaga Beach, Ontario, to Heston, Middlesex, took 30 h 50 min.

The last biplane fighter to serve with the RAF and FAA was the Gloster Gladiator, first flown as the Gloster SS.37 prototype on 12 September 1934. It entered service from February 1937. As newly-built aircraft, the RAF received 444 and the FAA 60 as Sea Gladiators, serving up to and during the early war years. The Gladiator is probably best remembered for its defence of Malta, when four of these fighters fought off large numbers of Italian aircraft.

Mainstay of the Soviet Union's tactical bomber force in 1941, the Tupolev-Arkhangelsky SB-2, was first flown in SB-1 (ANT-40.1) prototype form on 7 October 1934.

The first 'trans-World' air race was the MacRobertson Race from England to Australia which started on 20 October 1934. In March 1933 the Governing Director of MacRobertson Confectionery Manufacturers of Melbourne, Sir MacPherson Robertson, offered £15000 in prize money for an air race to commemorate the centenary of the foundation of the State of Victoria. The race was won by one of three specially built de Havilland DH88 Comets. A two-seat low-wing monoplane, it was powered by two 230 hp Gipsy Six R engines, each driving a variable-pitch propeller of unusual design. Set in fine-pitch for take-off, they were moved to the coarse-pitch cruise setting by compressed air after the machine was airborne and at suitable height; they could not be recycled back to the fine-pitch setting. Charles W.A. Scott and Tom Campbell Black were first to cross the finishing line at Flemington Racecourse, Melbourne, in the DH88 *Grosvenor House* (G-ACSS), having completed the 11333 miles (18239 km) from

Mildenhall, Suffolk, in 70 h 54 min 18 s at an average speed of 158·9 mph (255·7 km/h). Second home in the Handicap Race was, surprisingly, the Douglas DC-2 *Uiver* (PH-AJU) passenger transport aircraft of the Dutch airline KLM, flown by K.D. Parmentier and J.J. Moll.

The first flight by an aeroplane from Australia to the United States was made in the Lockheed Altair *Lady Southern Cross* by Sir Charles Kingsford Smith accompanied by Capt P.G. Taylor. Taking off from Brisbane on 22 October 1934, their flight ended successfully at Oakland, California, on 4 November after staging via Fiji and Hawaii.

One of the most enduring speed records was that set on 23 October 1934 by Italian Francesco Agello flying a Macchi MC72 seaplane. Still unbeaten in 1983, this world speed record of 440·683 mph (709·209 km/h) in FAI sub-class C-2 was achieved in the Macchi seaplane which had been intended to compete in the Schneider Trophy Contest of 1931.

The first regular weekly airmail service between Britain and Australia, from London to Brisbane via Karachi and Singapore, began on 8 December 1934. The participating airlines were Imperial Airways, Indian Trans-Continental Airways and Qantas Empire Airways. Mail which left London on 8 December reached Brisbane on 21 December.

The first woman in the United States to pilot an airmail transport aircraft on regular scheduled operations was Helen Richey. Her first scheduled flight, in a Ford Tri-Motor from Washington, DC, to Detroit, Michigan, was flown on 31 December 1934.

The Japanese Navy's last carrier-based biplane fighter, the Nakajima A4N1, began to enter service during 1935. Powered by a 770 hp Nakajima Hikari I engine it had a maximum speed of 219 mph (354 km/h), and about 300 examples were built. They first saw combat in 1937, during the Sino–Japanese war, operating from the aircraft carrier *Hosho*.

The first solo flight by a woman from Honolulu, Hawaii, to the United States was made by Amelia Earhart during 11–12 January 1935. Flying a Lockheed Vega, she landed at Oakland, California, after a flight lasting 18 h 16 min.

The existence of the Luftwaffe, created by Hitler's Germany, was announced officially on 9 March 1935.

The flying-boat produced in the greatest numbers was the Consolidated PBY Catalina. Excluding production in Russia, 1196 Catalina flying-boats and 944 amphibians were built, serving with the air forces and airlines of more than 25 nations. The prototype was first flown on 28 March 1935, and the initial production version had a maximum speed of 177 mph (284 km/h).

A privately-sponsored civil aircraft that led to one of Britain's main bomber types of the early war years was the Bristol 142. Ordered by Lord Rothermere of the *Daily Mail* as a six-passenger high-speed transport aircraft, at a cost of around £18 500, the 142 was flown first on 12 April 1935. Powered by two 650 hp Bristol Mercury engines, it proved to have a maximum speed of 307 mph (494 km/h). This was some 80 mph (128 m/h) faster than the RAF's latest fighter, the Gloster Gauntlet. On seeing that the Air Ministry was suitably impressed with his aircraft, Lord Rothermere gave the 142 to the nation and named it *Britain First*. A bomber derivative was soon on the production line as the Bristol Blenheim.

The first through passenger air service between London and Brisbane, Australia, was inaugurated on 13 April 1935 by Imperial Airways and Qantas Empire Airways. The single fare for the 12 754 mile (20 525 km) route was £195. However, owing to heavy stage bookings, no through passengers were carried on the inaugural flight. The journey took $12\frac{1}{4}$ days.

The first airline flight from the American mainland to Hawaii was made by a *Clipper* flying-boat of Pan American Airways during 16-17 April 1935. Taking off from Alameda, California, this was the airline's proving flight over this route, **representing the first stage in a transpacific route from the US to the Philippines.**

The first German monoplane fighter into squadron service with a fully enclosed cockpit and fully retractable landing gear was the Messerschmitt Bf 109B-1. The prototype Bf 109V-1 (D-IABI) was first flown on 28 May 1935, powered by a 695 hp British Rolls-Royce Kestrel V engine. The first production Bf 109B-1s were delivered to Jagdgeschwader 2 'Richthofen' in the spring of 1937, and this version was the first of the series to become operational in Spain with the Legion Condor during the civil war. The B-1 model was powered by a 635 hp Junkers Jumo 210D engine, had a top speed of 292 mph (470 km/h) at 13 100 ft (4000 m), and was armed with three 7·92 mm MG 17 machine-guns.

The first French monoplane fighter into squadron service with a fully enclosed cockpit and fully retractable landing gear was the Morane–Saulnier M-S 406. The M-S 405, from which the series was derived, first flew on 8 August 1935, and was **the first French fighter aircraft able to exceed a speed of 250 mph (402 km/h) in level flight.** The first production M-S 406 (N2-66) flew for the first time on 29 January 1939, and by 1 April 1939 a total of 27 had been delivered to the French Air Force. Powered by an 850 hp Hispano–Suiza HS 12Y-31 engine, the MS-406 had a maximum level speed of 304 mph (490 km/h) at 14 700 ft (4480 m), and was armed with one 20 mm HS 59 cannon and two 7·5 mm MAC machine-guns.

The first American monoplane fighter into squadron service with a fully enclosed cockpit and fully retractable landing gear (into fairings) was the Seversky P-35, the prototype of which was evaluated at Wright Field during August 1935. The production model, of which deliveries began in July 1937, was powered by a 950 hp Pratt & Whitney R-1830-9 engine. It had a top speed of 281 mph (452 km/h) at 10 000 ft (3050 m), and was armed with one 0·5 in and one 0·3 in machine-gun.

The Italian government declared war on Abyssinia on 3 October 1935, starting a campaign which was to last until 5 May 1936. The main Italian aircraft used in this conflict were the Caproni Ca 74, Ca 101, Ca 111 and Ca 133 bombers, and the Fiat CR20, CR30 and IMAM Ro 37 fighters.

The original British Airways was formed on 1 October 1935 from Hillman Airways, Spartan Air Lines and United Airways. It was to be merged with Imperial Airways in 1940 to form British Overseas Airways Corporation (BOAC).

The first British monoplane fighter into squadron service with a fully enclosed cockpit and fully retractable landing gear was the Hawker Hurricane. It was also **the RAF's first fighter able to exceed a speed of 300 mph (483 km/h), and the first of its eight-gun monoplane fighters.** The prototype was flown for the first time on 6 November 1935, and initial deliveries of production aircraft were made to No 111 Squadron at Northolt, Middlesex, during December 1937. The Hurricane I was powered by a 1030 hp Rolls-Royce Merlin II or III engine, had a top speed of 322 mph (518 km/h) at 20 000 ft (6100 m), and was armed with eight 0·303 in Browning machine-guns.

The first solo air crossing of the South Atlantic by a woman was accomplished by New Zealand's Jean Batten, flying a Percival Gull from Lympne, Kent, to Natal, Brazil, via Thies, Senegal, during the period 11–13 November 1935.

On 22 November 1935 and 21 October 1936, Pan American Airways inaugurated its first trans-Pacific mail service and passenger service respectively. The route was between San Francisco and Manila in the Philippines, via Honolulu, Midway Island, Wake Island and Guam, and took about six days. The aircraft used was the Martin 130 *China Clipper*, which was a high-wing monoplane flying-boat, powered by four 830 hp Pratt & Whitney Twin Wasp engines. Maximum cruising speed was 163 mph (262 km/h); range was 3200 miles (5150 km), and accommodation was for up to 43 passengers by day or 18 in a night sleeper layout.

The first flight of the Douglas DC-3 prototype was made on 17 December 1935, by Carl A. Cover from Clover Field, Santa Monica. A development of the DC-1 (Douglas Commercial No 1) and DC-2 the DC-3 first entered service with American Airlines. Its inaugural passenger-carrying service was from Chicago, Illinois, to Glendale, California, on 4 July 1936. Certainly the most famous airliner in aviation history, large numbers remain in civil and military service in 1983, 48 years after the prototype's first flight.

The first helicopter to fly successfully, although it was never developed beyond the prototype stage, was that built by Louis Breguet and flown in 1936. It featured contra-rotating rotors, an open framework fuselage, an aeroplane-type tail unit and wide-track main landing gear with additional nose and tail wheels. This helicopter flew for over an hour, during which it covered 27 miles (43·5 km).

The first entirely successful helicopter was the German Focke-Wulf Fw 61.

The RAF'S most famous and now legendary single-seat fighter of the Second World War was the Supermarine Spitfire, first flown as the Supermarine Type 300 prototype (K5054) on 5 March 1936. Its superb lines benefitted from the experience which its designer, R. J. Mitchell, had gained during the development of racing seaplanes to compete in the Schneider Trophy Contests; its power plant derived also from the Schneider Contests, its Merlin engine a direct descendant of the Rolls-Royce 'R' that had brought Great Britain permanent possession of the coveted Trophy in 1931.

The first case in Britain, involving the prosecution and punishment of an airline passenger for smoking on board an aircraft in flight, was heard at Croydon, Surrey, on 17 March 1936. The passenger, who had travelled on an Imperial Airways Paris–London flight aboard the HP45 *Heracles*, was fined the sum of £10.

First moves to institute Shadow Factories in Britain were made in April 1936, initially to establish aircraft engine production by motor car engine manufacturers. The scheme was later adopted for the production of aircraft.

The first work in Germany on the development of an aircraft turbojet engine began at Heinkel's Marienehe plant on 15 April 1936, when the German engineer Dr Hans Joachim Pabst von Ohain and Dipl Ing Max Hahn began work on such a power plant at the instigation of Ernst Heinkel.

The original British Airways airline began using Gatwick Airport, Surrey, as its operating base on 17 May 1936.

The first entirely successful helicopter in the world was the Focke-Wulf Fw 61 twin-rotor helicopter designed by Professor Heinrich Focke during 1933–34. The first prototype Fw 61VI (D-EBVU) made its first free flight on 26 June 1936 and was powered by a 160 hp Siemens-Halske Sh 14A engine. This aircraft, flown by Ewald Rohlfs in June 1937, established a world's closed-circuit distance record for helicopters of 76·025 miles (122·35 km) and a helicopter endurance record of 1 h 20 min 49 s. On other occasions it set an altitude record of 11 243 ft (3427 m) and a speed record of 76 mph (122 km/h). It gave a flying demonstration in the Berlin Deutschland-Halle during 1938 in the hands of the famous German woman test pilot Hanna Reitsch.

The first Short C-Type Empire flying-boat *Canopus* (G-ADHL) made its first flight on 3 July 1936 with John Lankester Parker, Short's Chief Test Pilot, at the controls. Its first flight with Imperial Airways was made on 30 October 1936. The Empire 'boats represented the last word in luxury air travel before the Second World War and, as their name implied, were flown on the Empire routes to Africa and the Far East. When 28 of these aircraft were ordered by Imperial Airways before the first aircraft was built, it **then represented one of the biggest gambles in commercial aviation history.**

Frenchman Henri Mignet's diminutive Pou du Ciel (Flying Flea), **virtually the first aircraft intended for amateur construction,** was the subject of an international air race. With several having been homebuilt and flown, an International Flying Flea Challenge Trophy Race was held at Ramsgate, Kent, on 3 August 1936 and won by Frenchman Edouard Bret.

The first large-scale military airlift began on 21 July 1936, when Junkers Ju 52/3m bomber/transports were used over a period of about six weeks to ferry some 7350 Nationalist troops,

Short C-Type Empire flying-boat Canopus *being refuelled at Dar-es-Salaam.*

with their artillery and other equipment, from Morocco to Spain at the beginning of the Spanish Civil War.

Formation of the Royal Air Force Volunteer Reserve was announced by the British government on 30 July 1936. It was to play a significant role in reinforcement of the Royal Air Force by the time of the outbreak of the Second World War.

The Spanish Republican Air Force mustered 214 obsolete aircraft at the outbreak of the Civil War. Additionally, the government had at its disposal 40 civil types of various designs. Between 1937 and 1939, 55 aircraft were built in the Republican zone. Aircraft despatched to Spain by friendly nations totalled 1947, of which 1409 came from Russia. The others included 70 Dewoitine D371, D500 and D510 fighters, Loire-Nieuport 46s and 15 S510 fighters from France; 72 aircraft, not including any fighters, from the USA; 72 aircraft from the Netherlands; 57 from Britain; and 47 from Czechoslovakia. Of these, some 400 are thought to have been destroyed other than in aerial combat, and 1520 were claimed shot down by Nationalist, German and Italian pilots.

The first Russian aircraft to enter combat in Spain in support of the Republican forces were the Polikarpov I-16 Type 6 fighters of General Kamanin's expeditionary command based at Santander. By September 1936, 105 of these aircraft had arrived in Spain and some 200 pilots and 2000 other personnel had also reached there from the Soviet Union. The I-16 first entered combat on 5 November 1936 and eventually a total of 475 were supplied. From March 1937 they were gathered in one formation designated Fighter Group 31, comprising seven squadrons of 15 aircraft each. More numerous was the I-15 biplane fighter, inferior to both the Fiat CR32 and Messerschmitt Bf 109, and no fewer than 415 were believed to have been lost in combat or on the ground. The most numerous Republican bomber type, the Soviet Tupolev SB-2, also fared badly; of 210 supplied, 178 were lost.

German intervention in the Spanish Civil War began in late July 1936 with the arrival of 20 Ju 52/3m bomber/transports, six Heinkel He 51 fighter biplanes and 85 volunteer air and ground crew. From this small beginning originated the Legion Condor, a balanced force of between 40 and 50 fighters, about the same number of multi-engined bombers, and about 100 miscellaneous ground-attack, reconnaissance and liaison aircraft, whose first C.-in-C. was Gen-Maj Sperrle. Volunteers from the ranks of the Luftwaffe served in rotation, to ensure the maximum dissemination of combat experience. Many of the major combat designs upon which Germany was to rely in the first half of the Second World War were first evaluated under combat conditions in Spain; the Heinkel He 111 bomber, Dornier Do 17 reconnaissance-bomber, Messerschmitt Bf 109 fighter, and the Henschel Hs 123 and Junkers Ju 87 ground attack aircraft were prominent. The contribution of the Legion Condor to the eventual Nationalist victory was considerable, but more important were the inferences drawn by Luftwaffe Staff planners. Valid lessons learned in Spain included the value of the dive-bomber in hampering enemy communications, and the effects of ground-strafing by fighters in the exploitation of a breakthrough by land forces. Less realistic was the impression

gained of the relative invulnerability of unescorted bombers and dive-bombers, an impression based on the lack of sophisticated fighter resistance. In the field of fighter tactics, and in terms of combat experience by her fighter pilots, the Spanish Civil War put Germany at least a year ahead of her international rivals.

Italian intervention in the Spanish Civil War began in August 1936 with the arrival of 12 Fiat CR32 biplane fighters. CR32s were later to become the Nationalists' main fighters, superseding the slower Heinkel He 51s. The eventual strength of the Italian Aviacion del Tercio in Spain was some 730 aircraft, all supplied by Italy and including Fiat CR32s, SM81s, SM79s, BR20s, R037s, Ba65s and a squadron of Fiat G50s. Of these, 86 aircraft were lost on operations and 100 from other causes, and 175 flying personnel were killed. A total of 903 enemy aircraft were claimed destroyed in aerial combat, and a further 40 on the ground.

The first Japanese Army Air Force low-wing monoplane fighter, and first with an enclosed cockpit, was the Nakajima Ki-27. The first prototype made its initial flight on 15 October 1936, and production aircraft entered combat in Manchuria during 1938. Powered by a 710 hp Nakajima Ha 1b engine, the Ki-27 had fixed landing gear and a maximum speed of 286 mph (460 km/h). In addition to its two 7·7 mm machine-guns, it could carry a bombload of 220 lb (100 kg).

The first intensive air bombardment of a city during the Spanish Civil War occurred on 6 November 1936, when Nationalist attacks were made on Madrid in attempts to dislodge Republican troops.

The first Imperial Airways all-air trans-Mediterranean service was flown on 12 January 1937 by the C-class flying-boat *Centaurus* as the final leg on an India-UK service.

The first monoplane to enter service with the Fleet Air Arm was the Blackburn Skua dive-bomber, of which the prototype was first flown on 9 February 1937. Deliveries of production aircraft began in November 1938; a total of 165 was built, these remaining in service until 1941.

The first aircraft turbojet engine in the world was bench-tested for the first time on 12 April

1937. A gas-turbine engine had been built previously but this, designed by Frank Whittle (later Sir Frank), was the first intended specifically for aircraft propulsion. In March 1938 Whittle received an Air Ministry contract for a production engine, and on 15 May 1941 the Gloster E.28/39, powered by this engine, took off at Cranwell flown by Flt Lt P.E.G. Sayer. **This was the first British turbojet powered aeroplane.**

The first aircraft with a completely successful pressurised cabin was the Lockheed XC-35. Built for research at high altitude, it was flown for the first time on 7 May 1937.

The inaugural flight of Britain's Empire Air Mail Programme was made on 29 June 1937, when the Imperial Airways C-class flying-boat *Centurion* (G-ADVE) left Southampton with 3500 lb (1588 kg) of unsurcharged mail.

The first two-seater fighter with a power-operated four-gun turret to serve with the RAF, the Boulton Paul Defiant, was first flown in prototype form on 11 August 1937.

The first North Atlantic trials involving the use of depot ships were started by Deutsche Luft-Hansa on 15 August 1937. These vessels were equipped to retrieve, refuel and catapult-launch four-engined Blohm und Voss Ha 139 seaplanes which had been developed specially for this purpose.

The first fully automatic landing by an aeroplane was made on 23 August 1937 at Wright Field, Ohio. This was accomplished by on-board equipment, without assistance from the pilot, and without radio control from the ground.

The first monoplane fighter to equip a US Navy squadron was the Brewster F2A Buffalo, flown for the first time in XF2A-1 prototype form during December 1937.

The first airmail and freight service between the United States and New Zealand was inaugurated on 23 December 1937 by the Pan American flying-boat *Samoa Clipper.*

The first Italian monoplane fighter into service with a fully enclosed cockpit and fully retractable landing gear was the Macchi C200 Saetta ('Lightning'). First single-seat fighter designed by Dr Mario Castoldi, the prototype was flown first on 24 December 1937. Deliveries of production aircraft began in October 1939, and these were powered by the 870 hp Fiat A74RC38 radial engine, giving the C200 a maximum speed of 313 mph (505 km/h) at 15 750 ft (4800 m). Armament consisted of two 12·7 mm Breda-SAFAT machine-guns.

The first flight refuelling test with a C-class Empire flying-boat of Imperial Airways was carried out under the supervision of Sir Alan Cobham, the founder of Flight Refuelling Ltd. The tanker used in these tests, started on 20 January 1938, was the Armstrong Whitworth AW 23 bomber/transport prototype which had been loaned to Flight Refuelling by the Air Ministry.

Concerned about a need to speed the re-equipment of the Royal Air Force, **a first British purchasing mission left for the United States** on 20 April 1938, under the leadership of Air Cdre A.H. Harris.

The Heinkel HeS 3B turbojet engine designed by Pabst von Ohain was flown for the first time during June 1938, a Heinkel He 118 serving as a testbed aircraft.

The first commercial use of composite aeroplanes in the world occurred during 21-22 July 1938, when the Short S21 *Maia* flying-boat and the Short S20 *Mercury* seaplane took off from Foynes, Ireland, the S20 upper component then separating and flying the North Atlantic nonstop to Montreal, Canada, with a load of mail and newspapers. It covered 2930 miles (4715 km) in 20 h 20 min, at an average speed of 140 mph (225 km/h). Numerous composite flights and separations were carried out and the pair of aircraft continued to operate on the Southampton to Alexandria air route until the outbreak of the Second World War. When launched from its 'mother-plane' *Maia*, the seaplane *Mercury* carried sufficient fuel to fly 5995·5 miles (9652 km) from Dundee, Scotland, to the Orange River, South Africa. In doing so, on 6-8 October 1938, it established a record that has never been beaten.

The first flight of a Danish airliner to the United Kingdom was made on 28 July 1938, the inaugural service made by the Focke-Wulf Fw 200

Caproni 161bis high-altitude biplane.

Condor *Dania* (OY-DAM) flying between Copenhagen and Croydon.

The last biplane to serve with the Fleet Air Arm was the Supermarine Sea Otter, first flown in prototype form on 23 September 1938. Production continued until July 1946, by which time 290 had been built, and the Sea Otter remained in service until the 1950s.

The greatest altitude ever achieved by a piston-engined aircraft is 56046 ft (17 083 m), set by a Caproni 161*bis* on 22 October 1938.

The largest airliner built for Imperial Airways between the wars was the Armstrong Whitworth Ensign, which entered service on the London–Paris route on 26 October 1938. Powered originally by four 850 hp Tiger engines, the Ensign was later re-engined with four 950 hp Wright Cyclones. Accommodation was for 27–40 passengers, according to the range of operation.

A new world distance record was established from 5 to 7 November 1938 by two Vickers Wellesleys of the RAF's Long Range Flight. Captained by Sqn Ldr R.G. Kellett and Flt Lt A.N. Combe, the aircraft landed at Darwin, Australia, after completing a flight of 7158·5 miles (11 520 km) from Ismailia, Egypt.

The first airliner with a pressurised cabin to enter service was the Boeing Model 307 Stratoliner, the prototype of which was flown for the first time on 31 December 1938. Derived from the B-17 Flying Fortress bomber, it was advertised as the first airliner to fly above most bad weather conditions because of its pressurised cabin. The first version to enter service, with Trans-Continental and Western Air in April 1940, was the Model 307B, accommodating 33 passengers.

Non-aviation inventions of the period

Insulin Isolated by Dr Frederick Banting and Charles Best in 1921, Toronto, Canada.

Television Demonstrated by John Logie Baird in 1926, London.

Antibiotics Penicillin discovered by Dr Alexander Fleming in 1928, London.

Frozen food Developed by Clarence Birdseye and tested in 1930, Springfield, Massachusetts.

Fluorescent lighting Demonstrated by the General Electric Company in 1935, Nela Park, Ohio.

Photocopier Successful copier developed by Chester Carlson in 1938, Pittsford, New York.

Progressive world absolute speed records achieved by man in the atmosphere

mph	km/h	Pilot	Nationality	Aircraft	Location of achievement	Date	
171·01	275·22	Sadi Lecointe	France	Nieuport-Delage 29		7 Feb	1920
176·12	283·43	Jean Casale	France	Blériot monoplane		28 Feb	1920
181·83	292·63	Baron de Romanet	France	Spad biplane		9 Oct	1920
184·51	296·94	Sadi Lecointe	France	Nieuport-Delage 29		10 Oct	1920
187·95	302·48	Sadi Lecointe	France	Nieuport–Delage 29		20 Oct	1920
191·98	308·96	Baron de Romanet	France	Spad biplane		4 Nov	1920
194·49	313·00	Sadi Lecointe	France	Nieuport-Delage 29		12 Dec	1920
205·20	330·23	Sadi Lecointe	France	Nieuport-Delage 29	Villesauvage, France	20 Sept	1922
211·89	341·00	Sadi Lecointe	France	Nieuport-Delage 29	Villesauvage, France	21 Sept	1922
222·93	358·77	Brig Gen W.A. Mitchell	USA	Curtiss HS D-12	Detroit, Michigan, USA	13 Oct	1922
233·00	374·95	Sadi Lecointe	France	Nieuport-Delage 29		15 Feb	1923
236·54	380·67	Lt R.L. Maughan	USA	Curtiss R-6		29 Mar	1923
255·40	411·04	Lt A. Brown	USA	Curtiss HS D-12	Mitchell Field, NY, USA	2 Nov	1923
267·16	429·96	Lt Alford J. Williams	USA	Curtiss R-2 C-1	Mitchell Field, NY, USA	4 Nov	1923
278·47	448·15	Adj Chef A. Bonnet	France	Ferbois V-2	Istres, France	11 Dec	1924
297·83	479·21	Maj Mario de Bernardi	Italy	Macchi M-52	Venice, Italy	4 Nov	1927
318·57	512·69	Maj Mario de Bernardi	Italy	Macchi M-52bis	Venice, Italy	30 Mar	1928
406·94	654·90	Flt Lt G.H. Stainforth AFC	GB	Supermarine S6B	Ryde, IoW, England	29 Sept	1931
423·76	681·97	Warrant Officer F. Agello	Italy	Macchi-Castoldi 72	Lago di Garda, Italy	10 Apr	1934
440·60	709·07	Lt F. Agello	Italy	Macchi-Castoldi 72	Lago di Garda, Italy	23 Oct	1934

Progressive world absolute height records achieved by man in the atmosphere

ft	m	Pilot	Nationality	Aircraft	Location	Date	
33113	10093	Maj R.W. Schroeder	USA	Lepere	Dayton, USA	27 Feb	1920
34508	10518	Lt J.A. MacReady	USA	Lepere	Dayton, USA	18 Sept	1921
35242	10742	Sadi Lecointe	France	Nieuport	Villacoublay, France	5 Sept	1923
36565	11145	Sadi Lecointe	France	Nieuport	Issy-les-Moulineaux France	30 Oct	1923
38418	11710	Lt C.C. Champion	USA	Wright Apache	Washington, USA	25 July	1927
39140	11930	Lt Apollo Soucek	USA	Wright Apache	USA	8 May	1929
41795	12739	W. Neuenhofen	Germany	Junkers W34	Dessau	26 May	1929
43166	13157	Lt Apollo Soucek	USA	Wright Apache	Washington, USA	4 June	1930
43976	13404	Capt C.F. Uwins	GB	Vickers Vespa	Filton, England	16 Sept	1932
44820	13661	G. Lemoine	France	Potez 50	Villacoublay, France	28 Sept	1933
47352	14433	Cdr R. Donati	Italy	Caproni 161	Rome, Italy	11 Apr	1934
4 609	14942	G. Détré	France	Potez 50	Villacoublay, France	14 Aug	1936

The fastest operational aircraft in the world is the USAF's Lockheed SR-71A strategic reconnaissance aircraft, capable of speeds beyond Mach 3.

In the 1960s Britain intended to develop a supersonic attack and reconnaissance aircraft for the RAF, as the BAC TSR 2. Though the single flying prototype proved highly successful, the project was cancelled before production got underway.

The world's first wide-body jet airliner was the Boeing Model 747, the first example of which is seen here in the company of a small chase plane to observe the flight. The 747 is the only airliner to offer seating for more than 500 passengers.

The largest American aeroplane is the USAF's Lockheed C-5A Galaxy transport, with a wing span of 222 ft 8½ in (67·88 m), a length of 247 ft 10 in (75·54 m), and weighing 769 000 lb (348 810 kg).

The most successful collaborative European civil aircraft projects resulted in the Airbus A300 and A310 airliners, of which many hundreds have been ordered worldwide. This A300B4-103 is operated by Korean Air Lines.

The Gates Learjet 24 is just one of several series of Learjet executive twin-jets, which are among the fastest aircraft of their type.

The latest helicopter from the British company Westland Helicopters is the Westland 30, seen here flying in support of a rig at sea.

BAe/Aérospatiale Concorde, the world's only operational supersonic airliner.

The first flying-boat to exceed Mach 1 was the Convair Sea Dart experimental fighter.

The world's first V/STOL combat aircraft was the British Aerospace Harrier. The first V/STOL aircraft to prove itself in combat was its naval counterpart, the Sea Harrier (as seen here).

One of the newest airliners available for purchase is the Boeing Model 767, a twin-turbofan medium-range transport with seating for up to 289 passengers.

Martin Marietta X-24A lifting-body research aircraft.

Britain's, West Germany's and Italy's first 'swing wing' combat aircraft is the multi-national Panavia Tornado, seen here in anti-shipping role with the German Marineflieger.

Space Shuttle Orbiter Columbia
lifts off on mission STS-4.

*Lunar Roving Vehicle used by
American astronauts on the Moon.*

Progressive world absolute height records achieved by man in the atmosphere

ft	m	Pilot	Nationality	Aircraft	Location	Date
49 944	15 223	Sqn Ldr S.R. Swain	GB	Bristol 138	Farnborough, England	28 Sept 1936
51 362	15 655	Lt Col M. Pezzi	Italy	Caproni 161	Montecelio, Italy	8 May 1937
53 937	16 440	Flt Lt M.J. Adam	GB	Bristol 138	Farnborough, England	30 June 1937
56 046	17 083	Lt Col M. Pezzi	Italy	Caproni 161 *bis*	Montecelio, Italy	22 Oct 1938

Progressive world absolute distance records achieved by man in the atmosphere

miles	km	Pilot/s	Nationality	Aircraft	Location of start	Date
1967	3166	Capts L. Arrachart and H. Lemaître	France	Breguet 19	Etampes, France	3–4 Feb 1925
2675	4305	Capt L. Arrachart and Adj Arrachart	France	Potez 550	Le Bourget, France	26–27 June 1926
2930	4715·9	Capt L. Girier and Lt Dordilly	France	Breguet 19	Le Bourget, France	14–15 July 1926
3215	5174	Lt Challe and Capt Weiser	France	Breguet 19	Le Bourget, France	31 Aug–1 Sept 1926
3353	5396	Capts D. Costes and J. Rignot	France	Breguet 19	Le Bourget, France	28–29 Oct 1926
3609·5	5809	Charles Lindbergh	USA	Ryan monoplane	New York to Paris	20–21 May 1927
3911	6294	C.D. Chamberlin and A. Levine	USA	Bellanca	New York, USA	4–6 June 1927
4466·6	7188·25	A. Ferrarin and D. Prete	Italy	Savoia-Marchetti S64	Rome, Italy	3–5 July 1928
4912	7905	Capt D. Costes and M. Bellonte	France	Breguet 19	Le Bourget, France	27–29 Sept 1929
5011	8065	R.N. Boardman and J. Polando	USA	Wright J6	Brooklyn, USA	28–30 July 1931
5309	8544	Sqn Ldr O. Gayford and Flt Lt G. Nicholetts	GB	Fairey Special monoplane	Cranwell, England	6–8 Feb 1933
5657	9104	Rossi and P. Codes	France	Blériot Zapata	New York, USA	5–7 Aug 1933
6306	10148	Col M. Gromov, Ing S. Daniline and Cmdt A. Youmachev	USSR	ANT-25	Moscow to San Jacinto	12–14 July 1937
6658·3	10715·5	Flt Lt H.A.V. Hogan and Mosson	GB	Vickers Wellesley	Ismailia to Koepang	5–7 Nov 1938
7158·4	11 520·4	Sqn Ldr R. Kellett and Flt Lt Gething	GB	Vickers Wellesley	Ismailia to Darwin	5–7 Nov 1938
7158·4	11 520·4	Flt Lt A.N. Combe and Bornett	GB	Vickers Wellesley	Ismailia to Darwin	5–7 Nov 1938

Second World War

By 1939 civil aviation was growing rapidly, and new generation transport aircraft, like the Boeing Model 247 and Douglas DC-3 monoplanes, were beginning to demonstrate that air travel could be safe and fast. The first links had been forged across the world's oceans, with design emphasis placed on the development of long-range flying-boats for operation over such routes. This then seemed fairly logical on the basis that seven-tenths of the earth's surface is covered by water, as well as by a long-held, but completely erroneous, belief that the surface of water would be more relenting than earth or rock in the event of a crash-landing.

Among the champions of water-based aircraft for world travel was the Frenchman, Jacques Schneider, son of a wealthy armaments manufacturer. In December 1912 he had offered a trophy valued at £1000 for annual international competition, plus prize money of £1000 annually for three consecutive years. Thus was born *La Coupe d'Aviation Maritime Jacques Schneider*—the Schneider Trophy—intended to spur the development of fast and reliable water-based aircraft. Its direct effect on the improvement of flying-boats was virtually nil, but in the search for more and more speed over the period from 1913 to 1931, new and important high-power inline aircraft engines were to emerge from the manufacturers of competing nations. These came, in particular, from America, Britain and Italy, the three nations that dominated the contests from 1919. At the same time, airframe construction had benefited from the need to design sleek, streamlined and drag-free structures.

Thus, with the outbreak of the Second World War in September 1939, major aircraft manufacturers had learned how to build robust monoplane structures and had available the powerplant to give them high performance. In the pages of this section can be found the military and civil developments that were squeezed into a mere six years.

The first helicopter to go into limited production was the Focke-Achgelis Fa 223. The experimental Focke-Wulf Fw 61 (q.v.) was not exploited commercially, being too heavy structurally to carry a payload. Instead, a commercially developed derivative, the Fa 266 Hornisse, appeared in 1939 as a prototype six-seat civil transport helicopter. **This was the first real trans-**

Mitsubishi A6M Zero-Sen, taxiing out on a Philippine airfield for a bombing mission. (US National Archives)

gear to enter squadron service was the Mitsubishi A6M2, known popularly as the Zero-Sen. The A6M1 prototype was flown first on 1 April 1939, and the '12-Shi fighter project', as it had been known, was adopted officially by the Imperial Japanese Navy on 31 July 1940, under the designation A6M2 Type o Carrier Fighter Model 11. The Zero was first used operationally on 19 August 1940, when a formation of 12 aircraft, led by Lt Tamotsu Yokoyama, escorted a force of bombers attacking Chungking. The A6M2 was powered by a 950hp Nakajima NK1C Sakae 12 engine, had a top speed of 332mph (534km/h) at 16570ft (5050m), and was armed with two 20mm Type 90 cannon (licence-built Oerlikons) and two 7·7mm Type 97 machineguns. Two 30kg bombs could be carried on an underfuselage rack.

The fastest aircraft to fly before the Second World War was a special development of the German Messerschmitt Bf 109 single-seat fighter. Bf 109s in Luftwaffe service at the outbreak of war included B, C, D and E series aircraft, the last with a maximum speed of 354mph

port helicopter. The Fa 266 first made a free flight in August 1940 and was redesignated Fa 223 Drache, by which time it had changed into a military helicopter. By 1942 the Fa 223 was ready for operational trials although only two examples had flown because of Allied bombing. Because of the bombing, the factory had been moved from Bremen to Laupheim and eventually finished up in Berlin. By the end of the war only a small number of helicopters had flown, three of which were used for transport duties by Luft-Transportstaffel 40.

One of the most unusual fighter aircraft to serve with the US Army Air Force during the Second World War was Lockheed's P-38 Lightning. Of distinctive twin-boom configuration, it was first flown in XP-38 prototype form on 27 January 1939.

The first Japanese monoplane fighter with a fully enclosed cockpit and fully retractable landing

The Messerschmitt Me 209 was designed only for record breaking and had a small airframe with very clean lines.

Pilot of the Me 209 for the world speed record of 26 April 1939 was Flugkapitän Fritz Wendel, here being congratulated by Willy Messerschmitt.

Focke-Wulf Fw 190, one of the classic German fighters of the Second World War. (US National Archives)

(570 km/h). However, on 26 April 1939, a much-changed Me 209 (Bf 109R) flew at Augsburg, Germany, at an FAI accredited speed of 469·22 mph (755·138 km/h), setting a record that was not beaten by another piston-engined aeroplane until 30 years later.

One of the Soviet Union's outstanding combat aircraft of the Second World War was the Petlyakov Pe-2, the VI-100 prototype of which was first flown on 7 May 1939. In production form, more than 11000 were built; they formed the backbone of Soviet tactical operations on the Eastern Front, but were used also in fighter, reconnaissance and trainer roles.

The first regular airmail service over the North Atlantic began on 20 May 1939 with the departure of the Pan American Airways' Boeing 314 *Yankee Clipper* (NC18603) from New York.

One of the classic German fighter aircraft of the Second World War, the Focke-Wulf Fw 190, flew for the first time on 1 June 1939. Entering service with the Luftwaffe in August 1941, Fw 190s were engaged in combat with Spitfires for the first time

on 27 September 1941. Their first major deployment was to provide an air umbrella for the German battleships *Gneisenau* and *Scharnhorst* and the cruiser *Prinz Eugen* during their 'Channel-dash' on 12–13 February 1942.

The first scheduled air mail service to be flown by a rotary-wing aircraft was recorded in the United States on 6 July 1939, by a Kellet KD-1B autogyro in service with Eastern Air Lines.

The first aircraft in the world to fly solely on the power of a turbojet engine was the German Heinkel He 178, which made its first true flight at Heinkel's Marienehe airfield on 27 August 1939. It was powered by a Heinkel HeS 3b engine designed by Dr Pabst von Ohain.

The Polish fighter most widely used at the time of the German invasion in September 1939 was the PZL P11, of which 128 were on strength on 1 September 1939. They equipped Nos 111, 112, 113 and 114 Squadrons of the 1st Air Regiment based at Warsaw, Nos 121 and 122 Squadrons of the 2nd Air Regiment based at Krakow, Nos 131 and 132 Squadrons of the 3rd Air Regiment at Poznan, Nos 141 and 142 Squadrons of the 4th Air Regiment at Torun, No 152 Squadron of the 5th Air Regiment in the Wilno/Lida area, and No 161 Squadron of the 6th Air Regiment based at Lwow. The P11/I prototype was flown for the first time during August 1931, and the first production P11as entered service in 1934. Definitive version was the P11c, powered by a PZL-built Mercury VI S2 radial engine of 645 hp, giving it a maximum level speed of 242 mph (390 km/h) at 18 000 ft (5485 m). Armament consisted of four 7·7 mm machine-guns, and two 12 kg fragmentation bombs could be carried beneath the wings.

The greatest single-day losses suffered by the Luftwaffe during the Polish campaign were those of 3 September 1939, when 22 German aircraft were destroyed. These comprised four Dornier Do 17s, two Fieseler Fi 156s, one Heinkel He 59, two Heinkel He 111s, one Henschel Hs 123, three Henschel Hs 126s, one Junkers Ju 52, three Junkers Ju 87s, two Messerschmitt Bf 109s and three Messerschmitt Bf 110s. One of the Messerschmitt Bf 110s was shot down accidentally by German troops near Ostrolenka. Luftwaffe personnel casualties on this day amounted to 34 killed, one wounded and 17 missing.

One of the few photographs of the Heinkel He 178 on its historic first flight.

The first occasion that a British aircraft crossed the German frontier during the Second World War was on 3 September 1939 when Blenheim IV (N6215) of No 139 Squadron, flown by Flying Officer A. McPherson, and carrying Cdr Thompson, RN, and Corp V. Arrowsmith, photographed German naval units leaving Wilhelmshaven.

The first leaflet raid over Germany in the Second World War was carried out by three Whitley IIIs of No 51 Squadron and seven Whitley IIIs of No 58 Squadron on the first night of the war, 3 to 4 September 1939. Approximately six million propaganda leaflets were dropped on targets in the Rhur and over Bremen and Hamburg.

The first British aircraft to drop bombs on enemy targets during the Second World War was a Blenheim IV (N6204), flown by Flt Lt K. C. Doran, leading a formation of five aircraft from No 110 (Hyderabad) Squadron in a raid on the German Fleet in the Schillig Roads, off Wilhelmshaven, on 4 September 1939. A formation of five Blenheims from No 107 Squadron also took part in the attack.

The first British aircraft to attack a German U-boat during the Second World War was an Avro Anson I of the RAF's No 500 (County of Kent) Squadron then based at Detling. On 5 September 1939, this aircraft made a bombing attack on the enemy submarine.

The first British gallantry decorations to be gaz-

etted during the Second World War were two Distinguished Flying Crosses on 10 September 1939 to Flying Officer McPherson and Flt Lt Doran (see above).

The first German aircraft to be shot down by British aircraft during the Second World War was a Messerschmitt Bf 109E, destroyed by Sgt F. Letchford, air gunner of a Fairey Battle (K9243) of No 88 Squadron, Advanced Air Striking Force of the RAF, over France, on 20 September 1939. The first Fleet Air Arm victory followed when three Dornier Do 18s of *Küstenfliegergruppe 506* were sighted by a patrol of Swordfish aircraft flying from HMS *Ark Royal* over the North Sea on 26 September 1939. Nine Skuas were launched immediately from the carrier and these succeeded in forcing one of the Dorniers (Werke Nr 731, of 2 *Staffel*, Kü F1 Gr 506) down on to the sea in German Grid Square 3440. The German four-man crew was later rescued and made prisoner on board a British destroyer.

The first British bombers to fly over Berlin in the Second World War were Armstrong Whitworth Whitleys of No 10 Squadron, which dropped propaganda leaflets during the night of 1–2 October 1939.

The first German aircraft shot down by an RAF aircraft operating from the United Kingdom during the Second World War was a Dornier Do 18 flying-boat destroyed by a Lockheed Hudson of No 224 Squadron. This occurred on 8 October 1939 during a patrol by the RAF aircraft over Jutland.

The first German aircraft shot down over British soil during the Second World War was a Junkers Ju 88A-1 of I/KG30, piloted by Hauptmann Pohl, and destroyed over the Firth of Forth by a Spitfire of No 603 (City of Edinburgh) squadron on 16 October 1939.

The most famous Japanese bomber aircraft of the Second War War, one of the outstanding aircraft of that war **and the most extensively-built Japanese bomber,** was the Mitsubishi G4M Navy Type 1 Attack Bomber. First flown on 23 October 1939, the G4M—known by the Allied codename *Betty*—was first used operationally in May 1941 in an attack on Chungking. In service throughout the entire Pacific War, the last opera-

tional flight of two G4M1s was to carry the Japanese surrender delegation to Ie-Shima on 19 August 1945.

The first enemy aircraft shot down by RAF fighters on the Western Front during the Second World War was a Dornier Do 17 destroyed over Toul on 30 October 1939. The victorious pilot was Pilot Officer P. W. Mould, flying a Hurricane of No 1 Squadron.

The first long-range anti-shipping squadron of the German Luftwaffe was formed in November 1939. In the absence of a more suitable aircraft, the unit was equipped with the Focke-Wulf Fw 200 Condor long-range civil transport. One of these aircraft, (D-2600) *Immelmann III*, was Adolf Hitler's personal transport. Though not ideal for military service, the Fw 200 was responsible for the destruction of an immense number of Allied merchant ships. The Condor unit I/KG40, controlled by the German Navy, claimed more than 363 000 tons (368 800 tonnes) of shipping destroyed during one six-month period.

The USAAF fighter with the most unusual power plant installation, flown in XP-39B prototype form on 25 November 1939, was the Bell P-39 Airacobra. This had its engine mounted in the rear fuselage, driving a conventional tractor propeller in the nose via a long extension shaft that passed beneath the pilot's seat.

The first loss suffered by the Finnish Air Force during the 'Winter War' with the Soviet Union in 1939-40 was Sergeant Kukkonen who, flying a Fokker D XXI of fighter squadron HLeLv24 near Viipuri, was shot down by his own anti-aircraft guns on 1 December 1939.

The first aerial victory claimed during the 'Winter War' between Finland and Russia was that of Lt Eino Luukkanen on 1 December 1939; flying a Fokker D XXI (*FR-104*) of Fighter Squadron HLeLv24, he destroyed a Russian SB-2 bomber.

The most extensively-built American aircraft of the Second World War, the Consolidated B-24 Liberator of which more than 18 000 were produced, was flown for the first time in XB-24 prototype form on 29 December 1939.

The first four-engined attack bomber to be designed for the Japanese Navy, and the first air-

Bell P-39 Airacobra Tarawa Boom Deay *at an airfield in Oahu, Hawaiian Islands.* (US National Archives)

craft with retractable tricycle landing gear to be built in Japan, was the Nakajima G5N Shinzan which flew for the first time in December 1939. Designed and built after examination of the American Douglas DC-4E prototype, it was found to have indifferent performance and only six were completed.

The first British naval fighter to be armed with a power-driven gun turret was the Blackburn Roc. Aircraft of this type entered service with the Fleet Air Arm in February 1940, but did not serve on board aircraft carriers. Proving unsatisfactory, they were retired in 1943.

The first British air combat victory of the Second World War to be recorded by a gun-camera was that showing the attack on and destruction of a Heinkel He 111 on 22 February 1940. This was achieved by Sqn Ldr Douglas Farquhar of No 602 (City of Glasgow) Squadron flying a Spitfire over Coldingham, Berwickshire.

The first Royal Air Force aircraft to drop bombs deliberately on German soil during the Second World War is believed to have been an Armstrong Whitworth Whitley (N1380, DY-R) of No 102 Squadron based at Driffield, Yorkshire. This squadron, in company with Whitleys of Nos 10, 51 and 77 Squadrons, and Handley Page Hampdens of No 5 Group, attacked the German mine-lying seaplane base at Hornum on the night of 19-20 March 1940.

The RAF's last operational biplane fighter was the Gloster Gladiator, of which production ended in April 1940. Only a few squadrons remained in service at the outbreak of the Second World War, but their classic exploits include operations from a frozen lake during the Norwegian campaign, participation in the surrender and capture of the Italian submarine *Galileo Galilei* on 18 June 1940, and the part played in the defence of Malta by the Sea Gladiators *Faith*, *Hope* and *Charity*.

The worst losses suffered by an air force in a single day's offensive operations, as a result of air combat and anti-aircraft gunfire, are believed to have been those of the Luftwaffe on 10 May 1940. On this day Germany invaded the Netherlands and Belgium and was opposed simultaneously by the air forces of Belgium, France, Great Britain and Holland. The Norwegian campaign, by then nearing its end, also claimed a small number of German victims on that day. According to its own records the Luftwaffe lost on 10 May:

	Destroyed	Damaged
Dornier Do 17 bombers	26	7
Dornier Do 18 flying-boat	1	
Dornier Do 215 reconnaissance aircraft	2	
Fieseler Fi 156 artillery support aircraft	22	
Heinkel He 111 bombers	51	21
Henschel Hs 123 dive-bomber		1
Henschel Hs 126 reconnaissance aircraft	1	3
Junkers Ju 52 transports	157	
Junkers Ju 87 dive-bombers	9	
Junkers Ju 88 bombers	18	2
Messerschmitt Bf 109 fighters	6	11
Messerschmitt Bf 110 fighters	1	3
Other types	10	3
Totals	304	51

Aircrew casualties amounted to 267 killed, 133 wounded and 340 missing; other Luftwaffe personnel casualties (Flak, engineers, etc) amounted to 326 killed or missing.

Apart from the historical interest of these figures, they indicate conclusively that the operations undertaken by the Luftwaffe on this day represented the true beginning of the *Blitzkrieg* against substantial opposition. On 10 May Germany suffered losses in excess of all previous cumulative losses since 1 September 1939, including the Polish campaign. Losses suffered by the Luftwaffe during the invasion of Poland may be summarised as follows:

Period	Aircraft destroyed	Aircrew killed	wounded	missing
1– 8 Sept	116	128	68	137
9–13 Sept	34	15	15	15
14–18 Sept	23	24	32	14
19–27 Sept	30	54	18	4

The greatest single victory achieved by the Royal Netherlands Air Force during the German invasion of the Low Countries was gained at 06.45 h on 10 May 1940 when a force of Fokker D XXIs intercepted 55 Junkers Ju 52/3m transport aircraft of KGzbV9. The Dutch pilots claimed to have shot down 37 of the formation, but German records indicate a total loss of 39 aircraft, 6 occupants killed, 41 presumed dead, 15 wounded and 79 missing.

The French military aeroplane most widely used at the beginning of the Battle of France on 10 May 1940 belonged to the Potez 630 series, of which a total of 1250 were built. The main variants were the 630 and 631 fighters and the 63/II reconnaissance aircraft. First flown in April 1936, the three-seat Potez 630 fighter, powered by two 640 hp Hispano-Suiza HS 14AB 10/11 engines, had a maximum speed of 280 mph (450 km/h) at 13 000 ft (3960 m). Standard armament comprised two nose-mounted Hispano 9 or 404 cannon, plus one MAC machine-gun for rear defence. Shortage of cannon made it necessary to arm many 630/631s with four machine-guns and when, in February 1940, it was decided to increase the fire power of these fighters, the cannon were supplemented by six machine-guns mounted beneath the wings.

The first British bombs to fall on the German mainland in the Second World War were dropped by eight or nine Whitleys of Nos 77 and 102 Squadrons, which attacked enemy lines of communication leading to Southern Holland on the night of 10–11 May 1940.

The first successful and practical helicopters to be designed outside Germany were those of the Russian-born American Igor Sikorsky. His first successful helicopter was the Vought-Sikorsky VS-300, which featured full cyclic pitch control and was powered by a 75 hp engine. This made its first recognised free flight on 13 May 1940,

British Fairey Battle light bombers and French-operated Curtiss Hawk 75 fighters go into action during the German invasion of the Low Countries. (Imperial War Museum)

Vought-Sikorsky VS-300 in original form, managing to lift from the ground in tethered flight for the first time on 14 September 1939. On 13 May 1940 the VS-300 made a recognised free flight.

although it had made a tethered flight on 14 September 1939. In May 1941 a 90 hp engine was installed and the VS-300 set up a new endurance record of 1 h 32 min 26 s. By 1942, after further improvement, the VS-300 became established as the first successful and practical helicopter.

The longest production run of any US fighter of the Second World War was that of the Vought F4U Corsair, first flown on 29 May 1940, at which time it was the most powerful naval fighter in the world. Initial deliveries to VF-12 (US Navy Fighter Squadron Twelve) began on 3 October 1942, the type remaining in production until December 1952. It was thus the last American piston-engined fighter to remain in production. Fastest of the series was the F4U-5N, powered by a 2300 hp Pratt & Whitney R-2800-32W radial engine with a two-stage supercharger, which gave a maximum level speed of 470 mph (756 km/h) at 26 800 ft (8168 m). In service with the British Fleet Air Arm on board HMS *Victorious*, Corsair Mk IIs took part in the attacks on the German battleship *Tirpitz* on 3 April 1944, this being the first operation flown with Corsairs from an aircraft carrier.

The first eight-gun fighter to enter service with the Fleet Air Arm was the Fairey Fulmar, which began to equip No 808 Squadron at Worthy Down in June 1940. Fulmars played a conspicuous part in the defence of convoys to Malta and Northern Russia.

First Allied aircraft to bomb Berlin during the Second World War was a Centre NC 223·4 civil transport (F-ARIN *Jules Verne*) which had been developed for transatlantic operations with Air France. Converted for operation as a bomber, on the night of 7–8 June 1940 this aircraft followed a circuitous route carrying a 4409 lb (2000 kg) bombload which it dropped on Berlin before returning over Germany and north-east France to land at Orly after a 13 h 30 min flight.

The first Victoria Cross to be won during the Battle of Britain was awarded posthumously to Acting Seaman J. F. (Jack) Mantle, RN, who was operating an anti-aircraft gun aboard HMS *Foyle Bank* in Portland Harbour, Dorset, on 4 July 1940. The ship, the only one in port with an anti-aircraft gun, became the focus of an enemy raid and was hit by a bomb which cut the power supply. Jack Mantle, though severely wounded,

continued to fire the gun, operating it manually; despite another direct hit upon the ship, which severed his left leg, he remained at his post until the end of the raid but succumbed to his terrible wounds almost immediately afterwards. His Victoria Cross was only the second to be awarded for an action in or over Great Britain, the first having been awarded to Lt W. Leefe Robinson of No 39 Home Defence Squadron, RFC, for his destruction of a Schutte-Lanz airship on the night of 2–3 September 1916 at Cuffley, Hertfordshire.

One of the first members of the Royal Air Force to be awarded the George Cross was Aircraftsman Vivian ('Bob') Holloway who, in July 1940, at Cranfield, Bedfordshire, entered a crashed and blazing bomber and extricated the pilot, and in so doing suffered severe burns to his hands. One month later, at the moment of returning from hospital, he again dashed into a blazing aircraft three times amongst exploding ammunition, and brought out three crew members. He survived his near-fatal burns despite having been on the danger list for 27 days.

The first Victoria Cross awarded to a pilot of RAF Bomber Command was that won by Flt Lt R. A. B. Learoyd. The award was made for gallantry when, on the night of 12–13 August 1940, Flt Lt Learoyd was flying Hampden P4403, as one of a force of five from Nos 49 and 83 Squadrons which dropped delayed action bombs on an aquaduct of the Dortmund-Ems Canal.

The only Victoria Cross ever to be awarded to a member of RAF Fighter Command was that won by Flt Lt James Brindley Nicholson, RAF, on 16 August 1940. A Flt Cdr of No 249 (Hurricane) Squadron, Nicholson was leading a section of three fighters on patrol near Southampton, Hampshire, when he sighted enemy aircraft ahead. Before he could complete the attack his section was 'bounced' from above and behind by German fighters which shot down one Hurricane and set Nicholson's aircraft ablaze. With flames sweeping up through his cockpit, the British pilot remained at his controls long enough to complete an attack on an enemy aircraft which had flown into his sights, and then baled out. Meanwhile, a detachment of soldiers on the ground, seeing Nicholson and his wingman descending on parachutes and believing them to be enemy para-

Refuelling RAF Hawker Hurricane I fighters during the Battle of Britain. (Charles E. Brown)

troops, opened fire with rifles. Nicholson was hit but survived his wounds and burns; but his colleague was dead when he reached the ground (whether or not he was killed by rifle-fire has never been established).

The first regular-serving American pilot to die in action during the Second World War was Pilot Officer William M.L. Fiske, RAF, who on 17 August 1940 died of wounds suffered in action the previous day at Tangmere, Sussex, during the Battle of Britain.

The first Second World War bombing attack on London was made by the Luftwaffe on the night of 24–25 August 1940.

The largest flying-boat to attain operational status during the Second World War was the German Blohm und Voss Bv 222 Wiking. Designed as a transatlantic civil transport for Lufthansa, the prototype (D-ANTE) first flew on 7 September 1940, but was quickly impressed into war service as a cargo transport. The final Bv 222C version had a wing span of 150 ft 11 in (46 m), gross weight of 108 000 lb (48 990 kg) and was powered by six Junkers Jumo 205C engines.

Development of the first rotary-wing man-carrying glider intended as a pilot escape system was started by a team led by Raoul Hafner in the UK on 3 October 1940. Named the Rotachute,

about 20 were built and tested but did not become operational.

The highest scoring Allied pilot during the Battle of Britain was Sergeant Josef František, a Czech pilot who served with No 303 (Polish) Squadron, RAF. His confirmed score of 17 enemy aircraft shot down was achieved entirely during September 1940; he was killed on 9 October 1940. The only British gallantry decoration awarded to František was the Distinguished Flying Medal, but he had been awarded previously the Czech War Cross and the Polish Virtuti Militari.

One of the best known Allied fighter aircraft of the Second World War, the North American P-51 Mustang of which more than 15 000 were built, was first flown in NA-73 prototype form on 26 October 1940. Designed to meet a British requirement for use in Europe, in its most extensively-produced versions, the P-51D/K, it became regarded as one of the classic fighter aircraft of the war.

The first air victory scored in the Greek-Italian campaign of 1940–41 was achieved by a Greek pilot of No 21 Squadron of the Royal Hellenic Air Force. Flying a Polish PZL P24, he destroyed an Italian aircraft north of Yannina on 1 November 1940.

The first organised transatlantic ferry flights of aircraft built in the United States, for service with the Allied nations involved in the Second World War, began on 10 November 1940.

The first American-built fighter aircraft in British service to destroy a German aircraft in the Second World War were two Grumman Martlets of the Royal Navy. Patrolling over Scapa Flow on 25 December 1940, Martlets of No 804 Squadron, flown by Lt L. V. Carver, RN, and Sub-Lt Parke, RNVR, intercepted and forced down a Junkers Ju 88. Known in US Navy service as the F4F Wildcat, this was Grumman's first monoplane fighter. Its first operational use in US Navy service was in the defence of Wake Island.

The first airborne operation carried out by British paratroops in the Second World War had the codename 'Operation Colossus'. On 10 February 1941 the paratroops were dropped by Whitley Vs of Nos 51 and 78 Squadrons in an unsuccessful attack against the viaduct at Tragino, Campagna, Italy.

First RAF squadron to fly four-engined bombers

operationally during the Second World War was No 7, which used three of its new Short Stirlings (led by Sqn Ldr Griffith-Jones) to bomb oil storage tanks at Rotterdam on the night of 10–11 February 1941.

The first 4000 lb 'block buster' bomb to be used operationally by the RAF was dropped by a Wellington of No 149 Squadron, during an attack on Emden on 1 April 1941.

The first aircraft designed as a jet fighter, and also the first twin-engined jet aircraft, was the German Heinkel He 280. The first prototype, the He 280V-1, was first flown on 2 April 1941 powered by two Heinkel HeS 8 turbojets, each developing approximately 1102 lb (500 kg) static thrust. Maximum level speed of the He 280V-5, with HeS 8A engines of 1650 lb (750 kg) static thrust, was demonstrated to be 510 mph (820 km/h) at 19 680 ft (6000 m). It did not achieve production status, being abandoned in favour of the Messerschmitt Me 262.

The first German turbojet-powered aircraft to enter operational service was the Messerschmitt Me 262A. The first flight of the Me 262V-1 prototype, powered by a single 1200 hp Junkers Jumo

The first German jet fighter-bomber was the
Messerschmitt Me 262A-1

piston-engine, was made on 18 April 1941. It was not until 18 July 1942 that the first flight with two turbojet engines was recorded, these being Junkers 109-004A-0 turbojets, each of 1848 lb (840 kg) static thrust. The first production aircraft had 109-004B-1 turbojets of 1980 lb (900 kg) thrust, which provided a maximum level speed of about 539 mph (868 km/h) at 23 000 ft (7000 m).

The Me 262A-2a Sturmvogel (Stormbird) fighter-bomber variant is believed to have entered service with Kommando Schenk in early July 1944, moving to Juvincourt in France on 10 July 1944 to begin operations with six aircraft. This suggests that the Me 262 was the first turbojet-powered combat aircraft to enter operational service. The Me 262A-1a Schwalbe (Swallow) entered operational service on 3 October 1944; a test unit was expanded and renamed Kommando Nowotny under the command of the Austrian ace, Major Walter Nowotny, and became operational on that date. One of the two Staffeln of the unit was based at Achmer, the other at Hesepe.

One of the outstanding US Army Air Force fighters of the Second World War made its first flight in XP-47B prototype form on 6 May 1941. This was to become known as the Republic P-47 Thunderbolt, which had been designed under the leadership of Alexander Kartveli, and of which more than 15 000 were built before production ended.

Three outstanding American long-range fighters of the war were the Republic P-47 Thunderbolt, Lockheed P-38 Lightning and North American P-51 Mustang (right). (US National Archives)

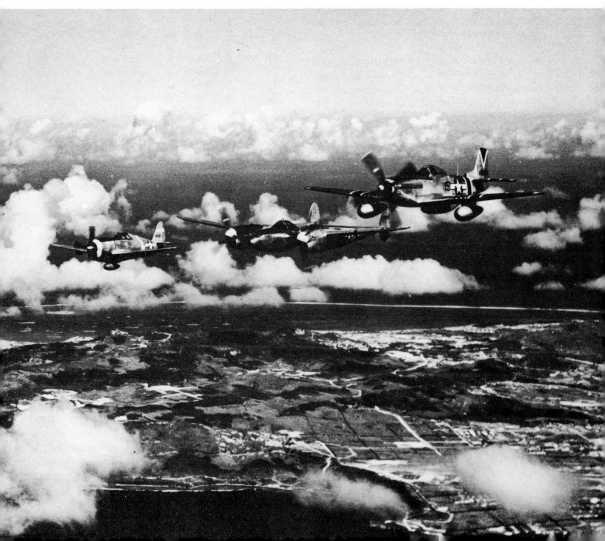

The largest airborne assault mounted by the Luftwaffe during the Second World War was operation 'Mercury', the landing of 22 750 men on the island of Crete beginning at 07.00 h on 20 May 1941. The Luftwaffe used 493 Junkers Ju 52/3m aircraft and about 80 DFS 230 gliders. The assault was made by 10 000 parachutists, 750 troops landed by glider, 5000 landed by Ju 52/3ms and 7000 by sea. The operation, although regarded as a brilliant success, cost Germany about 4500 men killed and some 150 transport aircraft destroyed or badly damaged, and effectively brought Luftwaffe paratroop operations to an end.

The greatest single loss of aircraft in any one day suffered by any nation involved in the Second World War occurred on 22 June 1941. On that day Germany began Operation Barbarossa, its invasion of the Soviet Union, and by nightfall Soviet aircraft losses amounted to 1811, of which 1489 were destroyed on the ground.

USS Shaw *explodes during the Japanese attack on Pearl Harbor on 7 December 1941.* (US National Archives)

The first combat mission flown by the Boeing B-17 Flying Fortress was a daylight raid at 30 000 ft (9150 m) against Wilhelmshaven by three aircraft of No 90 (Bomber) Squadron, RAF, on 8 July 1941. Twenty B-17Cs had been supplied to the RAF, and were used by that service under the name Fortress I. From 1942 onwards about 200 B-17F and B-17G aircraft were delivered to the RAF, which designated the 'Fs' as Fortress II and IIA, the 'Gs' as Fortress III. All of the II and IIA aircraft served with Coastal Command's Very Long Range force for mid-Atlantic patrol.

The first British single-seat monoplane fighter to serve on board aircraft carriers of the Royal Navy was the Hawker Sea Hurricane. The type equipped No 880 Squadron in January 1941 and was embarked in HMS *Furious* in July of the same year. They were used also aboard merchant ships and a number of small naval catapult ships under the 'Catafighter' scheme. Their first success in this role came on 3 August 1941 when the Sea Hurricane of HMS *Maplin*, flown by Lt R. W. H. Everett, RNVR, shot down a German Fw 200 Condor.

The first American-built aircraft to be used operationally by the RAF during the Second World War was the Lockheed Hudson, which entered service with No 224 Squadron at Gosport in the Summer of 1939. A Hudson operated by this squadron scored the first British victory over a German aircraft in the Second World War, directed Naval forces to the prison ship *Altmark*, and took part in the hunting of the battleship *Bismarck*. On 27 August 1941 a Hudson of No 269 Squadron caused submarine U-570 to surrender to it: the first U-boat captured in a solely RAF operation.

The first RAF Coastal Command aircraft to be equipped with ASV Mk II long-range radar were the Whitleys of No 502 Squadron. On 30 November 1941 one of the Squadron's aircraft, a Whitley VII (Z9190), made the Command's first ASV 'kill', sinking U-206 in the Bay of Biscay.

American participation in the Second World War resulted from the Japanese attack by carrier-based aircraft on the US Pacific Fleet and shore installations at Pearl Harbor, Hawaii, on 7 December 1941. The attack, made without any previous declaration of war, brought immediate reaction from the United States, which declared war on Japan on 8 December, marking the beginning of the Pacific War.

The last of the famous American Curtiss fighters to serve with the RAF was the Kittyhawk, which entered service in late 1941. A total of more than

3000 of these aircraft were delivered to Commonwealth air forces.

The Focke Achgelis Fa 330 Bachstelze was a single-seat gyro-kite designed in early 1942 and built by Weser-Flugzeugbau at Hoykenkamp near Bremen. Designed to be carried by Germany's ocean-going Type IX U-boats, it could be deployed when needed for observation duties, towed behind the surfaced submarine at a height of about 400 ft (122 m), to give its pilot a 25 mile (40 km) clear-weather field of view. It was, however, little used as U-boat crews believed it could pinpoint their position and also create crash-dive problems.

The greatest altitude from which anyone has ever jumped without a parachute and survived is 22 000 ft (6705 m). In January 1942 Lt I. M. Chisov of the USSR fell from an Ilyushin Il-4 which had been badly damaged. He struck the ground a glancing blow on the edge of a snow-covered ravine and slid to the bottom, sustaining a fractured pelvis and severe spinal damage. It is estimated that the human body reaches 99 per cent of its low-level terminal velocity after falling 1880 ft (573 m); this is 117–125 mph (188–201 km/h) at normal atmospheric pressure in a random posture, but up to 185 mph (298 km/h) in a head-down position. **The British record** stands at 18000 ft (5490 m) set by Flt Sgt Nicholas Stephen Alkemade, RAF, who jumped from a

US personnel crowd to view a Sikorsky R-4, the first helicopter to land in the fighter command area of Iwo Jima, March 1945. (US National Archives)

blazing Lancaster bomber over Germany on 23 March 1944. His headlong fall was broken by a fir tree, and he landed without a broken bone in an 18 in (46 cm) snow-bank.

The first helicopter designed and built for military service was the Sikorsky XR-4 which first flew on 13 January 1942. Its delivery flight from Stratford, Connecticut, to Wright Field, Dayton, Ohio, a distance of 761 miles (1225 km), was the first cross-country helicopter delivery flight, accomplished between 13 and 18 May 1942. As a result of military trials at Wright Field, a small development batch of these helicopters was used for limited service and training during 1944-45. R-4s were the first helicopters to fly in Alaska and Burma, first to be tried on board ship (1943), and the first to be flown by the British Fleet Air Arm.

The first transatlantic flight by a British Prime Minister was made by the Rt Hon Winston Churchill on 16-17 January 1942. The flight, between Bermuda and Plymouth, was made in the Boeing 314 flying-boat *Berwick* operated by British Overseas Airways Corporation (BOAC).

The last torpedo attack launched by the Fairey Swordfish was on 12 February 1942, when six unescorted aircraft of No 825 Squadron, led by Lt Cdr Eugene Esmonde, FAA, attempted to torpedo the German battleships *Gneisenau* and *Scharnhorst* and the heavy cruiser *Prinz Eugen*. This was in an attempt to prevent these warships from escaping through the English Channel, but without fighter escort the Swordfish faced a hopeless task, and all six were shot down by the protective umbrella of German fighter aircraft. Only five of the 18 crew members survived: all were decorated and a posthumous Victoria Cross was awarded to Lt Cdr Esmonde, the first to be won by a member of the Fleet Air Arm.

The need to gain knowledge of the capability of German radar installations resulted in the **first British combined operation against Europe during the Second World War.** British air, land and sea forces were used on 27-28 February 1942 to take vital components from a radar installation at Bruneval, northern France.

The first German U-boats to be destroyed by the United States Navy during the Second World War were sunk on 1 and 15 March 1942. These sinkings were achieved by Lockheed PBO-1 Hudson aircraft of the US Navy's VP-82 Squadron, based at Argentia, Newfoundland.

The first combat operation carried out by Avro Lancaster heavy bombers was a mine-lying sortie flown by No 44 (Bomber) Squadron, based at Waddington, Lincolnshire, over the Heligoland Bight on 3 March 1942. Their first night bombing attack was recorded when two of No 44 Squadron's aircraft took part in a raid on Essen on the night of 10-11 March 1942. The first of many famous raids involved 12 aircraft of Nos 44 and 97 Squadrons led by Sqn Ldr J.D. Nettleton, which made a low-level daylight attack on the MAN Diesel factory at Augsburg on 17 April 1942. Their first operation with the Pathfinder Force was made on the night of 18-19 August 1942.

A Handley Page Halifax (V9977) was **the first RAF aircraft to have the British H2S blind bombing radar system installed,** on 27 March 1942. This radar, in conjunction with the metal foil strips known as Window, dropped from the air to confuse enemy defensive radar, was first used with devastating success in an attack on Hamburg on 24-25 July 1943.

In an attempt to demonstrate US strike power against the Japanese mainland , on 18 April 1942 Lt Col James Doolittle led a force of 16 North American B-25 Mitchell bombers from the US Navy carrier USS *Hornet* to raid Tokyo. Unable to return to ship, most aircraft landed in China.

The first naval battle in which the issue was decided by aircraft alone was the Battle of the Coral Sea, fought on 7-9 May 1942, between US Navy Task Force 17 and Vice-Admiral Takeo Takagi's Carrier Striking Force (part of Vice-Admiral Shigeyoshi Inouye's Task Force MO). The battle was fought to prevent Japanese support of an invasion of Port Moresby and to disrupt plans to launch air strikes against the Australian mainland. In this respect the battle must be considered to have been an American victory, although the large American carrier USS *Lexington* was sunk—**the first American carrier to be lost in the Second World War.** The Japanese carrier *Shoho* was attacked and sunk by Dauntless and Devastator aircraft from the *Lexington* and *Yorktown*, becoming **the first Japanese aircraft carrier to be destroyed by American airmen.** A total of 69 American naval aircraft were lost during the battle, while the Japanese losses amounted to about 85 aircraft and some 400 naval airmen (many of whom went down with the *Shoho*). The Japanese carrier *Shokaku* was also damaged severely, but was able to limp home for repairs. The loss of experienced airmen

De Havilland Mosquito prototype, flown in November 1940.

and the absence of the *Shokaku* critically weakened Japanese naval forces that were to be involved in the vital Battle of Midway, fought 4–7 June 1942.

The only fighter of Australian design to fire its guns in anger during the Second World War was the Commonwealth CA-12 Boomerang, of which a total of 250 was built between May 1942 and January 1945. The first aircraft (A46-1) was first flown by Ken Frewin at Fisherman's Bend, Victoria, on 29 May 1942. Powered by an Australian-built 1200 hp Pratt & Whitney R-1830 engine, which gave it a top speed of 296 mph (476 km/h) at 7600 ft (2315 m), the Boomerang served eventually with Nos 4, 5, 83, 84 and 85 Squadrons, Royal Australian Air Force. Used principally as a ground-attack fighter, it is surprising that the Boomerang, which was frequently in action against Japanese aircraft, failed to destroy an enemy aeroplane in the air.

The first 'thousand bomber' raid against a German target was mounted by RAF Bomber Command. In the attack against Cologne on the night of 30–31 May 1942, 1046 aircraft were involved, of which 599 were Vickers Wellingtons.

The fastest aircraft in RAF Bomber Command for an entire decade, from November 1941 until introduction of the English Electric Canberra in 1951, was the de Havilland Mosquito. Entering squadron service with No 105 at Swanton Morley, Mosquitos made their first operational sortie on 31 May 1942, four aircraft making a surprise attack on Cologne just a few hours after the first 1000-bomber raid. Too fast to be intercepted during much of its wartime service, the Mosquito had the lowest loss rate of any aircraft in Bomber Command. Fighter variants of the Mosquito were no less successful, the Mk VI being the most extensively built, entering service with Fighter Command as a day and night intruder. Mosquitos served also as night fighters, responsible for home defence, and on the night of 14–15 June 1944 **the first V1 flying bomb to be shot down** was destroyed over the English Channel by a Mosquito of No 605 Squadron flown by Flt Lt J. G. Musgrave.

The first American naval aircraft to feature hydraulically-operated folding wings, and also the US Navy's first carrier-based monoplane torpedo-bomber to enter production, was the Douglas TBD Devastator. First flown in prototype form on 15 April 1935, the first production TBD-1s were delivered to US Navy Squadron VT-3 on 5 October 1937. Of 75 Devastators on strength with the US Navy on 3 June 1942, 37 were lost during the Battle of Midway (see below), Squadron VT-8 entirely destroyed and another squadron decimated in combat with Japanese Zero fighters. Following this action the type was withdrawn from operational use.

The first major naval battle of the Pacific War to confirm the lethal capability of an aircraft carrier strike force was that known as the Battle of Midway, fought off Midway island during 3 and 4 June 1942. In a first shattering blow, dive-bomber squadrons from the USS *Enterprise* and *Yorktown*, attacking from opposite directions to confuse Japanese defences, scored lethal hits on the Japanese carriers *Akagi*, *Kaga* and *Soryu*; within minutes they were blazing and out of action. Only *Hiryu*, some miles distant, had escaped but within the next two hours was spotted by scout planes from *Yorktown* and quickly put out of action by dive-bombers from the *Enterprise*. Before this happened, however, *Yorktown* had been damaged severely by aircraft from *Hiryu*, and was later sunk by the Japanese submarine I-168 while under tow for repair in Hawaii. From that moment the Japanese fleet no longer held the initiative; not only had Japan lost four of her six first-line aircraft carriers, but very large numbers of experienced naval airmen.

First night attack on a German U-boat in which a Leigh light was used to illuminate the target was made on the night of 3–4 June 1942 by a Vickers Wellington of No 172 Squadron, RAF.

The first single-engined American aircraft equipped with a power-operated gun turret, and also the first to carry a 22 in (55.9 cm) torpedo, was the Grumman TBF Avenger. First flight of an XTBF-1 prototype was made during August 1941. The first operational use of production aircraft was at the Battle of Midway, on 4 June 1942 (see above), when five out of six aircraft deployed were lost. Despite this inauspicious start, the Avenger became one of the most outstanding naval aircraft of the Second World War. Almost 10000 were built, of which nearly 1000 served in 15 first-line squadrons of the British FAA.

USAAF Boeing B-17Es flown on a mission over Germany.

The first aerial victories claimed during the 'Continuation War' between Finland and the Soviet Union, which broke out in June 1941, were two Soviet DB-3 bombers shot down by six Fokker D XXIs over the Riihimaki railway junction in the first air battle, which probably took place on 25 June 1942.

The most successful US Navy fighter aircraft of the Second World War was the Grumman F6F Hellcat, the prototype of which flew for the first time on 26 June 1942. US Navy statistics record that almost 75 per cent of all Navy wartime combat victories were achieved with Hellcats, of which 12 275 had been built when production ended in November 1945.

Following official formation of the **RAF's Pathfinder Force** on 15 August 1942, under the command of Air Cdre D. C. T. Bennett, the **first exploratory use** of this force was made on the night of 16–17 August 1942 in an attack on Emden, Germany.

The first Boeing B-17E to arrive in Britain was allocated to the USAAF's 97th Bombardment Group. This unit made its first operational sortie in Europe on 17 August 1942, when 12 B-17Es attacked Rouen.

The highest known interception by an unpressurised aircraft, its pilot G. W. H. Reynolds unaided by a pressure suit and breathing only a conventional oxygen supply, was that made at 49 500 ft (15 090 m) in a specially prepared Spitfire VC operating from No 103 MU near Alexandria, in late August 1942. A Ju 86P-2 high-altitude pressurised aircraft was destroyed in this interception.

The first RAF fighter capable of exceeding a speed of 400 mph (644 km h) was the Hawker Typhoon, which entered squadron service with No 56 at Duxford in September 1941. Armed with four 20 mm cannon, and able to carry two 1000 lb bombs or eight 60 lb rocket-projectiles beneath its wings, the Typhoon became famous for 'train-busting' activities and devastated German *Panzer* divisions at Caen and the Falaise gap after the Allied invasion of Europe.

The first and only time a Japanese fixed-wing aircraft attacked the continental USA during the Second World War occurred during June 1942. The aircraft, a Yokosuka E14Y1 ('Glen') light submarine-based reconnaissance floatplane launched from the Japanese submarine I-25, dropped four incendiary bombs on the wooded Oregon coast.

Probably the only captain of an aircraft to sink a U-boat from the air, and bring back a piece of the U-boat to prove it, was Sqn Ldr D. M. Sleep, RAF, flying an anti-submarine patrol in a Consolidated Liberator IIIA of RAF Coastal Command on 20 October 1942. Attacking the U-boat from low level, the explosion of the aircraft's bombs damaged the Liberator severely and it was a major feat for the crew to fly it some 800 miles (1287 km) back to base where it crashed on landing. It was discovered subsequently that a small piece of the submarine, identified by the Admiralty, had imbedded itself in the Liberator's tailplane.

First aircraft in the world to be equipped with crew ejection seats as standard, and also the

The first Lockheed Constellation transport in military colours.

Luftwaffe's first operational aircraft with retractable tricycle landing gear, was the Heinkel He 219, first flown in prototype form on 15 November 1942. A twin-engined night fighter, the He 219 became operational during June 1943.

Perhaps the most unusual aircraft to enter Luftwaffe service, in late 1942, was the Heinkel He 111Z. It consisted of two conventional He 111s, linked together by a new wing centre-section which carried a fifth engine. Intended to tow the Messerschmitt Me 321 Gigant glider, the He 111Z saw very limited service in this role and as a transport aircraft.

The first research aircraft to be designed for flight at 1000 mph (1600 km/h) was the Miles M-52. Development began in 1943, and by February 1946 the detail design was virtually completed. Construction was underway when the project was cancelled due to economic problems and the belief by some officials that it should have been designed with swept instead of very thin bi-convex straight wings. However, models of the M-52 flown during 1947–8 showed that the aircraft could have achieved its aim. Power for the M-52 was to have been provided by one Power Jets W2/700 turbojet engine, with augmentor and afterburner, developing up to 4100 lb (1860 kg) thrust.

Prototype Gloster Meteor Mk 1 jet fighter.

The first of Lockheed's famous Constellations, the Lockheed Model L-49, made its first flight at Burbank, California, on 9 January 1943. Designed and intended as civil transports, aircraft were commandeered off the production line by the USAAF, which found of great value the long-range capability of the 22 that it acquired and operated as C-69s.

The Royal Air Force heavy bomber with the greatest number of operational missions to its credit was the Avro Lancaster B Mark III, ED888, PM-M², of No 103 (Bomber) Squadron. Mike Squared, known alternatively as 'The Mother of Them All', made its first operational sortie in a raid on Dortmund on the night of 4–5 May 1943. By the time the aircraft was retired in December 1944 it had logged 140 missions. This number of missions was, however, exceeded by the de Havilland Mosquito B Mk IX light bomber LR503, GB-F, of No 105 Squadron and later 109 Squadron. Between 28 May 1943 and the end of the war, this aircraft completed no fewer than 213 operational sorties.

The first glider to be towed across the North Atlantic was an RAF Hadrian (American Waco CG-4) transport glider, its tug an RAF Dakota, which during June 1943 was flown in stages from Montreal to the UK in a flying time of 28 h.

The most successful Soviet woman fighter pilot of the Second World War,* and thus presumably the most successful woman fighter pilot in the world, served with the mixed-sex 73rd Guards Fighter Air Regiment. She was Jr Lt Lydia Lityvak, who was killed in action on 1 August 1943 at the age of 22, with a total of 12 confirmed victories while flying Yak fighters.

---

* During the Second World War, most Russian women combat pilots served with the 122nd Air Group of the Soviet Air Force. This all-female unit comprised the 586th Fighter Air Regiment, the 587th Bomber Air Regiment and the 588th Night Bomber Air Regiment. The 586th IAP (Istebitelnyi aviatsionnyi polk = fighter air regiment) was formed at Engels, on the Volga River, in October 1941; it was commanded by Maj Tamara Aleksandrovna Kazarinova. The pilots of this unit flew a total of 4419 operational sorties, took part in 125 air combats, and were credited with 38 confirmed victories. The unit flew Yak-1, -7B and -9 fighters. During the Second World War, 30 Russian airwomen received the gold star of a Hero of the Soviet Union. It is believed that 22 of them served with the 588th/46th Guards Night Bomber Air Regiment, which was equipped with Po-2 biplanes.

The fastest piston-engined fighter designed for the Luftwaffe, the Dornier Do 335, demonstrated a maximum speed of 474 mph (763 km/h) at 21 000 (6400 m). First flown in September 1943, the Do 335 Pfeil had a unique engine layout, one Daimler-Benz DB 603 being mounted conventionally in the nose, with a second DB 603 mounted in the rear fuselage and driving a pusher propeller through an extension shaft. It was developed too late to enter operational service.

The first specially-designed anti-submarine patrol aircraft for the Japanese Navy was the Kyushu Q1W Tokai, the prototype of which made its first flight in September 1943. Only a few Q1W1s entered service before the war's end, these being equipped with radar and magnetic anomaly detection (MAD) equipment.

The first operational use was made by the RAF of a 12 000 lb bomb, dropped by a Lancaster bomber on the Dortmund-Ems Canal on the night of 15–16 September 1943.

The first operational carrier-based fighter in the world with tricycle landing gear was the Grumman F7F-1 Tigercat. The first of two XF7F-1 prototypes made its first flight in December 1943, but rapidly changing requirements and alterations to specification meant that production aircraft entered squadrons too late to see operational service in the Second World War. A two-seat night-fighter variant (the F7F-2N) was also produced.

The first turbojet-powered fighter to enter operational service with the USAAF/USAF was the Lockheed P-80 (later F-80) Shooting Star. The first XP-80 prototype (44-83020) was flown for the first time on 8 January 1944, but although the Shooting Star was too late to see service in the Second World War, it was deployed operationally with considerable success during the Korean War.

The last scout aeroplane of the US Navy was the Curtiss SC Seahawk, designed for operation from battleships, carriers and from land bases. First flown on 16 February 1944, more than 500 were built for the Navy before cancellation of outstanding contracts after VJ-Day. The SC-1s were supplied in a landplane configuration and were converted to floatplanes, as required, in Navy workshops.

The first night bombing attack to be made from a US aircraft carrier was recorded on the night of 17–18 February 1944, when 12 TBF-1C Avengers from the USS Enterprise attacked Truk Island in the Pacific Ocean.

Making its first major daylight attack on Berlin, the USAAF deployed some 660 heavy bombers and escorting aircraft in this mission flown on 6 March 1944.

The first British twin-engined aircraft to land on the deck of an aircraft carrier was the pre-production prototype of the de Havilland Sea Mosquito (LR359) which, flown by Lt Cdr E. M. Brown, RN, landed on board HMS Indefatigable on 25 March 1944. Production Sea Mosquito TR33s first entered service with No 811 Squadron at Ford, Sussex, in August 1946.

Biggest amphibious assault in history, preceded by airdrops and Allied air force operations amounting to some 5000 sorties, the Operation Overlord landings on the Normandy coast began on D-Day, 6 June 1944.

The first operational use of composite combat aeroplanes was by the German Luftwaffe, during the Allied liberation of France in June–July 1944. Devised originally under a programme designated 'Beethoven-Gerät', it was known subsequently as the 'Mistel-Programm'. The biggest problem was to develop an effective system by which the pilot of the single-seat upper aircraft could control and effect separation of the two components. Initial operational Mistel Is comprised an upper piloted Bf 109F-4 and a lower Ju 88A-4 which carried a warhead containing 3800 lb (1725 kg) of high explosive. The weapon was first issued to 2 Staffel of Kampfgeschwader 101, commanded by Hauptmann Horst Rudat, which was formed in April 1944. The first operational use of the device, known unofficially as Vater und Sohn (Father and Son), was on the night of 24–25 June 1944, when five Mistels were deployed against Allied shipping in the Seine Bay. Later versions of the composite had Focke-Wulf Fw 190s as the upper component.

The first jet aircraft to enter operational service with the RAF was the Gloster Meteor Mk I, powered by two 1700 lb (771 kg) thrust Rolls-Royce W2B/23 Welland I turbojet engines.

Sir Frank Whittle (left), *photographed in 1982 with Michael Daunt* (right), *the second pilot of the Gloster E.28/39* (Britain's first jet aircraft, that first flew 15 May 1941). *Sir Frank Whittle had designed the first aeroplane jet engine to run, in 1937, which was the progenitor for the engines in the E.28/39 and Meteor jet fighter.* (Air Photo Supply)

Twenty Meteor Is were built, one of which was exchanged for an American-built Bell Airacomet—**the first US-designed and built jet fighter.** Three others were used for development purposes and the remainder (EE213–EE222, and EE224–EE229) were delivered to No 616 Squadron. The first two aircraft were delivered on 12 July 1944 to the Squadron, based at Culmhead, Somerset, under the command of Wg Cdr A. McDowall. The first combat sortie was flown from Manston by the Squadron on 27 July 1944

against V1 flying bombs but was unsuccessful owing to gun-firing difficulties. **The first combat success** was scored on 4 August 1944 by Flying Officer Dean who, after his guns had jammed, flew alongside the enemy bomb and, by tipping it with his wing, forced the missile into the ground. The aircraft was EE216.

The only known pilot who has been both gaoled and awarded his country's highest gallantry decoration for the same exploit was Lt Michael Devyatayev, a Soviet fighter pilot shot down by the Luftwaffe over Lvov on 13 July 1944. Taken prisoner by the Germans, Devyatayev escaped, seized a Heinkel He 111 bomber and flew nine other escapees back to Soviet-held territory. On regaining his freedom, the 23-year-old pilot was gaoled under the USSR criminal code which labelled him a traitor for having been taken prisoner. Nine years later, in 1953, he was freed under an amnesty prevailing at the time, and in 1958 was made Hero of the Soviet Union and awarded the Order of Lenin and Gold Star Medal.

During an attack on a fuel depot at Coutances, France, on 17 July 1944, USAAF P-38 Lightnings made the first operational use of napalm incendiary material.

The fastest twin piston-engined combat aircraft in the world to reach operational status was the de Havilland Hornet fighter which had a maximum speed of 485 mph (780 km/h) in 'clean' combat configuration. Powered by two 2070 hp Rolls-Royce Merlin 130 engines, the Hornet was armed with four 20 mm cannon, could carry up to 2000 lb (907 kg) of bombs or rockets on underwing pylons, and had a maximum range of over 2500 miles (4025 km). It was first flown by Geoffrey de Havilland Jr on 28 July 1944, but did not reach the first RAF squadron—No 64 (Fighter) Squadron at Horsham St Faith, Norfolk—until May 1946, after the end of the Second World War. The Hornet was the fastest piston-engined fighter to serve with the RAF and also the last piston-engined fighter to serve with RAF first-line squadrons.

The specially-prepared XP-47J Thunderbolt (43-46952), powered by a 2100 hp Pratt & Whitney R-2800-57 engine became, on 4 August 1944, the first piston-engined aircraft in the world to attain a speed in excess of 500 mph (805 kmh): 504 mph (811 km/h).

The first loss of a jet aircraft in aerial combat is thought to have taken place on 28 August 1944, when Maj Joseph Myers and Lt M. Croy of the 78th Fighter Group, US 8th Air Force, were credited with the destruction of an Me 262 operated by the Kommando Schenk.

The first aerial victory against another piloted aircraft to be gained by the pilot of a jet aircraft has never been identified positively, but was certainly achieved during the first week of October 1944 by a pilot of Kommando Nowotny, the target being a Boeing B-17 Flying Fortress of the US 8th Air Force.

The greatest number of enemy aircraft destroyed by a US Navy pilot in the course of a single sortie was achieved on 24 October 1944, when Cdr David McCampbell, accompanied by one other

aircraft, attacked a formation of 60 land-based Japanese aircraft approaching the US Fleet. Cdr McCampbell destroyed nine enemy aircraft and for this action, the destruction of seven enemy aircraft on 19 June 1944 and his inspired leadership of Air Group 15, he was awarded the Congressional Medal of Honor.

The first aviation unit formed specifically for suicide operations was the *Shimpu* Special Attack Corps, a group of 24 volunteer pilots commanded by Lt Yukio Seki, formed within the 201st (Fighter) Air Group, Imperial Japanese Navy, during the third week of October 1944. The unit, equipped with Mitsubishi Zero-Sen single-seat fighters, was formed for the task of diving into the flight decks of American aircraft carriers in the Philippines area, with a 250 kg bomb beneath the fuselage of each fighter. (*Shimpu* is an alternative pronunciation of the Japanese ideographs which also represent *kamikaze*, 'Divine Wind', the name applied more generally to Japanese suicide operations.) The first successful suicide attack was made on 25 October 1944 when five Zeros, flown by members of the Special Attack Corps, sank the US escort carrier *St Lo*, and damaged the carriers *Kalinin Bay*, *Kitkun Bay* and *White Plains*.

The first transpacific incendiary balloon attacks against the continental USA: see Lighter than air (3 November 1944).

The first jet fighter ace in the world has not been identified positively, but it is thought that he was one of the pilots of the Kommando Nowotny. The unit was withdrawn from operations following the death in action of Maj Walter Nowotny on 8 November 1944, and later provided the nucleus for the new fighter wing, Jagdgeschwader 7 'Nowotny'; III Gruppe JG 7 became operational during December 1944. Hauptmann Franz Schall is known to have scored three aerial victories on the day of Nowotny's death, and served subsequently with 10 Staffel, JG 7; it is therefore entirely possible that he was the first pilot in the world to have achieved five confirmed aerial victories while flying jet aircraft. Other known jet aces of the Second World War are listed below. The fragmentary records which survived the final immolation of the Luftwaffe in 1945 prevent the preparation of a complete list, and the following should be regarded only as a framework for further research:

Oberstleutnant Heinz Bar (JV 44)		16
Hauptmann Franz Schall (10/JG 7)		14
Major Erich Rudorffer (II/JG 7)		12
Oberfeldwebel Hermann Buchner (III/JG 7)		12
Leutnant Karl Schnorrer (II/JG 7)	not fewer than	8
Leutnant Rudolf Rademacher (II/JG 7)	not fewer than	8
Major Theodor Weissenberger (Staff/ JG 7)		8
Oberleutnant Walter Schuck (3/JG 7)		8
Oberst Johannes Steinhoff (Staff/JG 7, JV 44)		6
Major Wolfgang Spate (Staff/JG 7)		5
Leutnant Klaus Neumann (JV 44)		5

Boeing B-29 Superfortresses of the USAF's 21st Bomber Command, based on the Mariana Islands, launched the **first major attack on Tokyo** on 24 November 1944, a total of 88 B-29s being despatched on this operation.

The most successful destroyer of V1 flying-bombs in flight was Sqn Ldr Joseph Berry, RAF, who shot down 60 of these weapons during 1944.

The shortest elapsed time for the development of an entirely new jet fighter (which achieved combat status) was 69 days for the Heinkel He 162 Salamander. Conceived in an RLM specification issued to the German aircraft industry on 8 September 1944, the He 162 was the subject of a contract issued on 29 September 1944 for an aircraft capable of being mass-produced by semi-skilled labour using non-strategic materials. Sixty-nine days later, on 6 December 1944, the first prototype He 162V-1 was flown by Heinkel's Chief Test Pilot, Kapitän Peter, at Vienna-Schwechat. On 10 December the prototype broke up in the air and crashed before a large gathering of officials, and Peter was killed. Notwithstanding this set-back, the aircraft entered production and joined I and II Gruppen of

Jagdgeschwader I at Leck/Holstein during April 1945. III Gruppe of this Geschwader was under orders to receive the new fighter but was forestalled by the end of the war. Known also as the Volksjäger, or 'People's Fighter', it was intended that large numbers would be constructed, but only 116 A-series machines were completed. The Salamander was not a pleasant machine to fly, and as a result few of these aircraft were encountered in combat. Its single BMW 003 turbojet, rated at 1760 lb (800 kg) thrust, provided a maximum speed of 522 mph (840 km/h) at 19 685 ft (6000 m).

The largest military flying-boat built in Great Britain was the Short Shetland, of which only two prototypes were built. The first, designated Shetland I (DX166), flew for the first time on 14 December 1944, piloted by John Lankester Parker with Geoffrey Tyson as co-pilot. Designed for long-range maritime reconnaissance, both Shetland prototypes were powered by 2500 hp Bristol Centaurus engines, and their wing spans were 150 ft 4 in (45·82 m). The Shetland I had a maximum take-off weight of 125 000 lb (56 700 kg) and attained a maximum level speed of 263 mph (423 km/h). The first prototype was later destroyed by fire at its moorings. With the end of the war in sight it was decided to complete the second prototype as a civil transport, which was given the designation Shetland II. It was allocated the last constructor's number issued by Shorts at Rochester, S1313, and had the civil registration G-AGVD. It flew for the first time on 17 September 1947 and completed its preliminary trials, but lack of commercial interest in flying-boats after the end of the Second World War meant that it was scrapped in 1951 without ever having carried a fare-paying passenger.

The largest flying-boat to serve with the US Navy was the Martin JRM Mars. Twenty JRM-1 transports were ordered in January 1945 but only five were built, plus one heavier JRM-2. With a wing span of 200 ft (60·96 m) and gross weight of 165 000 lb (74 842 kg) in the JRM-2, the Mars flying-boat had a maximum speed of 225 mph (362 km/h). It was converted after the war for water-bombing of forest fires.

The first turboprop-powered aircraft to fly in the USA, albeit with a mixed powerplant, was the Consolidated XP-81 escort fighter prototype flown on 7 February 1945. This aircraft had a conventionally-mounted turboprop engine driving a tractor propeller, plus a turbojet engine mounted in the rear fuselage.

The first jet-driven helicopters in the world were the Doblhoff/WNF 342 (V1–V4) helicopters, built in the suburbs of Vienna between 1942 and 1945 by the Wiener Neustadter Flugzeugwerke (WNF). The jet power was produced by mixing compressed air (provided from a compressor driven by a piston engine) with fuel, which was then channelled through the three hollow rotor blades and burnt in combustion chambers at the rotor tips. The V1 was flown first in the spring of 1943 but was damaged slightly by air raids during 1944. The V2 was derived from the rebuilt and modified V1, the V3 destroyed itself by vibration, but the V4 flew well before development was stopped in 1945.

The last piston-engined fighter in FAA first-line squadrons was the Hawker Sea Fury. First flown on 21 February 1945, the type entered service with No 807 Squadron in August 1947 and operated with distinction throughout the Korean War. The Sea Fury flown by Lt P. Carmichael of No 802 Squadron destroyed the squadron's first MiG-15 on 9 August 1952.

The largest military flying-boat built in Germany during the Second World War was the Blohm und Voss Bv 238. The single prototype, powered by six Daimler-Benz DB 603 engines, was first flown in March 1945. Intended to fill a long-range reconnaissance or transport role, the Bv 238 had a wing span of 197 ft 4½ in (60·17 m) and a maximum loaded weight of 176 370 lb (80 000 kg).

The first successful tandem twin-rotor helicopter to be put into production was the Piasecki PV-3 (US Navy designation HRP-1) which first flew in March 1945. It was powered by a 600 hp Pratt & Whitney R-1340 Wasp engine and could fly at 120 mph (193 km/h). Designed to carry ten persons, six stretchers or cargo, the first production HRP-1 was completed on 15 August 1947. Versions of this helicopter served with the US Navy, Marine Corps, Coast Guard and Air Force.

The first test-drop of the 22 000 lb 'Grand Slam' bomb was made from an Avro Lancaster on 13 March 1945. The first operational drop of this bomb was made by Sqn Ldr C. C. Calder of No 617 (Bomber) Squadron, flying Lancaster BI

(Special) PD112. The bomb was dropped on the Bielefeld Viaduct on 14 March 1945, smashing two of its spans.

The first single-seat carrier-based dive-domber and torpedo-carrier in the US Navy, the Douglas AD-1 Skyraider was developed too late to see operational service in the Second World War. First flown on 18 March 1945, the Skyraider was to prove an important naval aircraft in the Korean and Vietnam conflicts. When supplied to the British Royal Navy under the MAP, it filled a unique position as an airborne early-warning aircraft. Designated AEW1 in British service, the Skyraiders were also the last piston-engined fixed-wing aircraft in first-line service with the FAA.

The first twin-engined single-seat fighter to operate from carriers of the Royal Navy was the de Havilland Sea Hornet F20, the prototype Sea Hornet (PX212) making its first flight on 19 April 1945. Aircraft of this type equipped No 801 Squadron, and were embarked in HMS *Implacable* in 1949, remaining in service until the squadron was re-equipped with Sea Furies in 1951. Production aircraft were powered by two 2030 hp Rolls-Royce Merlin 133s or 134s, and had a maximum speed of 467 mph (752 km/h) at 22 000 ft (6700 m).

The last U-boat to be sunk by RAF Coastal Command (the 196th) was destroyed by a Consolidated Catalina of No 210 Squadron on 7 May 1945. It was an RAF Catalina of No 209 Squadron which, on 26 May 1941, spotted the German battleship *Bismarck* after surface vessels had lost contact.

The only combat aircraft of canard configuration to be the subject of a production contract during the Second World War was the Japanese Kyushu J7W Shinden, intended as a heavily armed high-performance interceptor for use by the Navy. Powered by a 2130 hp Mitsubishi MK9D 18-cylinder supercharged radial engine, driving a six-blade pusher propeller, the prototype made its first flight on 3 August 1945. Only two more short flights were made before the Japanese surrender.

The only Japanese turbojet-powered aircraft to take off under its own power during the Second World War was the Nakajima Kikka. Designated Navy Special Attacker Kikka, its design was based on the Messerschmitt Me 262, but its development came so late in the war that the prototype flew only twice, on 7 and 11 August 1945.

The world's first operational atomic bomb was dropped on the Japanese city of Hiroshima on 6 August 1945, carried by the B-29 Superfortress *Enola Gay*, captained by Col Paul W. Tibbets Jr.

The second operational atomic bomb was dropped on the Japanese city of Nagasaki on 9 August 1945, carried by the B-29 Superfortress *Bock's Car*, captained by Maj Charles W. Sweeney.

The last Victoria Cross won during the Second World War was awarded posthumously to Lt Robert Hampton Gray, Royal Canadian Navy Volunteer Reserve (attached to the Fleet Air Arm), the pilot of a Corsair fighter-bomber who was killed in an attack on a Japanese destroyer in the Bay of Onagawa Wan on 9 August 1945 — after both atomic bombs had been dropped on Japan and only a few days before the Japanese surrender. Gray's VC was the only one awarded to a member of the Royal Canadian Navy during the Second World War.

The last sortie by suicide aircraft, according to Japanese accounts, was flown on 15 August 1945 by seven aircraft of the Oita Detachment, 701st Air Group, Imperial Japanese Navy, led in person by Adm Matome Ugaki, commander of the 5th Air Fleet. However, United States records fail to confirm any *kamikaze* attacks on this date.

The total number of suicide aircraft expended, and the results of these attacks, are believed to be as follows:

	Sorties	Aircraft returned	Expended
Philippines area	421	43	378
Formosa area	27	14	13
Okinawa area	1809	879	930
Totals	2257	936	1321

It has not proved possible to distinguish between actual suicide aircraft and escort fighters in the Okinawa operations and this must necessarily invalidate the total figures to some extent. A rough estimate would show that the usual ratio

Hiroshima after the first atomic bomb had been dropped. (US National Archives)

of escort fighters to suicide aircraft on most sorties was about three to two, although late in the campaign many sorties were flown entirely without escort.

The total number of American naval vessels sunk by suicide attacks from the air was 34, and 288 damaged. Those which were sunk comprised 3 escort aircraft carriers, 13 destroyers, 1 destroyer escort, 2 high-speed minelayers, 1 submarine chaser, 1 minesweeper, 5 tank-landing ships, 1 ocean tug, 1 auxiliary vessel, 1 patrol craft, 2 motor torpedo boats and 3 other vessels.

The first helicopter to cross the English Channel was a Focke-Achgelis Fa 223 (No 14) which arrived at Brockenhurst, Hampshire, in September 1945, piloted by a German crew of three. Fa 223 No 14 was first flown in July 1943 and with No 51 was confiscated by the Americans in May 1945. No 14 was destroyed in October 1945 during evaluation trials.

The end of the Pacific War became official on 2 September 1945, with Japanese signature of the surrender documents aboard the battleship USS *Missouri*, anchored in Tokyo Bay.

The first flight of an aircraft powered completely by turboprop engines was made by the 18th production Gloster Meteor F.1. Re-engined by Rolls-Royce with two RB.50 Trent turboprops, driving 7 ft 11 in (2·41 m) diameter five-blade propellers, it was flown for the first time on 20 September 1945.

The first post-war British survey flight to South America was made on 9 October 1945, when Capt O.P. Jones took off from Hurn, Hampshire, in the Avro Lancastrian G-AGMG.

The first American aeroplane to land under jet power on a ship was a Ryan FR-1 Fireball com-

The result of a kamikaze attack on USS Randolph. (US National Archives)

pound fighter, fitted with a conventionally-mounted Wright R-1820-72W radial piston-engine as well as a General Electric I-16 turbojet installed in the rear fuselage. This combination had resulted from US Navy doubts of the suitability of jet-powered aircraft for carrier operations. Flown by Ensign Jake C. West on to the escort carrier USS *Wake Island* on 6 November 1945, it had been intended to fly on using the reciprocating engine, but this failed on the approach and West landed under jet-power. **The first US (all-) jet aircraft to land on an aircraft carrier**, on 21 July 1946, was the McDonnell FD-1 Phantom prototype, which landed on the USS *Franklin D Roosevelt*. Production aircraft were redesignated subsequently FH-1.

The first two post-war world absolute speed records were established by Gloster Meteor F4 fighters. On 7 November 1945 Gp Capt H. J. Wilson established a record speed of 606 mph (975 km/h) at Herne Bay, Kent, flying the Meteor EE454 *Britannia*. On 7 September 1946 Gp Capt E. M. Donaldson raised the record to 616 mph (991 km/h) near Tangmere, West Sussex, in Meteor EE549. The three Meteors allocated to the re-formed RAF High Speed Flight (EE548-550), which was to make the attempt to set a new speed record in 1946, had their wings clipped, reducing wing span from 43 ft 0 in (13·11 m) to 37 ft 2 in (11·33 m). Unfortunately, it was discovered that this reduced their maximum speed by almost 58 mph (93 km/h) and full-span wings were used for the record attempt. Because the clipped-wing modification improved structural integrity, as well as rate of roll, it subsequently became standard on all but the earliest F4s. In 1948 Meteor F4s superseded F3s in the RAF's first-line fighter squadrons until they, in turn, were supplanted by F8s. In May 1950, the F4s which equipped No 222 Squadron at Leuchars

became the first jet fighters to be based in Scotland. Meteor F8s first entered service with No 245 Squadron at Horsham St Faith, Norfolk, on 29 June 1950. The Meteor F4 was powered by two 3500 lb (1587 kg) thrust Rolls-Royce Derwent 5 engines, the F8 by 3600 lb (1633 kg) thrust Derwent 8s. Meteor F8s of the Royal Australian Air Force were the only British jet fighters to see action in the Korean War.

The world's first pure jet aircraft to operate from an aircraft carrier was a de Havilland Vampire I, the third prototype (LZ551) which had been modified for deck-landing trials. It was first landed on HMS *Ocean*, a light fleet carrier of the Colossus Class, by Lt Cdr E. M. Brown, RNVR, on 3 December 1945. The first deck landing was followed by trials in which 15 take-offs and landings were made in two days.

The cartwheel manoeuvre (essentially performed in a twin-engined aeroplane) was first demonstrated by Jan Zurakowski in a de Havilland Hornet fighter (two Rolls-Royce Merlin engines) at Boscombe Down, Wiltshire, during 1945. The same pilot later gave demonstrations of the manoeuvre in a Gloster Meteor IV jet fighter at the annual SBAC Displays at Farnborough, Hants. It was performed during a vertical full-power climb to a point of near-stall by quickly throttling-back one engine and performing a controlled, vertical wing-over.

The most successful fighter pilot in the world, and Germany's leading ace in the Second World War, was Maj Erich Hartmann of Jagdeschwader 52. The first of only two fighter pilots in the world to score 300 victories, the achievement brought him into a select band of men—numbering 27 only—who wore the Diamonds to the Knight's Cross, the award being made on 25 July 1944. Hartmann eventually surrendered to American forces in Czechoslovakia during May 1945, by which time he had scored a total of 352 victories.

The most successful German fighter pilot in combat against the Western Allies during the Second World War was Hauptmann Hans-Joachim Marseille. In April 1941 he was posted to I Gruppe Jagdgeschwader 27 in Libya, and it was in desert warfare that he became a master. On 2 September 1942 he received the Diamonds to his Knight's Cross. Known as the 'Star of Africa', he died on 30 September 1942 when he baled out of his Messerschmitt Bf 109G but his parachute failed to open. Then only 22 years old, he had been credited with 158 victories, all of them gained in combat against the RAF and Commonwealth air forces.

The most successful English fighter pilot of the Second World War was Gp Capt James Edgar 'Johnnie' Johnson, credited with 38 confirmed aerial victories over German aircraft. Johnson remained in the RAF after the war, retiring finally with the rank of Air Vice-Marshal in 1966.

Luftwaffe fighter pilots with 150 or more confirmed victories during the Second World War and the Spanish Civil War

E = Eastern Front; W = Europe; Afr = North Africa; Gr = Greece; * = at least

✠✿✗♦ = Knight's Cross with Oak Leaves, Swords and Diamonds
✠✿✗ = Knight's Cross with Oak Leaves and Swords
✠✿ = Knight's Cross with Oak Leaves
✠ = Knight's Cross of the Iron Cross

Name, rank, decorations	Units	Total score	Day/ Night	Fronts	Four engined	With jet a/c
Major Erich Hartmann ✠✿✗♦	JG 52	**352**	352/0	352 E	0	0
Major Gerhard Barkhorn ✠✿✗	JG 52, 6, JV 44	**302**	301/1	301 E	0	?
Major Günther Rall ✠✿✗	JG 52, 11, 300	**275**	275/0	3 W, 272 E	?	0
Oberleutnant Otto Kittel ✠✿✗	JG 54	*267	267/0	267 E	0	0
Major Walter Nowotny ✠✿✗♦	JG 54, Kdo. Nowotny	**258**	258/0	255 E, 3 W	*1	3
Major Wilhelm Batz ✠✿✗	JG 52	**237**	237/0	232 E, 5 W	2	0
Major Erich Rudorffer ✠✿✗	JG 2, 54, 7	**222**	222/0	136 E, 60 W, 26 Afr	10	12
Oberstleutnant Heinz Bär ✠✿✗	JG 51, 77, 1, 3, JV 44	**220**	220/0	96 E, 79 W, 45 Afr	*21	16
Oberst Hermann Graf ✠✿✗♦	JG 51, 52, 50, 11, 52	**212**	212/0	202 E, 10 W	10	0
Major Theodor Weissenberger ✠✿	JG 77, 5, 7	**208**	208/0	175 E, 33 W	?	8
Oberstleutnant Hans Philipp ✠✿✗	JG 76, 54, 1	**206**	206/0	177 E, 29 W	1	0
Oberleutnant Walter Schuck ✠✿	JG 5, 7	**206**	206/0	198 E, 8 W	4	8
Major Heinrich Ehrler ✠✿	JG 5, 7	*204	204/0	204 E?	?	?
Oberleutnant Anton Hafner ✠✿	JG 51	**204**	204/0	184 E, 20 Afr	5	0
Hauptmann Helmut Lipfert ✠✿	JG 52, 53	**203**	203/0	majority E, *4 W	2	0
Major Walter Krupinski ✠✿	JG 52, 5, 11, 26, JV 44	**197**	197/0	177 E, 20 W	1	?
Major Anton Hackl ✠✿✗	JG 77, 11, 26, 300, 11	**192**	192/0	105 E, 87 W	32	0
Hauptmann Joachim Brendel ✠✿	JG 51	**189**	189/0	189 E	0	0
Hauptmann Max Stotz ✠✿	JG 54	**189**	189/0	173 E, 16 W	0	0
Hauptmann Joachim Kirschner ✠✿	JG 3, 27	**188**	188/0	167 E, 13 Gr, 6 W, 2 Malta	*2	0
Major Kurt Brändle ✠✿	JG 53, 3	**180**	180/0	160 E, 20 W	0	0
Oberleutnant Günther Josten ✠✿	JG 51	**178**	178/0	majority E	1	0
Oberst Johannes Steinhoff ✠✿✗	JG 26, 52, 77, 7, JV 44	**176**	176/0	148 E, 28 W & Afr	4	6
Oberleutnant Ernst-Wilhelm Reinert ✠✿✗	JG 77, 27	**174**	174/0	103 E, 51 Afr, 20 W	2	0
Hauptmann Günther Schack ✠✿	JG 51, 3	**174**	174/0	174 E	0	0
Hauptmann Emil Lang ✠✿	JG 54, 26	**173**	173/0	148 E, 25 W	?	0
Hauptmann Heinz Schmidt ✠✿	JG 52	**173**	173/0	173 E	0	0
Major Horst Ademeit ✠✿	JG 54	**166**	166/0	165 E, 1 W	0	0
Oberst Wolf-Dietrich Wilcke ✠✿✗	JG 53, 3	**162**	162/0	137 E, 21 W, 4 Malta	4	0
Hauptmann Hans-Joachim Marseille ✠✗✿♦	JG 52, 27	**158**	158/0	151 Afr, 7 W	0	0
Hauptmann Heinrich Sturm ✠	JG 52	**157**	157/0	157 E	0	0
Oberleutnant Gerhard Thyben ✠✿	JG 3, 54	**157**	157/0	152 E, 5 W	?	0
Oberleutnant Hans Beisswenger ✠✿	JG 54	**152**	152/0	152 E	0	0
Leutnant Peter Düttmann ✠	JG 52	**150**	150/0	150 E	0	0
Oberst Gordon Gollob ✠✿✗♦	ZG 76, JG 3, 77	**150**	150/0	144 E, 6 W	0	0

The most successful American fighter pilot of the Second World War was Maj Richard Ira Bong, whose 40 confirmed aerial victories are unsurpassed by any American military pilot of any war. Born at Superior, Wisconsin, on 24 September 1920, Bong enlisted as a Flying Cadet on 29 May 1941. After flying training at Tulare and Gardner Fields, California, and Luke Field, Ariz, he received his 'wings' and a commission (all American military pilots were automatically commissioned) on 9 January 1942. In May he was posted to Hamilton Field, California, for combat training on the Lockheed P-38 Lightning twin-engined fighter, and subsequently joined the 9th Fighter Squadron of the 49th Fighter Group, then based in Australia. All of his 40 victories had been scored by late 1944, in the Pacific theatre of war. General George C Kenney, his commanding officer, ordered him back to the United States in December 1944, with a recommendation for the Congressional Medal of Honor—which award was subsequently granted. Bong became a test pilot for Lockheed at Burbank, California; on 6 August 1945, the day the world's first atomic bomb was dropped on Hiroshima, he died when the engine of his P-80 jet failed. Many of his victories were gained while flying the P-38J *Marge* named after his fiancée.

The numbers of aircraft shot down by fighter pilots of the Second World War varied much more widely than was the case in the First World War, due to the enormous differences in conditions and standards of equipment in the various combat areas. Comparison of the lists of national top-scoring fighter pilots reveals the almost incredible superiority of German pilots in terms of confirmed victories—ie Major Erich Hartmann, the Luftwaffe's leading ace, is credited with nearly nine times as many victories as the leading British and American pilots, and 35 Germans are credited with scores in excess of 150.

Since the end of the war there have been persistent attempts to discredit these scores; but by any reasonable criterion, the figures must now be accepted as accurate. The Luftwaffe's confirmation procedure was just as rigorous as that followed by Allied air forces, and the quoted figures are those prepared at unit level and were not subject to manipulation by the Propaganda Ministry. The main reasons for the gulf between German and Allied scores were the different conditions of service and the special circumstances which existed on the Russian Front in 1941 and 1942. In Allied air forces an operational tour by a fighter pilot was almost invariably followed by a posting to a second-line establishment for several months. This process of rotating pilots to areas where they could recover from the strain of prolonged combat operations was unknown in the Luftwaffe; apart from very short periods of leave, a German fighter pilot was effectively on combat operations from the day of his first posting until the day his career ended – in death, serious injury or capture. The Luftwaffe fighter pilot's career was thus, in real terms, about twice as long as his RAF or USAAF counterpart.

When Germany invaded the Soviet Union in June 1941, the Russian Air Forces were equipped with very large numbers of obsolescent aircraft. They had no fighter whose speed and armament approached the performance of the Messerschmitt Bf 109E and Bf 109F, and their bombers in squadron service were markedly inferior to contemporary European designs. Thus, the Luftwaffe was presented with large numbers of easy targets—the perfect environment for the development of a fighter pilot's skill and confidence. The situation did not become significantly more challenging for many months, by which time many of the Jagdflieger had learned their trade so well that they retained the initiative. Despite this factor, one is left with the inescapable conclusion that Germany simply produced a group of officers who were fighter pilots of exceptional skill and determination.

The pilots who scored **100 or more victories against the Western Allies** in northern Europe, southern Europe, the Mediterranean area and North Africa were as follows (Western victories only, in cases of mixed service):

Hauptmann Hans-Joachim Marseille	158
Oberstleutnant Heinz Bär	124
Oberstleutnant Kurt Bühligen	112
Generalleutnant Adolf Galland	104
Major Joachim Müncheberg	102
Oberstleutnant Egon Mayer	102
Major Werner Schroer	102
Oberst Josef Priller	101

These figures become even more impressive if one reflects on the fact that Marseille achieved

151 of his victories between April 1941 and September 1942; and that Galland did virtually no combat flying between November 1941 and the end of 1944, while he occupied the post of General of Fighters.

Two categories of victories in northern Europe are worthy of special attention; those scored over heavy bombers, and those scored while flying jet aircraft. The achievements of the world's first generation of jet combat pilots are described· elsewhere in this chapter. The Luftwaffe placed great value on the destruction of the very heavily armed four-engined Boeing Fortress and Consolidated Liberator bombers which formed the United States 8th Air Force's main equipment in the massive daylight bombing offensive of 1943–5. Usually flying in dense formations protected by an enormous combined firepower—and, in the later months, by superb escort fighters—these large aircraft were obviously far more difficult to destroy than smaller ones. The leading 'heavy bomber specialists' among Germany's daylight home defence pilots included:

Oberleutnant Herbert Rollwage	.	44
Oberst Walther Dahl .	. . .	36
Major Werner Schroer	. .	26
Hauptmann Hugo Frey	. .	26
Oberstleutnant Egon Mayer	. .	25
Oberstleutnant Kurt Bühligen	. .	24
Oberstleutnant Heinz Bär	. .	21
Hauptmann Hans-Heinrich König	.	20
Hauptmann Heinz Knoke .	. .	19

The Great Air Fighters of the Second World War

The most successful fighter pilots of the Second World War, by nationality, are listed below: all scores are levelled down to the nearest unit: British gallantry decorations are quoted:

Country of origin		Aircraft destroyed in combat
Australia	Gp Capt Clive R. Caldwell, DSO, DFC*	28
Austria	Maj Walter Nowotny .	258
Belgium	Flt Lt Vicki Ortmans, DFC	11
Canada	Sqn Ldr George F. Buerling, DSO, DFC, DFM*	31
Czechoslovakia	Sgt Josef František, DFM	28
Denmark	Gp Capt Kaj Birksted	either 8 or 10
Finland	F/Mstr E. I. Juutualainen	94
France	Sqn Ldr Pierre H. Clostermann, DFC*	19
Germany	Maj Erich Hartmann .	352
Hungary	2nd Lt Dezjö Szentgyörgyi	43
Ireland	Wg Cdr Brendan E Finucane, DSO, DFC**	32
Italy	Maj Adriano Vinconti .	26
Japan	Sub-Officer Hiroyoshi Nishizawa	103
Netherlands	Lt Col van Arkel	12 V-1s and 5

Progressive world absolute speed records achieved by man in the atmosphe

mph	km/h	Pilot	Nationality	Aircraft
463·82	746·45	Flugkapitän Hans Dieterle	Germany	Heinkel He 100V-8
469·22	755·138	Flugkapitän Fritz Wendel	Germany	Messerschmitt Bf 109R

Second World War: No reliable international records

606·25	975·67	Gp Capt H.J. Wilson, AFC	GB	Gloster Meteor F4

Progressive world absolute distance record achieved by man in the atmosph

miles	km	Pilot/s	Nationality	Aircraft
7 916	12 739·6	Col Irving and Lt Col Stawley	USA	Boeing B-29 Superfortress

Country of origin		Aircraft destroyed in combat	
New Zealand	Wg Cdr Colin F. Gray, DSO, DFC**	27	
Norway	Flt Lt Svein Heglund	either 14 or 16	
Poland	Jan Poniatowski (rank unknown)	36	
Romania	Capt Prince Constantine Cantacuzino	60	
South Africa	Sqn Ldr M. T. St J. Pattle, DFC*	41	
United Kingdom	Gp Capt James E. Johnson, DSO**, DFC*	38	
United States	Maj Richard I. Bong	40	
USSR	Guards Col Ivan N. Kozhedub	62	

Fighter pilots serving with the Royal Air Force during the Second World War who achieved 25 or more confirmed aerial victories (countries of origin indicated in parentheses):

Sqn Ldr M. T. St J. Pattle, DFC*	41	(SA)	
Gp Capt J. E. Johnson, DSO**, DFC*	38	(UK)	
Gp Capt A. G. Malan, DSO*, DFC*	35	(SA)	
Wg Cdr B. E. Finucane, DSO, DFC**	32	(Ir)	
Sqn Ldr G. F. Buerling, DSO, DFC, DFM*	31	(Ca)	
Wg Cdr J. R. D. Braham, DSO**, DFC**, AFC	29	(UK)	
Wg Cdr R. R. S. Tuck, DSO, DFC**	29	(UK)	
Sqn Ldr N. F. Duke, DSO, DFC**, AFC	28	(UK)	
Gp Capt C. R. Caldwell, DSO, DFC*	28	(Au)	
Gp Capt F. H. R. Carey, DFC**, AFC, DFM	28	(UK)	
Sqn Ldr J. H. Lacey, DFM*	28	(UK)	
Wg Cdr C. F. Gray, DSO, DFC**	27	(NZ)	
Flt Lt E. S. Lock, DSO, DFC*	26	(UK)	
Wg Cdr L. C. Wade, DSO, DFC**	25	(US)	

Fighter pilots serving with the United States air forces during the Second World War who achieved 25 or more confirmed aerial victories:

USAAF:

Maj Richard I. Bong (CMH)	40
Maj T. B. McGuire (CMH)	38
Col F. S. Gabreski	31
Lt Col R. S. Johnson	28
Col C. H. MacDonald	27
Maj G. E. Preddy	26

USN:

Capt D. McCampbell	34

USMC:

Maj J. J. Foss	26
Lt R. M. Hanson	25
Lt Col G. Boyington	22

(Lt Col Boyington is known to have destroyed an additional six enemy aircraft while serving with the Air Volunteer Group under Chinese command.)

Location of achievement	Date
Oranienburg, Germany	30 Mar 1939
Augsburg, Germany	26 Apr 1939
Herne Bay, Kent, England	7 Nov 1945

Location	Date
Northwest to Washington	12 Nov 1945

Non-aviation inventions of the period

Nuclear reactor Uranium chain reaction demonstrated in 1942 by Italian physicist Enrico Fermi

Ball-point pen Patented in 1943 by Hungarian journalist Ladislao Biro

Artificial kidney First 'kidney machine' built in 1943 by Dutch doctor Wilhelm Kolff

Computer First electronic computer developed for US Army Ordnance Department in 1945

Post-war Aviation

For a second time in the brief historical period of less than three decades, the nations that had been involved in a major war began the process of facing up to a whole new range of problems. The return to peace was rather less of a shock than had been the case in 1919, with better plans for sailors, soldiers and airmen to be transformed back to civilians. But the six years of war had wrought tremendous changes in the field of aviation. Instead of the fairly parochial First World War, that which had just ended had been fought over a worldwide arena requiring the development of aircraft with far greater range capability. In the case of the United States, involved in European, Middle East and Far East theatres of action, it spurred the development of long-range transport aircraft, able to operate from and to land-aerodromes.

Longer-range operations brought the evolution of better communications and navigation systems; the need to attack targets by day or night and in all weather conditions improved instrumentation and hastened the development of airborne radar for navigation and blind bombing; and, of course, more potent weapons had been introduced as the war progressed. German and Allied research had shown that it would be possible to build new warplanes of increased speed and capability, and the development in Germany and Britain of gas turbine engines for aircraft propulsion meant that the powerplants needed by such advanced aircraft would soon be available.

All of this confirmed that the flying-boat was as dead as a dodo for long-range world travel; that a whole new generation of transport aircraft would need to be built to carry in peace the hundreds of thousands of ex-service men and women who had come to regard air travel as the norm; and that an equally large new generation of high-performance military aircraft, combining new technology and turbine engines, would very soon be required by the world's major air forces. The aviation industry got on with the task, and this section shows how it coped with the initial demands made upon it.

The first-ever Type-Approval Certificate for a commercial helicopter was awarded for the Bell Model 47 on 8 March 1946; this aircraft made its first flight on 8 December 1945 and provided the design basis for a family of Bell helicopters that has now continued in production for close on 40 years.

The first regular British air service to South America was inaugurated on 15 March 1946, the service flown initially by Lancastrians.

The Mikoyan MiG-9 and the Yakovlev Yak-15 were the first pure jet Soviet aircraft, both flown in prototype form on 24 April 1946. The Yak-15, designed by Alexander S. Yakovlev, was the first jet fighter to enter squadron service with the Soviet Air Forces when delivered to the IA-PVO in early 1947. Powered by a single RD-10 turbojet (a Russian adaptation of the German Jumo

004B engine) developing initially 1875 lb (850 kg) thrust, it was armed with two 23 mm Nudelman-Suranov NS-23 guns and had a top speed of 488 mph (786 km/h) at 16 400 ft (5000 m). Like the first Tupolev jet bombers, the Yak-15 was also the result of adapting a piston-engine airframe for jet propulsion. The prototype retained the wings, cockpit, tailplane and tailwheel landing gear of a Yakovlev Yak-3, the new engine being mounted in the forward fuselage. This meant that the jet efflux was below the pilot's cockpit, and production aircraft had the fuselage undersurface protected by heat-resistant stainless steel. It meant also that the first batch of production aircraft had an all-metal tailwheel. This proved unsatisfactory, and the Yak-15 was retrofitted with tricycle landing gear. A member of the company test team in 1947 was Olga Yamschikova, **probably the first woman in history to fly a turbojet-powered fighter aircraft.**

The first transatlantic arrivals at London's Heathrow Airport, opened officially on 31 May 1946, were Lockheed Constellations of Pan American Airways and American Overseas Airlines.

The first French aircraft to be designed specifically for stratospheric flight research was the Aérocentre Belphégor, which flew for the first time on 6 June 1946. Powered by a single Daimler-Benz DB 610 engine, developing 3000 hp, it had pressurised accommodation for five persons in its bulbous fuselage, including two research members; the pilot was situated in a cupola above the main cabin. With an all-up weight of 22 050 lb (10 000 kg), the Belphégor could fly to an altitude of 42 000 ft (12 800 m).

The first high-speed twin-engined strike aircraft designed specifically to operate from aircraft carriers of the Royal Navy was the Short Sturgeon. Originating from a wartime requirement, to operate from *Ark Royal* and *Hermes* class carriers, the war's end resulted in the Sturgeon being completed to satisfy a gunnery training and target-towing role. The first prototype made its maiden flight on 7 June 1946.

The first US airmail to be carried by turbojet-powered aircraft was that flown on 22 June 1946, by two USAAF Lockheed P-80 Shooting Star fighters, from Shenectady to Washington D.C. and Chicago, Illinois.

The most unusual bomber programme initiated after the Second World War involved the series of Northrop flying wings. The first full-size prototype XB-35 flew on 25 June 1946. Designed as a long-range bomber, it comprised a cantilever aluminium sweptback wing, constructed in one piece. Directional control was via drag-inducing double-split flaps at the wingtips, and elevons and leading-edge fixed wingtip slots were fitted. The crew of seven were situated in a centre-section nacelle; six electrically-operated gun turrets (four remotely controlled at outer wing stations) provided defensive armament. Powered by four turbo-supercharged Pratt & Whitney Wasp Major piston engines of 3000 hp each, the XB-35 had an all-up weight of 209 000 lb (94 800 kg) and a wing span of 172 ft (52·43 m). Its design had been started in 1942, followed by testing of four twin-engined scale models designated N-9M. Following the first flight of the prototype XB-35, 14 development aircraft were ordered by the USAF as YB-35s; two of these were converted into YB-49s, each with eight jet engines, and one into the YRB-49A with six jet engines. Although 30 RB-49s were ordered subsequently for operational service with the USAF, these were cancelled in 1949.

The last biplane in squadron service with the Fleet Air Arm was the Supermarine Sea Otter, a carrier-based or shore-based amphibian, of which production ended in July 1946. Used primarily for air-sea rescue and communications, its retirement was hastened by the introduction of helicopters to fulfil these roles.

The first American pure jet aeroplane to operate from a carrier was the McDonnell FH-1 Phantom, first operating from the USS *Franklin D Roosevelt* on 21 July 1946. It was also the first jet fighter to serve with first-line squadrons of the US Navy and the US Marine Corps.

The first recorded use of an ejection seat, to enable a man to escape from an aircraft in flight, occurred on 24 July 1946. This was the date when the first experimental live ejection was made, using a Martin-Baker ejection seat installed in a Gloster Meteor. With the aircraft travelling at 320 mph (515 km/h), 'guinea pig' Bernard Lynch ejected at a height of 8000 ft (2440 m). In subsequent tests, Lynch made suc-

The huge Northrop YB-35 flying wing bomber.

cessful ejections at 420 mph (675 km/h) at heights up to 30 000 ft (9145 m). It should be noted that the wartime Heinkel He 219 Uhu (Owl) was the first operational aircraft to be equipped with ejection seats; while no dates have been recorded, it is known that some lives were saved by this equipment in the He 219.

A unique post-war grouping of national airlines on 31 July 1946 brought about the formation of SAS (Scandinavian Airlines System), uniting the major operators of Denmark, Norway and Sweden.

The first manned test of an American ejection seat was made by Sgt L. Lambert, USAAF, who was ejected from a Northrop P-61 Black Widow on 17 August 1946. The two-seat aircraft was travelling at 300 mph (483 km/h) at 7800 ft (2375 m).

The first post-war long distance record for aeroplanes was set by a modified Lockheed P2V-1 Neptune maritime reconnaissance aircraft, the *Truculent Turtle*, which flew a distance of 11 236 miles (18 082 km) between 29 September and 1 October 1946. On 7 March 1949 a later-version P2V-2 took off from the carrier USS *Coral Sea* at the then record take-off weight from a ship of 74 000 lb (33 566 kg).

The first US experimental delivery of airmail by helicopter began on 1 October 1946; the operations were carried out in the Chicago suburbs in a combined exercise by the US Post Office and the USAAF.

The first non-stop flight between Hawaii and Egypt, over the North Pole, was made in a USAAF Boeing B-29 Superfortress on 6 October 1946, covering a distance of 10 873 miles (17 498 km).

The first aircraft to land on and take off from Mount Washington, New Hampshire, on 12 March 1947, was a ski-equipped Piper Cub flown by Carmen Onofrio.

Designed to obtain air-load measurements, the Douglas Skystreak raised the World Speed Record by 17 mph (27 km/h) to 640·60 mph (1030·95 km/h) on 20 August 1947, then to 650·78 mph (1047·33 km/h) on 25 August. The first of three Skystreaks flew initially on 28 May 1947, and automatic pressure recording was carried out via

Douglas Skystreak.

400 measurement points on the fuselage, straight laminar-flow wings and tail unit. In addition, strain gauges were attached to the wings and the tail unit.

The first six-turbojet bomber to fly in America was the Martin XB-48. Only two prototypes were built, the first of them flown on 22 June 1947, and both were powered by six wing-mounted Allison J35 turbojet engines.

The first flying-boat in the world capable of a maximum level speed of over 500 mph (805 km/h) was the British Saunders-Roe SR A/1 jet fighter flying-boat which first flew on 16 July 1947. Powered by two Metrovick Beryl axial-flow turbojets, the SR A/1, **which was also the world's first jet-powered flying-boat,** had a top speed of 512 mph (824 km/h) and an armament of four 20 mm guns. Three prototypes were built, but the project was abandoned when flight tests showed that the large flying-boat hull compromised both speed and manoeuvrability.

The Soviet Union's first jet-powered bomber to fly, on 24 July 1947, was the Ilyushin Il-22. However, early flight tests proved disappointing and its development was abandoned.

The first Russian jet bomber to achieve very limited production status was the Tupolev Tu-12, little more than a Tu-2 piston-engined bomber re-engined with gas-turbines. The prototype probably flew for the first time on 27 July 1947, powered by two 3525 lb (1600 kg) thrust RD-10 engines, derived from the Junkers 004B. Power plant of the later aircraft consisted of RD-500 engines, the Russian equivalent of the Rolls-

Royce Derwent 5, which developed 4410 lb (2000 kg) thrust.

The first British-designed and -built production helicopter was the Bristol Sycamore which first flew on 27 July 1947 and entered service with both the Army and Air Force. The Army versions were the HC10 ambulance and HC11 communications helicopters, the latter flying initially on 13 August 1950 and being delivered from 29 May 1951. The first RAF version, HR12, was sent to St Mawgan for trials on 19 February 1952.

British European Airways (BEA) began its first scheduled all-cargo services on 10 August 1947.

The United States Air Force came into being on 18 September 1947, as an **independent** member of the new unified US armed services and, **for the first time since its foundation,** was no longer under control of the Army.

The world's first scheduled helicopter service was inaugurated on 1 October 1947 by Los Angeles Airways (LAA), using a Sikorsky S-51. The CAB had awarded LAA a temporary (three-year) certificate for mail carrying, on 22 May 1947.

The North American F-86 Sabre, which was to become **the USAF's first sweptwing fighter, and its first fighter able to exceed a speed of Mach 1 in a shallow dive,** was flown for the first time in XP-86 prototype (NA-140) form on 1 October 1947.

The largest flying-boat in the world, the largest aeroplane ever flown, and the aircraft with the greatest wing span ever built was the Hughes H4 Hercules. The 180 ton (183 tonne) flying-boat was powered by eight 3000 hp Pratt & Whitney R-4360 piston-engines, had a wing span of 320 ft (97·54 m), and an overall length of 219 ft (66·75 m). Big enough to accommodate up to 700 passengers, it was intended primarily as a freighter and no cabin windows were provided. Piloted by its sponsor, the American millionaire Howard Hughes, it flew on only one occasion, covering a distance of about a mile, at a height of approximately 80 ft (24 m), over Los Angeles Harbor, California, on 2 November 1947.

The first piloted aircraft to be flown at twice the speed of sound was the Douglas Skyrocket, which flew for the first time on 4 February 1948. Designed to investigate sweptback wings, it was

Martin XB-48 six-engined bomber.

The largest flying-boat ever was the Hughes H4 Hercules, flown just once in November 1947.

powered by one Reaction Motors XLR-8 rocket motor of 6000 lb (2720 kg) thrust and one Westinghouse J34 turbojet engine of 3000 lb (1360 kg) thrust. The wings were of conventional subsonic configuration with a 35° sweepback. Altogether three Skyrockets were built, and on 31 August 1953 one reached an altitude of 83 235 ft (25 370 m). However, the most memorable flight of a Skyrocket was made on 20 November of the same year when the aircraft attained a speed of Mach 2·005 after being launched from a Boeing 'motherplane' at 32 000 ft (9750 m).

The world's first aircraft to fly on the power of a single turboprop engine was the Boulton Paul P.108 Balliol, a three-seat advanced trainer for service with the RAF. It was first flown with its Armstrong Siddeley Mamba turboprop engine on 24 March 1948.

The world's first turbojet-powered aircraft to exceed a speed of Mach 1 was the YP-86A prototype of the North American F-86 Sabre which, on 25 April 1948, attained supersonic speed in a shallow dive.

The first wind tunnel with a test section having a continuous capability of 3000 mph (4828 km/h) was that activated by the USAF at Aberdeen, Maryland, announced as being operational on 23 May 1948.

The first helicopter mail service in Great Britain was inaugurated on 1 June 1948 by British European Airways, with the Westland/Sikorsky S-51 (G-AKCU). Based at Peterborough, Northants, it served Norwich, Great Yarmouth and Kings Lynn.

The Berlin Airlift started effectively on 26 June 1948, when USAF C-47s based near Frankfurt made a first airlift of supplies into West Berlin.

The first east-west crossing of the North Atlantic by turbojet-powered aircraft was made by six RAF de Havilland Vampire F.Mk 3s on 14 July 1948, flying via Iceland and Greenland.

The first car ferry flight operated by Silver City Airways was made on 14 July 1948, the Bristol Freighter G-AGVC making the initial flight carrying two cars.

The world's first turboprop-powered civil transport (when it entered airline service) was the prototype Vickers Viscount (G-AHRF), first flown on 16 July 1948.

En route from Selfridge Field, Michigan, to Scotland, 16 Lockheed F-80 (formerly P-80) Shooting Star fighters of the USAF recorded the **first west-east crossing of the North Atlantic by turbojet-powered aircraft.**

The USAF's first turbojet-powered all-weather interceptor was the prototype of the Northrop XF-89 Scorpion, which recorded its first flight at Edwards AFB, California, on 16 August 1948. The Scorpion entered USAF service in 1950.

The first jet-powered fighter to be designed specifically as a parasite aircraft was the McDonnell XF-85 Goblin, which made its first flight on 23 August 1948. Designed to be carried inside the

Vickers Viscount G-AHRF, the first turboprop-powered civil transport. (Flight International)

forward bomb-bay of the Consolidated Vultee B-36 long-range bomber, the Goblin had an extremely short and stubby fuselage, with swept short-span wings and multiple tail surfaces. It was launched and picked up via a retractable 'skyhook' on the Goblin which hooked on to a retractable trapeze on the bomber. Following one abortive attempt to hook back onto the B-36, which nearly ended in disaster, the first successful hook-on was made on 14 October 1948. Although several more hook-ons were achieved, and the Goblin demonstrated a speed of 520 mph (837 km/h), the project was cancelled after only two Goblins had been built. One of them remains on view at the USAF Museum at Dayton, Ohio. The length of the Goblin was only 14 ft 10½ in (4·53 m); power was provided by a Westinghouse J34 engine of 3000 lb (1360 kg) thrust.

The first European swept-wing jet fighter to enter operational service after the Second World War was the Swedish Saab J-29. It first flew on 1 September 1948 and joined the Day Fighter Wing F13 of the Flygvapnet near Norrköping in May 1951. Nicknamed *Tunnan* (Barrel) and powered by a British de Havilland Ghost turbojet of 4410 lb (2000 kg) thrust, the J-29B possessed a top speed of 658 mph (1059 km/h) at 5000 ft (1525 m) or Mach 0·90 at the tropopause.

The first British jet-powered aircraft to exceed a speed of Mach 1 was the de Havilland DH108, three examples of which were built to investigate the stability and control problems of swept wings, so providing information for the design of the de Havilland Comet I airliner. The first DH108 made its maiden flight on 15 May 1946, using a standard de Havilland Vampire fighter fuselage and powered by one 3750 lb (1700 kg) thrust Goblin 4 turbojet engine. This first aircraft was used to provide data on the slow-flying characteristics of the swept wings; the second and third were used for high-speed flying. The last aircraft recorded a speed between Mach 1·0 and 1·1 on 6 September 1948 while in a dive from 40 000 ft (12 200 m).

A Vickers Viking carrying urgent medical supplies, and prevented by thick fog from taking off from Blackbushe, Surrey, on 30 November 1948, **became the first commercial aircraft to make use of the British wartime FIDO fog dispersal system to become airborne.**

The Northrop X-4 Bantam was designed to investigate the subsonic flight characteristics of aircraft with swept wings but without a tailplane. Two X-4s were produced, the first flying on 15 December 1948. The programme was completed successfully in April 1954, after some 60 flights had been made.

The first experimental night helicopter service was inaugurated on 14 February 1949 by British European Airways, flying the Westland-Sikorsky S-51 G-AKCU. The service, from Westwood, Peterborough, to Norwich, became regular from 17 October 1949 and continued until April 1950.

The first non-stop round-the-world flight was accomplished between 26 February and 2 March 1949. This was made by the Boeing B-50 *Lucky Lady II* with a crew commanded by Capt James Gallagher, USAF, and covering a distance of 23 452 miles (37 742 km) in 94 h 1 min. Taking off from and landing back at Carswell AFB, Texas, the B-50 was flight-refuelled four times.

A non-stop flight between Hawaii and Teterboro, New Jersey, representing a distance of 4957 miles (7978 km) was made by William P. Odom in a Beech Bonanza lightplane between 7 and 8 March 1949.

The peak day of the Berlin Airlift was recorded on 16 April 1949 when, during a period of 24 hours, a total of 1398 sorties was made by the international fleet of aircraft supplying West Berlin, and carrying in a total 12 940 tons (13 146 tonnes) of supplies.

Built as an experimental ramjet-powered aircraft, the French Leduc 0.10 made its first powered flight on 21 April 1949 after being released over Toulouse from a Languedoc motherplane. This carried the 0.10 above its fuselage on special mounting struts, providing the stream of air to flow into the engine which was necessary for the ramjet to work. On this occasion the 0.10 reached a speed of 422 mph (680 km/h) on 50 per cent power. Maximum speed achieved during a later flight was Mach 0·84. Three 0.10s were produced; each had a tubular double-skinned fuselage, the outer shell forming the annular ramjet duct and the inner shell accommodating the cockpit for the crew of two.

A flight-refuelled world endurance record of 1008 h 1 min was set in the US by Bill Barris and

From the Leduc 0.10 was developed the larger and more powerful Leduc 0.21, the two examples built seen here on top of their Languedoc carrier transports.

First prototype English Electric Canberra jet bomber.

Dick Reidel flying the Aeronca Chief lightplane *Sunkist Lady*. The six-week flight was achieved by flying low to the ground to haul up fuel and food four times daily from a jeep racing along the ground below.

The first jet bomber to be produced in the UK, and the first to serve with the RAF when it became operational in May 1951, was the English Electric Canberra. The prototype Canberra, the A.1, was first flown in prototype form on 13 May 1949.

The first helicopter station in New York, which had been established at Pier 41 East River, became operational on 18 May 1949.

A record total of 301 passengers and seven crew was carried by the US Navy's Martin Mars flying-boat *Marshall Mars*, flown from Alameda, Idaho, to San Diego, California, on 19 May 1949.

First flown in YF-94 prototype form on 1 July 1949, the Lockheed F-94 Starfire was **the first turbojet-powered all-weather interceptor to serve with the USAF's Air Defense Command.**

The de Havilland DH106 Comet I, which was to become the **world's first turbojet-powered airliner** when it entered airline service in 1952, was first flown in prototype (G-ALVG) form on 27 July 1949.

Flying at a speed of approximately 575 mph

(925 km/h) over South Carolina in a McDonnell F2H-1 Banshee, on 9 August 1949, Lt J.L. Fruin, USN, became the **first US airman to use an ejection seat for an emergency escape from an aircraft.**

The first British delta-wing research aircraft was the Avro 707, which made its first flight on 4 September 1949. Designed to gain data on the flight characteristics of delta wings at low speeds, the Type 707 was basically a scale model of the then-projected Vulcan bomber. Following its destruction in an accident, the Type 707B was produced to continue low-speed research, first flying in September 1950. Two Type 707As then followed for research into high-speed flight; and the series was completed by a single Type 707C, a two-seat version built to give pilots training in flying delta-wing aircraft. The 707C first flew in mid-1953, powered by a Rolls-Royce Derwent engine of 3600 lb (1635 kg) thrust.

The largest landplane ever built in Britain, the Bristol Brabazon I, which had a wing span of 230 ft (70·10 m), length of 177 ft (53·95 m) and maximum take-off weight of 290 000 lb (131 542 kg), was first flown as a prototype (G-AGPW) on 4 September 1949.

The first aircraft in the world powered by a coupled twin-turbine engine driving contra-rotating co-axial four-blade propellers was the Fairey Gannet, first flown on 19 September 1949. The unusual power plant was an Armstrong Siddeley Double Mamba, each of its two sections driving one propeller. Half of the engine could be shut down and its propeller feathered to provide a most economical cruise power setting.

The United Kingdom's first night airmail services to be operated by helicopter began on 17 October 1949, the inaugural flight being made by BEA's Sikorsky S-51 G-AJOV, flown by Capt J. Cameron.

The first helicopter to have the engine mounted in the nose of the fuselage was the Sikorsky S-55, which first flew on 7 November 1949. This layout provided increased cabin area for the accommodation of passengers or cargo.

The first aircraft to carry more than 100 passengers in flight across the North Atlantic was a USAF C-74 Globemaster I of MATS. Landing at Marham, Norfolk, after a non-stop flight from the US on 18 November 1949, the Globemaster had carried a total of 103 passengers and the aircraft's crew.

The 'Derry Turn' was evolved by John Derry, a test pilot of the de Havilland company, during 1949-50. It was a positive-G turn initiated by rolling in the opposite direction through 270°. A fairly spectacular manoeuvre, it was made possible only by the availability of sufficient excess engine power, allied with rudder control, to keep the nose of the aircraft up at the necessary late stage in the rolling manoeuvre.

Prototype de Havilland DH106 Comet jetliner.

The first helicopter in Great Britain to enter service with the RAF was the Sikorsky-designed Westland/Sikorsky Dragonfly (the S-51 built under licence by Westland Aircraft Ltd at Yeovil, Somerset). The first Westland-built S-51 was for commercial use and flew in 1948. The RAF's first Dragonfly HC Mark 2 (WF308) was powered by an Alvis Leonides engine and delivered in 1950; subsequent aircraft equipped No 194 (Casualty Evacuation) Squadron, the RAF's first helicopter squadron, on 1 February 1953.

Avro 707B, 707C and 707As accompany two early Vulcan V-bombers.

The Royal Navy's first all-helicopter squadron was No 705, formed at Gosport, Hampshire, during 1950. Equipped with the Westland Dragonfly, this type of aircraft soon demonstrated its value for 'plane-guard' duties and ship-to-shore communications.

First American-built aircraft to enter RAF service after the Second World War were ex-USAF B-29 and B-29A Superfortresses, given the RAF designation Washington B1. No 149 Squadron at Marham was the first squadron to receive these aircraft, in March 1950, and a total of 88 entered RAF service.

The first cross-Channel flight in a sailplane, between London and Brussels, was made by L. Welch on 12 April 1950.

The first scheduled helicopter passenger services in the UK were those made between 9 and 19 May 1950 during the British Industries Fair. The services were flown between London and Birmingham by a Westland/Sikorsky S-51.

The first sustained and regular scheduled helicopter passenger services in the UK, between Liverpool and Cardiff, began on 1 June 1950. The service was operated by British European Airways with Westland/Sikorsky S-51s, but due to low demand was terminated on 31 March 1951 after carrying 819 passengers.

The Korean War began on 25 June 1950, the first major confrontation in which newly developed aircraft were used, and one which highlighted the value of the helicopter for military operations, especially for casualty evacuation.

The first US Navy jet fighter to take part in air combat was the Grumman F9F-2 Panther, several of which took off from the carrier USS *Valley Forge* off Korea on 3 July 1950 and went into action against North Korean forces. A US Navy pilot of a Grumman Panther shot down a MiG-15 on 9 November 1950, and thus became the first US Navy pilot to shoot down another jet aircraft. The Panther was the first jet fighter designed by the Grumman Corporation, and the first two XF9F-2 prototypes were powered by imported Rolls-Royce Nene turbojets of 5000 lb (2268 kg) thrust.

The first turbine-powered airliner in the world to receive an Airworthiness Certificate was the Vickers V630 Viscount prototype (G-AHRF), with Rolls-Royce Dart turboprop engines, which was awarded Certificate No A907 on 28 July 1950. The following day British European Airways operated this aircraft to record the world's first scheduled passenger service to be flown by a gas-turbine powered airliner. Piloted by Capt Richard Rymer, the Viscount took off from London (Northolt) and flew to Paris (Le Bourget), carrying 14 fare-paying passengers and 12 guests of the airline. Capt Rymer was also the world's first holder of a pilot's licence for a turbine-powered civil transport aircraft.

The first non-stop crossing of the North Atlantic by a turbojet-powered fighter aircraft was recorded on 22 September 1950, when a Republic EF-84E Thunderjet with hose-and-drogue flight refuelling capability flown by Col David C. Schilling, USAF, flew from the UK to Limestone, Maine. The flight was achieved by making three in-flight refuellings *en route*.

The first aerial victory to be gained by the pilot of one jet aircraft over another was achieved on 8 November 1950, when Lt Russel J. Brown Jr of the 51st Interceptor Wing, USAF, flying a Lockheed F-80C, shot down a MiG-15 fighter of the Chinese People's Republic air force over Sinuiju on the Yalu River, the border between North Korea and China.

The first turbojet-powered night fighter to enter service with the RAF, serving with No 29 Squadron at Tangmere, Sussex, in January 1951, was the Meteor NF11, developed by Armstrong Whitworth.

The first jet aircraft to fly the North Atlantic non-stop and unrefuelled was an English Electric Canberra B.Mk 2 on 21 February 1951, which was flown from Britain to Baltimore and was later purchased by the USAF to become the first Canberra to carry American markings. Canberras were the first jet bombers produced in Britain and the first to serve with the RAF. The type had the unique distinction of being the first aircraft of non-US design to enter operational service with the USAF after the end of the Second World War. USAF approval for licence-production of the Canberra by the Glenn L. Martin Company was given on 6 March 1951, leading to a pre-production batch of eight B-57As (the original USAF designation), the first of these making its first flight at Baltimore, Maryland, on 20 July 1953.

The Fairey FD1 was a small delta-wing research aircraft that was conceived originally as a ramp-launched vertical take-off fighter. Powered by a single Rolls-Royce Derwent turbojet engine of 3600 lb (1635 kg) thrust, it made its first flight on 12 March 1951 at Boscombe Down. When the VTO project was abandoned, the FD1 was given conventional landing gear and used for research until it was grounded after a landing accident.

The first British V-bomber (so-called from the wing leading-edge plan-form) was the Vickers Valiant, of which the prototype (WB210) first flew on 18 May 1951. Two Mark 1 and one Mark 2 prototypes were built, and were followed by 104 production aircraft, the first of which (WP199) flew on 21 December 1953. They were powered by various versions of the Rolls-Royce Avon axial-flow turbojet, four such engines being located in the wing roots. The Valiant entered RAF service with No 138 Squadron at Gaydon, Warwickshire, in early 1955 and afterwards equipped Nos 7, 49, 90, 148, 207, 214 and 543 Squadrons. Production also included versions for photo-reconnaissance as the B (PR) Mark 1, and B (PR) K Mark 1 and BK Mark 1 tankers. Maximum speed was 567 mph (912 km/h) at 36 000 ft (11 000 m), Mach 0·84. Normal loaded weight with a 10 000 lb (4540 kg) bomb-load was 140 000 lb (63 560 kg). Range without external fuel tanks was 3450 miles (5550 km). A Valiant of Bomber Command carried Britain's

Camouflaged North American F-86 Sabre jet fighters at Suwon air base in Korea, September 1951. (US National Archives)

first operational atomic bomb, which was dropped over Maralinga, Southern Australia, on 11 October 1956.

The first jet fighter pilot to achieve five confirmed aerial victories over jet aircraft was Capt James Jabara, an F-86 Sabre pilot of the 4th Fighter Interceptor Wing, USAF, who shot down his fifth MiG-15 on 20 May 1951. Capt Jabara later went on to destroy a total of 15 MiG-15s, thereby becoming the second most successful Allied pilot of the Korean War.

The first solo trans-Polar flight was made on 29 May 1951 in a North American P-51 Mustang by American C. Blair from Bardufoss, Norway, to Fairbanks, Alaska.

The first jet aircraft flown with variable-geometry wings was the Bell X-5, which flew for the first time on 20 June 1951. Design of the X-5 began in 1948 and two were built, the first crashing on 13 October 1953. The X-5 was powered by a single Allison J35-A-17 turbojet engine; its wing span varied from 30 ft 10 in (9·39 m) to 18 ft 7 in (5·66 m) in unswept and swept positions respectively.

Britain's most successful military aircraft to be designed and built after the Second World War was undoubtedly the Hawker Hunter jet fighter, the first flight of the first of three prototypes (WB188) being made on 20 July 1951.

The first single-seat sweptwing interceptor jet fighter to enter service with the RAF was the Supermarine Swift, the prototype (WJ960) of which was flown for the first time on 5 August 1951.

The first freight service operated by turboprop-powered aircraft, between Northolt and Hanover, was flown by Rolls-Royce Dart-engined Douglas DC-3s of BEA. The first flight was made on 15 August 1951 by G-ALXN *Sir Henry Royce*. This aircraft and a second DC-3, G-AMBD *Claude Johnson*, had been used for development flying of the Dart power plants introduced on the Vickers Viscount.

The first standardised jet fighter to serve in FAA first-line squadrons was the Supermarine Attacker, which was also the first aircraft powered by the Rolls-Royce Nene turbojet. The type entered service with No 800 Squadron at Ford, Sussex, on 22 August 1951, and this was the

FAA's first operational jet squadron. When withdrawn from first line service, the Attackers were transferred to RNVR air squadrons: when No 1831 Squadron received these aircraft on 14 May 1955, it became the first jet fighter squadron of the RNVR.

The US Navy's first ASW helicopter squadron, Squadron HS-1, was commissioned at Key West, Florida Keys, on 3 October 1951.

The first British delta-wing interceptor fighter, and the first twin-jet delta fighter in the world, was the Gloster Javelin. First flight of the prototype (WD804) was made by Sqn Ldr W.A. Waterton on 26 November 1951. **The Javelin was also the RAF's first purpose-built all-weather interceptor fighter.** The use of the delta-wing posed many aerodynamic problems, early flights suffering from control surface vibration and buffeting. On the 99th flight, on 29 June 1952, both elevators were lost following violent flutter. By superb flying, Waterton managed to control the aircraft in pitch, by means of the variable incidence tailplane, and bring it in to a fast landing, which caused the landing gear to collapse. For his skill and courage in saving the aircraft and its flight recorder, Waterton was awarded the George Medal. **The first production Javelin**

Gloster Javelin WD804.

FAW1 (XA544), powered by two 8150 lb (3697 kg) thrust Armstrong Siddeley Sapphire AS Sa6 turbojet engines, made its first flight on 22 July 1954. First deliveries to No 46 Squadron at Odiham, Hampshire, began in February 1956.

The smallest piloted biplane ever flown was the Stits Skybaby, designed, built and flown by Ray Stits at Riverside, California, in 1952. It had a

Stits Skybaby, the smallest piloted biplane ever flown. (Howard Levy)

wing span of 7 ft 2 in (2·18 m) and a length of 9 ft 10 in (3·00 m). Powered by an 85 hp Continental C85 engine, it weighed 452 lb (205 kg) empty and had a top speed of 185 mph (298 km/h).

The first twin-rotor twin-engined helicopter to be designed and flown in Britain, the Bristol Type 173 prototype (G-ALBN), was flown for the first time at Filton, Bristol, on 3 January 1952.

The world's first Certificate of Airworthiness for a turbojet-powered civil airliner was awarded to the de Havilland Comet I on 22 January 1952.

The heaviest bomb-load carried by an operational bomber was that of the Boeing B-52 Stratofortress at 75 000 lb (34 019 kg); with this warload on board, the B-52 had a range of approximately 3000 miles (4828 km). Dubbed 'the big stick', the YB-52 prototype was first flown on 15 April 1952 by A.M. 'Tex' Johnson. The first of three production B-52As was delivered to the USAF's Strategic Air Command (SAC) on 27 November 1957. B-52s became subsequently the main flying deterrent of SAC and continue to have a significant strategic role in USAF planning.

The world's first turbojet airliner to enter commercial service was the de Havilland DH106 Comet I, powered by four de Havilland Ghost 50 turbojet engines. **The world's first regular passenger service to be flown by turbojet aircraft** was inaugurated by British Overseas Airways Corporation on 2 May 1952, using the de Havilland Comet I G-ALYP between London and Johannesburg, South Africa. Its route was via Rome, Beirut, Khartoum, Entebbe and Livingstone, and the aircraft was captained in turn by Capts A.M. Majendie, J.T.A. Marsden and R.C. Alabaster. It carried 36 passengers and the total elapsed time for the 6724 miles (10 821 km) was 23 h 34 min.

The first west-east crossing of the North Atlantic by helicopters was made in stages by two Sikorsky S-55s, between 13 and 31 July 1952.

A North American RB-45 reconnaissance aircraft of the USAF, flown between Elmendorf AFB, Alaska, to Yokota AB, Japan, on 29 July 1952, became **the first turbojet-powered aircraft to complete a non-stop transpacific flight.**

Saunders-Roe SR45 Princess flying-boat.

The first of three giant Saunders-Roe SR45 Princess flying-boats, and the only one to fly, made its maiden flight on 20 August 1952, piloted by Geoffrey Tyson. Because of the growing capability of landplanes for long-range intercontinental services, the three Princess flying-boats were scrapped.

The world's first large bomber to have a delta-wing plan-form was the Avro Vulcan B.1, the prototype of which (VX770) flew for the first time on 30 August 1952. Production aircraft entered service with RAF Bomber Command in May 1956, equipping No 230 Operational Conversion Unit at Waddington, Lincolnshire, and the type was to record more than a quarter-century of operational use by the RAF.

The Douglas X-3 was built to investigate the effectiveness of turbojet engines and short-span double-wedge wing and tail surfaces at very high altitudes, and to study thermodynamic heating at speeds up to Mach 3. Construction of the aircraft caused many problems, as it was built primarily of then little used titanium. To measure the pressure on the airframe during flight, a huge number of pin-hole orifices were positioned strategically over the airframe, and

temperature and stress were also measured at many locations. Powered by two Westinghouse J34 turbojets, the X-3 made its maiden flight on 20 October 1952. The programme was terminated in May 1956, after 20 flights had been made by NASA.

The heaviest aeroplane ever to serve as standardised equipment on board aircraft carriers was the Douglas A3D Skywarrior carrier-based attack-bomber. The first of two XA3D-1 prototypes was flown on 28 October 1952, and initial production A3D-1s (later A-3A) were first delivered to VAH-1 (US Navy Heavy Attack Squadron One) on 31 March 1956. The definitive production version, ultimately designated A-3B, served on board carriers of the Essex and Midway classes. The A-3B Skywarrior had a span of 72 ft 6 in (22·10 m), maximum loaded weight of 82 000 lb (37 195 kg), and was powered by two 12 400 lb (5624 kg) thrust Pratt & Whitney J57-P-10 turbojets, providing a maximum level speed of 610 mph (982 km/h) at 10 000 ft (3050 m).

The first commercial flights over the Polar regions between Europe and North America began on 19 November 1952. Flown by SAS (Scandinavian Airlines System) Douglas DC-6Bs, these first flights were unscheduled, but scheduled operations over this route were initiated during 1954.

Built to test the flight characteristics of swept wings at low speed, the Short SB5 produced data that was used in the design of the English Electric P1 prototype and, subsequently, the production Lightning fighter. The wings on the SB5 were tested at four different angles of sweepback, ranging from 50° to 69°, with combinations of a high or low mounted tailplane with various angles of incidence. After making its maiden flight on 2 December 1952, the aircraft was still flying experimentally in the early 1960s.

The third and last of the long-range medium bombers which had been developed **for the RAF's V-bomber programme,** the Handley Page Victor prototype (WB771) made its first flight on 24 December 1952.

The US Navy's first angled-deck aircraft carrier, the USS *Antietam*, began operational flight testing with Navy aircraft on 12 January 1953.

Designed as a mixed-power research aircraft, to provide data for future interceptors of similar concept, the French Sud-Ouest SO 9000 Trident first flew on 2 March 1953, powered initially by two wingtip-mounted Turboméca Marboré II turbojet engines. These were replaced later by Dassault Viper turbojet engines of nearly double the power, and an SEPR 481 rocket motor of 9920 lb (4500 kg) thrust was installed subsequently in the rear fuselage. Testing of the rocket power unit

French Sud-Ouest SO 9000 Trident experimental mixed-power research aircraft.

began in April 1955, and the Trident eventually attained a speed of 1055 mph (1700 km/h).

The world's first fatal accident involving a turbojet airliner occurred on 3 March 1953 when *Empress of Hawaii*, the de Havilland Comet I CF-CUN of Canadian Pacific Airlines, crashed on take-off at Karachi, Pakistan. This occurred during the aircraft's delivery flight from London to Sydney, its intended operating base, and all eleven occupants were killed. It was stated that the accident was caused by the pilot lifting the aircraft's nose too high during take-off, thereby causing it to stall.

The Convair Sea Dart was an experimental seaplane fighter fitted with delta wings and hydroskis. It set several 'firsts', being **the first delta-winged seaplane and the first seaplane to exceed the speed of sound.** The original aircraft was designated XF2Y-1 and made its first flight on 9 April 1953. It was joined subsequently by the development version, designated YF2Y-1, which exceeded Mach 1 on 3 August 1954 in a dive, shortly before being destroyed in an accident. Whereas the XF2Y-1 was powered by two Westinghouse J34 turbojet engines, each of 3400 lb (1542 kg) thrust, the later aircraft had two J46 engines of 6000 lb (2720 kg) thrust each, with afterburning. The YF2Y-1 proved sufficiently promising for the US Navy to order three more similar aircraft, but the whole concept of a seaplane fighter was soon abandoned.

The first scheduled flight on BEA's London-Nicosia route, made by the Vickers Viscount V.701 *Sir Ernest Shackleton* (G-AMNY) on 18 April 1953, marked the beginning of **the world's first sustained passenger service to be operated by turboprop-powered airliners.**

The first woman in the world to fly faster than the speed of sound was Miss Jacqueline Cochran, pilot extraordinary and American cosmetics tycoon who, flying a Canadian-built version of the North American F-86 Sabre, exceeded the speed of sound on 18 May 1953, and on the same day established a world's speed record for women of 652 mph (1049 km/h).

The most successful Allied fighter pilot of the Korean War was Capt Joseph McConnell Jr of the 39th Fighter Squadron, 51st Fighter-Interceptor Wing, USAF; an F-86 Sabre pilot, McConnell

scored his 16th and last victory on 18 May 1953, a day on which he destroyed a total of three MiG-15s. He was killed subsequently on 25 August 1954 while testing a North American F-86H.

The world's first fighter aircraft capable of sustained supersonic speed in level flight, the North American F-100 Super Sabre, was flown for the first time in YF-100A prototype form on 25 May 1953.

The first British transport aircraft designed specifically to air-drop heavy loads, and also the RAF's largest aircraft at the time of its introduction, was the Blackburn Beverley. Powered by four 2850 hp Bristol Centaurus 173 engines, the prototype (WZ889) flew for the first time on 14 June 1953. Able to carry a payload of almost 22 tons (22·4 tonnes), Beverleys began to equip No 47 Squadron Transport Command in March 1956.

When a USAF C-124 Globemaster II transport aircraft crashed on take-off from Tachikawa AFB, Tokyo, on 18 June 1953, its death toll of 129 represented **the first air disaster involving the death of more than 100 people.**

The Belgian airline Sabena operated **the first international helicopter flight into central London** on 7 July 1953. The flight was made by a Sikorsky S-55, between the Allee Verte Heliport in Brussels and London's South Bank Heliport near Waterloo.

The world's first 'over 700 mph' speed record was set at 715·60 mph (1151·64 km/h) on 16 July 1953. This was achieved by Lt Col W.F. Barnes, USAF, flying a North American F-86D Sabre.

The first US Navy pilot to achieve five air victories over Korea was Lt Guy Bordelon who, flying a piston-engined Vought F4U Corsair, shot down his fifth victim on 17 July 1953.

The world's first international helicopter service was inaugurated on 1 September 1953 by the Belgian airline Sabena, flying Sikorsky S-55s. Services included flights from Brussels to Lille, Maastricht and Rotterdam.

The first aircraft to test the practicability of the aero-isoclinic wing was the Short SB4 Sherpa, which made its maiden flight on 4 October 1953. The wing was designed as a partially flexible structure, with all-moving tips which were used as both ailerons and elevators. Flight testing showed that the handling characteristics of the aircraft were very satisfactory.

What was to become **the USAF's first operational delta-winged aircraft** when it entered service in April 1956, the Convair F-102 Delta Dagger, was first flown in YF-102A prototype form on 24 October 1953.

The only turboprop-powered flying-boat to serve with the US Navy was the Convair R3Y Tradewind, the first R3Y-1 making its maiden flight on 25 February 1954. A large transport with a gross weight of 160 000 lb (72 570 kg), the later R3Y-2s each had a nose door through which armoured vehicles could be disembarked directly on to a landing beach.

One of the smallest and lightest of the USAF's then modern combat aircraft was the Lockheed F-104 Starfighter, the XF-104 prototype of which was flown for the first time on 28 February 1954. Production F-104s, capable of Mach 2 performance, had a wing span of only 21 ft 10¾ in (6·67 m) and a maximum take-off weight for the F-104A of 24 804 lb (11 251 kg).

Probably the two most unusual experimental VTOL fighters built in America were the Lockheed XFV-1 and Convair XFY-1 'tailsitters'. Designed to the same specification, both had a maximum speed of about 500 mph (805 km/h) and were powered by Allison YT-40A turboprops driving co-axial contra-rotating propellers. The Lockheed XFV-1 was the first to fly, in March 1954; it had straight wings and a cruciform tail unit onto which sprung castoring wheels were fitted as the landing gear. The Convair XFY-1 made its maiden flight on 2 August 1954, and differed from its competitor mainly in having delta wings, with large delta tail surfaces above and below the fuselage forming a cruciform with the wings. Castoring wheels were positioned at the tips of these wing and tail surfaces, to form the vertical landing gear. The pilots of both aircraft sat on gimballed seats, enabling them to be in a near-upright position irrespective of whether the aircraft was in a horizontal or vertical attitude. The XFV-1 made only conventional take-offs; but many VTOL flights were made by the XFY-1, including transitions from vertical to horizontal flight, before the concept of a tail-sitting VTOL fighter was abandoned.

Convair R3Y Tradewind flying-boat with nose raised for straight-through loading.

The first turbojet powered all-weather fighter to serve with the Royal Navy was the de Havilland Sea Venom, which first entered service with No 890 Squadron, which re-formed at Yeovilton, Somerset, on 20 March 1954. At the end of 1958 three Sea Venoms of No 893 Squadron carried out the first firings of Firestreak missiles by an operational fighter squadron of the Royal Navy.

The last operational sortie by an RAF Supermarine Spitfire was that made in Malaya on 1 April 1954, the aircraft operating in a photo-reconnaissance role.

One of the most famous turbojet-powered transport prototypes in aviation history, the Boeing Model 367-80 ('Dash-Eighty'), made its first flight as the prototype of a flight refuelling tanker/transport for the USAF on 15 July 1954. Built extensively for the USAF in this form, it was to be developed simultaneously as the Boeing Model 707 civil transport, the founder member of a remarkable family of commercial transports now in worldwide use.

The first supersonic operational carrier-borne naval interceptor in the world was the Grumman F11F-1 Tiger of the US Navy. Designated originally F9F-9, this was changed after the first three production aircraft had been delivered and, in 1962, was designated finally F-11. The prototype, powered by a Wright J65-W-6 turbojet rated at 7800 lb (3538 kg) thrust, flew for the first time on

30 July 1954. The F-11A was capable of a speed of 890 mph (1432 km/h) in level flight at 40 000 ft (12 200 m), and was armed with four 20 mm cannon. Two or four Sidewinder missiles could be carried on underwing pylons. F11F-1s entered service with the US Navy's VA-156 Squadron in March 1957. Two F11F-1s were powered by 15 000 lb (6805 kg) thrust General Electric J79-GE-3A engines, and demonstrated Mach 2 performance in level flight.

The first supersonic single-seat fighter to serve with the RAF, the English Electric (later BAC) Lightning, designed by W.E.W. Petter, flew for the first time on 4 August 1954, piloted by Wg Cdr R.P. Beamont. Entering operational service with No 74 Squadron at Coltishall, Norfolk, in July 1960, it was the first RAF fighter capable of speeds in excess of Mach 2, and its first integrated weapons system. During the research which led to its contruction, Britain's first transonic wind tunnel was built.

The first aircraft to set a world speed record of over 1000 mph (1600 km/h) was the Fairey Delta 2, the first example of which made its maiden flight on 6 October 1954. Built originally to investigate the problems encountered during transition from subsonic to supersonic speeds, each Delta 2 was powered by a Rolls-Royce Avon turbojet engine. The first aircraft had an Avon RA5 which gave 12 000 lb (5445 kg) thrust, the second an RA28 which developed 1000 lb (450 kg) more thrust. The record was set on 10 March 1956, off the Sussex coast between Ford

Boeing Model 367-80, one of the most famous jetliners in aviation history.

and Chichester, Lt Cdr L. Peter Twiss flying the first aircraft (WG774) at an FAI accredited speed of 1131·76 mph (1821·39 km/h), the fastest of two runs made at 1147 mph (1846 km/h). Subsequently, this aircraft was converted into the BAC 221, with new delta wings and control surfaces, new landing gear, longer fuselage and a hydraulically-actuated drooping nose. Data gained with it were used in the development of the Concorde SST airliner.

The first man to escape from an aeroplane flying at supersonic speed and live was George Franklin Smith, test pilot for North American Aviation Corporation, who ejected from an F-100 Super Sabre on 26 February 1955 off Laguna Beach, California. After failure of the controls in a dive, Smith fired his ejector seat at an indicated speed of Mach 1·05 or more than 700 mph (1125 km/h). After being unconscious for five days Smith made an almost complete recovery from his injuries which included haemorrhaged eyeballs, damage to lower intestine and liver, knee joints and eye retina. Within nine months he was passed fit to resume flying.

The first jet fighter in the world with a variable-incidence wing was the Chance Vought (subsequently Ling-Temco-Vought, or LTV) F-8 Crusader supersonic air-superiority fighter of the US Navy. The operation of such a high-performance aircraft from the deck of an aircraft carrier meant that to achieve an acceptable landing speed an excessive nose-up attitude would result. The use of a variable-incidence wing provided the necessary compromise. The first of two XF8U-1 prototypes, powered by a Pratt & Whitney J57-P-11 turbojet engine, made its first flight on 25 March 1955. Deliveries of the production Crusader, under the designation F-8A, began to VF-32 (US Navy Fighter Squadron 32) on 25 March 1957, serving originally at sea aboard the USS *Saratoga*. This initial production version was powered by a J57-P-12 or -14 engine, providing a maximum level speed of 1100 mph (1770 km/h) at 40 000 ft (12 200 m). Armament comprised four 20 mm cannon and, on early models, a fuselage pack of 32 air-to-air rockets. Later F-8As carried two fuselage-mounted Sidewinder missiles.

The first post-war landing in the UK by a German civil-registered aircraft was made on 15

Two Crusader fighters of VF-62 with their angles of wing incidence increased.

April 1955. The aircraft was the Deutsche Luft-hansa Convair CV-340 D-ACAD on a route proving flight. The first regular post-war air services to the UK operated by Lufthansa began on 16 May 1955.

The first multi-engined monoplane airliner with its turbojet powerplant installed in pods, one on each side of the rear fuselage, was the French Sud-Est Aviation SE.210 Caravelle. The first of two prototypes made its maiden flight on 27 May 1955, powered by two 10 000 lb (4536 kg) thrust Rolls-Royce Avon RA.26 turbojets. This adoption of a rear-mounted engine installation was intended to ensure that the wing remained aero-dynamically 'clean', free from the interference to airflow caused by wing-mounted engines and nacelles. The Caravelle was the first French turbojet-powered airliner.

The first turbojet-powered airliner to enter service with Aeroflot was the Tupolev Tu-104, the prototype (SSSR-L5400) making its first flight on 15 June 1955. Its use on domestic routes was inaugurated by Aeroflot on 15 September 1956, thus the Soviet Union became the second nation in the world to introduce turbojet-powered civil transport aircraft. The use of the Tu-104 revolutionised Aeroflot's operations, these aircraft on long-range domestic routes providing a reduction of some 60 per cent in flight times by comparison with the piston-engined aircraft that they replaced.

The first member of the RAF to survive a super-sonic ejection (and the second man in the world) was Flying Officer Hedley Molland who escaped from a Hawker Hunter fighter on 3 August 1955. Flying at 40 000 ft (12 200 m), the aircraft went into an uncontrollable dive. All of Flying Officer Molland's efforts to regain control failed, and by the time he ejected his stricken machine was travelling at an estimated Mach 1·10, its height about 10 000 ft (3050 m). Descending in the sea he was picked up by a tug, and recovered in hospital from his injuries which included a broken arm (caused by flailing in the slipstream) and a fractured pelvis.

The first tilt-rotor convertiplane to be flown was the Bell XV-3. Two examples were built, the first making its initial vertical flight on 23 August 1955. Powered by a single Pratt & Whitney R-985 engine of 450 hp, the XV-3 had a large fuselage that could accommodate four persons, and had fixed wings of 31 ft 3½ in (9·54 m) span. The rotor/propellers were mounted at each wingtip and could be directed upward or forward by small electric motors for vertical or horizontal flight respectively. The first transition from vertical to horizontal flight was made on 18 December 1958; by 1966 more than 250 flights had been logged.

The world's first parachute escape from an aircraft travelling at speed on the ground was achieved by Sqn Ldr J.S. Fifield, on 3 September 1955, at Chalgrove airfield, Oxfordshire. This occurred when he was ejected from the rear cockpit of a modified Gloster Meteor 7, piloted by Capt J.E.D. Scott, Chief Test Pilot of Martin-Baker Ltd, manufacturers of the ejection seat. The speed of the aircraft at the moment of ejection was 120 mph (194 km/h) and the maximum height reached by the seat was 70 ft (21 m) above the runway.

The first supersonic tactical fighter-bomber to be designed as such, and in operational form one of the USAF's most important weapons in Vietnam, the YF-105A prototype of the Republic F-105 Thunderchief was flown for the first time on 22 October 1955. Exceeding Mach 1 during this flight, the definitive F-105D had a maximum speed in excess of Mach 2 and all-weather capability resulting from its fully integrated automatic flight and fire control systems.

One of the most bizarre air disasters in aviation history occurred on 1 November 1955, when a Douglas DC-6B of United Air Lines exploded in the air and crashed near Longmont, Colorado, killing all 44 occupants. It was established later that John G. Graham had introduced a bomb aboard to murder his heavily-insured mother who was a passenger.

The last British heavy bomber powered by piston engines was the Avro Lincoln four-engined aircraft. The Lincoln Mk I, known originally as the Lancaster Mk IV, was powered by 1750 hp Rolls-Royce Merlin 85 engines. This version had a maximum level speed of 319 mph (513 km/h) at 18 500 ft (5640 m), could carry 14 000 lb (6350 kg) of bombs and had defensive armament of six 0·50 in machine-guns in pairs in nose, dorsal and tail turrets. The last Lincoln was retired from Bomber Command in December 1955, when the RAF Command became an all-jet force.

The autogyro that has been produced in greater numbers than any other non-military rotorcraft is the Bensen B-8 Gyro-Copter, the prototype of which first flew on 6 December 1955. More than 7000 examples of the B-8M were built over the next two decades and the current version is usually powered by a 72 hp McCulloch Model 4318AX engine which gives it a maximum speed of 85 mph (137 km/h).

The first practical steps towards the creation of the post-war Luftwaffe came on 1 February 1956, when the West German Ministry of Defence initiated a pilot training scheme. The actual formation date of the Luftwaffe der Deutschen Bundesrepublik was on 24 September 1956.

The first rotating-wing aircraft to be literally a 'flying-boat' was the Bensen Model B-8B Gyro-Boat. Designed as a variant of the Gyro-Glider, this aircraft was basically a small dinghy that was fitted with a free-turning two-blade rotor and outer stabilising floats (in later models). The Gyro-Boat would take-off after being towed by a motorboat to a speed of 23 mph (37 km/h). The prototype first flew on 25 April 1956 and large numbers of these aircraft were built.

The world's first known air-transportable hydrogen bomb was dropped on 21 May 1956, from a Boeing B-52B flying at 50 000 ft (15 240 m) over Bikini Atoll in the Pacific Ocean.

The US Navy's first helicopter assault carrier, the USS *Thetis Bay*, was commissioned on 20 January 1956.

The first turbojet aircraft in the world to be used in the military transport role was a modified version of the de Havilland Comet Series 2, the first of which was delivered to RAF Transport

The Avro Lincoln was built also in Australia for the RAAF. This Lincoln was the first Australian Lincoln to complete 100 missions against bandits in Malaya.

Command at Lyneham, Wiltshire, on 7 July 1956.

The first non-stop transcontinental flight across the USA by a rotary-wing aircraft was made during 23 to 24 August 1956. This was accomplished by a specially-prepared Hiller H-21 ('Flying-Banana') twin-rotor helicopter, flying from San Diego, California, to Washington, D.C.

The first British atomic bomb was dropped by a Vickers Valiant (WZ366) of No 49 (Bomber) Squadron, RAF, captained by Sqn Ldr E.J.G. Flavell, over Maralinga, Southern Australia, on 11 October 1956.

Becoming the USAF's first supersonic bomber when it entered service in early 1960, the XB-58 prototype of the Convair B-58 Hustler, a four-turbojet delta-wing medium-bomber, was flown for the first time at Fort Worth, Texas, on 11 November 1956.

The first non-stop round-the-world flight by turbojet-powered aircraft, made by three USAF Boeing B-52 Stratofortresses, was completed on 18 January 1957 after a flight of 45 hr 19 min. Commanded by Maj Gen Archie J. Old, USAF, the 24 325 mile (39 147 km) flight was made at an average speed of 537 mph (864 km/h).

Built to test a turbo-ramjet engine, which was designed to form the bulk of the aircraft's airframe, the French Nord 1500-02 Griffon II was a direct development of the earlier Griffon I, which had been powered by a conventional turbojet only. The Griffon had a turbojet mounted inside the ramjet, to propel it to the speed at which the ramjet could ignite and provide power. It flew for the first time on 23 January

1957, and exceeded Mach 1 on 17 May, with its ramjet power on. Over 200 flights were made by the aircraft, culminating in a flight during which Mach 2·19 was attained on 13 October 1959, at which speed the ramjet developed four-fifths of the aircraft's total thrust.

The first use by BOAC of turboprop-powered aircraft came on 1 February 1957, when the airline introduced the Bristol Britannia Series 102 on its London–Johannesburg route. The inaugural flight of a thrice-weekly service was made by G-ANBI. Power for the aircraft was provided by four 3870 hp Bristol Proteus 175 engines.

The first British hydrogen bomb was dropped by a Vickers Valiant of No 49 (Bomber) Squadron, captained by Wg Cdr Hubbard, on 15 May 1957. The bomb was detonated at medium altitude over the Pacific in the Christmas Island area.

The first non-stop flight by an airliner from London to Vancouver, on the Pacific Coast of Canada—a distance of 5100 miles (8208 km)—was completed by the turboprop-powered Bristol Britannia 310 G-AOVA on 29 June 1957.

The first successful British convertiplane and first large VTOL transport was the Fairey Rotodyne, the prototype of which made its first flight on 6 November 1957. With accommodation for 40 passengers and a crew of two, the prototype Rotodyne Y was powered by two Napier Eland turboprop engines which were mounted below the fixed wings and drove tractor propellers. The large rotor mounted above the fuselage was driven by pressure-jets at the blade tips when required to be powered. In operation, the main rotor was usually powered for take-off and landing, but was allowed to autorotate in normal horizontal flight, the forward propulsion of the aircraft and much of the lift then coming from the turboprop engines and wings respectively. The first transition from vertical take-off to horizontal flight was made on 10 April 1958, and although potential operators were enthused with the Rotodyne, the project was cancelled under government economic cutbacks in 1962.

The first transatlantic passenger service to be flown by turbine-powered airliners was inaugurated by BOAC on 19 December 1957, using Bristol Britannia 312 turboprop aircraft. The

Fairey Rotodyne in horizontal flight.

Breguet 940 Integral.

first flight from London to New York was by G-AOVC captained by Capt A. Meagher.

The greatest altitude from which a successful emergency escape from an aeroplane has been reported is 56 000 ft (17 070 m). At this altitude, on 9 April 1958, an English Electric Canberra bomber exploded over Monyash, Derbyshire, and the crew, Flt Lt John de Salis and Flying Officer Patrick Lowe, fell free in a temperature of −70°F (−56·7°C) down to an altitude of 10 000 ft (3050 m), at which height their parachutes were deployed automatically by barometric control.

Flying a Lockheed F-104A Starfighter over Southern California on 16 May 1958, Capt W.W. Irvin, USAF, established **the first 'over 2000 km/h' world speed record,** ratified subsequently at a figure of 1403 mph (2259·18 km/h).

One of the first French research aircraft to give an effective STOL demonstration of the 'blown-wing' or 'deflected-slipstream' technique, the Breguet 940 Integral research aircraft was flown for the first time on 21 May 1958. It led to production of the similar Breguet 941S, four of which served with the Armée de l'Air in a transport role.

The first swept-wing single-seat fighter to be built for the Royal Navy, and the first to be capable of low-level attack at supersonic speed, attained in a shallow dive, was the Supermarine Scimitar. The first operational squadron, No 803, was formed at Lossiemouth, Scotland, in June 1958. The Scimitar was also the first British naval aircraft to have a power operated control system.

The last scheduled flight by an Airspeed Ambassador of BEA's Elizabethan class was made on 30 July 1958. In six years the 20-strong fleet had flown a combined distance of about 31 million miles (50 million km) and had carried almost 2½ million passengers.

The first aircraft to be designed and built in the Chinese People's Republic, a twin-engined light transport designated Beijing (Peking) No 1, made its first flight on 24 September 1958.

The termination of the Southampton-Madeira service of Aquila Airways, on 30 September 1958, represented **the end of UK commercial flying-boat operations.**

BOAC inaugurated the first transatlantic passenger services to be flown by a turbojet-powered airliner, the de Havilland Comet 4, on 4 October 1958. Simultaneous London–New York (Capt R.E. Millichap with G-APDC) and New York–London (Capt T.B. Stoney with G-APDB) services were flown.

Farthest travelling amateur-constructed aircraft is almost certainly the original Volmer VJ-22 Sportsman two-seat amphibian designed by Volmer Jensen in the United States. First flown on 22 December 1958, it has since logged more than 1700 flying hours, covering a total distance equal to six times round the world.

The last operational example of the Convair B-36, **the largest bomber aircraft to serve with the USAF and the largest operational bomber aircraft in the world in terms of wing span,** was retired from service on 12 February 1959. Spanning 230 ft (70·10 m), the B-36J version had a power plant of six 3800 hp Pratt & Whitney R-4360-53 piston-engines and four 5200 lb (2359 kg) thrust General Electric J47-GE-19 turbojet engines.

Achieving his first solo flight in a turbojet-powered trainer, on 13 March 1959, Aviation Cadet E.R. Cook became the US Navy's first student pilot to do so without previous experience in a propeller-driven aircraft.

The last operational use of water-based aircraft by the Royal Air Force was made on 15 May 1959 using a Short Sunderland of the combined Nos 205/209 Squadrons based at Seletar. The 'farewell' flight of the type was made 5 days later by ML797, bringing to an end 21 years of service.

The first turbojet-powered airliner service linking South America and the UK was inaugurated by Aerolineas Argentinas on 19 May 1959, the service between Buenos Aires and London flown by a de Havilland Comet 4.

The commercial transport aircraft with the world's highest sales total is the Boeing Model 727 three-turbofan short/medium airliner. Design of this aircraft, to complement the Boeing 707/720, was initiated in June 1959 and by 1983 more than 1800 had been delivered.

A remarkable lightplane non-stop distance record was established by American Max Conrad. Flying a single-engined Piper Comanche, he landed at New York on 4 June 1959 after completing a flight of 7683 miles (12 365 km) from Casablanca, Morocco.

Marking the 50th anniversary of Louis Blériot's flight across the English Channel, a London–Paris air race was sponsored by the *Daily Mail* during the period 13 to 23 July 1959. It was won by Sqn Ldr Charles Maughan, RAF, who combined a Hawker Hunter T.Mk 7, a Bristol Sycamore helicopter and two motor cycles to record a time of 40 min 44 s.

The longest recorded parachute descent was that by Lt Col William H. Rankin of the US Marine Corps who, on 26 July 1959, ejected from his LTV F8U Crusader naval jet fighter at 47 000 ft (14 326 m). Falling through a violent thunderstorm over North Carolina, his descent took 40 min instead of an expected time of 11 min, as he was repeatedly carried upwards by the storm's vertical air currents.

Australia's Qantas Empire Airways inaugurated its first transpacific service with tubojet-powered airliners on 29 July 1959, when the Boeing 707-138 *City of Canberra* was flown from Sydney to San Francisco.

The only known occasions on which inverted spins by high-performance jet aircraft have been demonstrated publicly, were the SBAC Displays at Farnborough, Hants, in September 1959 and September 1960. At these displays A.W. ('Bill') Bedford, Chief Test Pilot of Hawker Aircraft Ltd, used the demonstration Hunter two-seater G-APUX to perform inverted spins of twelve or 13 turns and used coloured smoke to trace in the sky the pattern of his recovery.

More than 30 years after being established as the hub of British civil aviation, London's Croydon Airport was finally closed down on 30 September 1959.

The first round-the-world passenger service by jet airliners was established by Pan American World Airways during October 1959. The inaugural service was flown by the Boeing 707-321 *Clipper Windward*.

The first nonstop flight between London and Bombay was recorded by a Boeing 707 during 20-21 February 1960, made during the course of the aircraft's delivery flight to Air India from The Boeing Company at Seattle, via London.

The first full transitions from vertical to horizontal flight, and vice versa, were made by the Short SC.1 VTOL research aircraft on 6 April 1960. The aircraft was powered by four Rolls-Royce RB.108 turbojet engines mounted to give vertical jet lift, and a fifth engine mounted horizontally to give forward flight.

H ('Jerry') Shaw who had piloted KLM's first Amsterdam–London service in 1920, was carried as a passenger on KLM's 40th Anniversary flight on 17 May 1960.

The greatest altitude from which a man has fallen and the longest delayed drop ever achieved by man was that of Capt Joseph W. Kittinger, USAF, over Tularosa, New Mexico, on 16 August 1960. He stepped out of a balloon gondola at 102 200 ft (31 150 m) for a free fall of 84 700 ft (25 816 m) lasting 4 min 38 s, during which he reached a speed of 614 mph* (988 km/h) despite a stabilising drogue and experienced a minimum temperature of −94°F (−70°C). His 28 ft (8·5 m) parachute deployed at 17 500 ft (5334 m) and he landed after a total time of 13 min 45 s. The step by the gondola was inscribed 'This is the highest step in the world.'

The world's first fully-successful experimental V/STOL fighter was the Hawker Siddeley P1127.

---

*The speed of 614 mph (988 km/h) reached by Kittinger during his fall represents a Mach No of 0·93 in the Stratosphere and would have been reached at an altitude of about 60 000 ft (18 300 m); thereafter his fall would have been retarded fairly rapidly to less than 200 mph (322 km/h) as he passed through the Tropopause at about 36 000 ft (11 000 m). The speed of 614 mph (988 km/h) almost certainly represents the greatest speed ever survived by a human body not contained within a powered vehicle beneath the interface (ie within the earth's atmosphere).

The first of two prototypes made its initial tethered hovering flight on 21 October 1960. In September 1961 the first transition flights from vertical to horizontal were made, and in 1963 the type was tested on board HMS *Ark Royal*. Several other development and evaluation models were built, with the name Kestrel, leading subsequently to the production Harrier. Power for the Kestrel was provided by one Bristol Siddeley Pegasus 5 vectored-thrust turbofan engine of 15 200 lb (6895 kg) thrust.

The last scheduled service operated by a piston-engined aircraft from London Heathrow was that flown by a Douglas DC-3 on 31 October 1960. Operating on a flight from London to Birmingham, it was also the last scheduled service by a DC-3 to be flown by BEA.

The world's first aircraft to incorporate a hinged tail for rear loading, the Canadair CL-44D-4, was flown for the first time on 16 November 1960. Powered by four Rolls-Royce Tyne 515/10 two-shaft two-spool turboprops, each rated at 5730 ehp, it had a range of 5660 miles (9110 km) with a 37 300 lb (16 920 kg) payload. Its maximum payload was 66 048 lb (29 960 kg).

Hawker Siddeley P1127, the first fully-successful V/STOL fighter, during deck landing trials on HMS Ark Royal.

Non-aviation inventions of the period

Automation Automatic assembly of motor car engines introduced by the Ford Company at Detroit, Michigan, in 1946.

Tubeless tyre The B.F. Goodrich Company of Akron, Ohio, developed the first successful tubeless tyre in 1947.

Credit card The Diners Club of New York introduced the first general-purpose credit card in 1950.

Microwave oven Patented in America during 1953 by the Raytheon Manufacturing Company.

Nuclear submarine The USS *Nautilus*, first nuclear-powered submarine in the world, was launched in the US during 1954.

Kidney transplant The first successful operation of this nature was carried out during 1954 at the Harvard Medical School, USA.

Progressive world absolute speed records achieved by man in the atmosphere

mph	km/h	Pilot	Nationality	Aircraft	Location of achievement	Date
615·65	990·79	Gp Capt E. M Donaldson, DSO, AFC	GB	Gloster Meteor F4	Rustington, Sussex, England	7 Sept 1946
623·61	1003·60	Col Albert Boyd	USA	Lockheed P-80R Shooting Star	Muroc, California, USA	19 June 1947
640·60	1030·95	Cdr T. F. Caldwell, USN	USA	Douglas D-558 Skystreak	Muroc, California, USA	20 Aug 1947
650·78	1047·33	Maj M.E. Carl, USMC	USA	Douglas D-558 Skystreak	Muroc, California, USA	25 Aug 1947
670·84	1079·61	Maj R.L. Johnson USAF	USA	North American F-86A Sabre	Muroc, California, USA	15 Sept 1948
698·35	1123·89	Capt J. Slade Nash, USAF	USA	North American F-86D Sabre	Salton Sea, California, USA	19 Nov 1952
715·60	1151·64	Lt Col W.F. Barnes, USAF	USA	North American F-86D Sabre		16 July 1953
727·48	1170·76	Sqn Ldr Neville Duke, DSO, OBE, DFC, AFC	GB	Hawker Hunter 3	Littlehampton, Sussex, England	7 Sept 1953
735·54	1183·74	Lt Cdr M. Lithgow, OBE	GB	Supermarine Swift 4	Libya, Africa	25 Sept 1953
752·78	1211·48	Lt Cdr J.B. Verdin, USN	USA	Douglas F4D-1 Skyray	Salton Sea, California, USA	3 Oct 1953
754·99	1215·04	Lt Col F.K. Everest, USAF	USA	North American YF-100A Super Sabre	Salton Sea, California, USA	29 Oct 1953
822·09	1323·03	Col H.A. Hanes, USAF	USA	North American F-100C Super Sabre	Edwards Air Force Base, California, USA	20 Aug 1955
1131·76	1821·39	Lt P. Twiss, OBE, DSC	GB	Fairey Delta 2	Chichester, Sussex, England	10 Mar 1956
1207·34	1943·03	Maj Adrian Drew, USAF	USA	McDonnell F-101A Voodoo		12 Dec 1957
1403·79	2259·18	Capt W.W. Irvin, USAF	USA	Lockheed F-104A Starfighter	Southern California, USA	16 May 1958
1483·51	2387·48	Col G. Mosolov	USSR	Mikoyan Type E-66	Sidorovo, Tyumenskaya, USSR	31 Oct 1959
1525·93	2455·74	Maj J.W. Rogers, USAF	USA	Convair F-106A Delta Dart	Edwards Air Force Base, California, USA	15 Dec 1959

Progressive world absolute height records achieved by man in the atmosphere

ft	m	Pilot	Nationality	Aircraft	Location	Date
59 445	18 119	J. Cunningham	GB	de Havilland Vampire I	Hatfield, England	23 Mar 1948
63 668	19 406	W.F. Gibb	GB	English Electric Canberra	England	4 May 1953
65 889	20 083	W.F. Gibb	GB	English Electric Canberra	England	29 Aug 1955
70 308	21 430	M. Randrup	GB	English Electric Canberra	England	28 Aug 1957
76 932	23 449	Lt Cdr G.C. Watkins	USA	Grumman F11F-1 Tiger	USA	18 Apr 1958
79 452	24 217	R. Carpentier	France	SO9050 Trident (F-ZWUM)	France	2 May 1958
91 243	27 811	Maj H.C. Johnson	USA	Lockheed F-104A Starfighter	USA	7 May 1958
94 659	28 852	Maj V. Ilyushin	USSR	Sukhoi T431	USSR	14 July 1959
98 556	30 040	Cdr L. Flint	USA	McDonnell Douglas F-4 Phantom II	USA	6 Dec 1959
103 389	31 513	Capt J.B. Jordan	USA	Lockheed F-104C Starfighter	USA	14 Dec 1959

Progressive world absolute distance records achieved by man in the atmosphere

miles	km	Pilots	Nationality	Aircraft	Location of start	Date
11235·6	18081·99	Cdr T. Davis and E.P. Rankin	USA	Lockheed P2V Neptune	Perth	29 Sept–1 Oct 1946

Progressive maximum speeds achieved by the American X-15 rocket-powered research aircraft

The record speed achieved by Captain Joersz and Major Morgan on 27 July 1976 represents the highest ratified speed record attained by an aeroplane which took off under its own power from the earth's surface. Between 1960 and 1967, however, the US Air Force conducted a substantial programme of manned flight trials with the North American X-15 and X-15A-2. Powered by a liquid oxygen and ammonia rocket engine, the X-15 was carried to altitude by a Boeing B-52 before embarking upon ultra-high-speed and high altitude flights, as summarised next.

mph	km/h	Mach No	Pilot	Date
2111	3397	3·19	J.A. Walker	12 May 1960
2196	3534	3·31	J.A. Walker	4 Aug 1960
2275	3661	3·50	R.M. White	7 Feb 1961
2905	4675	4·43	R.M. White	7 Mar 1961
3074	4947	4·62	R.M. White	21 Apr 1961
3300	5311	4·90	J.A. Walker	25 May 1961
3603	5798	5·27	R.M. White	23 June 1961
3614	5816	5·25	J.A. Walker	12 Sept 1961
3620	5826	5·25	F.S. Petersen	28 Sept 1961

mph	km/h	Mach No	Pilot	Date
3647	5869	5·21	R.M. White	11 Oct 1961
3900	6276	5·74	J.A. Walker	17 Oct 1961
4093	6587	6·04	R.M. White	9 Nov 1961
4104	6605	5·92	J.A. Walker	27 June 1962 (X-15A-2)
4250	6840	6·33	W.J. Knight	18 Nov 1966
4534	7297	6·72	W.J. Knight	3 Oct 1967 (X-15A-2)

Modern Aviation

The end to the Second World War came in Japan, undoubtedly hastened by the use of two operational atomic bombs, dropped over the cities of Hiroshima and Nagasaki. Nuclear weapons have dominated military and political thinking since that time but have, so far, prevented the eruption of a third and devastating World War. If the threat of such weapons is sufficient to prevent their use, and the beginning of a conflict that can only result in the end of 'civilisation' as we know it, then future generations may come to regard the physicists who developed them as saints and not sinners.

We still have localised wars, no less terrible for the men, women and children involved than a large-scale conflict, and those fought in Korea and Vietnam have had their impact upon aviation, particularly in the development and large-scale use of rotary-wing aircraft. Korea had shown their potential and Vietnam saw them used in growing numbers, bringing new capability and reliability. This can be illustrated by the fact that in 1974 the Bell Helicopter Company in the USA announced delivery of its 20 000th helicopter; of this total 16 000 had been produced in the single decade from 1964.

The teenagers of the 1930s, who became the servicemen and women of the Second World War, had run out into their gardens as children to see the unusual sight of an aeroplane flying past. They could never have dreamed they would live to see a day when air forces would fly, as routine, aircraft capable of speeds in excess of 1000 mph (1600 km/h), or deploy a single weapon that could virtually eliminate an entire city and its inhabitants. Nor could they have envisaged flying off on holiday to the other side of the world in an aircraft that seated 400 or more passengers, across an ocean once challenged only by such heroes as Alcock and Brown and the American Charles Lindbergh, or that one day men would land and walk on the Moon. . . .

Perhaps the most unusual helicopters ever produced, and certainly the lightest, are the Seremet strap-on helicopters, the first of which (the WS1) was tested in 1961. The last of the series would appear to be the WS8, flight testing of which began in 1975. It consists basically of a small engine mounted on a back-pack, the latter supporting also the twist-grip extended arm controls, the two-blade rotor, and the small tail rotor mounted at the end of a rearward extending single thin boom.

The first full-throttle test flight of the North American X-15A was made on 21 April 1961, piloted by Maj Robert White, USAF, when a speed of 3074 mph (4947 km/h) was attained.

The first specially designed anti-submarine helicopter ordered for the Royal Navy was the Westland Wessex, developed from the Sikorsky S-58. Equipped with an automatic pilot, the Wessex could be operated by day or night in all weathers. Earliest first-line squadron to be equipped was No 815, commissioned at Culdrose on 4 July 1961.

The current absolute world distance record in 1983 stands at 12 532.3 miles (20 168.78 km). This was established during 10–11 January 1962 by Maj Clyde P. Evely and his crew in a Boeing B-52H Stratofortress, flown from Okinawa, Ryukyu Islands, to Madrid, Spain.

The Convair B-58 Hustler, which was **the first supersonic bomber to enter production for the USAF,** had **unusual self-contained emergency escape capsules** that could be used at the aircraft's maximum speech of Mach 2. On 28 February 1962 the first manned test of one of these capsules was carried out, when Warrant Officer Edward J. Murray was ejected from a Hustler travelling at 595 mph (909 km/h) at 20 000 ft (6100 m). After a controlled time a parachute was deployed automatically to bring the capsule and its occupant safely to the ground. In a third test, on 8 June 1962, a capsule containing the chimpanzee Zena was ejected successfully at 1060 mph (1706 km/h), and this landed without causing any harm to its occupant.

The world's first specially designed low-level strike aircraft was the Blackburn NA39, subsequently named Buccaneer. The S1, powered by de Havilland Gyron Junior turbojets, first entered operational service with the FAA's No 801 Squadron at Lossiemouth in July 1962. The developed S2 version, with more powerful Rolls-Royce Spey turbojets, also entered service with No 801 Squadron, on 14 October 1965. Prior to that, on 4 October 1965, the first production aircraft (XN974) became the first FAA aircraft to make a non-stop crossing of the North Atlan-

tic without flight refuelling. The 1950 miles (3138 km) from Goose Bay, Labrador, to RNAS Lossiemouth were flown in 4 h 16 min.

The first outsize transport conversion of a Boeing Stratocruiser, designed by Aero Spacelines and then designated B-377PG (later named Pregnant Guppy), made its first flight on 19 September 1962. Derived Super Guppies are used currently by Airbus Industrie to transport internationally-built major assemblies of the Airbus to Toulouse for final assembly.

The first pilotless anti-submarine helicopter to enter service with the US Navy was the Gyrodyne QH-50A, in 1963; the Navy's drone helicopters each carried two homing torpedoes.

First pilot of a fixed-wing aircraft to gain 'astronaut's wings', for having attained an altitude of more than 50 miles (80 km) above the earth's surface, was NASA test pilot Joe Walker. They were awarded after he had flown the North American X-15A to a height of 271 000 ft (82 600 m) on 17 January 1963.

The first transpacific solo flight by a woman was achieved between 30 April and 12 May 1963 by

Jacqueline Cochran posing in the cockpit of her record-breaking Starfighter.

American Betty Miller. She flew from Oakland, California, to Brisbane, Australia, in four stages.

A 100-km closed-circuit world speed record for women was established on 1 May 1963 by Jacqueline Cochran, flying a Lockheed TF-104G Starfighter near Edwards AFB, California, at a ratified speed of 1203·686 mph (1937·14 km/h).

Regarded as one of the US Navy's 'finest air weapons' and the USAF's 'most effective fighter of the Sixties', the McDonnell Douglas F-4C Phantom II tactical fighter for the USAF was flown for the first time on 27 May 1963. This well armed and equipped aircraft had a maximum speed of Mach 2·16.

The first Fleet Air Arm helicopter used extensively from platforms on frigates, and smaller vessels, was the Westland Wasp. The first Small Ship Flight was formed on 11 November 1963. Though small, the Wasp could pack a hefty punch, carrying two homing torpedoes, or depth charges or air-to-surface missiles.

US airwoman Jerrie Mock became **the first woman to complete a solo flight around the world.** Landing at Columbus, Ohio, on 17 April 1964, this achievement had been completed in 29 days in her Cessna 180 lightplane, *Spirit of Columbus.*

Jacqueline Cochran, flying a Lockheed TF-104G Starfighter on 11 May 1964, **raised the women's world speed record** over a 15-25 km course to 1429·246 mph (2300·14 km/h).

A second solo round-the-world flight by a woman was completed on 12 May 1964. This was accomplished by American Joan Merriam who, flying a Piper Apache lightplane, took 56 days to cover the route which had been planned by Amelia Earhart.

Silver City Airways, which in mid-1948 had established the first UK cross-Channel car ferry, announced on 6 June 1964 that in its operations from that date a total of **one million cars had been carried between the UK and Europe.**

The first over 1000 km distance record by a sailplane was set in the USA. This was accomplished by A.H. Parker flying a Sisu-1A over a distance of 646 miles (1040 km).

The largest research aircraft ever built was the North American XB-70A Valkyrie, which was designed originally as a Mach 3 strategic bomber for the USAF, but modified subsequently into an aerodynamic test vehicle. Two Valkyries were built, the first flying on 21 September 1964. Each had large delta wings, with hydraulically drooping wingtips and twelve elevons and canard foreplanes. Power was provided by six General Electric YJ93 turbojet engines, each giving a thrust of 31 000 lb (14 050 kg) with afterburning. Mach 3 was achieved for the first time on 14 October 1965. One of the Valkyries was destroyed at a later date after colliding with its

The North American XB-70A Valkyrie, designed as the most formidable strategic bomber ever.

accompanying chase aircraft, and the programme was completed in 1969 after the surviving aircraft had completed more than 70 flights.

One of the most advanced two-seat all-weather supersonic attack/reconnaissance aircraft ever planned for service with the RAF, the BAC TSR.2, was cancelled for political and economic reasons after only one of a planned 20 development and pre-production aircraft had flown. The maiden flight of this aircraft (XR219) was made on 27 September 1964, and by the time the programme was terminated after a final sortie on 31 March 1965, 24 flights had been made and 13 h 14 min flying time accumulated. Powered by two Bristol Siddeley Olympus 22R turbojet engines, each developing 30 610 lb (13 885 kg) thrust with afterburning, advanced features of this aircraft included a navigation-attack system that would allow high or low level attacks to be made completely automatically without any visual reference, and a weapon delivery system that was stated officially to have an accuracy of 'tens of feet'.

The first flight of the USAF's variable-geometry Mach 2+ tactical fighter-bomber, the General Dynamics F-111A, was made at Fort Worth, Texas, on 21 December 1964. This was accomplished with the wing locked at a sweepback of 26°, and the first flight with the wings actuated through the full sweep from 16° to 72·5° was accomplished on 6 January 1965. Although their initial operational use in Vietnam appeared to be a failure, the aircraft has since been developed as a valuable component of the US armed forces, with some 400 in service in 1983.

The existence of a new US high-altitude high-speed reconnaissance aircraft, the Lockheed A-11, had been revealed by President Johnson on 29 February 1964. This had flown for the first time on 26 April 1962 but was to be developed as the somewhat larger but generally similar SR-71A two-seat strategic reconnaissance aircraft, first flown on 22 December 1964. Relying upon height and speed to provide invulnerability from interception, the SR-71A is capable of more than Mach 3 at optimum altitude, making it the fastest military aircraft in service. SR-71As hold the world absolute speed records, and one set a New York to London transatlantic record of 1 h 55 min 32 sec.

The McDonnell Douglas DC-9 twin-turbofan short/medium-range airliner, first flown on 25 February 1965, became the second of the world's commercial turbine-powered airliners to exceed a sales total of 1000.

The first non-stop helicopter flight across the North American continent was accomplished on 6 March 1965 in a Sikorsky SH-3A Sea King. The 2116 mile (3405 km) flight was made from the deck of the carrier USS *Hornet* at San Francisco, California, to the carrier USS *Franklin D Roosevelt* at Jacksonville, Florida.

In August 1965 Schramm Aircraft Company in the USA flew the Javelin single-seat helicopter designed by B. J. Schramm. In the early 1970s the company changed its name to RotorWay Inc and from the Javelin was developed one of the few helicopters to be designed for home construction, the RotorWay Scorpion Too. This is available currently under the name Scorpion 133, powered by a 133 hp RotorWay RW 133 engine which provides a cruising speed of 80 mph (129 km/h). The Scorpion 133 is basically of steel tube construction with a removable glassfibre cabin.

The first specially designed combat helicopter to go into large-scale service was the Bell Model 209 HueyCobra. First flown on 7 September 1965, six months after its development was started, the HueyCobra is a two-seat armed combat helicopter, designed for ground attack

The narrowness of the Bell Model 209 HueyCobra is clearly seen from these prototypes.

and escort duties. It can fly at over 200 mph (322 km/h) and can carry guns, a grenade launcher, rockets and missiles. One of the main features of the HueyCobra is that its fuselage is only 3 ft 2 in (0·965 m) wide, making it a difficult target to hit by ground fire and easy to conceal beneath trees or with small camouflage nets.

The last operational flying-boat in US Navy service, retired from first-line duties during 1966, was the Martin P5M Marlin. The first production P5M was flown initially on 22 June 1951, and the type saw extensive use for maritime patrol, ASW and air-sea rescue.

Sir Sydney Camm, one of Britain's most successful aircraft designers, died on 12 March 1966. He had joined the Hawker company in 1923 and was appointed Chief Designer in 1925, a position he held until being appointed Chief Engineer in 1959. In this remarkable 34-year period he had been responsible for design or design lead of a whole series of Hawker military aircraft that served throughout the world and the names Hart, Hurricane and Hunter, etched deeply in aviation history, form a fitting epitaph to a great designer.

The first British woman pilot to complete a solo round-the-world flight was Sheila Scott, who landed her Piper Comanche 260B *Myth Too* at London Heathrow on 20 June 1966. She had also established a new round-the-world record time for women of 33 d 3 min.

The world 'speed record' for parachute jumping is held by Michael Davis and Richard Bingham who made 81 jumps in 8 hr 22 min at Columbus, Ohio, on 26 June 1966.

The award of a contract to The Boeing Company for design and prototype construction of the first American supersonic commercial transport aircraft was made on 31 December 1966. The initial version planned was the Model 2707-200 with a variable-geometry wing, but this was later replaced by a fixed gull-wing in what was intended to be the production version, the Model 2707-300. President Nixon gave approval for the construction of two prototypes on 23 September 1969. These would have been powered by four General Electric GE4/J5P turbojet engines, each of some 68 600 lb (31 120 kg) thrust, and would have accommodated a crew of three and approximately 250 passengers. Despite the fact

Sheila Scott, the first British woman pilot to fly solo around the world.

that more than 120 deposits for aircraft had been received from 26 airlines, development of the 2707-300 was cancelled immediately after the US Senate voted against financial backing for the project, on 24 March 1971.

Because the prize offered by Mr Henry Kremer for a first significant man-powered aeroplane flight (a figure of eight covering 1 mile [1·6 km]) was still unclaimed, the Royal Aeronautical Society announced on 9 March 1967 that the total prize money available had been increased and that any nation was eligible to compete.

The first non-stop transatlantic flights by helicopters were made during 31 May to 1 June 1967 by two Sikorsky HH-3Es *en route* to the Paris Air Show. Air-refuelled nine times during their 4270 mile (6872 km) flight from New York to Paris, the journey was accomplished in 30 h 46 min.

The delivery of a Model 707-120B to American Airlines on 5 June 1967 marked a significant milestone for The Boeing Company, this being **the 1000th jet airliner produced by the company.**

The British record for a delayed drop by a group of parachutists stands at 39 183 ft (11 942 m), achieved by five Royal Air Force parachute jumping instructors over Boscombe Down, Wiltshire, on 16 June 1967. They were Sqn Ldr J. Thirtle, Flt Sgt A.K. Kidd, and Sgts L. Hicks, P.P. Keane and K.J. Teesdale. Their jumping altitude was 41 383 ft (12 613 m).

The first completely automatic approach and landing by a four-engined turbojet airliner with passengers on board was recorded by a Boeing Model 707-321B (N419PA) of Pan American Airways on 7 July 1967.

The lightest conventional fixed-wing aeroplane built and flown in Great Britain is the Ward P46 Gnome, built by Michael Ward of North Scarle, Lincolnshire, and flown on 4 August 1967. This has an empty weight of 210 lb (95·3 kg) and maximum take-off weight of 380 lb (172 kg). Its ceiling, imposed officially at 10 ft (3·05 m) because of the use of materials not covered by air regulations, **is probably the lowest ceiling of any aeroplane.**

The greatest number of parachute jumps made by one man is over 5000 by Lt Col Ivan Savkin of the USSR, born in 1913, who reached the figure of 5000 on 12 August 1967. It has been calculated that since 1935 Savkin has spent 27 h in free fall, 587 h floating, and has dropped 7800 miles (12 550 km). The largest number of jumps made by a Briton is believed to be the 1601

descents made by Flt Lt Charles Agate, all with packed parachutes, between 1940 and 1946.

In attaining the highest speed of its research programme on 3 October 1967—a figure of 4534 mph (7297 km/h) or Mach 6·72—the North American X-15A-2 became **the fastest manned aircraft to have flown.** It should be noted that while this speed is exceeded by the Space Shuttle, this latter vehicle is regarded as a spacecraft rather than a fixed-wing aircraft.

In early November 1967 the RAF used some 50 transport aircraft to withdraw British troops from Aden, **becoming involved in its largest transport operation since the Berlin Airlift** of 1948-49. This occurred when Britain gave up its sponsorship of the South Arabian Federation of Arab Emirates which had been set up in 1959.

The first variable-geometry ('swing-wing') aircraft of European design to fly was the Dassault Mirage G strike fighter prototype, which made its maiden flight at Istres, France, on 18 November 1967. This aircraft was lost in an accident on 13 January 1971, by which time it had accumulated some 400 hours of flight testing, and had demonstrated a maximum speed in excess of Mach 2.

The smallest ornithopter (flapping-wing aircraft) in the world is the record-breaking model

The initial 'swing-wing' configuration for the projected Boeing 2707–200 supersonic airliner.

Sikorsky HH-3E Jolly Green Giant helicopter moving in to refuel from a HH-130P Hercules tanker during the first non-stop transatlantic flight by helicopters.

built by Mr Kenneth B. Johnson of Cincinnati, Ohio, with a wing span of only 5·5 in (14 cm). Another of his model ornithopters, with a wing span of 1 ft 6 in (0·46 m) and weight of 0·25 oz (7·09 g), achieved a record flight of 5 min 15·2 s at Akron, Ohio, during 1968.

The first supersonic (in level flight) carrier-based interceptor fighter to serve with the Royal Navy was the McDonnell Douglas F-4K Phantom II (RN designation Phantom FG.1), of which the first three were delivered to RNAS Yeovilton, Somerset, on 29 April 1968. The Phantom FG.1, which equipped No 892 Squadron, was **also the FAA's last air superiority fighter,** a fact indicated by the Omega symbol on the tail fin (the last letter of the Greek alphabet). The Phantoms of No 892 Squadron served aboard the carrier HMS *Ark Royal* until this vessel was withdrawn from service in 1978.

First intimation of the intention to establish an RAF Museum at Hendon, North London, came on 4 April 1968 when Sir Dermot Boyle, Marshal of the Royal Air Force, launched an appeal for donations. One valuable source of funds for the Museum came from the sale of a series of commemorative 'first-day' philatelic covers flown in a variety of aircraft.

The first non-stop transatlantic flight by a turbine-powered executive jet was made on 5 May 1968. The flight from Teterboro, New Jersey, to London Gatwick, of 3500 miles (5633 km) was achieved by a Grumman Gulfstream II, powered by two Rolls-Royce Spey Mk 511-8 turbofan engines, each of 11 400 lb (5171 kg) thrust.

The important synthetic material known as carbon fibre, which is being used more and more extensively in aircraft structures, was developed by the Royal Aircraft Establishment at Farnborough, Hants, during 1963. It is some four times stronger than an equivalent weight of high tensile steel, and turbine engine compressor blades of carbon fibre reinforced plastics were shown for the first time at a Royal Society meeting on 16 May 1968.

The largest US landplane ever flown, in terms of overall dimensions and bulk, the Lockheed C-5A Galaxy, made its maiden flight on 30 June 1968. Powered by four General Electric TF39-GE-1 turbofan engines, each developing 41 000 lb (18 597 kg), it has a maximum take-off weight of 769 000 lb (348 813 kg). However, during the original development programme one take-off was made at 798 200 lb (362 057 kg), or 356·3 tons (362 tonnes).

Selected to power the Lockheed L-1011 TriStar, the **Rolls-Royce RB.211 high by-pass ratio (5:1) turbofan engine was bench tested successfully** for the first time at the company's Derby works on 31 August 1968. A turbofan engine generates more thrust at any given fuel consumption than a turbojet engine, and its large-diameter fan bypasses five times as much air around the gas turbine as is passed through the hot core of the engine. This cold airstream provides propulsive thrust and, mixed scientifically with the hot efflux from the core of the engine, reduces considerably the noise level of the engine.

The world's first supersonic transport aircraft to fly was the Soviet Union's Tupolev Tu-144, the prototype of which (SSSR-68001) flew for the first time on 31 December 1968. On 26 May 1970 this prototype became the **world's first commercial transport to exceed a speed of Mach 2,** by flying at 1335 mph (2150 km/h) at a height of 53 475 ft (16 300 m). The maiden flight of the prototype was also **the first time that its Kuznetsov NK-144 turbofan engines had been tested in the air.** Then rated at 28 660 lb (13 000 kg) thrust without afterburning and 38 580 lb (17 500 kg) thrust with afterburning, the four turbofan engines of production aircraft were each rated at 44 090 lb (20 000 kg) thrust with afterburning. **Regular supersonic flights, the first in the world** by an aircraft of this category, were started by Aeroflot on 26 December 1975, but were confined to the carriage of freight and mail. The first scheduled passenger flights began on 1 November 1977 and a total of 102 flights had been made by 1 June 1978 when the service was terminated. It is believed that the type has now been withdrawn from airline service due to uneconomic fuel consumption.

Believed to be the longest consecutive period of daily flying is the 1315 days recorded by Robert Armstrong. Owner of a small air service at Hutchinson, Kansas, he flew at least once every day between 1 June 1965 and 15 January 1969, a period of 3 years, 7 months and 15 days.

Soviet Tupolev Tu-144 supersonic airliner prototype.

The world's first wide-body commercial transport aircraft was the Boeing Model 747 'jumbojet', the first of which flew on 9 February 1969 from Paine Field, near Seattle, Washington. The first commercial service with the 747 was inaugurated by Pan American Airways on its New York–London route on 22 January 1970. Since that time, approximately 600 of these aircraft have been built in a number of versions for the world's airlines. In addition to standard passenger versions, combi or convertible variants are available for various and easily-changed permutations of cargo/passengers, as well as a purpose-designed freighter with a nose-loading door and a cargo handling system that enables two men to load or unload the aircraft in 30 min. Other versions include the 747SP low-weight long-range passenger transport, and during 23–24 March 1976 one of these aircraft on delivery to South African Airways **set a new world record for non-stop distance flown by a commercial transport.** Carrying 50 passengers, the aircraft was flown from Paine Field, Washington, to Cape Town, a distance of 10290 miles (16560 km). From 1 to 3 May 1976 a Pan American 747SP, commanded by Capt Walter H. Mullikin, completed a round-the-world flight in 1 d 22 h 0 min 50 s to **set a round-the-world record speed** of 502·84 mph (809·24 km/h). A 747SR short-range version is available. The 747 with the largest capacity is the 747-300, with a lengthened upper deck (seating 69). If required this could have a layout to accommodate 585 passengers. During engine certification tests, one 747-200B was flown at a maximum take-off weight of 850920 lb (385970 kg), equivalent to 379·9 tons (386 tonnes), which is **the greatest known take-off weight of any aircraft in the world.**

The largest helicopter flown anywhere in the world was the Soviet Union's Mil Mi-12, which took to the air for the first time on 12 February 1969. A twin-rotor aircraft with an overall span over the rotor tips of 219 ft 10 in (67 m) and fuselage length of 121 ft 4½ in (37 m), it was powered by four 6500 shp Soloviev D-25VF turbo-

Mil Mi-12, the largest helicopter ever built. (Brian M. Service)

Concorde 001 on its 28 min maiden flight.

shaft engines. First indication of the existence of this enormous helicopter to reach the West was in 1969, when Russia submitted to the FAI a number of payload-to-height records. Later, on 6 August 1969, the Mi-12 set a world record by lifting a payload of 88 636 lb (40 204·5 kg) to a height of 7398 ft (2255 m).

The world's first supersonic commercial transport to operate regular scheduled passenger services is the British Aircraft Corporation/Aérospatiale Concorde. The Aérospatiale 001 prototype made its first flight on 2 March 1969, and the BAC 002 flew for the first time on 9 April 1969. The Concorde test programme was the most comprehensive ever undertaken for a civil airliner, involving eight flight test aircraft plus two airframes for structural ground testing. Just prior to the type's entry into service, test aircraft had flown more than 5500 hours, of which more than 2000 hours were at supersonic speed. In route proving, test and demonstration flights, Concordes had then landed at 83 airports in 49 countries and had flown more than 5 million miles (8 million km). **The first passenger services were operated** on 21 January 1976, when simultaneous take-offs were made by Air France's 205 from Paris to Rio de Janeiro, via Dakar, and British Airways' 206 from London to Bahrain. Prior to that, on 1 September 1975, the fourth production Concorde became **the first aircraft in the world to record two return transatlantic flights (London–Gander–London), or four transatlantic crossings in a single day.** Due to different forms of opposition, primarily from environmentalists, it was not until 22 November 1977 that Air France and British Airways were able to inaugurate services to New York.

The world's first scheduled jet service within the Arctic circle was inaugurated by Nordair on 19 March 1969, providing a weekly return service between Montreal, Canada, and Resolution Bay, Cornwallis Island.

The most northerly parachute jump was made by Canadian Ray Munro, of Lancaster, Ontario, who on 31 March 1969 descended on the polar ice cap at 87° 30′ N. His eyes were frozen shut instantly in the temperature of −39°F (−39·5°C).

First European air force to introduce the Lockheed P-3B Orion ASW aircraft into operational service was the Royal Norwegian Air Force which, on 10 April 1969, received the first of an order for five.

An RAF Hawker Siddeley Harrier GR.1 made the first transatlantic crossing by the type on 28 April 1969, flying from Northolt, Middlesex, to Floyd Bennett Field, New York.

The greatest known landing altitude for a parachute jump was 23 045 ft (7134 m), the height of the summit of Lenina Peak on the borders of Tadzhikistan and Kirgiziya in Kazakhstan, USSR. It was reported in May 1969 that ten

Russians had parachuted on to this mountain summit but that four had been killed.

The Daily Mail Transatlantic Air Race, held between 4 and 11 May 1969 to celebrate the 50th anniversary of the first non-stop crossing of the North Atlantic by Alcock and Brown, required the winner to record the shortest time to travel from the top of the Post Office Tower, London, to the top of the Empire State Building, New York. It was won by Lt Cdr Brian Davis, RN, flying in the reverse direction in a McDonnell Douglas Phantom II. His time of 4 h 46 min 57 s for the Atlantic crossing was then a record, and his point to point winning time a remarkable 5 h 11 min.

A new world speed record for piston-engined aircraft was set on 16 August 1969 by US test pilot Darryl Greenamyer flying a modified Grumman F8F-2 Bearcat. Ratified by the FAI at 477·98 mph (769·23 km/h), this beat by some 8 mph (13 km/h) the record set in 1939 by a Messerschmitt Bf 109R. It has since been beaten and **the current record in this category,** of 499·047 mph (803·138 km/h), was established on 14 August 1979 by Steve Hinton, flying a specially prepared North American P-51D Mustang, powered by a 3800 hp Rolls-Royce Griffon engine.

The first land-based pure-jet aircraft in the world to be built for anti-submarine duties and long-range maritime patrol, the Hawker Siddeley Nimrod developed from the de Havilland Comet 4C, first entered service with RAF Strike Command on 2 October 1969. Powered by four Rolls-Royce RB.168-20 Spey Mk 250 turbofan engines, each of 12 140 lb (5507 kg) thrust, it has a typical operational endurance of 12 h.

The first airline in the world to introduce an inertial navigation system (INS) on scheduled passenger services was Finnair, on 20 October 1969, so dispensing with a navigator in the flight crew. In simple terms, an INS combines gyroscopes and accelerometers that provide data to a computer, and this in turn integrates the linear displacement from the start of the flight. Since the starting point is known, the INS can provide the exact position of the aircraft at all times, without any reference to an outside source.

An unrefuelled closed-circuit world distance record for piston-engined aircraft was set by Amer-

ican James Bede during 7–10 November 1969. This was achieved in his unorthodox BD-2 *Love-One* experimental aircraft which was intended for a non-stop unrefuelled round-the-world flight. Using the basic airframe of a Schweizer 2-32 high-performance sailplane, it incorporated a new high aspect ratio wing that was sealed to contain fuel, and carried additional fuel in the wingtips and fuselage to give a total of 565 US gallons (2138 litres). This provided a theoretical range of 28 500 miles (45 866 km). James Bede's distance record of 8973·4 miles (14 441·26 km) was to remain unbeaten for a period of 14 years.

An England–Australia Commemorative Air Race began on 18 December 1969, sponsored to mark the 50th anniversary of the first England–Australia flight by the brothers Ross and Keith Smith, as well as the bi-centenary of the discovery of Australia. It was won by Capts W.J. Bright and F.L. Buxton, flying the Britten-Norman BN-2A Islander G-AXUD.

The world's first all-paper man-carrying aircraft, assembled from paper, glue and masking tape as an aeronautical teaching aid at Ohio State University, flew on three occasions in August 1970. Towed into the air by a motor car, the all-paper glider had no wheels, but slid over the grass field on a fuselage undersurface of waxed corrugated paper. Maximum airspeed recorded was approximately 60 mph (96 km/h).

The first non-stop transpacific flight by rotary-wing aircraft was that completed on 22 August 1970 by two Sikorsky HH-3C helicopters. These two aircraft covered a distance of 9000 miles (14 484 km), flight-refuelled *en route* by Lockheed Hercules tankers.

The only mass hijacking of civil airliners involved a BOAC VC10, Swissair Douglas DC-8 and TWA Boeing Model 707. These were flown to a desert airstrip in Jordan known as Dawson's Field where, on 12 September 1970, they were destroyed by Palestinian guerillas.

Japan's first military jet transport of indigenous design and manufacture was flown for the first time on 12 November 1970. This was the first of two XC-1 prototypes which were designed and built by the Nihon Aeroplane Manufacturing

Company; C-1 production aircraft for service with the JASDF were built by Kawasaki.

The first round-the-world cargo service was inaugurated by Trans-Mediterranean Airways on 14 April 1971.

In the course of its development programme, the French-built **Concorde 001 prototype made its first completely automatic approach and landing** at Toulouse on 13 May 1971.

During the period 11 June to 4 August 1971, the British airwoman Sheila Scott, flying a Piper Aztec D, achieved the **first flight to be made by a lightplane from Equator to Equator via the North Pole.**

Japan's first supersonic aircraft of indigenous design and manufacture is the Mitsubishi T-2 twin-turbofan advanced trainer, in service with the JASDF. Flown initially in XT-2 prototype form on 20 July 1971, it was first flown supersonically in level flight on 19 November 1971. A single-seat close support version designated F-1 has been developed from this aircraft and the first of two prototypes was flown initially on 3 June 1975. Both versions are powered by two Rolls-Royce/Turboméca Adour 801A turbofans, or a licence-built version of this engine, each

developing 7070 lb (3207 kg) thrust with afterburning and providing a maximum speed at optimum altitude of Mach 1·6.

The first jet aircraft to be built in Brazil was the EMBRAER EMB-326GB Xavante (Servant) trainer and ground attack aircraft. Assembled under licence from Aermacchi of Italy, the first Brazilian-built example was flown initially on 3 September 1971, and the type serves with the Brazilian Air Force as the AT-26 Xavante.

The newest and most potent assault helicopter to be produced in the Soviet Union is the Mil Mi-24, development of which would seem to have started during 1972. Allocated the NATO reporting name *Hind*, it is approximately 55 ft 9 in (17 m) long and has a main rotor of the same diameter. It has auxiliary wings, each with three attachment points for a wide range of weapons. These allow the Mi-24 to be used for roles that include armed assault, accommodating eight fully-equipped troops in the main cabin; anti-tank/anti-armour warfare carrying laser-homing anti-tank missiles; and air-to-air combat against other helicopters and slow-flying fixed-wing air-

Mitsubishi T-2, Japan's first supersonic aircraft of indigenous design and manufacture.

craft. Known in the Soviet Union as the A-10, this helicopter has been used to establish a number of records, including an FAI-ratified speed of 228·9 mph (338·4 km/h).

Following NASA's research with aircraft such as the Martin Marietta SV-5P Pilot and Northrop/NASA HL-10 and M2-F2, **a $5500 million budget for the development of a reusable Space Shuttle was authorised** by a Presidential announcement of 5 January 1972.

The first aircraft to be flown in the United States with a fly-by-wire control system, on 29 April 1972, was a specially-equipped McDonnell Douglas F-4 Phantom II. Such a system replaces the conventional mechanical linkage for the operation of flight control surfaces by wires carrying electrical signals. Fly-by-wire offers many advantages, being lighter in weight, providing greater redundancy because cable runs can be duplicated or triplicated, and is ideal for integration with computer-controlled automatic flight control systems.

In early May 1972, the Cessna Aircraft Company became **the first aircraft manufacturer in the world** to deliver its 100 000th production aircraft. Ten years later the figure had risen to the remarkable total of almost 172 000 aircraft, but this rate of acceleration has since fallen as a result of the recession in general aviation activities.

The current world altitude record for helicopters of 40 820 ft (12 442 m) was established on 21 June 1972 by Jean Boulet of France, flying an Aérospatiale SA 315B Lama general purpose helicopter. A Lama carrying out demonstration flights in the Himalayas during 1969 **also made the highest landings and take-offs that have been recorded,** at an altitude of 24 600 ft (7500 m).

The Boeing Company announced on 22 September 1972 that with the receipt of its most recent order for the Model 727, placed by Delta Air Lines, this aircraft had become **the first jet-powered airliner in the world to reach a sales total of 1000.**

The first wide-body commercial transport aircraft produced by the aircraft industry of Europe is the Airbus Industrie A300 Airbus, the first example of which (F-WUAB) made its maiden flight on 28 October 1972. Bought initially by Air

France, it entered service with this airline on its Paris–London route on 23 May 1974. A truly international project, the A300 is built primarily by Aérospatiale of France, Deutsche Airbus of Germany, Fokker in the Netherlands, CASA in Spain and British Aerospace in the United Kingdom; other European countries are also involved in some sub-contract work. It is available with General Electric or Pratt & Whitney advanced technology turbofan engines in the 50 000 lb (22 680 kg) thrust class, and the A300 B2 and B4 can provide maximum seating capacity for 336 passengers. A variant flown on 6 October 1981 was **the first wide-body transport aircraft in the world to be specially equipped for operation by a two-man flight crew,** and certification in this configuration was gained on 8 January 1982.

The first two-crew man-powered aircraft to fly, on 23 December 1972 at Radlett, Herts, was the Hertfordshire Pedal Aeronauts Toucan. Its best flight, of 2100 ft (640 m), was made on 3 July 1973. It was superseded by the modified Toucan 2 which, with a wing span of 139 ft (42·37 m), **was the largest man-powered aircraft built.**

During its development programme, an Airbus Industrie A300B Airbus prototype recorded **the first fully automatic approach and landing to be made by the type,** on 8 May 1973.

The value of developing automatic landing systems for aircraft was amply demonstrated by a Pan American Boeing 747 on 26 June 1973. During its transatlantic crossing, the windscreen of the flight deck was damaged by a violent thunderstorm, completely cutting off all forward view. Carrying 220 passengers, this aircraft made a completely uneventful, fully automatic approach to and landing at London Heathrow.

The first at-sea deck landing by the Westland/Aérospatiale Lynx was made aboard the helicopter support ship RFA *Engadine* on 29 June 1973. One of three helicopters developed under the Aérospatiale/Westland co-production agreement, the British company had design leadership for the Lynx and, in terms of production, is built by Westland and Aérospatiale in proportions of 70 and 30 per cent respectively. First flown in prototype form on 21 March 1971, more than 300 Lynx helicopters have been ordered, serving with the British Army and Navy, and with the navies of Argentina, Brazil, Denmark, France,

Federal Germany, the Netherlands and Norway, and the State of Qatar Police.

The Sikorsky S-69 (XH-59A) helicopter, developed under a US Army contract, was flown for the first time on 26 July 1973 as a pure helicopter. Its unique feature is the rotor system, comprising two co-axially mounted contra-rotating three-blade main rotors, which eliminates the need for a tail rotor. For directional control the S-69 has a conventional tail unit, incorporating twin endplate fins and rudders. Power for the rotors is provided by an 1825 shp Pratt & Whitney Aircraft of Canada PT6T-3 Turbo Twin Pac, and following initial testing, the planned installation of two Pratt & Whitney J60-P-3A turbojet engines was completed. Mounted in pods, one on each side of the fuselage, the turbojets each have a thrust of 3000 lb (1361 kg). In this form the S-69 has demonstrated a maximum level speed of 303 mph (487 km/h) at optimum altitude, **making it the fastest pure rotating-wing aircraft to date,** that is **without the addition of wings.**

The US Navy's first helicopter mine countermeasures (MCM) squadron, HM-12, was established in late 1970. A special version of the Sikorsky S-65 twin-turbine helicopter was developed, with dual hydraulically-powered winches to stream and retrieve the tow, and the first of these RH-53D helicopters was delivered to Squadron HM-12 during September 1973. The special equipment deployed by the tow is designed to destroy acoustic, magnetic or mechanical mines. Since then the prototype of a more advanced version, designated temporarily as the CH/MH-53E, has been flown, for the first time on 23 December 1981. Based on the Sikorsky Super Stallion (CH-53E) three-turbine heavy-lift helicopter, the US Navy hopes to acquire some 200 examples of this aircraft.

The first electrically-powered manned aircraft to fly was the Austrian Militky MB-E1. Derived from the airframe of a Brditschka HB-3 sailplane, and powered by a Bosch electric motor driven by rechargeable batteries, it was flown for the first time at Linz on 21 October 1973.

An outsize repatriation task, carried out by two RAF Britannia transport aircraft, ended on 22 December 1973 with the return of these aircraft to their base at Brize Norton, Oxfordshire. Between 30 October and 20 December 1973 they had in 90 sorties ferried a total of 16 300 refugees between Karachi and Dacca and Chittagong and Karachi. The task was continued by two more Britannias at the beginning of 1974.

The first General Dynamics YF-16 lightweight fighter prototype, for competitive evaluation against the Northrop YF-17, made its first official maiden flight on 2 February 1974. An earlier 'unofficial' first flight had been made on 20 January 1974, when the aircraft had lifted-off while high-speed taxiing/braking tests were being carried out. The YF-16 was selected for production by the USAF and this led to **the largest single-aircraft production programme in the world.** It involves some 67 major and 3900 other sub-contractors to supply the General Dynamics plant at Fort Worth, Texas; in Europe there are an additional 33 major and 400 sub-contractors to feed the production lines in Belgium and the

Sikorsky S-69.

Netherlands. Designated officially as the F-16 Fighting Falcon by the USAF, this service plans to acquire some 2000 of these aircraft, the first production aircraft being delivered to the USAF on 17 August 1978. The first European-built F-16s were delivered to the air forces of Belgium, the Netherlands, Norway and Denmark on 26 January 1979, 6 June 1979, 25 January 1980 and 28 January 1980 respectively.

Europe's newest and most modern international airport, Charles de Gaulle at Roissy-en-France, which is some 15·5 miles (25 km) from the centre of Paris, was opened officially on 8 March 1974.

Following delivery of the company's 20 000th production helicopter, on 23 April 1974, Bell Helicopter's statistics showed that some 80 per cent of these had been delivered during the ten-year period from 1964. Sales of this proportion emphasise the enormous increase in the use of helicopters, particularly military use, that followed the post-war conflicts in Korea and Vietnam.

The longest association of a navigator and pilot must be that recorded by William G. Crooks, who retired from regular communication flights for Hawker Siddeley Aviation on 30 June 1974. After service in the RAF from March 1942, he first crewed with pilot R. J. Chandler in April 1948. From then, until his retirement, William Crooks recorded 6554 h as navigator/radio operator on flights with R. J. Chandler.

The growth of hang-gliding as an aviation sport was highlighted in Britain on 13 July 1974, when the first UK National Hang-Gliding Championships were held on the South Downs at Steyning Hill in Sussex. More than 100 pilots turned up for this inaugural competition and some 80 hang-gliders were involved in the event.

The first prototype of the Panavia multi-role combat aircraft (MRCA) made its first flight at Manching, Germany, on 14 August 1974. Designed to meet the requirements of the air forces of the Federal Republic of Germany, Italy and United Kingdom, and of the German Navy, the MRCA, since named Tornado, is a twin-engined two-seat supersonic aircraft. Its variable-geometry wings and advanced avionics, giving all-weather terrain-following capability, provide the necessary flexibility to meet the requirements

Rockwell International B-1B prototype.

of the user nations. The manufacture of more than 800 aircraft for these nations represents one of the largest aviation industrial programmes yet undertaken in Europe.

Just over 47 years after his greatest triumph—the first solo non-stop aeroplane flight across the North Atlantic—**the death was announced** on 26 August 1974 **of the American pilot Charles Lindbergh.** His achievement had not only captured the imagination of people around the world, but also marked the starting point of a significant growth in general aviation.

Two parachute jumps made by R. W. Mortimer of Folkestone, Kent, have probably **the longest recorded gap between them.** The first was made in Palestine during September 1946, the next 28 years later on 9 September 1974 at Lympne, Kent, in preparation for a voluntary fund raising project for a local charity.

The first prototype of the Rockwell International B-1 variable-geometry supersonic bomber made its maiden flight at Palmdale, California, on 23 December 1974. Despite steady progress of its development programme, US President Jimmy Carter cancelled B-1 production on 30 June 1977, the funding earmarked instead for the development of cruise missiles. However, in October 1981 it was announced by President Ronald Reagan that the programme was to be resumed and that 100 examples of a modified and advanced version designated B-1B were to be built for the US Air Force, with initial operational capability planned for August 1986. **The B-1B will be the USAF's first large supersonic bomber.**

US-1 version of the Shin Meiwa SS-2 flying-boat.

The first no-booking guaranteed-seat air shuttle service in Europe was inaugurated on 12 January 1975 by British Airways. Operated by Hawker Siddeley Trident I airliners, it links London Heathrow and Glasgow Airport, Scotland.

Lt Gen James M. Keck, USAF (Retd), and Maj Thomas J. Keck, USAF, are almost certainly the **only father and son to have individually flown an aircraft at a speed of more than Mach 3 in level flight.** Both flights were made in the Lockheed SR-71A strategic reconnaissance aircraft, father (James M.) flying first on 15 January 1975 and son (Thomas J.), assigned to Beale AFB, California, as an SR-71 pilot, making his first flight on 21 October 1977.

The lightest powered and piloted aeroplane to fly, with an empty weight of only 100 lb (45 kg), was the prototype of the Birdman TL-1. Designed and built by Emmett Tally of Dayton Beach, Florida, it was first flown on 25 January 1975. The later TL-1A had an empty weight of 122 lb (55·5 kg) and well over 300 have been built and flown by amateur constructors.

The largest military flying-boat in current service is the Japanese Shin Meiwa SS-2. Operated by the Japanese Maritime Self-Defence Force (JMSDF) under the designations PS-1 and US-1, signifying anti-submarine flying-boat and air-sea rescue amphibian respectively, the prototype of this four turboprop-powered aircraft made its first flight in the PS-1 configuration on 5 October 1967. With a wing span of 108 ft 8¾ in (33·14 m), the PS-1 has a maximum take-off weight of 94 800 lb (43 000 kg) and maximum ferry range

of 2948 miles (4744 km). The first US-1 was delivered to the JMSDF on 5 March 1975.

The first large aircraft with an air cushion landing system (ACLS) was the de Havilland Canada XC-8A Buffalo, a specially modified STOL transport developed with joint Canadian and United States funding, the first ACLS take-off being made on 31 March 1975. It was used in a programme to evaluate an ACLS for operation from such diverse surfaces as ice, rough fields, sand, snow, swamps and water. Prior to the XC-8A, Bell had flown a modified small Lake LA-4 with such a landing system, from September 1967, but even this was not the first aircraft with an ACLS. Earlier experiments included those in the Soviet Union before 1941, using a UT-2 monoplane trainer and a Pe-2.

The first solo Australia–England flight in an aircraft of amateur construction was completed on 1 July 1976. This was achieved by Clive Canning, flying his home-built Thorp T-18 Tiger, a two-seat all-metal sporting aircraft for which more than 1300 sets of plans have been sold. Just one month later, on 1 August 1976, Don Taylor set out to make a round-the-world flight in his Thorp T-18. This was completed successfully on 30 September 1976, the distance of 24 627 miles (39 633 km) completed in 171·5 flying hours, his T-18 becoming **the first home-built aircraft to circumnavigate the world.**

A new world speed record of 2193·17 mph (3529·56 km/h) was established by Capt Eldon W. Joersz and Maj G. T. Morgan Jr, USAF, flying a Lockheed SR-71A strategic reconnaissance aircraft on 28 July 1976. This straight-course speed is still **the current absolute world record for air-breathing aircraft.**

Most advanced helicopter built solely for testing rotor systems is the Sikorsky S-72 or Rotor System Research Aircraft (RSRA). The contract for two of these helicopters was placed by NASA in 1974, who ordered also a pair of General Electric TF34 turbofan engines in pods, for optional mounting on the sides of the fuselage of one helicopter, and two pairs of 41 ft 10 in (12·75 m) span wings. Each powered by two General Electric T58 engines of 1400 shp, the S-72s were delivered for use by NASA and the US Army in 1977, as test vehicles for new rotor systems under development or projected for future use. One of

the most important features of the design is the ability of the S-72 to fly as a conventional aeroplane, relying for lift and thrust on its wings and turbofan engines only. This enables experiments to be carried out on rotors that would be too small to keep the helicopter airborne. It also provides a safety back-up system if a new rotor under test should malfunction. Maximum speed of the S-72 is about 345 mph (555 km/h).

NASA's Space Shuttle carrier, a specially modified Boeing 747-123 operated formerly by American Airlines, flew for the first time following modification on 2 December 1976. Its first flight with the Space Shuttle Orbiter *Enterprise* carried 'piggy-back' above the fuselage was made on 18 February 1977. The first free flight, when the Space Shuttle was launched from the carrier at a height of 22 800 ft (6950 m) to glide in unpowered flight and make a successful landing at Edwards

AFB, was achieved on 13 August 1977. The Space Shuttle carrier is **the only modern aircraft to be used for piggy-back transportation.**

In bad weather and conditions of very poor visibility, an Airbus A300B2 operated by Air Inter made the **first fully-automatic landing of the type in commercial service.** This was recorded at Orly Airport on 22 December 1976.

The prototype of the Il-86, **the Soviet Union's first wide-body jet transport aircraft,** made its first flight from the old Moscow Central Airport of Khodinka on 22 December 1976. The Il-86, which has the NATO reporting-name *Camber*, is powered by four pylon-mounted Kuznetsov NK-86 turbofan engines, each of 28 660 lb (13 000 kg) thrust. With accommodation for up to 350 passengers, the aircraft is unique in having three low-level airstair-type doors, through which passengers can enter at ground level to leave their coats and hand baggage on the lower deck, before climbing one of the three fixed staircases to the main cabin.

Production flight testing of **the 10 000th Beech V-tailed Bonanza Model 35** was completed on 17 February 1977. The prototype of this four/five-seat light cabin monoplane was first flown on 22 December 1945.

The world's greatest air tragedy occurred on 27 March 1977 when, in conditions of bad visibility, two Boeing 747s collided on the runway at Santa Cruz, Tenerife, killing 579 people.

The first 1-mile (1·6-km) figure-of-eight flight by a man-powered aircraft was achieved on 23 Aug-ust 1977. This was accomplished in the Gossamer Condor aircraft, designed by a team in the United States under the leadership of Dr Paul MacCready. Spanning 96 ft 0 in (29·26 m) and having a gross weight of 207 lb (94 kg) including its pilot/power unit racing cyclist Bryan Allen, the 7 min 27·5 s flight between and around two pylons half a mile apart was made at Shafter, California, winning the £50 000 Kremer Prize.

The current world altitude record for air-breathing aircraft, ratified by the FAI at 123 524 ft (37 650 m), was set on 31 August 1977 by Alexander Fedotov in the Soviet Union, flying the specially prepared Mikoyan Ye-266M.

On 26 October 1977, the Russian parachutist E. Fomitcheva established **the present free-fall parachute record for women**, recording a free-fall distance of 48 556 ft (14 800 m) near Odessa. This has since been ratified by the FAI.

On 18 April 1978 the Vickers Viscount became **the first turbine-powered airliner to complete a**

Gossamer Condor in flight over the 10 ft (3 m) marker which checked the specified altitude was being attained.

Solar One with the solar cells clearly visible above the inner wing sections. (Flight International)

quarter-century of regular commercial airline service. The first service, on 18 April 1953, had been flown by Capts A.S. Johnson and A. Wilson in the Viscount G-AMNY *Sir Ernest Shackleton*, on BEA's route from London to Nicosia, via Rome and Athens.

The first crossing of the English Channel by a powered hang-glider was recorded on 9 May 1978 by David Cook flying a Volmer VJ-23 Swingwing. Its McCulloch MC-101B piston engine had been installed by David Cook, enabling him to complete the crossing from Walmer Castle, Deal, to Blériot Plage, France, in a flying time of 1 hr 15 min.

One of the most successful all-weather fighters of the years following the end of the Second World War was the McDonnell Douglas F-4 Phantom II. The 5000th example was delivered on 20 May 1978, within a week of the 20th anniversary of the maiden flight of the first prototype, which had been made on 27 May 1958.

During the period 1 to 19 July 1978, **two single-engined Beechcraft Bonanzas were flown around** the world in formation, from and to Addison, Texas, and covering a distance of 23 848 miles (38 380 km) in a flight time of 159 h 54 min. Throughout the flight, made by Frank Haile Jr with Walter G. Hedgren as co-pilot, and William H. Wisner with his 72-year-old father Bryce C. Wisner as co-pilot, all take-offs and landings were made in unison.

Claimed to be the first flight by a solar-powered aircraft, the Solar One designed by Freddie To made its first brief hop in the UK on 19 December 1978. A flight covering a distance of almost three-quarters of a mile (1200 m) was made from Lasham Airfield, Hampshire, on 13 June 1979. In this aircraft batteries are used to store the electricity generated by 750 solar cells, and as a result purists have argued that this is an electric- rather than solar-powered aircraft.

Despite the continued use of the Aérospatiale/BAC Concorde by Air France and British Airways for transatlantic services, the first flight of

Edgley EA7 Optica, designed to provide excellent visibility for the crew.

the 16th and last production Concorde, on 20 April 1979, **virtually marked the end of civil supersonic transport production programmes worldwide.**

Most extensively used man-powered aircraft was probably the *Chrysalis* biplane, built at the Massachusetts Institute of Technology. Flown for the first time on 5 June 1979, when dismantled three months later it had recorded a total of 345 flights which had been accumulated by 44 different pilots.

The world distance record for human powered flight was set on 12 June 1979 in the man-pow-ered *Gossamer Albatross*, designed by Dr Paul MacCready. Piloted and pedalled by Bryan Allen, the *Albatross* took off from Folkestone, Kent, at 05·51 h and landed 22·26 miles (35·82 km) distant at Cap Gris Nez, France, at 08·40 h. The duration was 2 h 49 min, and this achievement won the £100 000 Kremer Prize for **the first man-powered crossing of the English Channel.**

The first British Aerospace Sea Harrier for service with the Royal Navy was handed over on 18 June 1979. The first ship trials were carried out aboard HMS *Hermes* during November of that year. **First used in combat** during the Falkland Islands campaign (2 April to 14 June 1982), 28 Sea Harriers operating from HMS *Hermes* and HMS *Invincible* made 2380 sorties and destroyed 27 enemy aircraft in air-to-air combat without loss resulting from air-to-air combat.

A unique and easily recognisable aircraft, the British Edgley EA7 Optica made its first flight on 14 December 1979. Its three-seat cabin, mounted forward of a ducted propulsor unit, is of 'insect-eye' configuration, providing an unexcelled field of view for a fixed-wing aircraft. Powered by a five-blade fixed-pitch shrouded fan, driven by a 200 or 210 hp engine, the Optica is remarkably quiet and has a wing design which provides a speed range of 57 to 126 mph (92 to 203 km/h). Considered to be ideal for civil observation and survey tasks, the first deliveries of production aircraft were scheduled for mid-1983.

The MacCready Gossamer Penguin, an interim solar-powered aircraft converted from a three-quarter scale version of the *Gossamer Albatross*, made its first purely solar-powered flight on 7 August 1980. Piloted by Janice Brown, weighing 99 lb (45 kg), a straight flight of about 2 miles (3 km) was recorded. The *Gossamer Penguin* had flown earlier under solar power, on 18 May 1980, when a short climbing flight was made following an assisted take-off.

The de Havilland Comet 4C G-BDIW made the last revenue flight of the type from London Gatwick Airport on 9 November 1980. Just over 31 years earlier, on 27 July 1949, the Comet I prototype had made its first flight. Early development flying and initial in-service use suggested that Britain had a world-beating aircraft that would be built in large numbers. Unfortunately for de Havilland this failed to materialise, and it was the Boeing Model 707 and its successors that captured the lion's share of the commercial market for jet airliners.

A new woman's solo flight record between England and Australia was set by British pilot Judith Chisholm between 18 and 21 November 1980, flying a Cessna Turbo Centurion cabin monoplane. Although her 3 d 13 h record reflected the very considerable improvement in aircraft and facilities from the time that Jean Batten set the previous record, this in no way detracted from her achievement. She then set out from Australia to complete a solo round-the-world flight, landing back at London Heathrow on 3 December 1980. Judith Chisholm thus established **a new woman's solo round-the-world flight record** of 15 d 22 min 30 s, almost halving the previous record time set by Sheila Scott in 1966.

A first short-duration pure solar-powered test flight was made by the MacCready *Solar Challenger* on 20 November 1980. On 7 July 1981, piloted by Steve Ptacek (USA), the *Solar Challenger* became the first aircraft of this category to achieve a crossing of the English Channel. Taking off from Cormeilles-en-Vexin, near Paris, the aircraft was flown a distance of 163 miles (262 km) to make a landing at Manston aerodrome, Kent, 5 h 23 min later. Power for the *Challenger* was provided by fewer than 16 128 solar cells on the upper surfaces of the wings and tailplane, providing maximum power of 3 hp to the electric motor power unit.

After operating the Boeing 707 for just over 22 years, Pan American Airways flew its last revenue service with this type of aircraft on 26 January 1981.

An unusual record was established by British Airways on 30 January 1981, when aircraft operated by the airline made 96 automatic landings at London Heathrow. This occurred on a day when fog had virtually closed the airport to other airlines, the average RVR (runway visual range) throughout the day being less than 500 ft (152 m).

Taking off from Anchorage, Alaska, in a specially-prepared Rutan Long-EZ lightplane, **Dick Rutan established during 5–6 June 1981 a straight-line distance record** of 4563.7 miles (7344.56 km), ratified subsequently by the FAI under Class C-1-b. In a similar aircraft he had earlier set a closed-circuit distance record of 4800.3 miles (7725.3 km) in the same Class. From 15 to 16 December 1979, and with the Long-EZ aircraft with which he had set the straight-line distance record, he was also to gain FAI-ratified closed-circuit speed records for the class during 8–10 February 1982.

The Boeing Company recorded a major production milestone on 3 August 1981, when the delivery of a Model 727–200 for service with Ansett Airlines of Australia represented the 4000th production jetliner to be delivered by the company.

With the delivery to Swissair of a DC-9 Super 81

Jerry Mullen 'suited-up' in the cockpit of the Phoenix.

on 3 September 1981, McDonnell Douglas had attained the production of 1000 examples of this twin-turbofan short/medium-range airliner. The DC-9 thus **became the second production jetliner in the world to achieve sales in excess of 1000 aircraft.**

British Aerospace recorded the first flight on 20 September 1981 of a specially modified ACT (active control technology) fly-by-wire version of the SEPECAT Jaguar. Its advanced digital quadruplex-redundant fly-by-wire control system means that no mechanical backup is necessary, the system having the capability to survive and overcome automatically all probable failures. Following completion of an initial flight test programme with the aircraft in a stable condition, it was planned to begin a new programme in which the aircraft will be destabilised for use in a CCV (control configured vehicle) research programme.

The first hardened aircraft shelters in the United Kingdom, built at Honington, Suffolk, and intended to protect the occupying aircraft from nuclear blast, were put into use for the first time on 9 November 1981.

Attempting to set a new closed-circuit distance record for aircraft in the FAI sub-Class C-1-d, Jerry Mullen flying the *Phoenix*, an aircraft known formerly as the Bede BD-2 *Love one*, began his attempt on 5 December 1981. Landing on 8 December, after 73 h 2 min in the air, he had flown a record distance, since ratified by the FAI, of 10 007·12 miles (16 104·9 km).

A single-rotor helicopter, with no tail rotor to offset the effect of main rotor torque, was flown successfully on 17 December 1981. A modification of a US Army Hughes OH-6A helicopter, it has the tail rotor replaced by pressurised air ejected through a slot in the aircraft's tailboom.

During the period 8 to 10 January 1982 a Gulfstream III executive transport operated by the US National Distillers and Chemical Corporation, piloted by Harold Curtis, **established a new round-the-world speed record** in the FAI sub-Class C-1-k. Taking off from Teterboro, New Jersey, and landing back there 47 h 39 min later, the Gulfstream had recorded an average speed of 489·33 mph (787·5 km/h) for its circumnavigation of the world.

Exceeding the record set previously by the Mil Mi-12, a Mil Mi-26 heavy-lift helicopter, crewed by G.G. Alfeurov and L.A. Indeev, lifted a total mass of 125 153·8 lb (56 768·8 kg) to a height of 2000 m on 3 February 1982 at Podmoscovnoe in the USSR. The Mi-26, of which development began in the early 1970s, is **the heaviest production helicopter flown anywhere in the world, and was the first to operate successfully with an eight-blade main rotor.**

Following the invasion of the Falkland Islands by Argentinian forces on 2 April 1982, the main elements of the British task force, including the carriers HMS *Hermes* and *Invincible*, sailed from Portsmouth, Hampshire, on 3 April.

An attack on Argentinian positions on the airfield at Port Stanley, Falkland Islands, on 1 May 1982 by a single RAF Vulcan B2 operating from Ascension Island, ranks as **the longest ever operational sortie.**

Offering large potential savings in fuel costs, an Avco Lycoming engine was modified to operate with liquefied petroleum gas (LPG). Installed in a SOCATA TB 10 Tobago lightplane, this engine became airborne for the first time on 15 May 1982.

On 20 July 1982, Wg Cdr K.H. Wallis **set the latest in the series of world class records** established by the remarkable autogyros of his design

Jay Coburn and Ross Perot Jr, crew of the Bell
LongRanger that completed the first round-the-world
helicopter flight.

Spirit of Texas on display at the Air and Space
Museum, Smithsonian Institution, Washington DC,
under a suspended Boeing P-26 fighter (an example of
the USAAF's first all-metal monoplane fighter).

and development. Flying from Boscombe Down,
Wiltshire, he attained an altitude of 18 516 ft
(5643·7 m) in his Wallis WA-121/Mc which is
powered by a Wallis-McCulloch engine of about
100 hp. This aircraft has also exceeded unofficially the FAI-accredited records at present held
by the Wallis WA-116.

A round-the-world helicopter flight, completed
between 1 and 30 September 1982, was made by
the Bell 206L LongRanger II *Spirit of Texas* piloted by H. Ross Perot Jr, with J.W. Coburn as
his co-pilot. Flown from and to Dallas, Texas, it
established an FAI accredited round-the-world
speed record for helicopters in the sub-Class E-
1-d of 35·4 mph (56·97 km/h).

**The disbanding of the RAF's last Vulcan bomber
squadron,** No 44 at Waddington, Lincolnshire
(officially on 21 December 1982, representing the
end of a quarter-century of Britain's V-force),
was marked on 16 December 1982 when a force
of four Vulcans was scrambled for the last time.

**A total of 100 touch-and-go take-offs and land-
ings in a time of 2 min 46 s** is claimed by Ragnar
Stener of Drattinge, Huskvarna, Sweden. These
were made and witnessed on 20 March 1983, with
Ragnar Stener flying solo in an Eipper-Formance
Quicksilver MX2 microlight aircraft. The
touch-and-goes were made from the frozen surface of Lake Landsjon, the time recorded from
the moment before the attempt was made, when
the aircraft was standing still with the engine

running, until the aircraft was standing still
again after the final landing.

The civil Westland 30, the **newest transport helicopter of British design,** manufactured by Westland Helicopters at Yeovil, Somerset, entered
service with AirSpur Helicopters of Los Angeles,
California, on 10 May 1983. This represented
**the first use of the helicopter on scheduled opera-
tions.** Powered by two Rolls-Royce Gem 41-1
turboshaft engines, each with a maximum rating
of 1120 shp, the Westland 30 provides accommodation for a crew of two with a maximum of
19 passengers in a high-density seating layout.

It was reported on 23 July 1983 that Australian
millionaire Dick Smith, flying a Bell Model 206
LongRanger III, had **completed the first round-
the-world solo flight in a helicopter.**

Non-aviation inventions of the period

Word processor First introduced into America and Europe by IBM during 1964

Heart transplant Carried out in 1967 by Dr
Christiaan Barnard in South Africa

Microprocessor Patented during 1971 by
the Intel Corporation in the US

Videotex The transmission of Ceefax, Oracle
and Prestel first demonstrated in the UK during 1973–74

Progressive world absolute speed records achieved by man in the atmosphere

mph	km/h	Pilot/s	Nationality	Aircraft	Location of achievement	Date
1606·51	2585·43	Lt Col R. B. Robinson	USA	McDonnell F4H-1F Phantom II	Edwards Air Force Base, California, USA	22 Nov 1961
1665·89	2681·00	Col G. Mosolov	USSR	Mikoyan Type E-166	Sidorovo, Tyumenskaya, USSR	7 July 1962
2070·10	3331·51	Col R.L. Stephens	USA	Lockheed YF-12A	Edwards Air Force Base	1 May 1965
2193·17	3529·56	Capt E.W. Joersz / Maj G. T. Morgan Jr	USA	Lockheed SR-71A	Edwards Air Force Base	28 July 1976

Progressive world absolute height records achieved by man in the atmosphere

ft	m	Pilot	Nationality	Aircraft	Location of achievement	Date
113 891	34 714	Col G. Mosolov	USSR	Mikoyan E-66A	USSR	28 Apr 1961
118 898	36 240	A. Fedotov	USSR	Mikoyan E-266	USSR	25 July 1973
123 524	37 650	A. Fedotov	USSR	Mikoyan E-266M	USSR	31 Aug 1977

Progressive world absolute distance record achieved by man in the atmosphere

miles	km	Pilot	Nationality	Aircraft	Location of achievement	Date
12 532·3	20 168·78	Maj Clyde P. Evely	USA	Boeing B-52H	Okinawa to Madrid, Spain	10–11 Jan 1962

Rocketry and Spaceflight

The rocket is one of the oldest forms of artificial propulsion. For nearly one thousand years rockets have been used in warfare, the earliest examples recorded in the 11th century. But for hundreds of years the rocket possessed one serious drawback, the uncontrollable nature of its combustion. In the 17th and 18th centuries chemists were able to demonstrate the action of acids as potential propulsive agents (the earliest rockets had been fuelled by gunpowder), yet still the advance in metallurgy was not sufficient to enable these agents to be contained within a suitable combustion chamber. The development of the fully controllable rocket motor has been a triumph of our present century, but even today the handling of rocket fuels is treated with the utmost caution, so powerful is their interaction.

As mentioned previously, rockets were first used to add a new dimension to bombardment in warfare. As the centuries passed bombardment rockets were refined and more widely used, and it is perhaps surprising to many that among the ships of the Royal Navy that set sail for Boulogne in October 1806, during the Napoleonic war, were 24 carrying Congreve rockets. These rockets were fired from the ships against French vessels and the town of Boulogne, causing considerable damage.

Rockets were first used in aerial warfare during the First World War, when Le Prieur anti-balloon and anti-airship weapons were deployed on aeroplanes, but the rocket-powered and piloted interceptor aeroplane was a product of the following world conflict. Interestingly, although considerable time and expense were directed to rocket planes during the 1950s, no such aircraft has ever become operational outside Germany and Japan. However, the unmanned guided rockets that were also developed during the Second World War were to prove the progenitors of the surface-to-surface, surface-to-air, air-to-air, air-to-surface, and underwater missiles in widespread use today.

The first ever ballistic rocket was Dr Wernher von Braun's A-4 (V-2), which succeeded in lifting a payload into the upper atmosphere above the Baltic during the Second World War. This can be said to have marked the beginning of the conquest of space, with manned spacecraft subsequently being launched by the only two nations that could possibly afford the huge sums of money necessary for the hitherto fictional adventure—the USA and USSR. Von Braun, having made his way to America after the war, was the driving force for that nation's early space exploration effort, while other German scientists continued their work on launch vehicles in the USSR. Yet, despite the knowledge such men took with them, it was not until 1957 that the first man-made object was put into Earth orbit. However, once this had been achieved and space fiction became fact, it took just a dozen more years to put a man on the Moon. Now America has the world's first and only reusable spacecraft in the form of the Space Shuttle Orbiter, while the Soviet Union can boast the only continuously manned space station and the development of a remarkable space supply system using unmanned ferry spacecraft of the Progress series.

Recent reports have also given some details of a new Soviet reusable spacecraft, which is thought to be similar to the space Shuttle Orbiter.

The earliest recorded use of war rockets was described by Tseng Kung Liang of China in 1042. These were propelled by charcoal/saltpetre/sulphur gunpowder. The first Chinese rockets followed in about the 12th century and in 1232 the Chinese defenders of Peiping repelled a Mongol attack using rockets. Europe became aware of the rocket in 1258.

The first rocket-powered model was designed by the Italian Joanes Fontana in about 1420. This was designed as a model bird and an illustration of it appears in a manuscript held in Munich.

The first occasion British forces came under rocket attack was in 1780, when Hyder Ali of Mysore, India, repelled British forces at Guntur using iron-cased rockets. In 1799 British forces were again subjected to a rocket barrage in India, while challenging the forces of Tipu Sultan.

The pioneer of the British war rocket was Col Sir William Congreve, Bt, MP (1772–1828), head of the Royal Laboratory at Woolwich, London, and Inspector of Military Machines. Congreve developed a 6 lb (2·72 kg) rocket with a range of 6000 ft (1830 m), which was first tested in 1805. These were used for the first time on 8 October 1806, by Royal Navy ships attacking French vessels and the town of Boulogne.

The first massive rocket barrage by British forces occurred in 1807, when about 25 000 Congreve rockets were launched by the Royal Navy against Copenhagen. Interestingly, a Rocket Brigade of the British Army fought at the Battle of Waterloo in 1815.

The world's first successful liquid-propellant rocket was launched by the American Dr Robert Hutchings Goddard, on 16 March 1926, from a farm at Auburn, Massachusetts. Flying for just 2½ s, it reached an altitude of 41 ft (12·5 m) and travelled 184 ft (56 m) at a maximum speed of 60 mph (97 km/h). Goddard's previous achievements were as follows:

☐ On 7 July 1914 he received a patent for his two-stage solid-fuel rocket.

☐ On 10 November 1918 he demonstrated a solid-fuel rocket at the Aberdeen Proving Ground, Maryland, USA.

☐ On 8 March 1926 he statically tested at the Clark University a liquid-fuelled rocket which had an oxygen pressure feed system for the fuel.

The Society for Space Flight (VfR) was formed in Germany on 5 June 1927 and founded by Prof. Hermann Oberth, Rudolf Nebel, Willy Ley,

Dr Robert H. Goddard poses by his rocket at Auburn, Massachusetts. When launched, this became the world's first successful rocket to use liquid fuel.

Soviet GIRD-X semi-liquid rocket, launched in August 1933.

Max Valier, Herr Winkler, and Wernher von Braun.

The first full-size rocket-powered aeroplane in the world was the sailplane *Ente* (Duck), powered by two Sander slow-burning rocket motors and built by the Rhön-Rossitten Gesellschaft of Germany. Piloted by Friedrich Stamer, it made a flight of just over 0·75 mile (1·2 km) near the Wasserkuppe Mountain in about 1 min on 11 June 1928. The rocket-powered glider flown by Fritz von Opel at Rebstock, near Frankfurt, is often stated as being the world's first rocket aeroplane, but this did not fly until 30 September 1929. Known as the Opel-Hatry Rak-1, it however flew for more than 1·1 miles (1·8 km) and attained a speed of 100 mph (160 km/h). (It is worth noting here that Max Valier [see previous entry] had demonstrated rocket propulsion in Germany in 1928 and had received backing from Fritz von Opel for his work. Further, in 1929 Prof Hermann Oberth built a liquid-fuelled rocket while in Berlin.)

The first rocket to carry a camera was launched by American Dr Robert H. Goddard on 17 July 1929.

The world's first drome for launching rockets was opened on 27 September 1930 at Berlin-Reinickendorf.

Rockets for research and commerce. During the period 1931–34 a number of Europeans conducted experiments with rockets fired from the ground with the principal object of developing solid- and liquid-fuel motors as reliable power plants for air and surface vehicles. Some went further to suggest a commercial application.

The first successful firing of a ground-launched rocket in Europe for research measurements was achieved on 13 March 1931 by the German, Karl Poggensee, who fired a solid-fuelled rocket to a height of 1500 ft (460 m) near Berlin. It carried cameras and an altimeter and was recovered by parachute. Reinhold Tiling achieved a height of 6600 ft (2010 m) and a speed of about 700 mph (1100 km/h) with a rocket using solid fuel, launched at Osnabrück in April 1931 and which burned for about 11 s. Shortly afterwards he may have achieved an altitude of about 32 000 ft (9750 m) with another solid-fuelled rocket launched from the Frisian Island of Wangerooge.

The first rocket to be launched in the Soviet Union was the GIRD-X, a semi-liquid rocket developed by the Rocket Propulsion Study Group (GIRD) that had been formed in 1931. The launch took place on 17 August 1933.

The first attempt at a ground-to-ground rocket flight in the British Isles was undertaken by the German, Gerhard Zucker, on 31 July 1934. An attempt to fire a powder rocket from Harris to Scarp, in the Western Isles of Scotland, failed when the rocket exploded before take-off. Zucker had put forward the idea of sending mail by rocket across the English Channel, but his scheme never materialised. However, **the world's first experimental carriage of mail by rocket** had been recorded on 15 April 1931, launched from Osnabrück, Germany.

The initial development work which led to the German V-2 rocket commenced at Kummersdorf, near Berlin, during 1933–34, after Wernher von Braun had been invited to complete a thesis on rocket combustion in 1932.

The first German Army rocket, the A-1, was developed at Kummersdorf in 1933 but this never flew. Two A-2 rockets were fired from Borkum in December 1934 and achieved an altitude of about 8200 ft (2500 m). In April 1937 the Kummersdorf site was abandoned and von Braun took his team to Peenemünde on the Baltic coast. Here the A-3 and A-5 rockets were developed in preparation for the A-4. It was better known as the V-2, the initial V standing for *Vergeltungswaffe* ('reprisal weapon'). The first so-called 'reprisal weapon' was the V-1 flying bomb, better known to the British as the 'Doodlebug'.

The first successful launch of Goddard's gyroscopically controlled rocket was achieved in America on 28 March 1935. The altitude and speed attained by this rocket were 4800 ft (1465 m) and 550 mph (885 km/h) respectively.

Wernher von Braun made his first attempt to flight test his rocket motor on an aeroplane in March 1936, when he fitted a liquid-fuelled motor to a Heinkel He 112. The aircraft exploded but the pilot, Erich Warsitz, survived.

The German Research Institute for Rocket Flight was founded in April 1936.

The first known project to develop a specifically-designed rocket-powered manned aeroplane was begun in Germany as *Projekt X* by Dr Alexander Lippisch at the German DFS in July 1937. Though experimental, the resulting aircraft was the DFS 194, forerunner of the operational Messerschmitt Me 163 Komet rocket plane (see below).

The first specifically-designed rocket-powered and piloted aeroplane was the Heinkel He 176, which made its maiden flight at the secret German research establishment at Peenemünde on 20 June 1939. Piloted by Erich Warsitz, the He 176 was powered by a single Walter HWK R.I-203 motor.

The first successful use of air-to-air rockets against aeroplanes is believed to have taken place on the afternoon of 20 August 1939 when five Polikarpov I-16 Type-10 fighters, each fitted with underwing rails for eight 82 mm RS 82 rockets, went into action against Japanese fighters over the Khalkin Gol area of Mongolia. The unit, commanded by Capt Zvonariev, claimed the destruction of two Mitsubishi A5M fighters on this occasion.

The first successful liquid-fuel rocket aircraft in the world was the German DFS 194 which, having been conceived by a team under Dr Alexander Lippisch, was taken over by Messerschmitt A.G. at Augsburg and flown in August 1940 by Heini Dittmar. It was powered by a 600 lb (272 kg) thrust Walter rocket motor.

The world's first operational rocket-powered fighter was the Messerschmitt Me 163 Komet, first flown as a prototype **under full power** by Heini Dittmar at Peenemünde, Germany, on 13 August 1941. On one early flight Dittmar far exceeded what was then the official world speed record, attaining a speed of 571 mph (919 km/h); on 2 October 1941, after having been towed to altitude, he started the rocket motor and 2 min later recorded a speed of 623·85 mph (1004 km/h) in level flight. It was the success of these early trials that led to the Me 163 being developed as an operational rocket-powered interceptor.

The world's first strategic surface-to surface missile was the German V-2, developed under the supervision of Wernher von Braun. The first firing of a V-2 type (actually an A-4 rocket) took place on 13 June 1942, but the rocket failed, went out of control and crashed.

The first successful launching of a V-2 type (actually an A-4) occurred on 3 October 1942 when the rocket burned for just under 1 min, lifting it to over 50 miles (80 km) before it returned to earth nearly 120 miles (190 km) away downrange from Peenemünde. The operational V-2 was 46 ft 1 in (14·05 m) long and weighed 28 395 lb (12 880 kg), which included 19 115 lb (8670 kg) of alcohol and liquid oxygen propellants, and a warhead containing 2150 lb (975 kg) of explosive. Its range was between 190 and 200 miles (305 and 322 km).

The first air raid on a rocket research establishment was carried out by RAF bombers on the night of 17–18 August 1943 against Peenemünde. This followed air reconnaissance that had confirmed in June the existence of large rockets at the establishment.

The first operational use of rocket-powered and remotely controlled missiles took place on 17 August 1943, when the Luftwaffe carried out

V-2 launching site.

anti-shipping attacks on British vessels in the Bay of Biscay. The aircraft used for the raid were Dornier Do 217E-5s of II/KG 100, which launched Henschel Hs 293A-1 missiles. On 27 August 1943 an Hs 293 sank the Royal Navy corvette HMS *Egret* in the Bay of Biscay.

The first major warship to be sunk by air-launched missile was the Italian battleship *Roma*, struck by two Ruhrstahl/Kramer Fritz X-1 radio-controlled missiles launched from Luftwaffe Do 217K-2 bombers of III/KG 100 on 9 September 1943. *Roma* was one of many ships on their way to be surrendered to the Allies, and another, the *Italia*, was damaged by a Fritz X-1. As a matter of record, III/KG 100 had flown its first operational mission with Fritz X-1s over the Mediterranean on 29 August 1943.

The first American rocket-powered military aircraft was the Northrop MX-324, which was first flown under rocket power by Harry Crosby on 5 July 1944. It was powered by an Aerojet XCAL-200 motor, fuelled by monoethylaniline. It had originally flown as a glider in October 1943.

The first (and only swept-wing) rocket-engined aeroplane to enter operational squadron service with any air force was the Messerschmitt Me 163B-1 Komet interceptor fighter, first flown in prototype form in April 1941. It was powered by a Walter 109-509A-2 rocket motor, using the liquid propellants known as T-Stoff (hydrogen peroxide and water) and C-Stoff (hydrazine hydrate, methyl alcohol and water) to give a maximum static thrust of 3300 lb (1500 kg). Maximum speed of the Komet in combat was about 600 mph (965 km/h). The swept-wing, tailless Me 163B-1a was armed with two 30 mm MK 108 cannon; some machines are known to have carried various experimental armament systems in addition. The Komet equipped only one combat unit, Jagdgeschwader 400, which comprised eventually three Staffels. The whole unit was concentrated on Brandis in July 1944, and the first operation was flown against a group of

Messerschmitt Me 163B-1a Komet rocket-powered interceptor, with an endurance of only a few minutes.

B-17s on 16 August 1944, without any of the US bombers being destroyed. Although approximately 300 of these rocket-powered interceptors were built, JG 400 claimed only nine Allied aircraft destroyed and two probables before the units were disbanded in early 1945.

The first British commercial organisation to engage in the development of surface-to-air guided missiles was the Fairey Aviation Company which, in 1944, started work on a missile to counter Japanese suicide aircraft. The outcome of this was a general-purpose test vehicle named 'Stooge'.

The first country in the world to be subjected to an assault by ballistic rocket missiles was France. On the morning of 8 September 1944 the first V-2 rocket was fired against Paris. At about 18·40 h on the same day the **first V-2 to land in Britain** fell in Chiswick, London, killing two people and injuring ten. The last rocket to fall in Britain was at Orpington, Kent, at 16·54 h on 27 March 1945, killing one person and injuring twenty-three. Between the two dates 1115 rockets struck Britain (of which about 500 hit London), killing 2855 and seriously injuring 6268. **The worst incident** is believed to have occurred when a V-2 fell upon a Woolworth store at Deptford, killing 160 and injuring 135. **The worst-hit country** was, however, Belgium, more than 1500 rockets being launched against Antwerp alone.

The first interceptor designed to be piloted, rocket-powered and vertically launched was the German Bachem Ba 349 Natter, which was first launched as an unmanned prototype on 18 December 1944. The first piloted test flight took place on 28 February 1945, which was not successful and the pilot, Oberleutnant Lothar Siebert, was killed. Three launches in March were, however, successful and the Natter was thereafter approved for deployment against Allied aircraft flying over Germany. However, no Natter was used operationally. Designed to be semi-expendable, armament was 24 × 73 mm unguided rockets packed into the nose.

Fairey Stooge on its launcher awaiting test.

Japanese Yokosuka MXY-7 Ohka piloted flying bomb on display. (US National Archives)

The first purpose-designed suicide aircraft and the only rocket-powered aircraft to be used operationally outside Germany was the Japanese Yokosuka MXY-7 Ohka. This single-seater was powered by three small solid fuel rocket motors, which were ignited after the aircraft had been air launched from a carrier bomber and had travelled some distance in gliding flight. The first operational sortie by Ohkas was carried out on 21 March 1945 but was not successful. The first successful Ohka missions were flown on 1 April 1945, when the American battleship USS *West Virginia*, the British aircraft carrier HMS *Indefatigable* and other ships were damaged. On 12 April an Ohka sank the American destroyer USS *Mannert L. Abele* off Okinawa.

The first widespread operational use of air-to-air rockets against aeroplanes was by the Luftwaffe, probably by III/JG7 either in late 1944 or early 1945. The R4M unguided rockets, of which 24 were carried on racks under the wings of Messerschmitt Me 262A-1b jet fighters, were 55 mm folding-fin missiles aimed through a standard Revi gunsight. Fired in salvoes their effect was devastating, especially against the American formations of B-17 Flying Fortress and B-24 Liberator bombers.

The first American air-to-surface radar-guided missile was the Bat, an unpowered glide-bomb developed by Hugh L. Dryden. Carrying a 1000 lb (454 kg) warload, the missile was about 12 ft (3·65 m) long and, on being launched from its carrier aircraft, used radar to home on its target. It possessed a range of about 20 miles (30 km), and in April 1945 one such missile succeeded in sinking a Japanese destroyer at this range.

The first American surface-to-air anti-aircraft guided missile was the Western Electric SAM-A-7 Nike-Ajax, development of which was started by Bell Telephone Laboratories in 1945. Before the weapon entered service more than 1500 test rounds were fired, and by 1959 10000 had been delivered. Its place was taken in 1959-60 by the Nike-Hercules.

The first manned supersonic aeroplane in the world was the rocket-powered American Bell X-1. The second prototype made its first powered flight on 9 December 1946, piloted by Chalmers Goodlin, after being air-launched from a

Nike-Ajax missiles being raised to launch position.

Boeing B-29 Superfortress. Flown by Capt Charles 'Chuck' Yeager, USAF, the X-1 was taken progressively nearer to 'the speed of sound' and finally, on 14 October 1947, escaped from the buffeting of near-sonic compressibility into the smooth airflow of supersonic flight. The speed recorded for that historic occasion was 670 mph (1078 km/h) at a height of 42 000 ft (12 800 m), the equivalent Mach* number being 1·015.

The first launch of a ballistic missile in the USSR was made on 30 October 1947, when a reconstructed German V-2 was fired from Kazakhstan. (At the close of the Second World War, Soviet forces had captured Peenemünde, the secret German rocket research establishment, together with missiles and technical data.) The V-2 formed the basis of the first Soviet ballistic missile, deployed with an improved missile known as Pobeda which had a range of 559 miles (900 km). The Pobeda was designed under the direction of Sergey Korolev and the first test

missile was launched in 1948. It was in mass production by 1950 and subsequently was allocated the code name *Shyster* by NATO. Pobeda missiles were also the first to be used in launching experiments with dogs, between 1949 and 1952. The first Soviet intercontinental ballistic missile was test launched successfully in August 1957.

The first British air-to-air guided missile to destroy a target aircraft was the Fairey Fireflash (code-named 'Blue Sky'). Work on this started in 1949 but it never achieved operational status; it was, however, ordered into production and, fitted to Swift Mark 7 fighters, used by an RAF squadron to develop interception tactics with missiles. Fireflash was a 'beam-riding' missile which in fact carried no sustainer motor but was boosted by two cordite rockets and then coasted along a coded radar beam.

The first ballistic missile to enter service in the United States was the Firestone SSM-A-17 Corporal, a liquid-fuelled rocket-propelled (unboosted) missile which entered service with the US Army during the early 1950s and subsequently with the British Army. It had a range of about 75–100 miles (120–160 km).

The first surface-to-surface weapon to enter service with the US Air Force was the Martin TM-61A Matador 'flying-bomb' which joined Tactical Missile Wings in the USA, Germany, Korea and Taiwan from 1951. By 1957 Martin's Baltimore factory had delivered 1000 Matadors.

The first operational pilotless long-range ground-to-air interceptor was the Boeing IM-99 Bomarc. The first prototypes, designated XF-99s, were tested in 1952. Launched vertically, the Bomarc was powered by two Marquardt RJ43-

*The use of the Mach scale for aircraft speeds was introduced by Prof Ackeret of Zürich, Switzerland. The Mach number is the ratio of the velocity of a moving body to the local velocity of sound. This ratio was first employed by Dr Ernst Mach (1838–1916) of Vienna, Austria, in 1887. Thus Mach 1·0 equals 760·98 mph (1224·67 km/h) at sea-level at 15°C, and is assumed, for convenience, to fall to a constant 659·78 mph (1061·81 km/h) in the stratosphere, i.e. above 36 089 ft (11 000 m).

Capt Charles 'Chuck' Yeager enters the small cockpit of the Bell X-1.

MA ramjets and incorporated a Westinghouse guidance system. Its cruising speed was Mach 2·8 and maximum range varied from 200 miles (320 km) for the IM-99A to 400 miles (640 km) for the IM-99B.

Claimed to be the first rocket-powered rotary-wing aircraft to fly, on 13 May 1954, the American Kellett KH-15 research helicopter had a small liquid propellant rocket motor mounted at the tip of each of its main rotor blades.

The first aircraft to fly at over Mach 3 in level flight was the Bell X-2, two examples of which were built for continued research at transonic and supersonic speeds. Built with a K-monel metal fuselage, and stainless steel swept wings and tail unit, the first X-2 was destroyed after an explosion in its B-50 motherplane which resulted in the research aircraft being jettisoned. The second X-2 made its maiden flight on 18 November 1955, but after several successful flights this too was destroyed, on 27 September 1956, at the end of a test in which it recorded Mach 3·2.

The first air-to-air guided missile to be adopted by the US Air Force was the Hughes GAR-1 Falcon, six of which were carried in wing-tip

Fairey Fireflash beam-riding missiles carried by a Vickers Supermarine Swift Mk 7 fighter.

Boeing Bomarc missile operated by the 46th Air Defense Missile Squadron at McGuire Air Force Base.

pods on the Northrop F-89H Scorpion all-weather fighter. They entered operational service in 1956.

The first-ever firing of a nuclear-tipped air-to-air missile was carried out on 19 July 1956 when a Northrop F-89J Scorpion discharged a Douglas MB-1 Genie at 15 000 ft (4500 m) above Yucca Flat, Nevada, in the USA. This missile incorporated a warhead of about 1·5 kilotons yield and the fighter turned away sharply to avoid the missile's blast. The warhead was detonated after having travelled about 3 miles horizontally, but USAF observers standing directly below the explosion reported no ill-effects from fall-out.

The world's first true stand-off bomb to achieve operational status was the Bell GAM-63 Rascal on which, under the original designation XB-63, work started in 1946. Powered by three liquid-fuel rockets, this bomb was first delivered to the US Strategic Air Command at Pinecastle Air Force Base, Florida, on 30 October 1957, and was carried operationally under Boeing DB-47E Stratojet bombers of SAC. Its warhead was either atomic or thermonuclear, as required, and its range was about 100 miles (160 km).

The first operational French ground-to-air guided missile was the DEFA (Direction des Etudes et Fabrications d'Armement) PARCA

(Projectile Autopropulsé Radioguidé Contre Avions) liquid-fuel rocket weapon, which entered service with the French Army in about 1957. It had an effective ceiling of 82 000 ft (25 000 m).

The first man-made satellite, *Sputnik I*, to enter an orbit round the Earth was rocket-launched from the Soviet Union on 4 October 1957. Weighing 184·3 lb (83·6 kg), the satellite was a metal sphere 23 in (58·42 cm) in diameter which orbited the Earth in 96 min at 142–588 miles (228·5–945·6 km) perigee and apogee. Its purpose was to measure and transmit information on the density and temperature of the upper atmosphere, as well as to measure the concentration of electrons in the ionosphere. It completed about 1400 circuits of the Earth before re-entering the lower atmosphere and burning up on 4 January 1958.

The first living creature carried into space from Earth to experience orbital flight was a Russian bitch, Laika, which was carried aloft in the second Russian satellite, *Sputnik 2*, launched on 3 November 1957. The purpose of this satellite was to measure and transmit readings of cosmic radiation and on the behaviour of the creature

The world's first official missile mail was carried by a US Regulas I missile on 8 June 1959. This illustrates a letter carried on the flight and addressed to Chairman of the Chance-Vought board.

during space flight. The satellite weighed 1120·6 lb (508·3 kg) and orbited the Earth in 103·7 min at 140–1038 miles (225–1670 km) perigee and apogee. By regulated feeding, supply of oxygen and by other devices, the dog was kept alive for seven days in space, during which time telemetered information on respiration and heart behaviour was transmitted back to Earth. This satellite completed 2370 orbits of the Earth before it re-entered the denser atmosphere and burned up on 14 April 1958.

The first American satellite was *Explorer 1*, launched on 31 January 1958. This discovered the Van Allen radiation belts.

The first British air-to-air guided missile to achieve operational status was the de Havilland Firestreak (code-named 'Blue Jay'). Incorporating an infra-red heat-seeking guidance system, the Firestreak equipped squadrons of Gloster Javelin 7s and 8s of the RAF in 1958 and 1959, and also de Havilland Sea Vixens of the Fleet Air Arm. It continues to arm RAF Lightnings.

The first live animals launched in an American satellite were four mice carried by *Discoverer 3*, launched on 3 June 1959.

The first television pictures taken of the Earth from space were accomplished by the American satellite *Discoverer 6*, launched on 7 August 1959.

The first British surface-to-air guided missile to enter service was the Bristol/Ferranti Bloodhound (code-named 'Red Duster'), powered by

The X-15 on its public debut, with Capt. Robert White in attendance.

two Bristol Thor ramjets (and four solid-fuel booster rockets), which equipped the experimental RAF missile station at North Coates, Lincolnshire, in June 1958.

The first British surface-to-air guided missile ordered for the British Army was the English Electric Thunderbird (code-named 'Red Shoes') which entered evaluation service in 1959.

The first operational sub-surface-to-surface ballistic missile in the world was the American Lockheed Polaris FBMS ('Fleet Ballistic Missile System'), of which the first test firing was carried out in 1959. Sixteen such missiles were carried on board each of the special class of nuclear-powered submarines built for the US Navy and Royal Navy.

The fastest aeroplane ever flown is the rocket-powered North American X-15A-2 research aircraft. Three X-15s were built during the late 1950s and the first free flight was made on 8 June 1959. Just over three months later, on 17 September, the second craft made the first powered flight. Because the 60 000 lb (27 215 kg) thrust Thiokol XLR99-RM-2 rocket engine was not ready, two XLR11-RM-5 engines powered X-15

556th Strategic Missile Squadron training to operate the SM-62 Snark.

No 2. Despite the fact that these gave a combined thrust of only 33 000 lb (15 000 kg), a speed of Mach 2·3 was recorded. By December 1963, then powered by the XLR99, speed had climbed to Mach 6·06, and a surface skin temperature of 1320°F (715·6°C) had confirmed yet another problem associated with very high-speed flight. Following a landing accident to No 2, it was rebuilt and various modifications introduced. Redesignated X-15A-2, this machine made its first flight on 28 June 1964. The highest altitude it attained was 354 200 ft (67·08 miles) on a flight by J. A. Walker on 22 August 1963, and the highest speed was 4534 mph (Mach 6·72) by W. J. Knight on 3 October 1967. A full list of the progressive speeds achieved by these aircraft is given at the end of an earlier section.

The first man-made satellite to impact on the Moon was the Soviet *Luna 2*, launched on 12 September 1959 and hitting the Moon's surface on the 14th. Prior to impact, *Luna 2*'s instruments sent important information back to Earth.

The first American missile with intercontinental range was the Northrop SM-62 Snark, an aeroplane-configured missile with a thermonuclear warhead and capable of a range of more than 6 300 miles (10 140 km). Snark first became operational in 1959, with the 702nd Strategic Missile Wing, Presque Isle Air Force Base.

The first operational British stand-off bomb was the Hawker Siddeley Dynamics Blue Steel, of which test firings were made from Avro Vulcan and Handley Page Victor bombers in mid 1960. It entered service with Vulcan Mark 2s of No 617 (Bomber) Squadron in 1962, becoming operational in the following year. Initially powered by a 16 000 lb (7 260 kg) thrust Bristol Siddeley Stentor BSSt.1 liquid-fuel rocket motor, it had a stand-off range of about 200 miles (320 km).

The first living creatures carried into Earth orbit and safely recovered were the bitches Belka and Strelka. Launched on 19 August 1960, the *Sputnik 5* (Spaceship 2) which carried them for 17 orbits of the Earth, re-entered the atmosphere on the following day. The capsule containing the two dogs separated from the re-entry vehicle and, when it was opened, Belka and Strelka were found to have survived their ordeal in space without coming to any harm.

The first British ballistic missile was the Hawker Siddeley Dynamics Blue Streak which, though started in 1955, was cancelled as a military project in 1960. It was, however, adopted as the launch vehicle for the ELDO (European Launcher Development Organisation, or Conseil Européen pour la Construction de Lanceurs d'Engins Spatiaux CECLES). Its first test launch was conducted on 5 June 1964, but in 1970 British participation in ELDO was withdrawn.

The first large living creature to be launched into space by America and safely recovered was a chimpanzee named Ham. Launched by NASA in *Mercury-Redstone 2* on 31 January 1961, the animal was recovered after a 420 mile (676 km) down-range flight with no ill effects, even though it had been subjected to 17g at launch.

The first human to enter space was the Russian cosmonaut Flt Maj Yuriy Alexeyevich Gagarin

Blue Steel under the fuselage of a Vulcan bomber.

(aged 27, born Friday, 9 March 1934 near Gzatsk, died in a jet crash on Wednesday, 27 March 1968). Launched at 09·07 h, Moscow time on 12 April 1961, from Baikonur, East Kazakhstan, in the 10 417 lb (4725 kg) *Vostok 1* spacecraft, Gagarin completed a single orbit of the Earth, making a safe landing in the USSR 1 h 48 min later.

The first American to enter space was Alan B. Shepard who, on 5 May 1961, was launched in a sub-orbital trajectory of 297 miles (478 km). In his 15 min 22 s journey in the *Mercury* capsule *Freedom 7*, Shepard had attained a height of 118 miles (190 km) and travelled at a speed of 5188 mph (8350 km/h). (The third man into space was also an American, Virgil Grissom, who travelled in sub-orbital flight on 21 July 1961.)

Cosmonaut Flt Maj. Yuriy Gagarin. (Soviet Weekly)

1 d 10 h 19 min 49 s and covered 22 orbits. During the flight he carried out experiments connected with navigation and guidance in space and made a manual re-entry. During the mission Cooper was monitored by television.

The first woman to enter space was the Russian cosmonaut Jr Lt Valentina Vladimirovna Tereshkova, aged 26, who, in *Vostok 6*, was placed in Earth orbit on 16 June 1963 and completed 48 orbits in 70 h 41 min.

The first multi-crew space mission was achieved by the Soviet Union, following the launch of the three-man *Voskhod 1* on 12 October 1964. Crewed by cosmonauts Vladimir Komarov, Konstantin Feoktistov and Boris Yegorov, the mission (without use of spacesuits) lasted 1 d 17 min and covered 16 Earth orbits.

The first ever EVA (Extravehicular Activity) or 'spacewalk' was accomplished by Soviet cosmonaut Alexei Leonov who, with Pavel Belyayev, crewed *Voskhod 2*. Launched on 18 March 1965, the flight lasted 1 d 2 h 2 min, during which

Mercury capsule Freedom 7 *being readied to carry America's first man into space.* (US National Archives)

The first manned space flight lasting more than one day was accomplished on 7 August 1961, when Soviet cosmonaut Herman Titov became that nation's second man in space. He made a space flight lasting 1 d, 1 h and 11 min. Titov completed 17 orbits of the Earth, compared to Gagarin's one. His spacecraft was *Vostok 2*.

The first American astronaut to go into Earth orbit was Lt Col John H. Glenn who, on 20 February 1962, completed three orbits in *Mercury* capsule 6 *Friendship 7*. The flight lasted 4 h 55 min 23 s.

The first co-orbit rendezvous by two spacecraft was achieved by the Soviet Union after launch on 11 and 12 August 1962. *Vostok 3*, crewed by Andrian Nikolayev, and *Vostok 4*, crewed by Pavel Popovich, came within 3 miles (5 km) of each other and provided the **first TV transmission from a manned space vehicle**.

The first American spaceflight lasting more than one day was achieved by *Mercury* capsule 9 *Faith 7*, crewed by astronaut Gordon Cooper. Launched on 15 May 1963, Cooper's flight lasted

Leonov spent 23 min 41 s in a spacesuit outside the craft but tethered to it by a 16 ft (5 m) line.

The first American multi-crew mission and the first mission to perform manned orbital manoeuvres was *Gemini 3*, a two-man spacecraft with astronauts Virgil Grissom and John Young on board. The first mission to begin with a launch using a huge Titan II booster, it was made on 23 March 1965 and lasted 4 h 53 min.

The first American 'spacewalk' was performed by Edward White who, with James McDivitt, crewed *Gemini 4*. Launched on 3 June 1965, the mission lasted 4 d 1 h 56 min, during which White made a 21 minute 'spacewalk'.

The first recognised manoeuvred rendezvous in space was achieved by American spacecraft *Gemini 6* and *Gemini 7*, launched on 15 December and 4 December 1965 respectively. During the mission, which lasted 13 d 18 h 35 min for *Gemini 7*, *Gemini 6* was manoeuvred to within 6 ft (1·8 m) of *Gemini 7*. *Gemini 6* and 7 were crewed by Walter Schirra and Thomas Stafford and Frank Borman and James Lovell respectively.

The first docking of spacecraft in space was achieved by America's *Gemini 8* and an Agena docking target. Launched on 16 March 1966, *Gemini 8* was crewed by Neil Armstrong and David Scott. The docking, however, had to be terminated almost immediately as the spacecraft began spinning uncontrollably.

The first unpowered flight of the Northrop/ NASA M2-F2 lifting-body re-entry research vehicle was made on 12 July 1966, following launch at 45 000 ft (13 710 m) from a B-25 'motherplane'. Representing one of the stages in development of NASA's Space Shuttle, it had a fuselage structure D-shaped in cross-section with the straight side of the 'D' forming the upper surface. After five unpowered flights it was dismantled for examination and then rebuilt, as the M2-F3, with power provided by an 8000 lb (3629 kg) thrust Thiokol XLR-11 rocket engine. The M2-F3 made its first powered flight on 25 November 1970, achieving a speed of Mach 0·8 at 53 000 ft (16 150 m). When the programme terminated in December 1972, a total of 20 powered flights had been made.

Three 'spacewalks' and a docking manoeuvre

were performed by the crew of *Gemini 12* (James Lovell and Edwin Aldrin), during a 22 h 34 min mission which began on 11 November 1966.

The world's first experimental space bomb was launched on 25 January 1967 as Cosmos K-139 by the Soviet Union. A version of the SS-9 *Scarp* intercontinental ballistic missile, it became known as FOBS (Fractional Orbital Bombardment System). It is believed that this system did not become operational.

The first spaceflight fatality was Soviet cosmonaut Col Vladimir Mikhailovich Komarov. Launched on board *Soyuz 1* on 23 April 1967, he met his death after being in orbit for more than 25 h, when his craft impacted on the final descent due to parachute failure.

The first American three-man mission began on 11 October 1968, when *Apollo 7* was launched with astronauts Walter Schirra, Don Eisele and Walter Cunningham on board. The mission lasted for 10 d 20 h 9 min.

The first manned flight around the Moon was performed by American spacecraft *Apollo 8*, launched on 21 December 1968 with astronauts Frank Borman, James Lovell and William Anders on board. Flying around the Moon on 24 December, they returned to Earth on the 27th. Mission time was 6 d 3 h 1 min.

The first manned spacecraft to go into lunar orbit was *Apollo 10*. Launched on 18 May 1969 with astronauts Thomas Stafford, Eugene Cernan and John Young on board, this was a Moon landing rehearsal, during which Stafford and Cernan made two descents to within 8·7 miles (14 km) of the Moon's surface in the Lunar Module. The mission lasted for 8 d 3 min.

The first human to set foot on the Moon was the American astronaut Neil A. Armstrong, aged 38 (born on Tuesday, 5 August 1930 at Wapakoneta, Ohio). At 02·56 h 20 s GMT on Monday, 21 July 1969 Armstrong stepped on to the Moon's surface from the lunar module *Eagle*, an event watched through television by 600 million viewers 232 000 miles away on Earth. Shortly afterwards his colleague Edwin E.A. Aldrin joined him on the Moon, while Michael Collins remained in Moon orbit in the command module *Columbia*. The entire flight to the Moon by *Apollo 11* had been a complete success, having

Astronaut Edwin Aldrin deploys the Passive Seismic Experiments Package during Apollo 11's Moon mission. (NASA)

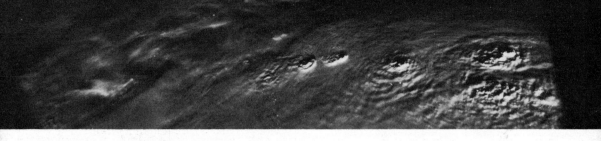

Soyuz 19 during the joint US/USSR ASTP mission, photographed from the Apollo *craft while in Earth orbit.* (NASA)

any mission, and Schmitt was the 12th man to set foot on the Moon. They performed a 21 h 31 min 44 s EVA (Extra Vehicular Activity) and collected a record 253 lb (114·75 kg) of rock and soil. A Lunar Roving Vehicle was used.

The first combined US and USSR space mission was the ASTP (Apollo-Soyuz Test Project), during which the crews of *Soyuz 19* and the *Apollo ASTP* docked in orbit for astronaut/cosmonaut exchanges and combined experiments. *Soyuz* was launched on 15 July 1975 with Alexei Leonov and Valeri Kubasov on board, and the same day America launched the *Apollo* with astronauts Thomas Stafford, Vance Brand and Donald Slayton. The mission ended on the 24th.

The world's first reusable spacecraft is America's NASA Space Shuttle Orbiter *Columbia*, which was launched on its first mission (STS-1) on 12 April 1981. Crewed by John Young and Robert Crippen, *Columbia* took off under the power of its own engines and those of two jettisonable boosters and made 37 orbits before landing 2 d 6 h 21 min later as an unpowered aircraft on the dry bed of Rogers Lake, Edwards Air Force Base, California, on the 14th.

The first commercial mission for the Space Shuttle Orbiter was mission STS-7, launched on 18 June 1983 and crewed by Robert Crippen, Frederick Hauk, Sally Ride and John Fabian. Sally Ride thus became **the first American woman in space.**

The greatest endurance in Earth orbit is 185 d, achieved by the Soviet cosmonauts Valeriy Ryumin and Leonid Popov. They were launched on

Columbia *arriving at Complex 39 Pad A in preparation for STS-1.*

board *Soyuz 35* on 8 April 1980 and subsequently docked with the *Salyut 6* space station. They returned to Earth on 11 October 1980.

The greatest aero-spacecraft mass lifted to altitude was the Space Shuttle Orbiter *Columbia*, launched on 11 November 1982 at a weight of 235 634 lb (106 882 kg). The absolute world record for manned spacecraft lifted to altitude is *Apollo 8*, launched on 21 December 1968 at 282 147 lb (127 980 kg).

The heaviest man-made object in space at the time of writing was the Soviet *Salyut 7* orbital scientific station, launched on 19 April 1982. It is an improved development of the earlier *Salyut 6* station, with two docking ports for manned and unmanned spacecraft and incorporating new systems. *Salyut 7* is likely to be similar in size to *Salyut 6*, which was 49 ft 2½ in (15 m) in length, with folding solar panels that spanned 55 ft 9¼ in (17 m), and with a weight of 41 670 lb (18 900 kg). This, however, is not as large as America's former Skylab I station, which was launched on 14 May 1973 and fell to Earth on 11 July 1979.

The Soviet scientific station Salyut 7 during final testing before launch into space. (US Department of Defense)

Aircraft Index

Notes: This index includes all forms of aircraft, including fixed- and rotary-wing aeroplanes, balloons and dirigibles; it includes also aircraft powerplants; missiles; satellites and spacecraft

The following space-saving abbreviations are used for both the Aircraft and General Indexes:

A	aeroplane or aircraft		P	powerplant
AC	aircraft carrier		RLG	retractable landing gear
AF	aeroplane fixed-wing		RTW	round the world
AR	aeroplane rotary-wing		S	satellite/spacecraft
ASW	anti-submarine warfare		UK	signifies England, Scotland, Ulster & Wales individually or collectively
F	flight/flown/fly		v.	in combat against
H	helicopter		WS	warship
LTA	lighter-than-air craft		WSR	world speed record
M	missile		1WW	First World War
NS	non-stop		2WW	Second World War

General Index